# Introduction to African American Studies

## Cultural Concepts and Theory

by

D1560537

Talmadge Anderson
Departments of Comparative
American Cultures
and Marketing

*Washington State University*
*Pullman, Washington 99164*

KENDALL/HUNT PUBLISHING COMPANY
4050 Westmark Drive    Dubuque, Iowa 52002

# DEDICATION

To my mother, Viola L. Anderson
and my children:
Rose, Ramona, Talmadge
Tammie, Rhunell and Raul

Cover art: *Following the Path,* Oil, 20 1/2″ × 32,″ Copyright 1988 by Earl Jackson. Used by permission.

# *Table of Contents*

## Chapter 1 ▪ Nature, Scope and Foundation of African American Studies

## Chapter 2 ▪ Initiation and Development of African American Studies

# Chapter 4 ▪ Sociological Perspectives of African Americans

# Chapter 5 ▪ Black Psychology and Psychological Concepts

# Chapter 6 ▪ Politics and African Americans

# Chapter 7 ▪ Black Economic and Entrepreneurial Concepts

# Chapter 8 ▪ African American Arts and Humanities

# *Preface*

The purpose of this book is to provide students and other readers historical, theoretical and philosophical concepts of the African American experience from a Black perspective. Thus, much of the theories, concepts and perspectives discussed are those of African American scholars and writers who by their apparent philosophy and professional work have demonstrated a proclivity towards social and psychological Blackness. Yet, a work of this nature could not have been possible without including the studies and perspectives of respected non-Black or White scholars who, because of their racial fairness and academic integrity, have also contributed much towards demystifying the African American past and present.

However, the honesty and sincerity of a few cannot fully erase or rectify the African disparagement and racism that many European and Euro-American scholars have accorded the black race under the myth of value-free or objective study and research. Consequently, the reader may discover throughout the book critical and uncompromising concepts by Black social theorists that are intended to be vindicative and corrective of the ethos of African people, their achievements and worldviews.

*Introduction to African American Studies* is based on the premise that the culture, experience and values of Blacks/Africans are funda-mentally different from those of Whites/Europeans and other races of people. If this is not the case, there is little rationale for a separate field of African American studies. A more significant justification for African American or Black studies is that it has been historically misrepresented, neglected or excluded in American education.

The approach to the study of Black Americans in this text was inspired by the independent educational philosophy and attitude of Carter G. Woodson who founded America's foremost Black scholarly organization, the Association for the Study of African American Life and History. The book has also drawn upon the concepts of eminent Black studies authorities such as Nathan Hare, who was the first coordinator of Black studies; Maulana Karenga, who established the cultural mode of the field; William E. Nelson, organizer of one of the first Master's degree programs; and Molefi Asante, head of Temple University's Ph.D. program of African American studies, and leading proponent of Afrocentricity.

The organization and development of the contents of the book adhere closely to the curriculum guidelines of the National Council for Black Studies. While all Black social theorists may not concur with some of the ideological concepts presented, the text does represent theories and perspectives of a growing number of Afrocentric oriented scholars and education professionals.

Too often, an introductory course of African American studies is taught or discussed only from a mono-disciplinary approach, i.e. history, sociology, or humanities. However, in a sequence of chapters, this book is organized to provide basic instruction that is related to the philosophy, origin, history, sociology, psychology, politics, economics, and humanities areas of African American studies. Thus, students who may pursue an academic degree or career in any one of the traditional disciplines will be prepared to apply or relate a Black perspective to a particular field.

Chapter 1 follows the pattern of most introductory texts by stating the nature and scope of the field and by setting forth the biographies and philosophies of the early exponents and intellectuals who have contributed towards its development. Chapter 2 describes how African American or Black studies was initiated, and how programs or departments were developed and established at major colleges and universities throughout the nation. This chapter also presents and discusses various academic models and approaches and states some of the methodological problems that characterize Black studies development.

Chapters 3 and 4 on African American history and sociology are the most lengthy because they constitute the crux of Black life. These subjects were also of principal concern in the early demands for Black studies. In relation to the study of Blacks, African American social and behavioral theorists have challenged the traditional paradigms and approaches of sociology and psychology more than in any of the other fields. Consequently, a school of Black scholars in each of these disciplines have declared respectively, a Black sociology and a Black psychology. Chapters 4 and 5 relate to African American differentiations in sociology and psychology.

Chapters 6 and 7 are about theories, ideologies and concepts toward Black political empowerment and economic development. Chapter 8 treats the Black aesthetic and African American creativity in the visual, performing and literary arts.

It should be noted that the terms African American and Black or used interchangeably throughout the text. "Black" is always capitalized when intended for use as a proper noun. The identity and identification of African Americans are explained and discussed more fully in Chapters 1 and 2.

Each chapter of the text presents only a summary survey of each subject area. It would be virtually impossible to include or to discuss adequately all of the pertinent information and data related to the various subjects on African Americans in a single book. The book is designed for use by undergraduate and graduate students and for other persons who seek a general interdisciplinary overview of the Black American experience. It is deliberately written with an ideological tone to provoke student or reader discussion and debate. The questions and exercises at the end of each chapter are purposed to encourage constructive comment or dissent, and to motivate research in the various subject areas. Meticulous effort has been made to provide proper and sufficient notes and references to facilitate this purpose.

Finally, it must be recognized that full measures of civil rights, social justice, and politico-economic equity have yet to be achieved by African Americans. The author hopes that this work will provide enlightenment on facets of African American history and thought from a perspective that has been too often muted. In studying the text, it is certain to reveal to the student or reader that much work needs to be done in the areas of racial understanding and race relations in the United States.

# Acknowledgments

This book was written under considerable time constraints. I felt I had a duty to the contributors and readers of a journal I edit and manage to see that their quarterly issues were not interrupted even while I took leave to accomplish this work. Under such conditions, I am indebted to a few persons for their kind assistance and moral support. Without their interest and help in large and small ways I would not have been able, spiritually, to write this book.

I am indebted to Nathan Hare, the vanguard leader and first coordinator of Black Studies, for the information he readily furnished me on the early struggles for African American studies. I thank Robert Staples, a life long friend and colleague, for his valuable insights and consultations on the subject of Black sociology. I am also grateful to Daudi Ajani ya Azibo for his contributions on the subject of Black psychology. I thank William E. Nelson, Jr. for his superb letter of confidence in my ability to write this book.

I appreciate Evelyn Nash, Maja Keech, Willie Leanna Miles, and Naomi Nelson, for their various interest and support. The publisher's staff editors were also supportive and accessible. And, finally, I thank William M. Harris for his friendship and constant encouragement throughout this effort.

# Chapter 1

## Nature, Scope and Foundation of African American Studies

### INTRODUCTION

*African Americans.* Over thirty million citizens of the United States of America are descendants of the continent of Africa. Identified principally by skin color and differentiated mostly socio-politically and economically, they are, indeed, Africans in America or at most African Americans. America's population, historically and contemporarily, is comprised of immigrants with the exception of the few millions of Native Americans relegated to exist mostly on reservations throughout the country. However, African Americans are clearly distinguished from other racial-ethnic groups because of their involuntary immigration and initial slave status. Although history reveals that there were Africans accompanying the early European explorers of the Americas a hundred years preceding the landing of the first

captives at Jamestown in 1619, Blacks were the first numerically significant involuntary immigrants to the New World. Other immigrant groups, with the exception of African Americans, chose voluntarily to come to America in pursuit of political freedom and economic opportunity. Conversely, the African presence in America was based upon the denial of freedom and economic exploitation.

Africans in America were divested of their humanity and converted into capital goods (slaves) in order to promote the economic growth and development of America and Europe. The nature of their subjugation and treatment at the hands of white European-American slavemasters represented a form of "racism" based on color never practiced anywhere in the world. The African immigrants were forcibly denied their language, history, culture, ancestral ties and homeland affiliations. African American women were raped and subjected to slavemaster miscegenation

1

and the sale of their offspring or family members as chattel property. While these extreme oppressive conditions and inhuman acts may no longer prevail, the legacy of slavery and its effect still lingers and impacts, even today, upon the psyche and social orientation of African Americans.

Furthermore, Emancipation, the period of Reconstruction, the Civil Rights Movements and resulting laws and enactments have failed to accord to African Americans total equality of opportunity or a full measure of social justice. Institutional racism, prejudice and discrimination continue to impede the advancement of African Americans in the areas of education, employment and political empowerment.

In spite of a legacy of slavery, segregation and the on-going disheartening effects of discrimination, African Americans have proven their tremendous capacity for perseverance and resiliency against oppression and overwhelming odds. History does not reveal any other people who were captured, shipped thousands of miles and sold like cattle, and who endured 400 years of enslavement and racial degradation, yet, survived, achieved and progressed in the same land and in the presence of the former slaveholders. This phenomenon should be considered in any comparison of the African American experience with other immigrant groups.

*Racial Identification.* Africans in the New World were deprived of human recognition and the status of a national origin. Consequently, their identity, designation or name was arbitrarily decided upon by the captors and enslavers. Africans in Europe and America were called by or given negative and colloquial titles or names such as: nigger, darkie, colored, negro, etc. The debate and dilemma of a racial/national identity or name for American residents of African descent has not yet been, unanimously, resolved.

Sterling Stuckey has written perhaps one of the most comprehensive historical accounts of the dilemma and controversy of Black naming and identity in his book, *Slave Culture: Nationalist Theory & the Foundations of Black America.* Beverly H. Wright suggests that American Blacks' choice of a label for racial identification has been influenced by their social and political environment and effected by locus of control and by changes in ideology reflected in each stage or era of progress or movements.[1] During the height of the Civil Rights Struggle of the 1960s, millions of Black Americans embraced the ideology of Black Power and Self-Determination. Thus, any name or identity imposed upon them by white Americans was emphatically rejected.

The 1960s might be characterized as an era of social and political reformation of the American polity. Reformation was demanded and agitated for by first and second generations of American Blacks who insisted that the gulf between the theoretical precepts set forth by the U.S. Constitution for equality and justice for all citizens, and America's practice and conformance to the law be closed. For Americans of African descent, it was a period of active rebellion against all forms of white racism and the prevailing ideology of white supremacy.

The Civil Rights Movement of the sixties signaled a rebirth of African Americans' pride in their race, history and culture that was reflective of the Harlem Renaissance. A faction of African American participants of the drama of the 1960s revived the ideology of self-empowerment, self-sufficiency, self-determination, self-help and self-respect. More importantly, they felt like it was the time for the descendants of Africa to reassert their own identity. It was the time for **Self-Naming.**

In European and Western historical thought and folklore, the term "black" and color black have negative and ominous meanings. **Black** connotes that which is soiled, dirty, foul, horrible, wicked, evil or bad. The European concept of the devil is black.[2] Thus, it has been easy for white Americans and Europeans to associate their negative connotations of blackness to the dark-skinned peoples of Africa. Furthermore, as a religious rationale for the unjust and oppressive treatment of African people, whites introduce the Biblical myth of Noah's son Ham. The story states that God willed that Ham's son and all his descendants would be black, and he banished them into the depths of Africa (Egypt). Older generations of African Americans had been socialized in the belief that blackness was bad and that the pigmentation of their skin was disadvantageous. Many engaged in the futile attempt of skin lightening and of revering white or light-skinned persons.

However, it was in defiance of the white European-American conceptualization of *black* that caused citizens of African descent to reject, permanently, the traditional term of "Negro" and replace it with *Black*. Stokely Carmichael and Charles V. Hamilton state in their book, *Black Power: The Politics of Liberation in America,* that "Black people must redefine themselves, and only they can do that . . . There is a growing resentment of the word "Negro," for example, because this term is the invention of our oppressor."[3]

The underlying motive or reason for the adoption of the term Black as the new racial identification was also psychological. After centuries of being socialized into believing that the term and color black have derogatory implications, American Blacks needed a form of "reverse psychology" to correct the negative imagery. Therefore, during and after the 1960s period, exclamations, slogans and cliches such as, "Black Power", "Black Pride", and "Black is Beautiful" have served to reverse and to supplant all Eurocentric negative connotations of the word black. The new identification of Blacks in America was almost immediately accepted and initiated nationwide and internationally. Blacks refused to respond to or initial any forms or documents having the term Negro or Colored. Consequently, all federal, state and local government offices, schools and colleges, private organizations and enterprises were compelled to revise various forms and documents to comply with the new self-definition and identity of Black Americans.

The adoption of the identity of Black was not intended in any way to cease or to diminish the use of the term African when referring to Black people. The terms African, Afro-American, and African American have always been used by Black Americans. Many Black institutions and organizations were chartered under the name of African. (For example: The African Methodist Episcopal Church) However, prior to the Civil Rights Movement of the 1960s, few whites used the term African in reference to Black citizens in any form or circumstance.

In 1988, a group of Black leaders met in Chicago to discuss national goals and objectives. The Rev. Jesse Jackson, a prominent Black political figure, suggested that all Blacks be identified officially as *African Americans.* In Jackson's words, "To be called African Americans has cultural integrity. It puts us in our proper historical context."[4]

The debate and discussion on the designation or use of the terms Black or African American pose no real dilemma. Both terms are proper and correct depending upon their application or intent. The identification of African American is appropriate if it is used only to apply to Black citizens of the United States or North America. The term may be also applicable to Blacks living in South America. African American is not sufficient or correct to refer or relate to Black people in Africa or in diaspora. The term Black is universal in concept and is meant to include all Black people of African ancestry.

This book is entitled, *Introduction to African American Studies* because it treats primarily the history, culture and experience of Blacks in the United States of America. In any event the word Black should be capitalized when used as a proper noun or adjective in reference to a race of people of African descent. It is also important that students of the African American or Black experience not become confused and automatically associate the term "minority" as a synonymous racial identification for Black people in the United States or for Africans throughout the world. The word minority has been bureaucratically, conveniently and expeditiously coined by federal agencies and intended to refer to all non-white citizens. In recent years, Blacks have become increasingly apprehensive when they are referred to or perceived as minorities for the following reasons: First, minority is a derivative of the word minor which means *less than, under,* or *subordinate to.* Minority also is used commonly to refer to one who is under full legal age and, thus, being *child-like* or not fully grown. Secondly, the term minority can be psychologically detrimental to a people if they are socialized into believing that they are perpetually perceived as and relegated to a minor rank or role in the society. Psychologically and politically, the term may have been initiated and designated for this purpose. A third reason for the inappropriateness of the word minority as a racial identification for African Americans is that it falsely assumes that a group or population of people is in the minority at all times and in all situations. Furthermore, African people are not a world minority. However, white or European people are minorities in comparison to African and Asian world populations.

Finally, any current identifications of Black Americans of African ancestry may be transitional. If racism is eradicated from American society, and if total freedom, justice and equality is accorded Blacks in America; the term American may then sufficiently apply to all citizens.

# DEFINITION, SCOPE, PURPOSE AND OBJECTIVES

*Definition.* The meaning of African American Studies and the holistic concept, Black Studies, was developed during and after its advent at schools, colleges and universities in the United States. The lag towards the formulation of a definitive concept was due to the racially intense and catalytic socio-political environment out of which it was demanded and hastily developed. A discussion of the era and origin of African American Studies follows later in this chapter. However, the dynamic and socially furious events and circumstances leading to its inception do not in any way diminish its significance as a field of study.

It was established initially that the defining and conceptualizing of African American or Black Studies was logically and necessarily the task and challenge for Black Americans and other black people of African origin. Others may contribute their perspectives, but the initiative and final definition must be from an African ethos or worldview. Over time and through the process of academic maturation, functional definitions and a consensus of concept have been achieved. The eventual unified approach towards defining and developing African American Studies contributed to its phenomenal development and institutionalization.

African American Studies may be defined as a field of study that systematically treats the past and present experiences, characteristics, achievements, issues and problems of Black citizens of the United States who are of African origin and background. The study does not begin with their enslavement in America, but with their heritage and ancestral roots in Africa. African American Studies concentrates on both the distinctiveness of Black people from, and their interrelationship with white American society as well as with all other American racial-ethnic groups.

Vivian Gordon further defines and explains the broad scope and nature of African American or Black Studies. She writes:

> [African American] Black Studies may be defined as an analysis of the factors and conditions which have affected the economic, psychological, legal and moral status of the African in America as well as the African in diaspora. Not only is Black studies concerned with the culture of the Afro-American ethnic, as historically and sociologically defined by the traditional literature, it is also concerned with the development of new approaches to the study of the Black experience and with the development of social policies which will impact positively upon the lives of Black people.[5]

Gordon submits that her definition may be imprecise and concedes that it may remain so long into the foreseeable future since the boundaries of the field of study are subject to debate.

*Scope.* The transitory nature of Black American identification is reflected in the various titles used to demarcate and to identify the academic area treating the study of African people in America and in diaspora. Of the more than 200 programs relating to Black Americans surveyed, the most common descriptive titles used to identify them are: African American Studies; Afro-American Studies; African American and African Studies; African and African American Studies; Africana Studies; Black Studies; and Pan-African Studies. The range of differentiated titles exists mostly for the purpose of defining or explicating the geographical scope of each program or curriculum. For example, the program at the University of Wisconsin-

Milwaukee parenthetically augments the title of Afro-American Studies with the term (Africology). Thus, the definition of the program reads:

> Afro-American Studies *(Africology)* is the normative and empirical inquiry into the life histories and life prospects of peoples of primary African origin, especially those who live in the United States and Canada, Africa, the Caribbean, as well as Central and South America. Its purpose is to educate students to describe, explain, evaluate and predict actions, events and phenomena that structure the life experiences and possibilities of [B]lacks in the several societies in which they live.[6]

In Abdul Alkalimat and Associates' book, *Afro-American Studies: A Peoples College Primer,* it is stated that "Afro-American Studies covers the entire American hemisphere, including North, Central, and South America, the Caribbean, and northern countries like New Foundland and Greenland".[7] It is clear from the titles of identification that Africa and the ethos of African peoples are the foundation of and dominate the theme of academic programs instituted to study the life and history of Black Americans. The root or origin of the identity, culture, history, and philosophy of Blacks in the United States is Africa. Any academically legitimate or valid study of Black people in America must include, to some extent, a study of the customs, characteristics, traditions, languages and mannerisms of the peoples native to the continent of Africa. For even after 400 years of white American and European cultural hegemony, African traits are still identifiable in Black Americans.

The contextual scope of African American studies is developed academically and pedagogically within an interdisciplinary framework. This means that African American studies relates to the established and traditional academic disciplines of Western societies.

Thus, a comprehensive approach to African American studies deals with the historical, sociological, psychological, political, and creative cultural aspects of the Black experience.

It is essential in a contextual sense to include the African past and culture. However, the greater emphasis and investigation of African American studies must begin, historically, with the slave trade and slavery; slave resistance; Civil War; Emancipation and Reconstruction; segregation and discrimination; overt racism and oppression; protest and desegregation and the civil rights movements. Sociologically, the survival of the Black family; Black male/female relationships, sex roles and patterns, racism and discrimination; community growth and development; education; health and welfare; church and religion; and crime and delinquency factors are relevant areas of study. Behavioral studies may focus on the psychology of oppression; socialization affects; personality development and alienation; and self-concept and identity. Theories and ideologies of Black empowerment; electoral participation and influences; employment; and entrepreneurship are examined and discussed in relation to the political science and economic disciplines. The cultural dimensions of African Americans are reflected in their literature, poetry, music, dance and other performing and visual arts. These cultural attributes of American Blacks might be categorized as Afrocentric creative arts or as the humanities of African Americans.

Chapter two will reveal and point out the necessity of adopting the premise that Black Americans are not of European but are of African origin. Therefore, theoretical bases and constructs; research and analyses of African Americans should be founded, substantially, upon African or Afrocentric values, culture and norms and not entirely on white European standards.

A common misperception of African American studies is that it is limited in scope to the study of only the Black experience and culture. Its scope, breadth and depth is much more expansive. African American studies is a component and integral part of the American and world human experiences. The Africans' involuntary immigration to the New World and subsequent enslavement are indictments of the moral depravity of mankind not only in the Americas, but also of Europe, Asia and Africa. The Atlantic slave trade effected the political and economic destinies of millions of people and several countries throughout the world. The liberation struggles and civil rights movements of African Americans have provoked international concern and continue to have worldwide implications. Black Americans have effected and impacted upon American foreign policy decisions in many areas, especially, those related to South Africa and the Third World. The study of the American political economy is incomplete without an acknowledgement and inclusion of the role and contributions of African Americans. Furthermore, the political tactics, music, dance and entertainment talents of African Americans have permeated world cultures and are admired and imitated. Indeed, the scope of the African American experience is universal.

*Purpose and Rationale.* African American studies warrants particular academic interest because it is a branch of knowledge that was deliberately slighted or expunged from the American scheme of education. Critical issues pertaining to its development and social problems between black and white Americans will continue as long as the field of study is treated outside the main sphere of the educational process. In fact, the ignoble and deplorable history and contemporary state of race relations in the United States might be attributed to the failure of the educational system to reveal and to treat with integrity the African experience in America. This statement can be made with certitude and without qualification because of the nature and role that education plays in developing the minds, attitudes and values of a society.

Education is a process of learning and development; therefore, through its execution, it can instill the rules, rank and order of human interpersonal relationships. Education is the social vehicle by which values and culture are transmitted, but it can mean much more. It can be used as a political tool for the rallying, uplifting and glorifying of one group while at the same time alienating, oppressing and denigrating another. Either one of the results may be achieved through the omission of truth and facts and by the commission of inequitable educational policies and falsehoods. Figuratively, African American studies was born because it lacked revelation and because its existence, validity and legitimacy as a component of the total American experience could no longer be denied.

In the classic, *Introduction to the Foundations of American Education*, by James A. Johnson et al., the role, commitment and purpose of American education through schools are very clearly and cogently stated. The role of education is not only perceived as being a preserver of traditions and heritage, but also it is expected to be readaptive to present times and situations. More importantly, education should function as a positive change agent for society. American education holds that it has a commitment to the universality of education, social and economic liberation, and equality of opportunity in consistence with the democratic principles of the Republic. One of its most important purposes is that it seeks to satisfy the normative and psychological needs of students.[8]

The education system has failed, substantially, to fulfill its role, commitment and purposes as they relate to 30 million or more citizens of African descent. America has never been fully committed to proportioning or equalizing educational resources, facilities and opportunities for Black Americans. When one examines the textbooks and curricula of American public schools, colleges and universities, it will be discovered that, basically, the only tradition and heritage that are preserved are those of white Americans. The influence of their European heritage is predominant. In spite of the monumental role Africa and Africans have played historically and presently in the development of America into a superpower, it is scarcely if ever acknowledged or noted in the educational literature. American education is slow and even ineffectual in readjusting to modern perceptions and realities of race and culture, especially, in relation to African Americans, Africans and the Third World. After centuries of racial oppression, exploitation, injustice, violence, hatred and discrimination that have marked American history, education has not succeeded in effecting change in racist attitudes, values and ideology that still permeates the society. African American studies is a positive modification of the status quo in race relations and is serving the purpose of effecting change by educationally correcting historical omissions, distortions, oversights and cultural myths pertaining to Black Americans and other peoples of African descent.

American education has only partially and ineffectually provided the societal enlightenment and moral guidance towards the achievement of political, social and economic liberation for Black Americans. The reason is that school boards, textbooks and, generally, white faculty members give only minimum and cursory attention to the factors of discrimination and institutional racism which have historically and contemporarily affected the social and economic status of African Americans. Therefore, the essence and content of African American studies have a somewhat different social and political orientation. African American or Black studies must study the effects and implications of racism, inequality and injustice that have impacted in the past and continue to impact upon the daily life of Black people.

Few may argue the contention, that the purpose of education or any school system is to attempt to fulfill or provide for the positive socio-psychological needs of students. Yet, the casual, slight and often stereotypical treatment of Blacks in the educational curricula and textbooks negatively affects the social psychology of the African American student. Furthermore, the omission, distortion and depreciation of the role and contributions of Black Americans instill within the minds of white students the false notions of white supremacy and European ethnocentricity.

The education that American students receive in the traditional disciplines of the social and behavioral sciences and in the humanities cannot be postulated as complete without taking into account or integrating the African American contribution and experience. Africans, as well as Europeans, constitute the reality of America's social, cultural, political, scientific and economic development. For instance, the enslavement of Africans, abolition, emancipation and the many subsequent civil rights struggles and movements have had and continue to have a direct and profound effect on American religion, politics and economics. Who would deny that the African American/African ethos and culture have influenced the arts of white America?

Yet, the dominant society's proclivity towards ethnocentrism and institutional racism has virtually precluded any significant treatment of the Black American's contribution or position relative to the social, behavioral, applied sciences and cultural arts. This fallacy in American education has not only affected the self-concept of Black Americans, but has contributed to the miseducation of Whites.

The purpose, function and rationale for African American or Black studies are to expand and impart knowledge through scholarly research, theoretical inquiry and analyses of

the field. However for the sake of authenticity, African American studies must extend beyond traditionalism. Having been suppressed and denied academic legitimacy for so long, African American studies is further purposed to be historically revealing, educationally corrective, and socially reformative. African American studies has undertaken the mission of revealing and disclosing the past and present roles of Black people in American society. In the process it performs the necessary function of correcting the myriad of distortions, stereotypes and myths maliciously attributed to people of African descent by white Americans and Europeans. In comparison, the most challenging purpose and rationale for African American studies is its potential for effecting social reform of the racist tradition of American society.

*Objectives and Uses of African American Studies.* When considering any one of the various academic disciplines or fields of study, a student or other interested person is logically concerned relative to its societal objectives and practical application in the scheme and function of life. Opponents and skeptics of the newly emergent programs and departments of African American or Black studies questioned the academic validity and professional application of a body of knowledge oriented almost exclusively towards people of African descent.

First, African American studies is a branch of knowledge in the broad and infinite realm of education. African American studies was initiated on the campuses of educational institutions nationwide because it is the function of schools and colleges to educate. In addition to the role, commitment and purposes of education discussed above, education is a process of developing one's knowledge, mind, skills and character. Education may be superior to training because it prepares one to think creatively, theoretically and intellectually on a broad range of subjects and human phenomena. Thus, when one receives a degree or certificate in African American studies, his or her education is not usually limited to courses related only to Black or African people. Like any other curriculum or program the student is required to take courses in mathematics, science, and a core of subjects in the traditional disciplines of the social and behavioral sciences, and the humanities. If one chooses to concentrate more on a subject area such as African American studies, the objectives of an education are still being served, and theoretical or philosophical thought is not diminished. Society seeks and requires foremost and simply an *educated* person. The primary objective of an African American studies curriculum, regardless of race or color, is education for positive and productive citizenship.

The question what practical occupational use is African American or Black studies can also be asked of Shakespearean studies, Medieval Literature or American Studies. Yet, most of the hundreds of annual graduates in these fields find gainful employment not only in academe but in government, industry and many other occupational categories.

For African Americans, Black studies is as essential to their normative and psychological well being as White studies is to white Americans or Europeans. The concept of universal education requires that one should be acquainted with the culture of other races and ethnic groups. However, it is socially and psychologically dysfunctional to be unfamiliar or alien to one's own culture and heritage.

In addition to endowing students with intellectual marketable skills, African American studies was initiated and developed with several other objectives in mind. During the early 1970s, a task force funded by the U.S. Department of Health, Education and Welfare was charged with the responsibility of making a limited but systematic inquiry into the status of Black (Afro-American) Studies Programs at a selected number of American institutions of higher education. The task force was concerned with the definition, purpose and objectives of a significant number of programs. A list of the task force's statement of objectives and a few from other sources are as follows:[9]

- To provide an understanding of the life, history and culture of Afro-Americans—an awareness of the Black experience.
- To develop the tools of inquiry necessary for research and publication.
- To provide an opportunity to acquire skills and knowledge for building the Black community.
- To provide an understanding of the current social, economic, and psychological condition of Black people.
- To provide an understanding of racism as an element in American life.
- To liberate Black people.
- To provide specialized training and to develop professionals.
- To humanize American education and American society.
- To explode myths about Blacks.
- To help fashion a Black identity.
- To provide an opportunity to experiment with art forms expressing the Black experience.
- To academically scrutinize the entire ethical and economic structure of the United States, exposing the gulf between the ideals of the Constitution and the actual practice of human equality and social justice.
- To reveal the personal and social consequences of racism and to prepare students for the work which will help destroy that aspect of American society.
- To provide interdisciplinary study in the arts, sciences and humanities from Black perspectives.
- To provide meaningful human study experience which in itself might serve as a

career or complement the professions in the fields of sociology, psychology, social work, politics, economics, education, law and the humanities.

The goal and utility of African American studies are to serve as an educationally beneficial and intellectually broadening field of study for all students regardless of race or ethnic origin. As an interdisciplinary program, African American studies may enhance the self-concept and self-esteem of the Black American, but conversely, it serves to eliminate the negative and stereotypic attitudes that white people may have relative to Black life and history and, especially, towards the Black community.

## FOUNDATION AND PHILOSOPHY

*Basis and Development of Thought.* African American studies does not attribute the basis of its foundation and philosophy to that of any of the classical European Greek and Roman philosophers. Such medieval philosophers were persons of a leisure class sustained by a rank and order system of feudalism. Aristotle, Plato and others wrestled philosophically with the ontological and theological facets of human existence. Somehow in their profound musing, they theorized and developed a rationale for human servitude and subjugation based upon superiority and inferiority of biology, heritage, value and culture. The reasoning of these early white European philosophers provided the basis and academic framework for a succession of eighteenth, nineteenth and early twentieth century white European and American scholars who depreciated Africa and dehumanized its people.

Hegelianism and Darwinism philosophies and theories imply that there exists a so-called natural hierarchy among human races

with Europeans or Caucasians being at the apex. In subsequence, European intellectuals such as David Hume, Thomas Arnold, Count de Gobineau, and Houston Stewart Chamberlain; and Americans such as Professor John Burgess of Columbia University, undoubtedly, related to Hegel and Darwin in their denigratory theories of the Black race or African people.[10] Therefore, African American or Black Studies is significantly antithetical to the racist social theory of European philosophers and intellectuals. African American studies is founded and grounded in an African or Afrocentric world view.

The philosophy of African American studies as a field or discipline is to be differentiated from the study of African American philosophers. However, the philosophy of African American or Black studies grew out of the collective philosophical thought, writings and rhetoric of Black ideologists and intellectuals from the slave, abolition, Emancipation, Reconstruction eras; through the Harlem Renaissance; and to the past and present civil rights movements. Much of the content and social theory of African American studies reflects to some extent the oppressive social, political and economic experiences of Black Americans during these periods. Although protest, petition and racial vindication are thematic in African American studies, its philosophical foundation is much broader.

Philosophy in this discussion refers to how a people perceive and interpret the nature of human existence, world phenomena, human conduct and creativity. The history, culture and status of a people within the world community effect their worldview and perception of reality. The perceptions and interpretations of those at the top or vantage of the social, political or economic order may be different from those at the bottom. Black Americans have had to interpret the world from an oppressed state and within a hostile environment. The thought and perceptions of Black intellectuals are not any less profound or invalid simply because they may express social protest and racial vindication. Furthermore, the orientation and foundation of African American studies provides the intellectual framework for the interpretation of Black art and literature.

African American studies is based upon the philosophy, culture, aesthetic, and historical experiences of Black people in America. Historically or contemporarily, there has never existed a unanimity of Black American philosophy. Socio-political concepts and issues such as: slavery, racism, segregation, desegregation integration, separatism, civil rights, Black Power, Black art, Black capitalism, Black nationalism, affirmative action, equal education opportunity, etc., have evoked a myriad of divergent philosophical responses from Black Americans. African American studies attempts to treat and to place into perspective the philosophies and ideological leanings of eminent Black intellectuals, writers, artists, and social and political activists from 1619 to the present time. African American studies is also inclusive of the works of all writers and scholars regardless of race or national origin that have contributed toward the revelation and development of the Black experience without stereotypical prejudice and racist intent.

For the purpose of African American or Black studies, the terms philosophy or philosopher must not be defined or perceived totally from the scientific ideal or value neutrality standard of Eurocentric academic ideology. White American and European scholars or intellectuals have traditionally viewed African American and African philosophic perspectives with disdain and regarded them as insignificant relative to universal learning and knowledge. Black writers and intellectuals have not generally been concerned with Eurocentric futuristic and abstract social and political theory but have concentrated more or less on philosophical subjects of protest, race survival and liberation. Their perspectives and concepts mirror their true socio-political and economic status in American society.

Because of the protest, race vindicative and controversial nature of much of Black philosophical perspectives, white social scientists often dismiss it as being polemical, propagandistic or unscholarly. Thus, the Black or African philosophical perspective is excluded from the generally accepted textbooks of American social theory. Leonard Harris writes in his book, *Philosophy Born of Struggle*, that the world

. . . refuses to see Afro-Americans as humans and as peers. It is a world unduly reluctant to embrace, and unwilling to avow, messages of truth, insight, sound arguments or cogent methods because of their source. Yet that world fraudulently prides itself on color-blindness and universality.[11]

In the context of African American studies, a Black philosopher may be one with acuity of perception, clarity of diction and integrity of purpose who has contributed profound perspectives and concepts toward the understanding of world phenomena and human conduct, especially, those affecting the existence and survival of people of African descent. The person may be without formal education as was Malcolm X or may have earned a Harvard Ph.D. such as Alain Locke. African American studies does not depend solely upon those who have historically and traditionally denied the human equality and views of Black people to validate its foundation and philosophy or to sanction the purveyors of its perspectives and concepts.

Philosophical concepts, writings and studies of Africans in America or Black Americans existed centuries before the first formal academic program was initiated in 1968. It may be useful to become familiar with some of the most eminent African American scholars, writers, intellectuals and ideologists before treating the controversial origin of African American/Black studies programs at colleges and universities throughout America.

**Black Philosophers and Philosophy of the 18th and 19th Centuries.** In consistence with the above definition of an African American philosopher or Black philosophy relative to this text, numerous persons of the eighteenth and nineteenth centuries have contributed to the philosophical orientation and foundation of African American Studies. It is not important whether such persons are recognized as philosophers or intellectuals in the classical Eurocentric tradition. What is essential is that the proponents of African American or Black studies are intellectually liberated enough to define terms and concepts within an independent Afrocentric framework. The eighteenth and nineteenth centuries were the most oppressive eras for Africans in America. However, there arose from the masses of subjugated Africans persons of great insight and intelligence. They were insightful because they sought learning and knowledge. They were intelligent because it is unintelligent not to resist oppression. Many Africans in America resisted oppression and espoused ideological theories and concepts of liberation. To this extent and in the context of African American or Black studies, these Blacks were philosophic and prophetic. Because of the deliberate and intensive efforts of early American historians to create and sustain the image of African inferiority, history may never reveal all of the philosophical attributes and literary contributions of Blacks of the eighteenth and nineteenth centuries. However, it was impossible to suppress the liberationist thought and writings of some because of their impressive logic, eloquence and dynamism.

Historically, much of African American philosophy has been concerned with the deliverance of Blacks from bondage and oppression and related to social theory and political protest. Most African American leaders and intellectuals of the eighteenth and nineteenth centuries were noted for their stirring and prophetic speeches, writings and rhetoric of abolition or abolitionist philosophy. Some of the most notable of these exponents were David Walker, Henry Highland Garnet, and Frederick Douglass. There are many others whose philosophies and ideologies will be mentioned or alluded to throughout this text.

## David Walker (1785–1830)

An author and abolition activist, David Walker could aptly be called the father of militant Black liberation ideology. He was one of the most eminent, if not the first, African American to foster pride of Blackness, Black unity and Black consciousness. His belief that Africans were being exploited and oppressed throughout the world caused him to plea for the universal emancipation of Black people. This concept may have planted the seed for the development of the Pan-Africanism movement which emerged in the twentieth century.

Walker was born in Wilmington, North Carolina, of a free mother and a slave father. After traveling and living many years in the South, he moved to Boston in 1827. From what is known about his early life, he was a self educated man. He became famous and revered among many Africans in America for his book titled, *David Walker's Appeal: To the Coloured Citizens of the World, but in particular, and very expressly, to those of The United States of America.* It was candid and inflammatory in its condemnation of white Christianity which aided and abetted slavery, and in its appeal to Blacks to resist bondage and overthrow their slaveholders. The book was circulated, clandestinely, to Blacks and whites in the North and South, but more particularly in the southern states. *David Walker's Appeal* sparked a tide of panic among white government officials and citizens of the southern states. The book marked the end to the philosophy of moral suasion to end slavery. Instead, more violence and oppression followed. A price was placed on Walker's head, and although he was urged to flee to Canada for safety, he remained in Boston. After completing a third edition of his book, the work of David Walker ended when he was found dead under mysterious circumstances in 1830.

## Henry Highland Garnet (1815–1882)

Being an African and yet an American resulted in conflicting personalities and extremely contrasting ideologies for many of the Black intellectuals and abolition activists of the nineteenth century. It reflects a behavioral phenomenon that W.E.B DuBois in the twentieth century was to describe as "double consciousness" or twoness of thought. Henry Highland Garnet represented a case in point. He was born a slave in Maryland and subsequently escaped slavery with his parents and moved to Pennsylvania in 1824. He had a thirst for knowledge and education, and eventually graduated from Oneida Institute in 1840. Undoubtedly at Oneida, he was exposed to the classical studies of Greek and Latin. He was a "refined" man and became an outstanding scholar, minister, writer and educator. He seemingly had faith in American institutions and believed that ultimately the principles of the Declaration of Independence and the American Constitution would be realized. He recruited Black troops for the Union Army, and ended his career as an American emissary to the republic of Liberia.

Yet contrastingly, he vehemently opposed whites and advocated revolution to overthrow the slave system. He rejected the spirit of democratic capitalism and materialism. Garnet must be recognized as the forerunner for the advocacy of the political militancy of the Black Church. He is attributed by many as the father of Black nationalism because he promoted and supported the ideologies of Black self-determination, self-reliance, self-esteem, self-defense, and the emigrationist schemes of the back-to-Africa movements. Garnet's nationalist philosophy and ideology preceded those of Marcus Garvey, Malcolm X and many others of the twentieth century. He is known most for his inflammatory anti-slavery speech titled, *Address to the Slaves of the United States of America*, delivered at the Convention of Free Colored People in Buffalo, New York. Garnet admired David Walker and, after Walker's death, reissued the second edition of *David Walker's Appeal* and included his own, *Address to the Slaves of the United States of America*, in the book.

## Frederick A. Douglass (1817–1895)

The social philosophies and political objectives of African Americans today are as variant and diverse as those of Black 18th and 19th century ideologists. While a significant percent of African Americans subscribe to the Africanist/Black Nationalist, separatist and militant philosophies of David Walker and Henry Highland Garnet, an equal number may embrace the integrationist, assimilationist and Afro-Saxonist ideologies of Frederick Douglass. In fact, the integrationist/assimilationist ideals of Douglass greatly influenced the social philosophy and political objectives of African Americans throughout much of the twentieth century until the 1960s. He was born into slavery in Tuckahoe, Talbot County, Maryland. During his tenure as a bondservant, he witnessed and endured some of the most brutal and inhuman treatments ever recorded in history. However, he escaped slavery in 1838 and lived in New York and eventually joined the abolitionist movement. Mostly self-educated, Douglass became one of the most articulate and

Photo 1  Frederick A. Douglass. Courtesy of National Archives.

impressive orators of the period. He captured the attention of the leading and formidable white abolitionist, William Lloyd Garrison, editor of an abolitionist newspaper called, *The Liberator*. Douglass fell under the influence of Garrison and they worked together as abolitionists until differences in ideological approaches to end slavery caused a break in their relationship. Garrison's philosophy of using moral suasion, appeal to the brotherhood intuition of mankind and non-violence, greatly shaped Frederick Douglass's thinking and political ideology on slavery. Garrison, like contemporary white liberals, did not encourage or support the idea of Blacks using political processes and militancy toward achieving abolitionist objectives. Douglass, however, felt that moral suasion alone was insufficient.

Having spent over twenty years of his life under abject slavery, only the influence of William Lloyd Garrison upon Douglass may explain why he formed and advocated integrationist and assimilationist philosophy. Douglass did not approve of any organization that was distinctively racial. He believed that the slave system deprived master and slave of human dignity. He always fostered the notion of Black/White equality and challenged the ideology of white supremacy and the myth of Black/African inferiority. Yet, Douglass harbored a rather Eurocentric perception of Africa. He opposed most colonization or back-to-Africa movements. A significant number of his speeches and campaigns was devoted toward the support of women's suffrage and equal rights crusades which were totally dominated by white women. After the death of his first wife, he married a white woman. Douglass's philosophical ambivalence relative to race consciousness reflects the duality of the psychological and cultural realities of the African American's existence and experience in America.[12]

David Walker, Henry Highland Garnet and Frederick Douglass are given particular biographical treatment here because of their eminence as Black philosophers and ideologists during the 18th or 19th centuries. It is not the intention to imply that they were the only players in the drama of Black struggle and liberation during the slavery, Emancipation and Reconstruction eras. Sojourner Truth, Harriet Tubman, Ida B. Wells Barnett, Martin R. Delaney, George T. Downing, James McCune Smith and Alexander Crummell—All intellectuals, philosophers or activists—who complemented and contributed toward the freedom aspirations of African Americans. Black abolitionists of the eighteenth and nineteenth centuries developed the philosophical foundation for the social philosophy and political ideology of African Americans of the twentieth century. Their philosophical legacy and those of twentieth century scholars, intellectuals and ideologists provided the historical and cultural basis for the demand and eventual institution of African American and Black Studies. The succeeding discussion focuses on six Black intellectuals and one charismatic leader of the late 19th and early 20th centuries. They contributed significantly to the philosophical and literary foundation for the study of Black Americans long before the formal advent of African American or Black studies programs at colleges and universities in the United States.

**Late 19th and Early 20th Century Black Philosophers and Intellectuals.** A f r i c a n American philosophers and scholars of the early twentieth century were fundamental to the origin and development of African American studies. This period produced a cadre of Blacks educated at America's prestigious universities under the tutelage of eminent white professors, and trained in the academic regimen of "scientific idealism" or abstract, objective and empirical methodological research. Late nineteenth century African American philosophers and philosopher-intellectuals of the early twentieth century provided the basic social theory and ideological bases upon which African American studies was founded. Particular biographical references are given under this topic for W.E.B DuBois, Booker T. Washington, Charles S. Johnson, E. Franklin Frazier, Carter G. Woodson, Alain Locke, and Marcus Garvey.

Black sociologists and historians have played a principal role in the areas of research and development of the African American or Black studies idea and in its realization as an academic field of study. Three of the exponents treated here were sociologists: W.E.B. DuBois, Charles S. Johnson, and E. Franklin Frazier. Although DuBois earned his Ph.D. in history, he functioned as a sociologist and his works are characterized as sociological in nature. The sociologist, Nathan Hare, who will be discussed in the next chapter, is recognized as being the father of formal Black/African American studies in the United States. Sociology, simply defined, is the study of group life and human interaction. Since much of African American philosophy has been related to social theory, social analysis and social protest, sociology has been a suitable discipline for research of Black social organization and culture.

Carter G. Woodson, a historian, is acclaimed as the father of modern Black historiography. However, Woodson was only one of many Black and white authors of *new* perceptive historical works on African Americans that proliferated in the twentieth century. Woodson is extolled not only because of his contributions to Black history, but because of his philosophy of African American education and independent Black thought.

Booker T. Washington might appropriately be considered as a nineteenth century exponent. However, his controversial accommodationist philosophy carried over far into the twentieth century. If only from an Afrocentric perspective, Marcus Garvey was an intellectual and a great philosopher. His Black cultural nationalist ideology was the underlying motivation of the Black Power and Black Studies advocates and activists of the 1960s. Mention of Alain Locke is significant because he was formally or academically trained in traditional European and American philosophy at Harvard University. Nevertheless, much of his work related to the value and heritage of African American culture.

## William Edward Burghardt DuBois (1868–1963)

DuBois might be acknowledged as an outstanding scholar, author, social critic and egalitarian social activist. Having received the Ph.D. at Harvard University, he was firmly established in the tradition of the scientific method of research and empiricism. He authored numerous books, many reflecting his empiricist orientation towards studying and researching the life and history of Black Americans.

DuBois possessed a kind of philosophical ambivalence relative to the integration and eventual assimilation of Blacks into the mainstream of white society. He advocated and worked towards the realization of integration, yet on the other had, rationalized for the necessity of Blacks to maintain a measure of separate institutions endemic to the Black community. He was one of the founders of the National Association for the Advancement of Colored People (NAACP) an organization that was and continues to be totally dedicated towards the achievement of total integration of Blacks and whites. His exaltation of Black culture, color and consciousness, and insistence on the retention of separate Black organizations and institutions led to his eventual defection from the NAACP. Prophetically, he feared the negative psychological effects of African Americans being totally socialized and mentally inundated with white and European history,

Photo 2   W.E.B. DuBois. Courtesy of National Archives.

culture and social values. DuBois was not the absolute integrationist and assimilationist aspirant as was Frederick Douglass. He was, however, a philosophical and psychological example of his own theory of Black "double-consciousness . . . two-ness . . . and . . . warring ideals . . ."[13]

Contrary to what some may argue, DuBois was not the originator or forerunner for the advocacy of Black cultural consciousness or awareness and Pan Africanist ideology. Much of the DuBoisian philosophy had already been expressed by David Walker, Henry Highland Garnet and Frederick Douglass. Indeed, recognition and lionization of DuBois as a major proponent of African American studies ideology developed and increased vigorously after the initiation of formal academic programs. DuBois perhaps led other Black scholars in performing specific studies of African Americans in the United States during a certain era. His work did not lead to or constitute the formalization of academic programs in Black Studies during his academic tenure or life time. However, he did urge and propose a plan for the initiation of a Black oriented curricula at predominantly Black colleges. His efforts were not realized because of his retirement and a reduction of funds allocated for the project.[14]

Ideologically, DuBois believed that there should be a cadre of intellectuals produced among the Black race in America dedicated toward uplifting the social, economic and political condition of the Black masses. He referred to this cadre as, The Talented Tenth. He warned that this group should not perceive its self as elitist and detached, but as servants to the oppressed and uneducated Blacks.[15] His philosophy of Black liberation conflicted sharply with the leading Black ideologist of that era, Booker T. Washington. The distinctiveness and definitiveness of DuBois's philosophy is revealed in his acute opposition to the accommodationist ideology of Booker T. Washington.

## Booker T. Washington (1856–1915)

The "accommodationist" philosophy of Booker T. Washington had an immeasurable effect on the lives and condition of millions of African Americans. Accommodationist is the term historians use to describe Washington's philosophy of capitulating to white racism, oppression and segregation in the South. His ideas were expressed in a speech he made at the Cotton States Exposition in Atlanta in 1895. Whites praised Washington's address and hailed him as a prudent leader of the Negro people. The speech propelled Washington into national fame. W.E.B DuBois later described the speech as the "Atlanta Compromise." In essence Washington stated that Blacks: 1) would accept second-class citizenship and segregation; 2) should not agitate for desegregation and political equality; and 3) must limit their education to agriculture, the industrial arts and crafts and the professions. The statement Washington made that, "In all things that are purely social, we can be as separate as the fingers, yet one as the hand in all things essential to mutual progress," drew the loudest applause from the hundreds of whites in the audience.[16]

Many Blacks, including W.E.B. DuBois, viewed the ideas and implications of Washington's speech socially retrogressive and predicated on "Uncle Tomism." Others surmised that the opinions of Washington were practical considering the reality of the circumstances at that time. Some aspects of his philosophy may have appealed to some Black entrepreneurs and professionals because, ironically, their success or the profitability of their businesses depended partly and unfortunately on the oppressive and exploitative system of segregation.

In a sense, a notion of Black independence or domestic nationalism was implicit in Washington's philosophy. His speech alluded to nationalist tenets of self-help and self

Photo 3   Booker T. Washington. Courtesy of National Archives.

determination. Washington stressed the importance of economics and Black entrepreneurship. He founded the Negro Business League whose members included African American business proprietors. It might be said that Booker T. Washington originated the concept of Black capitalism. Washington's philosophy of accommodation still is considered by many as a betrayal of the ideals of human equality and civil rights. However, the eventual effects of his ideas and influence cannot be definitively assessed. His social and economic philosophies continue to spark much debate and controversy in African American studies.

Washington was an educator and the builder of the Tuskegee Institute in Alabama. His educational accomplishments as principal of the Institute caused him to have much influence among southern Blacks. He had a substantial number of Black professionals who supported him and his ideology. Washington and his supporters represented a formidable political force known as the "Tuskegee Machine."[17] After his Atlanta speech, whites crowned him the national leader of the Black race.

Booker T. Washington may not be perceived as an intellectual. But certainly he was a cunning practical philosopher who used his ideas to win influence among white Americans. This in turn, endowed him with power among Blacks. He used his power to overtly and covertly force his will or political ideology upon a large segment of the Black population. Like Frederick Douglass, he was born a slave and, also like Douglass, his particular philosophy had a profound impact on the social and political conditions of African Americans for almost a century.

## Carter G. Woodson (1875–1950)

Woodson is acclaimed by African Americans as the father of Black history. There is no question that he was pioneering and assertive in re-establishing the long neglected heritage and history of Black people. However, it is equally significant to note that Woodson provided the philosophical basis and rationale for Black intellectual and educational independence. Since white and Jewish scholars held virtually complete control and authority over African American and African studies, it was difficult for African Americans to achieve any measure of scholarly independence and recognition of their works. More importantly, few Blacks had the insight and courage to challenge white control of Black scholarship.[18]

Rightfully, Woodson may be acclaimed as a philosopher and historian, scholar-educator and intellectual activist. He earned the Ph. D. degree at Harvard University in 1912 and, subsequently, studied at the Sorbonne in Paris. In 1915, he founded the Association for the Study of Afro-American Life and History. This organization was chartered not only for the study of Black history, but for the study of all aspects of African American life and experience. In 1916, he founded and published the *Journal of Negro History* and in 1920, he established the Associated Publishers as an independent publishing affiliate of the Association for the Study of Afro-American Life and History. In 1926, Woodson initiated the national observance and celebration of *Negro History Week*, now changed and termed **Black History Month**. In 1937, he founded the *Negro History Bulletin*.

Carter G. Woodson was decrying the irrelevancy of traditional American education to Black life in 1933, long before 1968 when Black students demanded African American/Black studies. In his classic work titled, *Mis-education of the Negro*, Woodson with simplicity and candor explains how American education and Black educators have failed African American youth. The inference is that although Blacks have been physically emancipated from slavery, they have been

Photo 4  Carter G. Woodson. Reprinted with permission from The Associated Publishers, Inc.

socialized into remaining in intellectual bondage. He wrote:

> When you control a man's thinking you do not have to worry about his actions. You do not have to tell him not to stand here or go yonder. He will find his "proper place" and will stay in it. You do not need to send him to the back door. He will go without being told. In fact, if there is no back door, he will cut one for his special benefit. His education makes it necessary.[19]

Like W.E.B. DuBois, he perceived that the role of the Black intellectual is to serve rather than to be elitist and detached from the Black masses. Woodson was astutely philosophic and prophetic in his criticism and theories relative to the social, political and economic conditions and challenges of Black people in America. His book, *Mis-education of the Negro*, is a synthesis of the wisdom, ideologies and prophesies of David Walker, Henry Highland Garnet, Frederick Douglass, W.E.B. DuBois and Booker T. Washington.

## E. Franklin Frazier (1894–1962)

Early Black philosophers and intellectuals functioned outside the realm of the university establishment and without the influence and authority that academe endowed. Their writing and oratory was related almost entirely to abolition, social protest and social reform issues. Beginning with the early twentieth century, more Blacks were admitted to northern white universities and some earned advanced or doctorate degrees. Equipped with academic rank and authority, they applied their university training and research methodology toward the social analysis, organization and culture of African Americans. E. Franklin Frazier was productive and prolific in the study of African American life, condition and experience from a sociological perspective.

Frazier earned the Ph.D. in sociology from the University of Chicago. He was chiefly in-
fluenced by Robert E. Park, and also by other eminent white sociologists of the University of Chicago sociological school of thought. Frazier's research and publications focused principally on the Black family, Black intra-class structure, and institutions in the Black community, specifically, Black business and the Black Church. Moreover, he was ideologically an integrationist, and his integrationist orientation and philosophy permeated and influenced his works. His studies and conclusions on the Black family, the Black middle-class, and Black businesses sparked the most debate, at least, among African American scholars and intellectuals.

Some of Frazier's studies might easily be interpreted as being highly critical and even satirical of the life, condition and experience of African Americans. In his book, *The Negro Family in the United States*, he submits that social factors such as the high incidence of female-headed households, children born out of wedlock, divorce, poverty, crime and delinquency has resulted in the *disorganization* of the Black family. Daniel Moynihan, author of a United States Labor Department report on the Negro family, used Frazier's analysis to state in the *Moynihan Report* that the Black family was a "tangle of pathology" and rendered further dysfunctional because of its matriarchal structure or pattern. Black civil rights proponents viewed the *Moynihan Report* as an attack on the Black family and a distraction from the real issue of racism in American society.

It was Frazier's contention, also, that slavery had destroyed all vestige of African heritage and culture relative to Black behavioral and social patterns. This theory was criticized by many African American scholars and firmly rejected by those of the late twentieth century. The meticulous and comprehensive research of Melville J. Herskovits, a white anthropologist was accepted by many Black intellectuals as a contradiction to Frazier's thesis of the destruction of African culture.[20]

*Black Bourgeoisie*, a book published by Frazier in 1957, provoked the wrath and resentment of the African American social strata to which it was directed, the middle-class. The work may be interpreted as a sardonic and satirical literary ridicule of the Black middle-class' diminutive efforts towards imitating white culture and simulating white social and economic institutions. The book generated class antagonism between low-income and middle-class African Americans. Many low-income Blacks who felt that the well-to-do Blacks were indifferent to their plight praised the book, especially, during a period of the 1960s' civil rights movement. *Black Bourgeoisie*, could be applicable or descriptive of any oppressed or colonized group that aspires to emulate the coveted position of their oppressor. However, one must realize that E. Franklin Frazier was an ardent integrationist and visionary assimilationist. As an integrationist, he believed that Blacks must *fully* and *successfully* adopt and practice white middle-class values and culture if the ultimate goal of assimilation is ever to be achieved. The statement that Frazier makes in *Black Bourgeoisie*, is that African Americans have not been sufficiently successful or expeditious enough in the mastery of white middle-class values and culture. Frazier's philosophy and advocacy of integration as the panacea for the race problem in the United States moderated or changed prior to his death in 1962.

Regardless of the debate and controversy some of Frazier's works provoked, his books and articles proved to be valuable resources towards the academic development of African American studies. They provide students with the opportunity to study and critique social theory authored by an African American and analyzed within an intra-racial context.

## Charles S. Johnson (1893–1956)

Research methodology and analytical technique have historically been acquired by African American scholars at major American and European universities. The standard for these processes are based upon approaches and paradigms consistent with European scientific social theory. Objectivism, empiricism and statistical analysis and inference are imperatives in the determination of good scholarship. Charles S. Johnson acquired *good* research skills and abilities while studying at the University of Chicago. While at the university, he became associated with Robert E. Park and other eminent professors of the Chicago school.

Johnson was able to resist protest ideology for the sake of having his work "accepted" as being professional, in spite of the climate of intense racism and segregation under which most of his studies were conducted. Nevertheless, Johnson's work relating to Black rural and urban life is important to the sociological field and, particularly, to African American studies. He is credited with having created broader interest in social research and analysis of the Black community. He was not ideological or particularly philosophical in an explicit or direct sense. However, he used the inferences from the statistical and empirical analyses of his studies to show evidence of and provide rationale for rallying public opinion against the evils of racism and the injustice of segregation. The lack of even hints of protest or ideological militancy in his works may be attributed to the fact that financial support for many of his studies came from governmental sources or white philanthropy.[21]

Charles S. Johnson, E. Franklin Frazier and W.E.B. DuBois were useful to their mentors or white researchers because of their indigenousness to the Black community. Race of interviewer is important in order to achieve greater reliability of responses from African Americans. The slave experience, repression and fear has always encouraged Blacks to respond differently to questions asked by a white rather than a Black interviewer. This may be true even today.

W.E.B. DuBois' study, *The Philadelphia Negro*, provided the model for research of the Black community that was subsequently followed by Johnson and Frazier. Johnson never earned a degree above the B.A. Yet, his studies were as perceptive, interpretative of the ethos of Blacks, and eloquently written as W.E.B. DuBois.

## Alain Leroy Locke (1886–1954)

From an academic perspective, Locke was formally educated and trained in the field of philosophy. He received his Ph.D. degree at Harvard in 1918. He was a philosopher and an intellectual in the vein of that which archetypal universities like Harvard, Oxford and the University of Berlin can produce. His philosophical interest and contributions were in the area of value theory. His theories of values, value conflict and resolution, contributes much toward the analysis of American racism and an enlightenment of the contemporary concept of cultural pluralism. He wrote several books and numerous articles relating to the social and behavioral sciences, humanities, education and religion.

It is important to recognize Alain Locke as a major contributor to the theoretical foundation of African American studies. In spite of the fact that he may not be widely known or acclaimed, he was a contemporary of DuBois, Washington, Woodson, Frazier, Johnson and Marcus Garvey. Locke maintained a quiet "presence" among these men and his works influenced or complemented their ideologies in a reasoned, but elitist way. Furthermore, his entire professional career was spent at the predominantly Black Howard University as a professor of philosophy. While at Howard he, undoubtedly, effected the philosophical orientations of thousands of Black students and other intellectuals who would, after his demise in 1954, become participants and professionals in the field of African American or Black studies.

He was a strong advocate of Black education, adult education and, particularly, Black culture *in* education. Locke was indeed philosophically prophetic in view of what he wrote of and described in his most profound work, *The New Negro*. In this essay, he apparently foresaw the restlessness and growing intolerance of Blacks to white racism and the eventual Black revolt and American reform movements of the 1960s. He was also insightful relative to the race value arguments brought on by Affirmative Action initiatives and programs of the 1960s and continuing in the 1990s. Locke is referred to by many as the interpreter of the Black American's culture.[22]

## Marcus Garvey (1887–1940)

The philosophy and foundation for the study of Black people in the United States would be incomplete without taking into account the charismatic and dynamic influence of Marcus Garvey. While he may not have been considered as intellectually astute as his contemporaries or peers, he equalled them or even excelled them in ideological keenness and persuasiveness. In a technical sense, Garvey was not an American, but he was Black and his ethos was indisputably African. However, the economic and social courses of action he proclaimed or advocated have made an indelible impression upon the philosophy and ideological opinions of millions of African Americans during the early twentieth century—and even today.

He was born and received his early education in Jamaica, West Indies. He became a printer by trade and made several attempts and achieved some success at starting newspapers. Garvey was reared under the exploitative rule of British colonialism and began early to protest and organize against poverty and bad working conditions. He left Jamaica in 1909 and travelled abroad to Costa Rica,

Photo 5  Marcus Garvey. Courtesy of The Library of Congress.

Panama and several other Latin American countries. There he witnessed much of the same demeaning and oppressive treatment accorded people of African descent by the European colonial powers. He, subsequently, lived in England for a few years and attended London University. Upon his return home, he organized the Jamaica Improvement Association which later was to serve as a model for an American branch of the organization called the Universal Negro Improvement Association (UNIA). The UNIA became the ideological base for the launching and development of the era of Garvey and Garveyism. The provocative and idiomatic slogans of "back to Africa," "Africa for Africans" and "Black is Beautiful" were the rallying themes of the UNIA, and Black self-sufficiency and self-determination was its motivating economic objective.

Black leaders, foes and friends; integrationist, separatists, Pan-Africanists and nationalists acclaimed him as the greatest boaster of the African American's spirit of self-pride. He instilled within them a notion and spirit of defiance against white racism and white supremacy in the United States. W.E.B. DuBois and E. Franklin Frazier, although critical of Garvey's personality, ego, and administrative incompetency, hailed him as a leader of the Black masses across all socio-economic strata or income groups. Frazier noted that "The Garvey Movement is a crowd movement essentially different from any other social phenomenon among [Blacks]."[23]

Garvey instilled within the hearts and minds of Black people not only a philosophy and ideology of freedom, but also a *psychology* of liberation. Garvey and Garveyism emerged during the cultural revival and revelation period of the Harlem Renaissance. The splendor and the enchantment of the "Black Pride" ideology of the Garveyites accentuated and complemented the cultural creativity of African American writers and artists of the Harlem Renaissance.

The Garvey movement and the UNIA co-existed with other Black freedom type organizations. While the other leaders and organizations focused and fought for social and political enfranchisement, Garvey's emphasis and priority were economic. He understood, clearly, that for the masses of Blacks, social integration and politics were secondary to their impoverished economic status. Garvey introduced to the Black masses the idea that capitalism practiced and mastered by Blacks can operate to uplift and dignify African people. Conversely, he taught them that monopoly capitalism controlled by whites was being used to exploit and oppress Blacks. Harold Cruse describes civil rights initiatives and programs that do not recognize or prioritize the economic factor as "non-economic liberalism."[24]

In many ways the philosophy of Marcus Garvey and Booker T. Washington were similar, especially in terms of separatism and economic emphasis. Cruse alludes to their similarities when he writes, " . . . it was not so much that Washington was against civil rights as he was *instinctively* opposed to the ideals of noneconomic liberalism that dominated the civil rights traditions . . ."[25] It may seem paradoxical that Booker T. Washington was condemned by many Blacks for his acceptance of white separatist ideology, yet, Marcus Garvey was lauded by the Black masses for his advocacy of race separation. The difference, of course, is that Washington endorsed unequal or inequitable segregation or separation of the races. Garvey's separatism demanded race equality. Moreover, there is a fundamental difference between forced segregation and voluntary separation.

Garvey's mis-management of his Black Star Shipping Line and a myriad of other economic ventures; covert and overt persecution by American and British governments; and a growing resentment by Black leaders for his endorsement of white racist segregation policies led to the decline and demise of

Garveyism and Garvey. However, Garvey predicted that his cause would rise again.

This prophecy was realized during the 1960s when African American students and Black Nationalists such as Stokely Carmichael, Elijah Muhammad, Malcom X, and many others espoused many of the philosophies and ideologies of Marcus Garvey. The concept of Black Nationhood, and the symbolic Garvey colors of red, black and green were flaunted and flourished during the civil rights revolt of the 1960s and 1970s. The philosophy and idealism of Marcus Garvey are embraced today by millions of Black Americans and represent a significant political factor and social paradigm in the foundation of African American studies.

### African American/Black Philosophy and Social Change.
A people's philosophy is derived from exposure to physical, social, cultural, political and economic phenomena or experiences unique to their own survival or existence. Their experiences forge upon their mind and intellect a perception of the universe and universal relations that forms a world view or philosophy of life. Thus, the philosophy of one group may not be practical or relevant, in a generic sense, to all people. The African American experience is certainly different in many significant aspects to the life and history of white Americans and Europeans. It is an aberration of psyche reality for the oppressed to hold the same worldview of life as the oppressor. Neither are life chances and outlook the same for the impoverished and the wealthy. A different product of wisdom and understanding emerges from each group depending upon their relative status or condition in world society.

Philosophy is transmissible and transient. White American philosophy and worldview did not begin with the landing of the Pilgrims on the Mayflower. Correspondingly, the genesis of African American thought and intellect was established long before the first

slaveship arrived in America. In spite of the denial of the equality of African peoples by Europeans and the destruction of much of African civilization, there was and still exists an African philosophy as opposed to European. The written and unwritten thought, knowledge and wisdom of Africans have been passed down from generation to generation. Great African thinkers have always existed in the societies of the Egyptians, Bantus, Zulus, Tauregs, Kikiyus, Sudanese and countless others. The ancient African empires of Ghana, Mali and Songhay were once the centers of African thought and intellect. The Songhay Empire, and the University of Sankore at Timbuctoo, were in existence over a hundred years after the slave trade started.[26]

There is no reason for African Americans or Black people to relate *solely* to European or American classical and neo-classical philosophers for enlightenment relative to their own plight and destiny. The philosophies of Socrates, Plato, Aristotle, Hegel and Marx relative to virtue and morality grew out of a social milieu of leisure-class and feudalism or bourgeois and proletariat human relationships. Their axioms and prescriptive assessments of human conduct are almost incomparable and, certainly, not completely applicable to the chattel slavery, racism, segregation and discrimination experiences of Africans in America.

As stated above, philosophy is not only transmittable but transient. After successive civil and human rights struggles and triumphs, culminating with the Civil Rights Movement of the 1960s, African American thought and philosophy began to change from purely social protest to a new stage of liberation ideology. The new philosophy is not focused essentially on social, but it is predicated towards the achievement of complete political and *intellectual* liberation. The 1960s also introduced the long neglected subject of women's liberation and, especially, Black women's liberation.

The thought and activities of protest of African American women of the 18th and early 19th centuries were unheralded and sometimes unpublicized. Black women like Harriet Tubman, Sojourner Truth, Anna Julia Cooper, Mary Church Terrell, Ida B. Wells, Maria W. Stewart and many others played major roles toward the formulation of an African American philosophy and of laying the foundation for African American studies. These women projected their philosophy through their activities if not always by oratory or in the "learned" literature.

The discovery or rediscovery, revelation, analysis and interpretation of the works and activities of historical and contemporary African American philosophers, writers and artists are a major mission and research task of African American or Black studies. The idea of making this knowledge a part of world history, and making American education relevant to Blacks formed the intellectual "liberated" basis for the institution of African American and Black Studies in the United States. The first formal academic program in Black Studies was initiated in 1968.

## · QUESTIONS AND EXERCISES ·

1. What factors differentiate the history and experience of African Americans from that of Asian, Hispanic, and Native Americans?

2. Define African American or Black Studies and enumerate the major educational and social objectives.

3. If the term "Black" is used to *name* a race of people in America, should it be capitalized as a proper noun or uncapitalized as a common adjective?

4. Providing the history and experience of Black citizens of the United States were integrated fully and equitably into American textbooks, would it obviate the need for a separate discipline of African American studies?

5. Prepare a brief paper differentiating between the social, political and economic philosophies of Booker T. Washington, W.E.B. Dubois and Marcus Garvey.

6. Study the histories or biographies of early Black women human rights activists such as Harriet Tubman, Sojourner Truth, Anna Julia Cooper, Mary Church Terrell, Ida B. Wells and Maria W. Stewart. What were their social, political or economic philosophies besides or beyond the abolition of slavery?

7. Obtain a copy of *David Walker's Appeal* or Henry Highland Garnet's *Address to the Slaves of the United States of America*. Compare their philosophies and rhetoric with that of Black civil rights activists of the 1960s such as Malcolm X, Stokely Carmichael, Angela Davis or Martin Luther King, Jr.

# ▪ NOTES AND REFERENCES ▪

1. Beverly Hendrix Wright, "Ideological Change and Black Identity during Civil Rights Movements." *The Western Journal of Black Studies.* 5/3 (Fall 1981) 186–95. Also see Sterling Stuckey's *Slave Culture: Nationalist Theory & Foundations of Black America* (New York: Oxford University Press, 1987), pp. 193–244.

2. See Joel Kovel, *White Racism: A Psychohistory* (New York: Vintage Books, 1971), pp. 62–63. In fact, the *Oxford English Dictionary* and *Websters Dictionary* define the term black as evil, wicked and bad in addition to other meanings.

3. Stokely Carmichael and Charles V. Hamilton, *Black Power: The Politics of Liberation in Americas Politics.* (New York: Vintage Books, 1967). p. 37.

4. Lynn Ludlow, "Assorted Reaction to Calling Blacks African Americans." *The San Francisco Examiner.* (December 22, 1988) p. A-4.

5. Vivian Gordon, "The Coming of Age of Black Studies." *The Western Journal of Black Studies.* Vol. 5, No. 3, (Fall 1981) p. 233.

6. Cited from program announcement, "Opt for Undergraduate Studies in Afro-American Studies," College for Letters & Science, The University of Wisconsin-Milwaukee, 1991.

7. See Abdul Alkalimat and Associates, *Introduction to Afro-American Studies: A Peoples College Primer,* (Chicago: 21st Century Publications. 1986).

8. James A. Johnson et al., *Introduction to the Foundations of Education.* (Boston: Allyn and Bacon, 1969). pp. 12–13.

9. The objectives listed here and other findings of the Task Force can be found in the published report, *Black Studies: Issues in their Institutional Survival,* U.S. Department of Health, Education, and Welfare. Washington, D.C. (October 1976).

10. For a comprehensive study of how European and American philosophers and intellectuals introduced racism and degraded Africa, see St Clair Drake, *Black Folk Here and There,* (Los Angeles: University of California, Center for Afro-American Studies, 1987), pp. 13–42. Also, Chukwuemka Onwubu, "The Intellecutal Foundation of Racism," in *Black Studies: Theory, Methods and Cultural Perspectives,* ed. Talmadge Anderson (Pullman, WA: Washington State University Press, 1990) pp. 77–88.

11. Leonard Harris, *Philosophy Born of Struggle,* (Dubuque, Iowa: Kendall/Hunt Publishing Company, 1983) p. ix.

12. Biographical data on Walker, Garnet, and Douglass are common and numerous. See *The International Library of Afro-American Life and History* (Washington, D.C.: The Assn. of Afro-American Life and History, 1976); Sterling Stuckey, *Slave Culture* (New York: Oxford University Press, 1987); and Philip S. Foner, *The Life and Writings of Frederick Douglass,* ed. Vol. 1–4. (New York: International Publishers, 1975).

13. DuBois stated his theory of double-consciousness in his book, *The Souls of Black Folk.* These quotes are from W.E.B. DuBois. *The Souls of Black Folk,* (New York: Signet Classic, The New American Library 1969) p. 45.

14. See W.E.B. DuBois. *The Autobiography of W.E.B. DuBois.* (New York: International Publishers, 1968) pp. 313–330.

15. Manning Marable, *W.E.B. Du Bois: Black Radical Democrat,* (Boston: Twayne Publishers 1986) p. 147.

16. Bernard A. Weisberger. *Booker T. Washington*. (New York: Mentor Book, The New American Library 1972). pp. 83–87.

17. Marable, *W.E.B. DuBois*, 42, 43.

18. For a profound study of the plight of the Black intellectual, see Harold Cruse, *The Crisis of the Negro Intellectual*. 1967. (New York: William Morrow & Co. Reprint. New York: Quill 1984) pp. 96–111, 451–475.

19. Carter G. Woodson, *Mis-education of the Negro* (Washington, D.C.: The Associated Publishers, Inc. 1933. Reprint 1969) p. xxxiii.

20. See G. Franklin Edwards, "E. Franklin Frazier" in *Black Sociologists* ed. James E. Blackwell and Morris Janowitz (Chicago: The University of Chicago Press 1974) pp. 92–97. Also, Melville J. Herskovits, *The Myth of the Negro Past* (Harper & Brothers 1941. Reprint. Boston: Beacon Press 1958).

21. Ibid., 72–73. Richard Robbins in *Black Sociologists*.

22. See Johnny Washington, *Alain Locke and Philosophy: A Quest for Cultural Pluralism* (New York: Greenwood Press 1986) 78–98, 120–131.

23. See John Henrik Clarke, *Marcus Garvey and the Vision of Africa*, ed. (New York: Vintage Books 1974) 3–9, 237.

24. Harold Cruse, *Plural But Equal* (New York: William Morrow and Co., Inc. 1987) 293, 325.

25. Ibid.

26. John Henrik Clarke, "The University of Sankore at Timbuctoo: A Neglected Achievement in Black Intellectual History." *The Western Journal of Black Studies*. 1(2) (June 1977) 142–146.

# Chapter 2

## Initiation and Development of African American Studies

### DEMAND, CONTROVERSY, AND INSTITUTIONALIZATION

*Evolution of the Student Movement in America.* African American or Black Studies was instituted at American colleges and universities through the educational demand of Black students with the support of the Black community, and with nominal assistance from white student organizations. The initiation of African American studies programs and departments at institutions of higher learning followed a non-traditional or inverse process in comparison to traditional disciplines or fields of study. The idea and efforts toward establishing African American studies did not originate with academic administrators and faculty as custom would require. Demands for the formalization of programs and curricula relating to the study of African Americans

began with Black students who were aided and abetted not only by professional, common, and "street" people of the Black community, but also by enlightened white students. The emergence of student power and, particularly, the effect that Black students had upon the moral consciousness of white America compelled schools, colleges and universities to reassess their academic mission and social objectives.

Historically, human progress and social change have been effected by students steeped in the classical philosophies of their teacher mentors, and guided by the traditional purpose and role of institutions of higher learning. However, in numerous countries throughout the world, students have rebelled against tradition and effected change in social customs and political policies through organized protest, rioting and strikes. Until the 1960s, American students, seemingly, accepted the role and objective of the college or university as being a bastion of the privileged elite and purposed for the pursuit of liberal education and professionalism.

The 1960s was an era marked by the emergence of student power. Students began to challenge the meaning and purpose of education, and forced colleges and universities to reexamine their role and function in American society. Students not only questioned the societal tradition and purpose of institutionalized education, but sought to reform the college or university structure and curriculum. African American students at, historically, Black institutions initiated the student revolt by challenging the racist and segregationist traditions of the American south. These students demonstrated that education should and did serve to enlighten a people relative to their civil rights and social justice, and gave them the courage of free expression and the determination to seek truth.

White students were concerned with free speech, shared student-university governance, ideological diversity, social idealism, and humanitarian goals and objectives. They also questioned the morality of the complicity of the university, corporation, military and Central Intelligence Agency (CIA), especially in relation to the Vietnam War. While white students sought to legitimize radical politics and to revolutionize the system, Black student protest and demands were clearly focused on American racism, segregation, civil rights, discrimination and the initiation of Black or African American studies. In many instances, white students joined and supported the civil rights and Black studies initiatives of African American students. Student demands, protest and rebellions did not always occur within a peaceful milieu. The Student Power Movement of the 1960s provoked unprecedented campus and community incidents of violence and disruption.[1]

A sequence of historical events in the struggle for civil rights and social equality preceded and influenced the student rebel-

lions that, subsequently, led to the demand and formal initiation of African American studies. The socio-economic and political status of Blacks have tended to improve after each American War or international conflict. Blacks have always served loyally and valiantly in the armed forces, fighting to protect the liberty and rights of others abroad that were denied to them at home in America. Upon their return to the United States or discharge from the armed services, they have been less prone to accept the degrading affects of racism and the inequitable status of second-class citizens. This was particularly evident in the aftermath of World War II and even more after and during the Korean Conflict. Moreover, African Americans inevitable participation in the work force of wartime industries, improved their economic means and resources. In spite of the vast economic disparity that existed between the two races, the minor gains that accrued to Blacks as a result of World War II sparked new hopes and fueled their determination to resist segregation and to fight the dehumanizing institution of racism. Civil rights organizations such as the National Association for the Advancement of Colored People (NAACP) renewed their legal initiatives and appeals in the courts to end racial discrimination and segregation. It was the sons and daughters of those Black parents who gained new courage and means to fight racism and segregation during the war and post-war periods who precipitated the student movements and rebellions of the 1960s.[2]

One of the most phenomenal events that was to be a seed for the Black student rebellion of the sixties was the *Brown v. Board of Education of Topeka* decision by the United States Supreme Court on May 17, 1954. This decision by the Supreme Court ruled that racial segregation in public schools was unconstitutional. The ruling provoked a wave of white protests and a series of lynchings, bombings and other violent and repressive activities by white supremacist groups directed toward African Americans in the southern United States. White southern lawyers hastened to prepare briefs and suits to appeal, forestall or resist the school desegregation ruling. Black civil rights organizations and their attorneys began to attempt implementation of the law by initiating test actions or cases in the elementary and secondary public schools in the eleven hard-core segregationist states of the South.

Efforts of school boards to comply with the law were obstructed by avid segregationists and met with terror and violence. One of the most notable resistance cases occurred at Central High School in Little Rock, Arkansas where the state's National Guard had to be federalized to enforce the law and allow Black students to enter. Similar scenarios of resistance, confrontation and enforcement were repeated in the arena of higher education when African Americans attempted to enroll as students at the Universities of Alabama, Georgia and Mississippi. The gauntlet for integration and equality was cast with Black students serving as both pawns and protagonists.

Less than two years after the *Brown vs Board of Education* Supreme Court ruling, a Black woman named Rosa Parks challenged the segregation policy of Montgomery, Alabama by refusing to move to the back of the bus to provide a seat for a white man. When she adamantly refused to move to the rear of the bus after repeated requests by the bus driver the police were summoned and she was arrested. This incidence incited an unprecedented stance of unity among the Blacks of Montgomery and triggered a mass Black boycott of the city's transit system. The boycott was formally organized under the title of the Montgomery Improvement Association. The young clergyman Martin Luther King, Jr. was elected to head the boycott movement. Through his leadership, rallying and fund raising efforts, the Montgomery Boycott achieved national and world attention and

support. The Montgomery Bus Boycott ignited the spirit of defiance to racism in Black America and similar resistance movements were started all over the country. King adopted the Mahatma Gandhi philosophy of nonviolent protest during the boycott. His tactics and strategies of nonviolence and civil disobedience became a model for future protest movements in the United States, especially, for dissident students of the 1960s.

The favorable school desegregation decision of the Supreme Court and the triumphant result of the Montgomery boycott swelled the liberation aspirations of the younger Black generation. They became impatient with the slow pace of securing freedom through the courts and the "gradualism" philosophy of traditional civil rights leaders and organizations. African Americans felt betrayed because of the ineffectiveness and lack of enforcement of the *Brown* decision. Four years after the ruling southern schools and universities remained virtually segregated and unequal.

On February 1, 1960, four students from the historically Black North Carolina Agricultural and Technical College at Greensboro seated themselves at the segregated lunch counter of a Woolworth store. They were refused service but, yet, they sat quietly and read their textbooks. In spite of being jeered and threatened, they sat passively. The counter was closed, however, they returned the next day. The students exercised the techniques and tactics of nonviolent protest and passive resistance. When news of the sit-in was disseminated in the media, thousands of students began similar sit-ins in towns and cities where Black colleges were located. Within weeks from 50,000 to 70,000 persons had participated in sit-ins or demonstrated on behalf of the movement. Thousands were arrested and several killed. Police brutality was rampant.

The dynamic growth and spread of the sit-ins throughout the South led to the formation of one of the most formidable African American student organizations in the history

Photo 6  Resistance to School Desegregation. Courtesy of The Library of Congress.

of America. Martin Luther King, Jr. and Ella Baker of the Southern Christian Leadership Conference (SCLC) called a meeting of student representatives from all Black colleges. Over two-hundred people attended the conference in Raleigh, North Carolina, April 15, 1960. Out of this meeting the Student Nonviolent Coordinating Committee (SNCC) was born.[3]

There is an extensive and indirect relation to SNCC and the eventual establishing of African American/Black studies programs and departments in educational institutions in the United States. The sit-ins, organized and led by SNCC, had begun a student revolutionary movement purposed towards fighting and abolishing all forms and practices of racial segregation and discrimination. During the Spring and Summer of 1961, SNCC participated with the Congress of Racial Equality (CORE) in the execution of the dangerous and sometimes violent Freedom Rides throughout the South. The Freedom Rides were activities designed to exercise the rights of Blacks to travel interstate on public transportation without segregation or discrimination. Although the Supreme Court had ruled segregation in carriers and terminal facilities unconstitutional fourteen years earlier, fear and the threat of arrest or violence inhibited Blacks from exercising the right in the deep South. SNCC diversified its concerns and activities from Freedom Rides to Black voter registration and political reform throughout the South.

SNCC, in association mostly with CORE, organized grassroots Blacks and coordinated massive voter registration drives. Their efforts were met with terror and violence from southern whites who were resistant and recalcitrant in relinquishing their hold on White Supremacist politics. SNCC was instrumental in organizing an independent Black political organization in Lowndes County, Alabama called the Black Panther Party. By the mid 1960s, under the leadership of Stokely Carmichael, the ideological bent of SNCC had changed from integration to independent Black politics, self-determination and economic self-sufficiency. Carmichael defined the new ideology with the slogan of *BLACK POWER*. The term Black Power was a controversial one and was the subject of various interpretations. However, its implications reintroduced Marcus Garvey's concepts of race pride, self-respect, self-help and "black" consciousness.

The impact, achievements and social revolutionary roles that SNCC played in the liberation of African Americans during the 1960s are too voluminous to treat in this book. However, it is important to state that the influence and social revolutionary ideology of Black students were not limited to the geographical confines of the Southern and Eastern United States but also took root in the West. The new nationalist and militant emphasis of SNCC, in all probability, influenced the formation and ideology of a more radical Black student/community organization in California. The Black Panthers, founded in Oakland California in 1966, adopted the name and symbol of the defunct SNCC Black Panther political party of the Lowndes County Freedom Organization in Alabama.[4]

By 1967 the concept of Black Power—interpreted as African Americans having control of the social, political and economic institutions in their community—began to make sense and gain support throughout Black America. However, it was evident that if the goals of Black self-determination and self-sufficiency were to become a reality, African Americans would have to become educationally and technologically competent. Consequently, the strategy and base of operations of the student movement generally shifted from the town to the campus. When students redirected their attention to the campus, they discovered that the educational policies and academic curricula of the colleges and universities represented and promoted the same racial inequities and social injustices as the broader society. American institutions of higher education, perhaps more than any other institution, denigrated the humanity of Black people and posed as the most formidable barrier to the realization of Black pride, self-development and self determination. In order for education to benefit African Americans, it had to become more responsive to the needs of the Black community and more relevant to Black culture. Thus the students began to organize, to demand and negotiate change. The most popular name for these organizations was Black Student Union. The gauntlet had been cast and the course set that would bring about a revolution in American education.[5]

***Black Studies at San Francisco State College: The Genesis.*** It was merely incidental that the first Black or African American Studies academic program was initiated at San Francisco State College. The shift of Black students' focus from social and economic integration to educational reform, academic parity and Black Power was a national phenomenon. The nature and intensity of racism at predominantly white colleges and universities caused African American students to revel in their African heritage and culture. Therefore, it was inevitable that the lack of any curricula treatment of the culture and experience of Africans in America would become a burning issue and demand. Indeed, almost concurrent with San Francisco State College's concession to the demand for and adoption of a Black Studies Department in 1968, students at other major institutions were using disruptive tactics and making similar and related appeals. For instance, students at Stanford, Columbia, Northwestern, Cornell, and Ohio State universities were concerned with the adoption of Afro-American history courses, recruitment of more Black students, employment of initial or additional Black faculty or the provision of special buildings for Black American culture or habitation. Of course after the historic strike and political controversy over African American studies and other social issues at San Francisco State College had occurred, the demand and establishment of Black Studies programs and courses accelerated throughout the nation.

Before a summary account of the factors leading to the establishment of the first Black Studies Department is given, the identity or, indeed, the position of *student* should be examined. The term student defines the abstract quality of one who, occupationally, acquires knowledge. One who is the processor and product of studying. When one enrolls as a student in an educational institution, his or her status as a civilian is viewed as suspended relative to certain civic responsibility or accountability. In essence, students are favored with a mythical shield of invulnerability. Therefore, students are effective quasi-civilian agents for promoting and making social change.

Economic paradoxes and race/class income differentials of the 1960s exacerbated the deteriorating social conditions of racial-ethnic minorities in the United States. This gave rise to increased student discontent with the role and performance of higher education institutions. In California and, particularly, in the Black and other Third World communities near San Francisco State College, students began to develop their own idea relative to the college's role and responsibility for reaching out to the educationally deprived and economically disadvantaged.

During periods of economic upturn and prosperity, many affluent white students tend to relax their materialistic pursuits and adherence to the principles of the "establishment" and become more socially oriented and committed. Conversely, the paradox of inflationary-recession raises the unfulfilled socioeconomic expectations of the underclass and provoke unrest and discontent in Black and Third World communities. The tax cut and accelerated expenditures of the Vietnam War which took place during the mid and late 1960s produced an aura of economic optimism among some groups of white students and they focused their attention on social or war and peace issues.

The student government at San Francisco State had a significant fund of $300,000 obtained through compulsory student body fees. White student activists were able to direct much of these funds toward the development of a Tutorial Program to help ghetto children and the underprivileged and for the support of other educational and socio-political community programs including the Mississippi Summer Project. The student programs included the creation of an Experimental College for the purpose of social and educational indoctrination which they hoped would lead to social reform. The idea and success of these white student programs in conjunction with the initiation and rise of the Black Student Union (BSU) and its Black consciousness and Black Power orientation set the stage for the unfolding drama of African American Studies. Black student activists co-opted the model of the white student programs and, with the support of the student government fund, launched a number of Black arts and culture courses in the Experimental College. In the summer of 1966 Jimmy Garrett, a SNCC organizer from Watts, founded the BSU at San Francisco State. He was not content with confining the Black studies courses to the Experimental College. Garrett vigorously campaigned for the incorporation of the Black studies courses into the academic departments of the college. However, the ultimate goal was for the establishment of a Black Studies Department.[6]

By December 1967, under constant pressure and provocation from the Black Student Union, the Acting President of the College, S. I. Hayakawa had virtually conceded a Black Studies Department. On February 9, 1968, Hayakawa had made the independent decision to appoint Dr. Nathan Hare to develop and coordinate a Black Studies curriculum. However, the Board of Trustees forestalled or postponed implementation of the program. Having exhausted all viable means and appeals, Black students became exasperated and called a strike on November 6. The college was effectively closed.

The strike called by the Black Student Union was based on a myriad of issues and grievances affecting various campus groups. However, the most incisive demand among the issues was the demand for the immediate establishment of a Black Studies Department. The strike gained the support and joint participation of various third world student organizations including the Asian-American Political Alliance (AAPA), Mexican-American Student Confederation (MASC), Latin American Student Organization (LASO), Philippine-American Collegiate Endeavor (PACE), and the Intercollegiate Chinese for Social Action (ICSA). In coalition with the Black Student Union, these groups formed an umbrella organization called the Third World Liberation Front (TWLF). The combined organizations submitted a list of 15 non-negotiable demands to the Administration. The Students for a Democratic Society (SDS), a radical white student organization supported and participated in the strike, as well as other unaffiliated white students.[7]

The strike was successful and the students were victorious. By the end of 1968, San Francisco State College was the first institution of higher education to formally establish a Black or African American Studies program, and Nathan Hare was the first coordinator or head. After the 1968 student rebellion and strike, the number of Black/African American courses, programs and departments proliferated not only in institutions of higher education, but units and courses were adopted also in many elementary and secondary schools. Moreover, African American studies served as the vanguard and model for the subsequent implementation of Chicano Studies, Asian American Studies, Native American Studies and even Women Studies.

# AFRICAN AMERICAN STUDIES AND EDUCATIONAL DEMOCRACY

*Democratization of American Education.* The demand for and establishment of African American Studies signaled the waning influence of Frederick Douglass' integrationist or assimilationist philosophy. Integration and

Photo 7   Nathan Hare. Courtesy of Nathan Hare.

the remote hope of assimilation had been the primary social and political objectives of Black civil rights movements since Emancipation. Although the accommodationist-segregationist philosophy of Booker T. Washington and the subsequent Black nationalist-separatist ideology of Marcus Garvey had widespread appeal and support among certain socio-economic classes of African Americans, racial integration had always been perceived by most as the panacea for race problems in America. However, the integration oriented campaigns of Black students changed when their attention shifted from town to campus. In fact, their educational demands were quite separatist and Garveyian in nature. For one to understand the complexity of the paradoxical change of Black student emphasis from integrated to race-specific educational concerns, it is necessary to discuss the race-exclusive nature of American education.

American education professes to the ideals of democracy, equality of opportunity, and the rights and dignity for all citizens. These ideals are ignored relative to their application to America's more than 30 million citizens of African descent. Black Americans are almost compelled to subscribe to and adopt white Western Anglo-Saxon history and culture, yet, they are denied equal opportunity and access to social and political power. "Americanization" for Blacks requires their social and cultural adaptation to White middle-class norms and European values. Thus, the White ethnocentric character of American education, in cause and affect, gives rise not only to White nationalism but, also, to institutional racism. The exclusion of the African American experience belies the democratic intent of education and makes the social platitude of integration a myth.

Democracy fosters the principle of equality of rights, opportunity and treatment. Although democracy is based on the theory of majority rule, its egalitarian orientation provides for the maintenance and protection of minority rights and dignity. The race-specific or separatist implications of African American studies may well be interpreted as a cry for the fulfillment of the democratic principles of education. Educational exclusivism and racism were the bases of the demand for African American Studies. Any policy of integration that requires African Americans to relinquish their heritage, culture and racial identity and have them to become fused or extinct within the culture of the dominant society is undemocratic.

The establishing of African American or Black studies programs was, and still is, perceived by some as a trend towards separatism or even segregation. The democratic implications inherent in the institution of African American studies have been lost because of the confusion over the definitions or differences between the terms segregation and separatism from a Black perspective. Segregation is a policy of enforced apartness (apartheid) under the control of an oppressor or dominant race. Separation refers to the voluntary act of a race collectively separating in pursuit of their own social, economic or political freedom and self-actualization. Nathan Hare writes that:

> Segregation exists when somebody sets you apart for characteristics they deem to be inferior. Separation is the act of moving away or seeking independence of mind or space yourself, for your own reasons at your own time. There is a crucial psychological difference between the two which is too often missed.[8]

Unresponsiveness of Whites to the demand of Blacks to end educational racism and to include African American life and experience into the history and development of the United States led to a series of separatist demands on campuses nationwide.

At the height of the Black/African American studies movement Preston Wilcox observed that:

The rash of Black Studies programs is a direct reflection of the failure of "integrated," white supremacist education. Black students are refusing to attempt to fully integrate themselves into racist institutions which educate Black students to hate themselves as Blacks. White controlled institutions of higher education have systematically overlooked the intellectual and political interests of [30] million Black people and persisted in talking about the right of free inquiry and academic freedom.[9]

Black students and the Black community took American schools, colleges and universities to task for teaching the equality of mankind while, at the same, institutionalizing inequality in the educational curricula.

Race-specific studies related to African Americans and to other American racial-ethnic populations were instituted to exist, in a relative sense, with studies of white Americans. The various ethnic-racial studies programs represent a giant step towards democratizing American education. However, the educational system remains as one of the major institutions perpetuating racialist and racist ideas and implications. The system continues to focus almost solely on the White American-Eurocentric experience while neglecting or ignoring the presence, interests and contributions of African Americans. The only other democratic and viable alternative to separate African American studies programs is to *equitably* integrate in the educational curricula the life, experience and contributions of Black Americans into the total history and development of the United States.

**Relationship of Race and Educational Relevance.** The race of an individual or group is of primary concern and importance in American society. Race determines, collectively, the level of social attainment, the degree of political empowerment and, the opportunity for economic advancement of many racial-ethnic groups in the United States, especially of African Americans. When a person's or group's life-choices, political and economic status or condition are affected or determined by race, the resulting social phenomenon is racism. Those who have the power to implement and enforce the policies and conditions of racism are oppressors or racists. The human objects or victims of racism become the oppressed. Therefore, if education is purposed to serve as a liberating agent and is designed to satisfy the normative and psychological needs of persons, it is logical to assume that the education which is relevant to the oppressor might be much different or even irrelevant to the oppressed.

Race, particularly, in America is a biological, social and cultural reality. The biological characteristics of a race are hereditarily transmitted while those that are socio-cultural and attitudinal might be acquired or learned. Of most significance in the theory of race and racial characteristics, is color. Euro-Western anthropologists generally describe three main races: The Negroid or "black," the Mongoloid or "yellow-brown," and the Caucasian or "white."[10] The inference or conclusion is that the "color" of the different races is directly related to their continent of origin, Africa, Asia or Europe. In the United States where race and color, particular of African Americans, are of immense social and political significance, the demand for educational relevance according to race has unequivocal validity.

The prospect for universal education is diminished when world human phenomena or "civilization" is viewed from only the white American-European perspective. Increasingly during the twentieth century, the world is influenced more by White Western art, technology, thought, socio-political experiences, and religious or moral values. But the Caucasian or "white" race should not be and is not the only model for human development and achievement. In the words of Alioune Diop the European [white race] "has crushed the language of others, has violated the spirituality of others, devalued the technological or artistic experience of others, humiliated and paralyzed the creativity of others."[11] Diop's implication of the perpetration of cultural genocide by Europeans upon others is, especially, relevant to Africans and African Americans.

U.S. textbooks and public education glorify the American and European nexus, but are virtually mute on the African's or Black race's concomitant role in America's development and influence upon its art and culture. John H. Bunzel, a White author, captured the essence of the Black students' concern for educational relevance when he wrote that, ". . . the Black Students' Union, their educational problem at San Francisco State is clear and unambiguous: they read *white* literature, study *white* families, analyze *white* music, survey *white* civilizations, examine *white* cultures, probe *white* psychologies. In a word, the college curriculum is white-culture-bound."[12]

In a multi-racial society, education must be made relevant to the cultural, political, and social interests and aspirations of all the races. An educational system must be pedagogically designed to positively influence the cognitive and affective learning outcomes of all the racial-ethnic groups in relation to ethos and culture. Academic programs and curricula which have the effect of abetting oppression are irrelevant to the oppressed race. Such an educational system benefits the vested interests of only the race it is designed to serve.

It is educationally sound and beneficial to teach and to study race and races providing racial ethnocentrism, domination and superiority are critically analyzed, and emphasis is placed upon the equality, interrelatedness and interdependence of all races. Cultural, technological and social borrowing or exchanges have taken place between the races ever since the beginning of time. To presume that all customs, arts, science and technology that are worthwhile and deserving of mention are the product of the culture, ingenuity and intellect of the white race or Europe is preposterous. African or Africa was among the early contributors to the culture, science and technology of world civilization. Yet in American textbooks there is little, if any, positive inclusion or treatment of any other race except white or European. This does not mean that the white race's culture is bad or negative. However, it does imply that no single race's culture can meet the needs or serve the interests of all mankind. In the absence of a philosophy of cultural/racial relativism, cultural hierarchy determines the character of race relations. Cultural ranking produces the bases for racism. Racism, inevitably, results in the inequitable sharing of economic goods and political power. Thus, there is a direct relationship between race and educational relevancy. Education has the potential of fostering the cultural supremacy of one race while making the culture of another race irrelevant.

# CONTEMPORARY CONCEPTS AND APPROACHES

*Black Consciousness and Community Orientation Concept.* Nathan Hare, a sociologist and the initial curriculum developer, emphasized that "blackness" and Black community base and focus are the measures of an authentic Black or African American studies program. Blackness or Black consciousness is proposed as necessary to counterbalance the longstanding psychological affects of White cultural imperialism. For the same reason, African American education should be primarily concerned with or centered in the Black community. Education and research are primary functions. However, these functions are to be applied towards Black community problem solving and social action. Hare's concept of Black Consciousness and Community Orientation (BCCO) is consistent with the theory of "relevance" in education.[13] The emphasis placed upon Black culture and the Black community in no way makes African American studies irrelevant to white society. In addressing the issue of Black studies relevance to Whites, Hare states:

> However, a racist society cannot be healed merely by solving the problems of its black victims alone. The black condition does not exist in a vacuum; we cannot solve the problems of the black race without solving the problems of the society which produced and sustains the predicament of blacks. At the same time as we transform the black community, through course-related community activities, white students duplicating this work in their communities—predominantly—may operate to transform the white community and thus a racist American society.[14]

In other words, African American studies cannot be relevant to the needs of the Black community if it is not dedicated towards the task of bringing about political and social change within the entire society. Universal relevance is achieved under the Black consciousness and community concept by including research and analyses on the white, red, yellow, and any other generally defined races. African American studies is virtually of little value if it engages only in the study of the Black condition (victim analysis). Hare's initial curriculum included courses related to the study of oppressed peoples in all parts of the world, their liberation movements past and present, those that succeeded and those that failed. The BCCO concept of African American studies is implicitly separatist in theme and tone although, in reality, it has promoted democracy and equitable integration. This concept of Black studies, and others, whetted

the intellectual curiosity and social awareness of millions of Whites. Not only were African American studies classrooms integrated, but the movement resulted in the hiring of a few thousand Black faculty and staff at, previously, all-white colleges and universities. Thus, the instituting of Black or African American studies accomplished, relatively, more integration in higher education than centuries of integrationist-assimilationist appeals and ideology.[15]

From its inception, the Hare philosophy or model of Black studies was socially and politically revolutionary. It was educationally based on ideological and pedagogical blackness, but not limited merely to the study of blackness or Black history and culture. There is an expressive or affective phase which was designed to give African Americans a knowledge of their history and instill within them a sense of self-pride and collective destiny. On the other hand, it indirectly benefits Whites by helping to change their false notions of superiority and correcting many of their distorted views of African American life and history. A second phase might be termed functional or pragmatic. It serves the purpose of increasing professional, scientific and technical skills in the Black community through the use of new teaching techniques and methodology relevant to and in terms understood by Black people. Courses producing these socio-economic skills might be entitled, black politics, black economics, black science or blacks in mathematics, etc. The objective being that as African American studies or education is made more relevant to the Black community and its needs, the community, then, is made more relevant to (or involved in) the educational process.[16] Nathan Hare's ideas and concepts which were based on the student movement and Black Power philosophy of the 1960s, significantly, influenced the curricula development of African American studies.

## The Kawaida Theory of Maulana Karenga.

A somewhat different concept effecting the ideological course and development of Black and African American studies has been the Kawaida theory of Maulana Karenga. Kawaida is basically a synthesis of Black nationalist, Pan-Africanist and socialist thought and practice. Kawaida theory and Hare's concept differs, partly, in their diagnostic, prescriptive and critical assessment of African American culture and condition in American society. Karenga posits that African American culture and African consciousness have been, dysfunctionally, affected by the dominant European American society. Therefore, in order to rectify the socio-cultural imbalance and counteract the psychological affects of oppression, theories and programs of sociocultural reconstruction must be developed. In brief, Kawaida theory asserts that Africans in diaspora are estranged from their natural or positive values and, thus, there is the need for cultural and social reconstruction. Kawaida theory describes and critiques the African American experience and condition and, then, prescribes corrective social and cultural theory.[17]

Karenga's perspective of African American culture is reflective of E. Franklin Frazier's view (see Chapter I) that Blacks in America have suffered the loss of their African culture and social heritage. Consequently, his theory of Black culture has attracted some critics. *Kawaida Theory* maintains that:

> The key crisis in Black life is the cultural crisis, i,e., the crisis in views and values. The vision crisis is defined by a deficient and ineffective grasp of self, society and the world, and the value crisis by incorrect and self-limiting categories of commitment, and priorities which in turn limit our human possibilities.[18]

The critical aspect of Karenga's work lies in his assertion that views and values are the only determinants of culture when, indeed,

these are only a few among a myriad of other elements. Furthermore, Kawaida seems to imply that the cultural crisis and the deficient and ineffective self-conception that Blacks suffer are to be blamed on African Americans, rather than on the racist nature and affects of American society.

In spite of a degree of technical criticism of Kawaida theory, its principles have served as a guideline for the initiation of Black studies courses and as a basis for much philosophical thought and discussion. As a corrective for real or perceived dysfunctions of Black social organization, Kawaida submits seven fundamental tenets (*The Nguzo Saba*) for a new value system. Without full explication of each one, they are listed here as:

1. Umoja (Unity)
2. Kujichagulia (Self-Determination)
3. Ujima (Collective Work and Responsibility)
4. Ujamaa (Cooperative Economics)
5. Nia (Purpose)
6. Kuumba (Creativity)
7. Imani (Faith)

These principles are popular referents in discussions and analyses of African American family life or Black male/female relationships not only in Black studies courses, but among many Black nationalist oriented individuals and households throughout the United States. Numerous Black studies curricula or textbooks are organized around Kawaida's seven basic areas of culture: Mythology, History, Social Organization, Economic Organization, Political Organization, Creative Motif, and Ethos.[19]

The Black studies ideologies of Maulana Karenga and Nathan Hare are somewhat different, however they are not uncomplementary or contradictory. They differ primarily in political leanings and social focus. While Karenga and Hare appear separatist in social viewpoints or anti-integrationist, Hare is not an avid Black cultural nationalist. Implicit in Hare's works is the notion, that African American history and African culture are means but are not the major objectives or the end in the struggle for Black liberation and education.

### The Afrocentric Concept and Approach.

Afrocentricity or (Africentricity), as an intellectual foundation of the African American experience, has existed since the 18th century. Implications of Afrocentricity were evident in the abolitionist and emigrationist oratory, thought and philosophy of David Walker, Henry Highland Garnet, Martin Delaney and numerous other Black philosophers of that period. More pronounced inferences of the theme of Afrocentricity were evident in the political ideologies of prominent figures such as Marcus Garvey, Elijah Muhammad, Malcolm X, and Stokely Carmichael. However from a modern and more clearly defined academic perspective, Molefi K. Asante is regarded as the leading theoretician of the Afrocentric concept. He is theoretically supported by a significant number of Black behavioral and social scientists. Leading Afrocentric psychologists include Joseph Baldwin, Na'im Akbar, Linda James Myers, Wade Nobles and Daudi Azibo. The works of contemporary Black social scientists Leonard Jeffries, Dona Richards, Ronald Walters, James Turner, Jacob Carruthers and many others, reflect the Afrocentric perspective.

Molefi Asante, in essence, defines Afrocentricity as a way of viewing and interpreting universal phenomena from African historical and cultural perspectives. Thus, African American studies must be viewed as an extension of African history and culture beginning with the primacy of the classical African civilizations. Any analysis of Black or African American culture and experience that is not based on Afrocentric theory and philosophy may lead to erroneous results or conclusions.[20]

The fundamental premise of the Afrocentric approach to African American and Black studies is that each race or racial-ethnic group of mankind is endowed with its own insight and interpretation of the environment and the world. Different racial-cultural groups or populations have distinct ways of conceiving their existence and the order of the universe. The term used to describe the various conceptions racial-cultural groups hold relative to nature and the universe is "worldview". In other words, worldview includes cosmology, epistemology and ontology. A people's worldview will cause them to respond to and to place different values on social, spiritual, physical and material realities in conformance with their history and culture.[21]

The principles of Afrocentricity complements the educational objectives of the Kawaida theory of Maulana Karenga. Kawaida may build upon the theoretical posture of Afrocentricity. Afrocentricity provides for the correction of the cultural crisis and deficiency of views and values that Kawaida theory ascribes to African Americans.

Insofar as Afrocentricity and the development of African American studies, it means that African thought, philosophy and values are a valid frame of reference for study and research. Afrocentrist proponents maintain that prior to the academic formalization of African American or Black studies, what was taught was White studies of Blacks which was, essentially, Eurocentric concepts and perspectives of Afrocentric peoples. However, the argument for Afrocentric courses and programs is not one that opposes Eurocentricity. Afrocentric oriented African American studies promotes the idea that along with Roman, Greek or European culture and civilization— African culture, myths, legends, literature and thought can either be integrated or allowed to coexist. The white race's or European world view, in totality, is not universally applicable to all peoples.

# TOWARD NEW PARADIGMS AND METHODOLOGIES

***Developing New Research and Analytical Frameworks.*** It is evident from the preceding discussions that African American studies originated out of the throes of a social movement. The field was established before its theoretical objectives and paradigmatic means of development were clearly defined. However, the initial proponents and architects of African American or Black studies were soon convinced that many of the traditional Euro-American research models used to investigate and analyze the Black experience were flawed or inappropriate. Indeed, much of the racist and stereotypical theory relating to the African American experience was the result of the Euro-American scholar's flawed analyses based on the so-called, "value free", scientific method.

Historically, much of the implicit racist social and governmental policies affecting the quality of life of African Americans and Africans have been based upon theoretical constructs used by white Americans and Europeans which are inconsistent with the social and cultural realities of Black people or the Black community. Since Blacks are, in general, oppressed then a value-free, objective or "detached" approach and methodology toward the liberation of Black people from oppression would be, for the African American scholar, insensible if not even masochistic. Incisively, one of the most salient purposes of African American studies is to effect social, political and economic change. But in the absence of values those who are a part of the system, and who benefit from institutional racism, may employ paradigms and research methodology that may tend to sustain the socio-political and economic status quo in order to preserve their self interests.

Many African American studies theorists have rejected the comparative, order and value-neutrality paradigms and methodologies of white social science. The comparative approach attempts to use White middle-class norms and values as the standard for analyzing and evaluating Black social and behavioral characteristics. The order-equilibrium model is, essentially, conformance and assimilationist oriented. There are, also, serious deficiencies inherent in the objective or value-neutrality methodology in relation to the life and condition of African Americans.[22]

Racism, neo-colonialism, prejudice and discrimination impact upon the life condition and affect the worldview of Black people. Consequently, new study models and research methodologies may have to be constructed or traditional ones will have to be modified to take into account the different social reality of African Americans. Nathan Hare, in his initial conception of Black studies, challenged African American social theorists to the task of formulating new or alternate research models toward the study of Blacks. He stated:

> The black scholar must develop new and appropriate norms and values, new institutional structures, and in order to be effective in this regard, he must also develop and be guided by a new ideology. Out of this new ideology will evolve new methodology, though in some regards it will subsume and overlap existing norms of scholarly endeavor.[23]

The development of new or modified theoretical and empirical paradigms for authenticating and explicating the African American experience is necessary if the Black Consciousness and Community Orientation concept of Nathan Hare; the Kawaida (corrective) Theory of Maulana Karenga; or the Afrocentrists' school of thought are to be realized. African Americans are not Europeans nor are they the "natural" adapters of

Western culture. Any study of Black Americans must take into consideration their unity of African origin and Afrocentric ethos or worldview.

**Paradox of Cultural Pluralism, Diversity and Americanization.** The American population is comprised of many diverse racial and ethnic groups. Yet, the educational system has not moved, progressively, towards formulating curricula models, pedagogical approaches and methodological designs to equitably serve all citizens. The "melting pot" theory that postulates a homogeneous or national culture is a mythical concept relative to African Americans. African Americans, perhaps more than any other American racial-ethnic group, have little if any possibility of ever being assimilated. The reason being a matter of "color" and the derogatory status white Americans impute to black people. Therefore as a result of social alienation and political and economic disfranchisement, Black Americans have, either voluntarily or necessarily, opted for a separate social, cultural and *national* identity.

A course of separate racial or ethnic social/cultural assertion have not only been pursued by African Americans, but have been adopted to some extent by various other "conspicuous" American minority populations. However, separate racial-ethnic cultural assertion by specific non-white populations conflict with the goal of a national homogeneity or the "Americanization"[24] of all citizens of the United States. Americanization, in essence, means conformance by all citizens to the dominant or majority American culture. The term American is, implicitly and almost exclusively, meant to refer to white Anglo-Saxons. Because of political and patriotic reasons, America expects Blacks to become Americanized without according them full rights and privileges of citizenship. Whites offer to Blacks the opportunity for Americanization while the equitableness of integra-

tion is denied and assimilation is, virtually, impossible.

The socialization objective of American education has produced in African Americans the feeling of ambivalence. As a solution to the cultural and identity dilemma, African American studies was demanded and established to co-exist as an auxiliary to American education. Separate racial-ethnic cultural programs have been instituted with the idea and intent of promoting cultural pluralism. Although cultural pluralism is espoused as an educational means of improving race relations and preserving national unity, the practice and implications of cultural pluralism are paradoxical to the concept of Americanization.

In referring to racial stratification and education, John Ogbu suggests that Blacks, particularly, have had to forge their own collective social identity and cultural frame of reference. What has resulted is an opposing or oppositional Black cultural identity in relation to White culture and society.[25] Black Americans have little hope of ever, collectively, becoming assimilated into the mainstream of White American society. Consequently, many have subscribed to a form of African American nationalism in response to European American nationalism or Anglo-Saxon Americanism. Increasingly, Africa is being proposed as the historical, social and psychological frame of cultural reference in the study and research of Black Americans.

Racial and ethnic assertion in the United States has not been limited only to African Americans. Native Americans, Asian Americans, Mexican Americans, and Hispanic Americans have observed the cultural pluralist (separatist) or cultural nationalist trend of Blacks and have moved toward a greater degree of racial-ethnic assertion. The goal of Americanization for achieving a national homogeneity is giving way to an oppositional heterogeneity of races and ethnic groups. For the most part, Blacks have been unwilling to submerge or lose their African heritage and culture in exchange for an *inequitable* measure of Americanization or integration. Furthermore, cultural pluralism and "cultural diversity," will inevitably lead to some extent of functional separateness among racial and ethnic minorities. The social product of the promotion of cultural diversity is cultural specificity.

Demographers project that if current Hispanic, Asian and Black immigration and birth rates continue to increase at the present rate, that by the year 2080 Whites (non-Hispanic) will represent less than half of the total U.S. population. Clearly, there is a need to develop new or alternative theoretical formulations and research paradigms for differentiating, analyzing and explicating the diverse populations of America. The historical and continuing maladies of racism, dis-

crimination, prejudice and racial conflict in American society encourages and, indeed, compels Blacks and other oppressed minority groups to respond with racial-ethnic assertion or separatism. Thus, the growth and development of African American studies and other ethnic studies programs continues.

The socially curative propositions of cultural pluralism, cultural diversity and integration have not, substantially, effected the unequal social, political and economic conditions of African Americans. Until institutional racism, anti-Black and anti-African attitudes and sentiment no longer persist in the United States, the trend towards Black cultural assertion and Afrocentricity will, probably, increase. For African Americans there is, contemporarily, no viable alternative.

---

# · QUESTIONS AND EXERCISES ·

---

1. What were the fundamental social and educational concerns of Black students that caused them to the petition and protest for the development of African American studies during the 1960s?

2. Why did so many White students advocate and support the move to establish Black studies programs at predominantly white colleges and universities?

3. Relate the educational rationale for African American studies to the political and economic objectives of the Civil Rights Movement of the 1950s and 1960s.

4. Who was the "Father" of formal Black studies programs in the U.S.? Name other major proponents of the Black studies movement.

5. Are cultural pluralism, multi-ethnicity, and cultural diversity synonymous terms relative to American education?

6. Write a summary position paper on culture, race and educational relevance.

7. Give an analysis and evaluation of Nathan Hares' (BCCO), Maulana Karenga's (Kawaida), and Molefi Asante's (Afrocentric) paradigms or approaches to African American studies.

8. Is the American educational system free of political influence, political content and White nationalistic orientation? Discuss.

9. Historically and universally, students have effected social and political change through protest and demonstration. What gives

students this unique ability, power and influence?

10. What did you learn from textbooks or was taught about African Americans in elementary and secondary schools?

## · NOTES AND REFERENCES ·

1. For a dialectical study of student-university and societal conflict, see Edward J. Bander, *Turmoil on the Campus*, ed. (New York: The H.W. Wilson Co. 1970).

2. See Benjamin Quarles, *The Negro in the Making of America*. (New York: The Macmillan Co. 1969) Collier Books 1970. pp. 215–38. Also compare Lerone Bennett Jr. *Before the Mayflower*. (Chicago: Johnson Publishing Co., Inc. 1982) Penguin Books 1984. pp. 360–85.

3. Howard Zinn, *S N C C—The New Abolitionists*, (Boston: Beacon Press 1965). 16–39.

4. Sol Stern, "The Call of the Black Panthers" in *Black Protest in the Sixties*, ed. August Meier and Elliot Rudwick (Chicago: New York Times Company 1970) Quadrangle Books 230–242.

5. See also Harry Edwards, *Black Students* (London: The Free Press. Collier-Macmillan 1970).

6. James McEvoy and Abraham Miller. *Black Power and Student Rebellion*, ed. (Belmont CA: Wadsworth Publishing Co. 1969). Barlow & Shapiro, 286–97, Gitlin, 298–306.

7. Ibid. pp. 278–79.

8. Nathan Hare, *The Hare Plan* (San Francisco: The Black Think Tank 1991) 56–57.

9. Preston Wilcox, "Integration or Separatism in Education: K–12." *Integrated Education: Race and Schools* (Jan–Feb 1970) Issue 43, Vol. VIII, No. 1. Reprint, Integrated Education Associates, Chicago.

10. See Ruth Benedict, *Race: Science and Politics* (New York: The Viking Press 1945) 9–18, also, Otto Klineberg, *Race Differences* (New York: Harper & Brothers Publishers 1935) 20–24.

11. Alioune Diop, "Cultural Well-Being," *First World*, Vol. 2, No. 3. (1979) 8–9.

12. John H. Bunzel, "Black Studies at San Francisco State," *The Public Interest*. (date unavailable, est. August 1968) p. 26–27.

13. Much of the information explaining this concept has been obtained by the author in discussion with and from materials furnished by Nathan Hare, a colleague and friend.

14. Nathan Hare, "Questions and Answers About Black Studies." Reprinted from, *The Massachusetts Review*, "Directions in Black Studies." (Autumn, 1969) p. 733.

15. See Nathan Hare, "The Meaning of Black Studies," *The Graduate Journal*. The University of Texas at Austin. (1971) VIII/2. 453–56.

16. Hare, "Questions and Answers About Black Studies." p. 727.

17. Maulana Karenga, *Kawaida Theory: An Introductory Outline* (Inglewood, CA: Kawaida Publications 1980).

18. Ibid. p. 17.

19. Ibid. pp. 17–22, 44–46.

20. See Molefi K. Asante, *Afrocentricity: The Theory of Social Change* (New York: Amulefi Publishing Company 1980) 5–26. Also, Ellen Coughlin, ". . . the Life and History of Black Americans." *The Chronicle of Higher Education*. 1987. (October 28).

21. Dona Richards, "Implications of African-American Spirituality," in Molefi K. Asante

and Kariamu W. Asante, *African Culture: The Rhythms of Unity*. ed. (Westport: Greenwood Press 1985). 207–10.

22. See Ronald L. Taylor, "The Study of Black People: A Survey of Empirical and Theoretical Models," (pp. 10–15) and Terry Kershaw, "The Emerging Paradigm in Black Studies," (pp. 16–24) in Talmadge Anderson, *Black Studies: Theory, Method, and Cultural Perspectives*, ed. (Pullman, WA: Washington State University Press 1990).

23. Nathan Hare, "The Challenge of a Black Scholar." *The Black Scholar*. (December 1969) p. 6.

24. William Peterson, Michael Novak, and Philip Gleason, *Concepts of Ethnicity* (Cambridge: The Belknap Press of Harvard University Press 1982) 84–89.

25. John U. Ogbu, "Racial Stratification and Education" in Gail E. Thomas, *U.S. Race Relations in the 1980s and 1990s*. ed. (New York: Hemisphere Publishing Corp. 1990) 15–18.

# Chapter 3

# History of Africans in America

## THE HERITAGE OF AFRICA

*African Civilizations Before European Domination.* If the concept of civilization means a people who have reached a high stage of social and cultural development and who functions under a high order of social organization, then early African civilizations equaled and, in many aspects, surpassed the much acclaimed civilizations of ancient Europe and Asia. The myth that Africa had no history or civilization of world significance was perpetrated by Europeans for the purpose of self-glorification and to establish White cultural hegemony over Africa and its peoples. Furthermore, the denigration of African history and culture served as a moral or religious rationale for Europe's colonization of Africa and initiation of the slave trade.

In fact, Africans were among the first builders of dynamic civilizations and establishers of great cities, city-states, kingdoms and empires. They were also the early developers of agriculture involving the cultivating of soil and the growing of domestic crops. Animal domestication, iron-smelting and tool-making appeared among various African populations from about 4300 to 250 B.C. Africans were the forerunners or concurrent contributors in science, engineering, metallurgy, medicine, architecture and the fine arts.

Findings of twentieth century anthropologists and archaeologists support the theory that African peoples were the earliest fabricators of wood, stone and other natural materials into survival tools and devices. In 1959 Louis S. B. Leakey, a noted British anthropologist, discovered the fossil remains of a prehistoric humanlike creature in Olduvai Gorge in Tanzania, East Africa that he named *Homo habilis* meaning skillful man. The skull and teeth construction of Homo habilis were adapted for meat-eating which would indicate a reliance on tools or animal killing devices. The fossil also had hands with opposable thumbs and forefingers necessary for tool-making. The earliest Stone Age culture has been established in Africa and evidence of stone or pebble-like tools have been found throughout the African continent. Since Homo habilis dates back over two millions years ago, scientists believe that humans or mankind began in Africa and migrated out to Asia, Europe and other regions of the world. Before Leakey's discovery of Homo habilis, it was believed that mankind began in Asia because of the fossil remains of Peking Man and Java Man that were excavated in that part of the world. It is not known precisely when Africans became regular uses of fire. However, objects or devices made from iron have been found to exist in Egypt as early as 2000 B.C. The aesthetic or functional expressive nature of the prehistoric Black man are revealed in the rock paintings, etchings and engravings of animals, and other figures, that have been discovered in several African countries. Historical and contemporary research and discoveries attest to the early evolution of African civilization.[1]

Because of the undeniable advanced civilization of the Egyptians, White historians have attempted to claim Egypt as an extension of European culture. Obviously, the question or point of concern is the matter of which race or color are the Egyptians. If the Egyptians are, historically, proven to Black, it would destroy the European myth of African intellectual inferiority. The Egyptians were of mixed racial stock having physical and genetic characteristics of Africans and Europeans. However, Greek writers and philosophers described Egyptians as being black. Drawings, etchings and sculptures discovered by archaeologists and other researchers are mostly Negroid in feature, although it may be argued that some may show European and Asian characteristics. The Sphinx is the image of a Pharaoh having the head of a Black. The massive migration of Black Ethiopians during the time of the Hyksos invasion (c.1700–1500 B.C.) made Egypt more African than ever. Ethiopians is a name the ancient Greeks used to describe Africans of dark hue. Ethios meaning "burnt" and ops referring to face, thus, burnt-faces. Ethiopians eventually dominated the political life and organizations of Egypt. By the eight century before Christ, Ethiopia had gained complete control of Egypt and ruled for more than a century until their conquest by the Assyrians.

Black people contributed significantly towards the ingenious achievements of ancient Egypt. The Egyptians invented a form of alphabet, made paper from certain plants and, also, developed ink from the juices of various plants. Egyptians are most noted for their construction of the great pyramids (tombs) or monuments, method of preserving the dead, invention of the calendar and contributions to mathematics. The Egyptians were advanced in the use of metals and in the creation of jewelry and objects in gold and silver. The Black or African cultural influence permeated the Egyptian civilization. While much focus and credit has been placed on the achievements of the Egyptians, it must be understood that countries to the south of Egypt had developed various elements of civilization independent of Egyptian influence. Kush, Nubia, and Ethiopia contributed to and participated in the cultural and technological achievements of the Egyptians. Egypt, racially (mixed), culturally and geographically, is an integral part of Africa.

Throughout the span of human existence trade, commerce in conjunction with waterways and land routes have been the motivating factors in the human formation of villages, towns, cities, states nations or empires. Ancient Africa followed this natural course in the development of socio-political and geographical units which out of each emerged various cultures or civilizations. The phenomenal development of Egypt or Northeast

Africa may be attributed to the transitory and migratory nature of the people who traveled within its fluctuating borders and who affected its state of existence from without. Geographically, Egypt was centrally located at the crossroads leading from all directions into Africa from Asia and Europe. The Nile River connected Egypt, economically and socially, with southeastern African nations and kingdoms. The progressive agricultural economy derived from the fertile land of the overflowing Nile, and the gold mines below the First Cataract of the Nile provided the sources of wealth necessary to develop a great civilization. Commerce flourished and attracted not only Africans from the south, but European traders from the North via the Mediterranean Sea and Asians from the Red Sea. However, it was gold which drew Caucasian peoples from many countries near and far. As the numbers of white and Asiatic peoples increased in Egypt, the fortunes and statuses of Blacks declined.[2]

The development of African civilizations was not limited to Egypt and northeastern Africa. Social, political, agricultural and commercial development of northern interior and western Africa occurred contemporaneously with that of Egypt and territories along the Nile. Carthage, a city-state established by the Phoenicians in the year 814 B.C., was a major trading post and entrepot in the western Mediterranean Sea before and after its conquest by the Romans in 146 B.C. Commerce was the foundation of the Carthage economy and they practiced a unique silent bartering practice with interior Africans. Carthaginians sought to establish markets along the Atlantic coast of Africa, however, the extent of success of their efforts is not known.

The western Sudan from Lake Chad to the Atlantic abounded in gold, ivory and various agricultural products. Trade routes were established along the Atlantic coast of Africa and as a result, numerous African groups, villages, towns and cities emerged from the

Western Sahara to Equatorial Guinea. Goods and products originating in the west and western Sudan were sold to the North Africans (Berbers) who in term traded them with the Europeans and Asians. In most cases, gold was the principal export and salt, skins, cloth, jewelry, weapons and metal cooking utensils were imported.

Africa is a vast, topographically varied, and humanly complex continent. The history of its peoples and of the development of the thousands of its ancient cities, kingdoms and empires would require hundreds of volumes. The purpose of the preceding and following discussions is to reveal that prior to the European conquest and institution of slavery, progressive and dynamic African civilizations existed that contributed immensely toward the development of world society. The ancestral roots of African Americans are likely to be traced from West Africa, since this is the region where most slaves bound for the Americas were purchased, captured and shipped. Consequently, the remainder of this section will highlight three great Western Sudan or West African empires that rose and declined from the beginning of the eighth to the end of the eighteenth century. Some historians refer to the period as the Golden Age of West Africa.

*Ghana*

One of the oldest and most significant West African political state of record is the ancient kingdom of Ghana. The date of origin of Ghana is not precisely known. However, the recovered records do show that by the year 300 A.D. Ghana had been ruled, successively, by more than forty-four kings. It was located in the western Sudan northeast of the Senegal River and northwest of the Niger River. At the height of the Ghanian empire, it covered the territory that now encompasses today's Mali, Guinea, Gambia, Senegal and a portion of Mauritania. The expansion of the

Ghanian empire, territorially, resulted mostly from peaceful alliances with neighboring cities and states but there were some conquests.

The Ghanians were an agricultural and trading people. The country was strategically located along the trans-Saharan trade routes. Gold was the principal commodity that contributed to the wealth and power of Ghana. Although Ghana may not have had complete control of what was called the Wangara gold mines, it reaped immense profits through the levying of import and export taxes on traders passing through Ghanian territories. Gold was so abundant that it was decreed that only the king could possess gold bars and the people could use only the gold dust. This was necessary to circumvent the erosion or depreciation of the value of gold. Gold was the primary medium of exchange but salt, a product not plentiful in Ghana, was also valuable and used for exchange purposes.

The economy of Ghana was diversified and, therefore, gold was not the only metal it produced and benefitted from. Ghana had engaged in iron mining and manufacturing for over a thousand years. Its skill in iron making enabled it to form a powerful large army equipped with awesome weapons which intimidated any neighboring countries or potential enemies. Besides having astute traders and merchants, Ghana was known to have expert craftsmen such as goldsmiths, blacksmiths, coppersmiths, potters, weavers of cloth, stonesmiths, carpenters and makers of furniture. Ghana was a trading empire that sold not only agricultural, consumer and commercial products, but also slaves. However, it must be pointed out here that slavery in connotation and practice was different from the European and American institutionalized slavery initiated during the sixteenth to the nineteenth centuries.

During the year 1062 a Moslem religious sect, the Almoravides, began to invade Ghana with the intent of forcing its people to submit to Islamic or Muslim conversion.

Although the empire of Ghana put up strong resistance for more than ten years, the capital of Ghana Kumbi fell to the invaders in 1077 A.D. The Almoravide Muslin movement disintegrated when their leader died in 1087. However because of dissidence among its former member states and the destructive affects of the Almoravides, Ghana failed at attempts to restore the empire. By the year 1240, Ghana entered into a period of economic decline which was compounded by a series of droughts.

*Mali*

Succeeding the destruction and decline of Ghana, small kingdoms formerly under the Ghanaian empire, competed for its wealth and position in the Western Sudan. The Black kingdom of Mali emerged as the stronger organized state in the year 1235 A.D. However, the origin of Mali dates back to the seventh century. Unlike Ghana, Mali's kings or (mansas) embraced the Muslim religion and this served to strengthen its ties with the Islamic world. Basically, only the Malian rulers adopted the Muslim faith while the masses remained paganistic in their beliefs. Nevertheless Sundiata, the king of Mali, formed alliances with neighboring Islamic rulers and soon became the most influential and powerful person in West Africa. He subdued all of the smaller states—Kaniaga, Diara, Soso, and Galam—which formerly constituted Ghana and took control of the gold mining regions of Wangara. Mali was primarily an agricultural economy, yet, there was a substantial skilled craft sector including weavers, dyers, tanners, blacksmiths, goldsmiths, silversmiths and coppersmiths.

A ruling successor to Sundiata, Mansa Musa I, made the Mali empire renown not only in Africa, the Middle East and in Europe. One of the most significant events that occurred during the reign of Mansa Musa was his historic pilgrimage to Mecca in 1324.

It was unusual because it may have been the first time a Black Sudanic king ever travelled from western Africa through Egypt to visit Mecca. The Mansa Musa entourage to Mecca consisted of more than 70,000 persons including soldiers, logistical personnel and servants. He took with him 24,000 pounds of gold borne by 80 camels. He gratuitously distributed gold and gifts to his hosts and to prominent citizens along the way. On his return, he was accompanied with Islamic scholars, one named es-Saheli, a poet and architect. The architect supervised the construction of several magnificent temples and buildings throughout the empire, but especially in Timbuktu. The University of Sankore was located at Timbuktu and it became an international intellectual center, attracting students and visitors from northern Africa, the Middle East and Europe.[3]

The geographical extent of the empire of Mali equalled the size of western Europe. It covered what later became French West Africa, including Senegal, Gambia, Mali, and parts of Nigeria and the Upper Volta. The empire of Mali began to decline by the year 1550, weakened by the incursions of the Songhay, attacks from the Mossi and the malicious designs of the Portuguese.

## Songhay

The rise and fall of the Songhay empire is particularly significant in reflecting on the medieval history of Black people. The decline and eventual destruction of Songhay was a turning point in the educational and intellectual advance of Africans which may have ever since affected their image and plight in world society. Contrary to common belief, Africans were one of the world's first peoples to foster the concept of the university. Black people as a race were learned in literature, art and the sciences long before came under the influence of Western European culture. Before the fall of Songhay and under the aus-

pice of the Islamic religion, Africa was well on its way towards rivaling or even surpassing European or Western civilization.

The history of the kingdom of Songhay probably began in the early eighth century at Gao, a rather centrally located city in the Western Sudan. However, its emergence as a kingdom capable of challenging the empire of Mali did not occur until the fifteenth century. Mali and Songhay had been parts of the Ghanian domain. Following the decline of Ghana, Songhay had developed into a formidable kingdom and became a matter of concern to the Mansa Musa of the ascended empire of Mali. On the return of the Mansa Musa from his pilgrimage to Mecca, he visited the captured city of Gao and took two of the King of Songhay's sons as hostages to assure the loyalty of Songhay to Mali. After the death of the Mansa Musa, one of the sons escaped and in 1355 founded a dynasty called the "Sunni" (meaning replacement) that, subsequently, challenged and brought about the downfall of the Malian empire.

Under the rule of one of the succeeding monarchs, Sunni Ali, Songhay conquered and incorporated most of the cities and kingdoms of the former empire of Mali and the Niger region. Among the cities Sunni Ali had captured by 1469 were Timbuktu and Jenne. These two cities had already become renown educational centers that were established during the reign of the empire of Mali. The University of Sankore was located at Timbuktu. After conquering the kingdom of Mali, Songhay became the dominant and most revered empire of West Africa.

When Sunni Ali died in a drowning accident in 1492 his son, who was not a devout Muslim, succeeded him on the throne. His failure to become converted to the Islamic faith led to his dethronement and a Muslim general, Askia Mohammed, became the ruler of Songhay. Askia Mohammed was an, exceptionally, competent ruler and continued the conquest and expansionary objectives of

Sunni Ali. He brought the Mossi territory and most of the Hausa States under his rule. Being a devout Muslim, Mohammed made a pilgrimage to Mecca in similar style and fashion as the Mana Musa of Mali had done in 1324. He returned with a host of Islamic scholars, teachers, scientists and professionals to aid him in structuring an efficient centralized administration, and in developing cultural and intellectual centers of education at Timbuktu and Jenne and at various other major cities of the Songhaian empire.

The establishment of schools, colleges and universities and the reinstitution of Black intellectualism are the most significant contribution that the Songhaian Empire made to African peoples and to African history. Courses were offered in law, literature, astronomy, medicine, music, mathematics and in all of the subject areas that now constitute modern school and college curricula. The University of Sankore at Timbuktu and other schools attracted students and scholars from all over Africa, the Middle East and Europe. Emphasis and achievements in education and scholarship were not the only attributes of the Songhay Empire. It consolidated all of the agricultural, trade and commercial interests of the former empires of Ghana and Mali and became the economic hub and power of Western Africa.

A series of disruptive and destructive events caused the decline and fall of the empire of Songhay. Askia Mohammed was dethroned by his eldest son. Civil wars and invasions by the Moroccans weakened Songhay beyond its ability to ever recover. The Moroccans with a smaller army, but aided by Spanish mercenaries with firearms, defeated the Songhaian army. The invaders plundered and destroyed the established educational institutions including the libraries and original works of many scholars. However, the ruins of some of the buildings that once housed the University of Sankore still stand in the Mali Republic.

The number of early African cities, kingdoms and empires and the extent and quality of their civilizations are not limited to the northeast, north and the western Sudan regions of the continent. Several states rose and declined in the fifteenth century among the Hausa people in the region east of Songhay which now constitutes the nation of Nigeria in modern Africa. Encroaching upon the Hausa land east and west of Lake Chad was the Kanem-Bornu empire which existed under King Idris Alooma between 1580 and 1617. Several Black kingdoms were developed in the thirteenth and fourteenth centuries south of the Sudan along the Guinea coast which included the forest states of Dahomey, Ife, Oyo and Benin. South from the mouth of the Congo river was the Kingdom of the Congo, a confederation of several smaller states. It was one of the first African regions to come under the influence and domination of the Europeans. South of the Congo in the region now called South Africa, there were kingdoms inhabited by Black people including the Zulu, Basuto and Hottentot peoples. Medieval East African states developed and civilizations emerged much in the same manner as northern and western Africa. The drama of cultural evolutions included the same players of African, Arab Islamic and Asian backgrounds and influences. In relation to African Americans, West Africa has the greatest significance. The majority of Black slaves forcibly imported to America from Africa, embarked on slaveships from the region south of the Sudan and west along the bend of the Atlantic coastline.

African civilizations, like European, Asian and other cultures of the world, developed in relation to their own climate, physical phenomena and environmental conditions of life. Pre-European or pre-colonial African peoples were not all racially or ethnically homogeneous in a *pure* sense. Yet, there exists among Black indigenous peoples of Africa a common psyche and a very similar philosophical, ideological and cultural worldview. This worldview was derived from the physical attributes of the continent. The climates, rivers, desert, mountains, lakes, forests, animals, minerals, metals, wildlife and insects of Africa are unique in comparison to others countries and continents. The imperialistic intrusion of the Europeans and the cultural hegemony that they imposed upon Black peoples further strengthened the common thread of African unity. All of these factors culminated into what modern Black social theorists describe as the *Afrocentric* worldview in reference to the unity of origin and the common struggle of African peoples.

The dynamic and stifling influence of Islamism did not significantly affect the lay or common peoples of ancient Africa. Their leaders, dynasties and kings subscribed or adopted the Muslim religion for the economic and political benefits it provided. In fact the Islamic religion, generally, fostered and practiced equalitarianism and in a reciprocal way, enhanced the educational and economic conditions of Blacks. On the other hand, Christianity as introduced by Europeans claimed the doctrine of equality in theory, but practiced Black domination and White Supremacy.[4]

Pre-colonial Africans functioned under similar traditions of social organization, religion, political structure, judicial practice and arts creation. Throughout most of Africa, the family, community, village, state and kingdom were formed and functioned under an hierarchal system of kinship. The family was the beginning, nucleus and basis of social organization. Various African groups and nations practiced the patrilineal or the matrilineal family systems of authority and descent in accordance to their different ethnic and cultural traditions. Polygamy was a functional family pattern that was allowed in most societies. However, socially imposed economic conditions discouraged its widespread practice. The monogamous nuclear familial

structure did not become a social standard until after the European Christian influence dominated the African continent. Agricultural production and guild practice (arts, crafts) followed the lines of the kinship system through the extended family. The kinship and amalgamated kinship systems of pre-colonial Africa were rigid institutions. Kinship lines were often the basis of political rulerships or dynasties. An individual had little status or security outside the family clan.

Contrary to Western European notions, ancient Africa was rich in its own traditions of religion, philosophy, creative arts and literature. African religious beliefs and customs, prior to and independent of Islamism, were comparable to those of other peoples of the world. Many African societies embraced common beliefs of deism and creation or mythologies of creation and animistic worship. The most widespread indigenous religious practice of Africans was ancestor worship. They believed that the spirits of their ancestors exercised surveillance and influence over their daily lives. In spite of the heterogeneity of ancient Black states or peoples, there existed a collective African philosophy that was transmitted from generation to generation— written and unwritten. Just as in Europe and Asia, there were great African philosophers in Egypt, the Western Sudan and in southern and eastern Africa. These great thinkers expounded and prophesied on life, death, love, beauty, good, evil and other aspects of human reality. Literature, mostly oral, in the form of proverbs, parables, folktales, short stories, myths and legends abounded throughout Africa. Literature, art, music and dance served functional purposes in African societies.

Before the imperialistic and hegemonic intrusion of Europeans into Africa, Black societies and kingdoms possessed all of the elements that Whites ascribe to civilization. Yet, European historians wrote of world civilizations without acknowledging that there existed any civilizations in Africa except that of

Egypt. Even today, white scholars and historians deny or reluctantly admit the Blackness and African ancestry of the Egyptians. In antiquity, Africa gave to Europe and the rest of the world in terms of culture and civilization as much as it has received.[5]

*Background and Beginning of the African Slave Trade.* Slavery, described as one group of humans subjugating other humans for the purpose of forcing them to perform labor, work or services without pay or compensation, has been known to exist since the history of mankind. This form or practice of slavery existed many millennium before the Middle Ages in Europe, Asia and Africa. Ancient practices of slavery were not based, specifically, on the race or color of individuals or groups. Whites, Blacks and other peoples enslaved members of their opposite race or color and each other. For the most part and prior to 1500 A.D., European and African traders and merchants negotiated and traded in gold, agricultural products and slaves without color and race being a fundamental factor or social condition. Persons conscripted into slavery were generally captives who had been conquered or subjugated as a result of intergroup and intragroup conflicts or warfares. In particular, no systematic or automatic subordinate social or political role was assigned to Africans because of their race or color. However prejudice based on a myriad of human elements including religion, myths and stereotypes, are seemingly inevitable sociopsychological traits of mankind.

Slavery in any form is cruel and oppressive. But early slave customs and practices were more humane in comparison to the turn human bondage took during and after the sixteenth century. Slaves were often of the same race and nationality of their slaveholders. In some societies their slave status had a term or specified tenure. They could purchase their freedom and could and often did inter-marry with slavemasters, they could own property

and possessed certain rights as human beings. The basis, nature and character of early slavery were to be changed drastically by the Europeans upon their interest and forage into Africa.

Europe and the Americas benefitted developmentally and most economically from the "new" discovery, exploration and exploitation of Africa and Africans from the fourteenth to the early nineteenth century. A more succinct statement is that Europe and the Americas developed at the cost of the underdevelopment of Africa. Several European peoples including the English, Portuguese, French, Spanish, Dutch and Swedes participated and profited from the rape of Africa's physical resources and the marketing of Black human bodies. It might be said that Portugal was in the vanguard but, eventually, England and the United States of America would emerge as principal beneficiaries and victors of the Atlantic Slave Trade.

A member of the Portuguese royal family, Prince Henry the Navigator, is the primary character responsible for opening the veil of West Africa to the Europeans and revealing its substantial materials resources and economic potentials. Prince Henry's preoccupation with ocean navigation or the maritime arts led to the unprecedented exploration of Africa by white people which eventually resulted in the Atlantic slave trade. Henry had learned from his school of sailors about the trade routes of the Western Sudan which led to the great city of Timbuktu and about the legendary gold mines of Wangara. Portugal was perhaps the most familiar with northwest Africa bordering the Atlantic because its historical military encounters with the Muslims and Berbers. Having either defeated or made peace with Islamic forces, the Portuguese were heady with the prospect of foreign exploration.

The Portuguese developed sturdy, easy-navigable ships called caravels which facilitated their efforts towards exploring the West African Atlantic coast in search of gold and adventure. After numerous failed attempts at penetrating beyond the coast of Morocco, one of the voyages was successful in sailing beyond the Western Sahara and reporting to Prince Henry the discovery of people and cities. In 1441, a Portuguese caravel brought back a few captives which included Black Africans. As the expeditions of the Portuguese increased further south towards the coast of Guinea, they were encouraged to capture and return with more of these Black inhabitants. A Portuguese captain named Lancarote planned and executed a series of kidnapping raids off the coast of Guinea. He brought back to Portugal and to Prince Henry in 1444, over two-hundred African men, women and children for public auction. A scholar of the African slave trade, Oliver Ransford writes

> . . . August 1444 remains one of the saddest dates in the history of man—white as well as black, and we are still paying for what followed that auction in the meadow outside Lagos. For the profit made that morning by Lancarote's sailors and the enormous financial potential it disclosed, committed western Europe to the continuance of this trade in human flesh.[6]

England's ascendancy to a world power began near the end of the fifteenth century and after the reign of Elizabeth I. Wars and domestic disorganization initially prevented England from participating competitively in the exploration of Africa and the "New World". (The term New World applies to the European perception of the Americas and the West Indies. Obviously, the land was not "new" to its original inhabitants). However after the defeat of the Spanish Armada and Henry VIII's unification of England under Protestantism during the early fifteenth century, the British were prepared to challenge the naval and commercial advance of Portugal, Spain, France and other Europeans nations. England moved aggressively during the sixteenth century to establish colonies in the

West Indies and in North America. English and French plantation colonies produced tobacco as a major cash crop until the market price fell and, thus, created the need for a new product or diversification. The Dutch introduced sugar to the French and English colonies. There was a profitable and booming world market for sugar. Sugar cultivation in the West Indies was a major factor and rationale for the development of the Atlantic slave trade.

Sugar production requires large capital outlays, land areas and laborers. Consequently, the settlers and planters were insufficient in number to fertilize, grow, weed, harvest and process the sugar cane into sugar. In order to sustain the commercial and industrial revitalization of Europe, there was no hesitancy on the part of the colonizers in demanding African slaves as the solution to the labor problem. All of the European colonizers of the West Indies, North America and South America resorted to slavery as the solution to their labor problems.

It might be postulated that Spain and Portugal initiated the derogatory and demeaning attitudes toward Africans that tended to make Blacks the most select and optimum victims of enslavement. Portugal's warring experience with the dark-skinned Islamic Moors of Northwest Africa had accustomed them to capturing Black people as prisoners of war and, subsequently, relegating them to serfdom or slavery. While color or race may not have been the basic reason for their denigratory treatment of Africans, Black became a symbol of subordinate status. Indeed, domestic servitude and slavery without regard to race or color was common in Europe. The systems of slavery of medieval Europe, Asia and Africa were more humane. Slaves were favored with the tradition of being vested with certain rights. They often became simply menial residents of an estate or their period of servitude had a definite tenure. History reveals several variations of human slavery which does not in anyway diminishes the cruelness of its practice.[7]

Differences and the demographical results of Spanish and Portuguese slave traditions provide interesting analyses and contrast for historians and social theoreticians. However after the discovery of the vast and rich agricultural resources of North America and the West Indies, it was the English, French and, subsequently, white Americans who introduced the concept of racism. They morally rationalized that the race and color of Africans made them inferior beings and, therefore, appropriate for slavery. The Protestant and Catholic clergy of Europe sanctioned and even encouraged the enslavement of Blacks on the grounds that the African heathens needed to be brought under the influence of Christendom and civilized.

The underlying motive for African slavery was that the economic and industrial development of Europe was substantially based and dependent upon the plantation economies of the New World and the West Indies. Relatively, England benefited more from African slavery than other European countries. During the seventeenth century, more than a fourth of all British imports and exports of merchandise and agricultural products were produced by the British slave colonies. The British economy was significantly based upon the enslavement of Africans. Slavery was imperative for the development of Europe and, eventually, the United States. To sustain the new commercial renaissance and expansionist designs of the Europeans new markets, produce, materials and lands were required. These needs and demands created a market for slaves and, thus, the beginning of the Atlantic slave trade.[8]

The actual number of slaves transported from Africa to the Americas and the West Indies cannot be determined. However the consensus, even from modest estimates, suggests an average number above ten millions. This figure includes only the approximate number of Africans who actually survived the voyages. Millions more were murdered, died from sickness and suicide. The period of the slave trade extended for more than four centuries. Few may deny that African chiefs or rulers were guilty of complicity with the Europeans in the *initial* stages of African slavery. War captives and criminals detained in some African societies were exchanged with the Europeans for trinkets and other valuables. The greed that influenced African chiefs to cooperate with the European slave traders is humanly inexcusable. However, the chiefs or co-conspirators could not have known of the unprecedented inhuman and cruel slave system that awaited their African kinsmen in the New World. When African societies awakened and became conscious of the magnitude and horrors of slave marketing, it was too late. The naval, military and firearms superiority of the Europeans rendered Africans helpless to bring about a cessation to the trade. The English, French and Dutch established trading posts or forts along the coast of Western Africa to engage in and to defend this sordid trade.

Neither can it be denied that the British invented the efficient and profitable triangular, three-way profit system of exchanging goods that were produced in the slave colonies for more slaves, which in turn were sold and traded for sugar and tobacco destined for English ports. Providing the demand and markets for sugar, tobacco, cotton and condiments had not existed, slavery on such vast scale would not have developed. If morals had triumphed over markets, there would have been no slave trade. The slave colonies of the New World existed for the purpose of supplying goods to the mother countries that the colonial powers could not produce or provide for themselves.

It would be difficult for one to imagine the terror, horror and suffering the slave experienced in captivity while waiting for embarkation to points unknown to them, and to

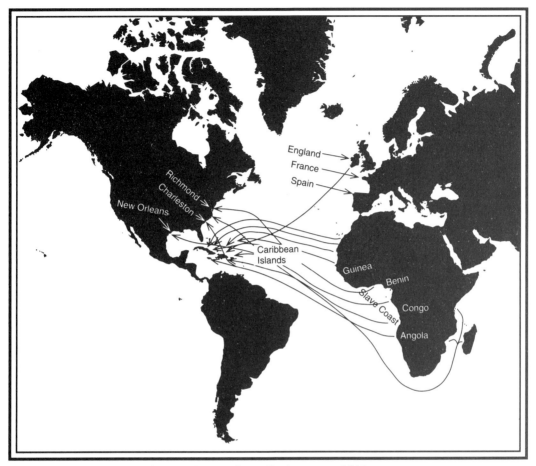

General Atlantic Slave Trade routes of Africans
to America, direct and via the Caribbeans.

Figure 1  Atlantic Slave Trade Routes.

uncertain fates and destinies. The slaves were collected, chained, branded and guarded while waiting for slaveships to stop at the European commercial depots or forts located along the West African coast from Senegal to Angola. The captives represented a variety of backgrounds, languages and cultures. Not all were prisoners of war or incarcerated offenders. Many were farmers, merchants, artisans, members of rival royal families and common people captured especially for the slave trade. They were found along the coastal regions and many were marched from the deep interiors of the African forests. Generally, it is assumed that the majority of African Americans originated from West Africa. However, it would be practically impossible to determine any Black American's precise cultural state, city or clan of origin.

On the voyage to the New World, Blacks were packed like sardines below the main deck of the slave vessels, and chained together by their legs, wrists or necks. Sickness and epidemics often afflicted the slave cargo and crew. The air was foul and poisonous compounded by the extreme heat. Naked men and women lie for hours and days in their own defecation, blood and mucus which covered the floors. Thousands committed suicide or died from harsh and cruel treatment and punishment. Resistance, revolt and mutiny were not uncommon and thousands died in these attempts. The estimate is that only one out of five slaves survived a voyage.

The Atlantic slave trade was a system founded on human-to-human cruelty and exploitation motivated by economic greed, social deviance, and psychological and moral unconscionableness. The capitalistic minded enslavers were unwilling or unable to pay for the labor required for the production of goods and services necessary to sustain a market economy. The Europeans conceived the moral rationale that Africans were savage, barbarious and less *civilized* than themselves. It is interesting to note that Europe's intensification of African slavery occurred concurrently and before the decline of one of Africa's greatest academic and intellectual civilizations—the empire of Songhay and its University of Sankore at Timbuktu.

## AFRICAN BONDAGE AND OPPRESSION IN AMERICA

*The Institution of Slavery in America: 1619–1783.* Africans began their horrid experience of servitude and slavery in America in 1619 at Jamestown, Virginia. Historians may be technically correct in qualifying the status of the first twenty Blacks who disembarked from a Dutch vessel at Jamestown as indentured servants, but not slaves. Nevertheless, most writers concur that these Africans were brought to the English colony of Virginia against their will. The various literature suggest that they had been captured by the Dutch privateers, sold to the colonial

government and then distributed among the white settlers. If they were indentured servants it simply meant that they had a binding and legal obligation to work for another person until their fixed term of indenture had expired. Thus, since there are no records of their eventual disposition or fate, they may have become "free" at some time in their lives. There is a fine line of distinction between involuntary servitude and slavery, especially, when human beings can be captured, transported and sold against their free will. At the time of the twenty Africans arrival in Virginia, there existed no formal recognition or authorization of slavery. Slave laws were to be enacted some forty years later.

A few years prior to 1619, the settlers of the colony of Virginia had discovered the profitability of raising and exporting tobacco to England. The producing of tobacco required and demanded laborers and hundreds of white voluntary and involuntary workers and servants were shipped to the colonies from England. Plantations developed around a base crop, for example: tobacco in Virginia and Maryland, rice or indigo in South Carolina, and sugar in the West Indies. The colonial government allotted to the planters or settlers fifty acres of land per servant or worker. The more servants a settler could acquire the more land he could own. Indians (Native Americans), who fought unsuccessfully with the English colonies, were captured and reduced to involuntary servitude. However, the Indians proved to be "unbreakable" or unsuitable for plantation labor and the fixed term of white indentured servants would expire after five or seven years. The genesis of the involuntary arrivals of Africans in 1619 was timely and opportune for the settlers. Millions of Africans would follow those initial twenty to America and their status and treatment would become more clearly defined as *slave*.[9]

The influx of millions of Africans into the southern colonies of America occurred partly as the result of England's unmanageable circumstances in the West Indies and the Caribbeans. England had reigned supreme and prospered, overwhelmingly, from sugar production on its West Indian and Caribbean island plantations. Millions of slaves had been brought from Africa to British colonized Barbados, Jamaica, Bermuda, the Bahamas, Trinidad and many of its other colonial islands. Millions more were imported to Spain's Cuba and Puerto Rica, and to French colonized islands including Guadeloupe and Martinique. The fact is that there existed a surplus of African slaves. In many instances, slave populations outnumbered slaveholders on the hundreds of plantations. Consequently, slave uprising, revolts and runaways became epidemic.

To suppress the soaring African populations and uprising, the most inhumane, brutal and cruel punishment and death ever imagined were inflicted upon Black men, women and children. They were burned, whipped, hanged, tongues and noses slit, and clubs were used to break their arms, legs and backs in order to impress upon them the might of white people. However, such sadistic and inhumane treatment did not stem the tide of insurrections and runaways. One group the "maroons" won their independence by escaping into the forests and mountains and repelling European military expeditions. Other slave insurrectionist groups were also successful in achieving independence.[10] The slave control problem, Anglo-French conflict in the West Indies and Caribbeans, in addition to the eventual market glut of sugar, caused England to direct more attention to its North American colonies. Slave trafficking continued from the west coast of Africa to the New World. When the prosperity of the West Indies and Caribbeans declined, millions of Africans from these British possessions began their involuntary importation to the North American colonies.

Analysis of the landing of the first Black indentured servants at Jamestown, Virginia is important because their reception and treatment determined the status and fate of the millions that would follow. Their arrival introduced ambivalent but not new racial attitudes among the English settlers. The Portuguese had instilled in the minds of Europeans the concept of African subordination ever since 1444, when Prince Henry's sailors kidnapped, auctioned and traded Black slaves from the west coast of Africa. Therefore, Africans brought to the southern colonies were immediately relegated to a subordinate status beyond that of indentured servant. Because they were black, conspicuously different and could not blend in with the Indian and white indentured servants who were almost physically indistinguishable from the settlers, escape was virtually impossible. The colonists realized very early that it was much more profitable and convenient to conscript Africans into slavery in order to satisfy their ever increasing demand for free workers. Slavery was a permanent solution to their labor problems.

As Professor St. Clair Drake and other scholars of race have pointed out, racial slavery per se may not have originated in the American southern colonies. However, the American practices of confining racial slavery exclusively to Blacks, perpetual servitude, forbidden assimilation, and the predication of African subjugation on the ideology of white supremacy revolutionized world traditions of human bondage.

If there was any ambivalence on the part of the Virginia colony towards the status and treatment of the initial Africans to American soil, it was soon resolved. By the year 1750, slavery was recognized and sanctioned by law in all the American colonies. These laws clearly differentiated the status and treatment of Black slaves from other types of servants. Especially in the southern colonies, African slaves had no rights except those arbitrarily determined by the individual slavemasters. Blacks, their children and future descendants were purchased and sold into perpetual slavery as chattel property with no legal rights as human beings.

The conditions, treatment and experiences the slaves endured in each colony or colonial region depended upon a myriad of domestic and international economic or commercial factors. The growing of tobacco, cotton, rice, indigo, timber, pitch and turpentine in Maryland, Virginia, the Carolinas and Georgia was labor-intensive and differed in nature and climate from the agricultural and more industrialized economies of the middle and New England colonies. Furthermore, the intensity and severity of the work imposed upon the slaves was related mostly to the market demand of England for a specialized crop or product. The British economy depended heavily on the plantation colonies and their increased use of slave labor. Not only were tobacco, cotton and other commodities produced for export to England, but there developed complementary and reciprocal markets between the southern, middle and New England colonies. The colonies provided for each other the products which each independently could not or did not produce in sufficient quantities for domestic consumption.[11]

The importation and use of African slaves in the middle colonies of New York, New Jersey, Pennsylvania and Delaware; and in the New England colonies of Massachusetts, Connecticut, New Hampshire and Rhode Island have been recorded as earlier as 1636. However, it is estimated the population of Blacks in colonial New England never exceeded 20,000. Early cargoes of slaves to the northern colonies received much the same status and treatment as those of the southern colonies. However after 1750, regional differences in the commercial and industrial economies, and in the social traditions of the American colonies resulted in some degree of variations in the treatment of slaves. For example, the

non-agriculturally based or more commercial-industrialized economies of the Middle and New England colonies contrasted vastly with the labor-intensive agricultural plantations of the south. The nature of much of the work in the colonies north of Maryland required that the slaves possess limited reading ability and education. What resulted was probably a more humanitarian type of slavery.

Another factor which contributed towards a comparatively milder form of slavery in the Middle and New England colonies was the religious influence of the Quakers and Puritans. The English Quakers of the Middle colonies constantly tried to improve the plight of the slave by providing them with religious education and in promoting anti-slavery sentiment. This was particularly true in Pennsylvania, Delaware and New Jersey. Consequently, the slave populations in these three colonies never reached significant proportions. The colony of New York maintained the most strict and harsh slave system of the Middle colonies. During the early seventeenth century slave codes were enacted in New York forbidding the congregation of more than three slaves, legalizing the whipping of those guilty of the slightest infractions, setting curfews and nullifying any regard for Blacks as a result of baptism. These laws were enacted to control the increasing number of Africans who began to stage a number of rebellious actions and insurrections. Perpetrators of rebellious acts and insurrections were subjected to horrifying punishment or death.

By 1771, discontent over the importation of African slaves surfaced in all of the colonies. The discontent was based on the fear of Black uprising as a result of the increasing proportion of slave populations. Slave management concerns and policies always followed a similar course. Whenever slave populations threatened the security of the white colonists, cruel and restrictive slave codes were enacted and brutal punishment was prescribed to

contain or control any potential Black insurrections. Another method of control was to
restrict slave importations. Moreover, the
looming specter of the Revolution generated
a freedom consciousness.

The Revolutionary War (1775–1783) for
freedom and independence from Britain created for the American colonists a paradox of
moral consciousness relative to their own enslavement of Africans. The institution of
slavery maintained by the American colonies
was inconsistent with the petition and principles of freedom that they submitted to England for American independence. Consequently, the Revolution served to increase
the slowly developing anti-slavery sentiment.
Nevertheless, the Revolution caused a dilemma as to whether or not to permit the enlistment and arming of Blacks in the war
against England.

Black participation in colonial military
ventures was not new. Blacks had served in
the Anglo-French conflict, Indian and colonist battles, and in all colonial wars between
1689 and 1763 including the French and Indian War (1755–1763). In many campaigns,
Blacks fought alongside whites and received
equal pay. If they distinguished themselves in
the line of duty, they were usually given their
freedom. However, Blacks fought, initially,
only a few weeks in the Revolution before
being excluded.[12]

In the summer of 1775, General George
Washington issued an order not to enlist
Blacks into the military. Subsequent policies
of the council of war rejected the use of both
slave and free Blacks in the army. However
in order to capitalize on the American colonists rejection of Blacks for military service,
Lord Dunmore, the British governor of Virginia, issued a proclamation in November
1775 inviting all able bodied indentured servants and Blacks, free or slave, to serve in
the British military. The move by the British
to enlist Blacks provoked the concern of the
colonial army since it was logical to assume

that hundreds of Africans would flock to join
his Majestic's troops. Thus, General Washington sought to reverse his previous order re-
jecting Black enlistment. In January 1776,
Congress granted Washington's request to enlist only free Blacks in the continental army.
Prior to the American colonists reversal of
policy, hundreds of Black run-aways and
slaves from Virginia, Maryland and the Carolinas had escaped to the British lines. They
bolstered the British position to the extent
that the colonists further reversed their policy
and permitted the recruitment of both free
and enslaved Blacks to join their ranks. However, Georgia and South Carolina never *formally* approved of Black enlistment and service in the military. Approximately 5000
Blacks served in both the American and British armies during the duration of the war.
Thus, Blacks were used as pawns fighting for
the British and American oppressors with the
hope of being rewarded, eventually, with
manumission (freedom) if they survived the
war.[13]

*Slavery After the American Revolutionary
War.* The American War for Independence
had given hope to millions of Africans that
their history of suffering and human bondage
would end or be ameliorated. Such expectations soon proved to be contrary to the majority will of the now independent America.
The feelings of guilt and hypocrisy that
fueled the anti-slavery sentiment before and
during the war faded with the British surrender at Yorktown. What resulted after the war
was regional reinterpretations and modified
forms of slavery and human oppression. The
North responded by gradually and theoretically declaring slavery illegal. Even before the
cessation of the war, Vermont had moved to
abolish slavery in 1777 and Pennsylvania followed in 1780 with a gradual emancipation
plan. Immediately after the war the state of
Massachusetts declared slavery unconstitutional. Subsequently, New Hampshire,

Connecticut, Rhode Island, New York and New Jersey provided for the gradual manumission of slaves. By 1807, the Northern states had passed emancipation laws. There emerged in the North a category of Africans that Professor John Hope Franklin described as "Quasi-free Negroes".[14] In 1787, the new national government of the former 13 colonies enacted statutes stipulating that the Northwest Territory be exclusive of slavery. Eventually this meant that the five states carved out of the Northwest Territory: Indiana, Illinois, Ohio, Michigan and Wisconsin became non-slave states upon their admission to the Union.

The South not only did not make any move to abolish slavery, but it became even more recalcitrant to the idea of manumission and vengeful towards the slaves. The axiomatic expression, "all men are created equal," expressed by Thomas Jefferson and incorporated in the Declaration of Independence, did not wield the same moral force in the South as it may have had in the North. The apparent ambivalence between Jefferson's egalitarian philosophy of freedom and his adamant practice of slavery, served to reinforce the will of the South to resist all anti-slavery notions and to pursue human bondage and oppression with even a greater passion.

The founding fathers of America in drafting the new Constitution ignored totally the question of slavery except through their *implicit* recognition and treatment of Africans as chattel property. The Constitution was predicated on compromise and reconciliation of the interests of the North and South in order to preserve the American union. On the matter of representation and taxation based on population, there arose the problem of counting in the "free" North versus the non-free South. As a compromising measure the Constitution, without mentioning slavery or race, relegated the status of a Black to "three-fifths" of a person. Further compromises were

evident in the dispute over the continued importation of slaves and in the adjudication of rights in the case of escaped "indentured" servants or laborers. The constitutional problem of dealing with escaped slaves was to resurface again under the Fugitive Slave Law of 1850.

In essence, white America's independence from the tyranny and oppression of Britain resulted in few changes in the plight of Africans, especially, in the southern United States. To the contrary, the freedom gained by white Americans from the War of Independence made them freer than ever to suppress and deny to Africans the same human dignity and freedom that they had so valiantly sought and fought for from England. In the aftermath of the Revolutionary War, slavery grew and intensified in the South and *real* freedom was not enjoyed by the "free" Blacks in the North. From American independence grew the seeds of the most unique forms of racial slavery and racism ever to be practiced in the world.

The Middle and New England colonies had begun to render slavery unconstitutional during the Revolutionary War period, and by the end of the war—at least on paper—human bondage above the Mason-Dixon line had come to an end. Out of the quasi-free Post-Revolutionary War milieu of the northern states emerged viable free African communities and Black personages of distinction. Religious organizations, anti-slavery groups, and persons of anti-slavery sentiment increased their efforts to provide the opportunity for Blacks to learn to read and write or to obtain an education. Often on their own initiative, Blacks became self-educated. Various white religious denominations and churches permitted Africans membership and allowed them to participate on a subordinate basis. With this modicum of opportunity and freedom, quasi-free or former ex-slaves developed a spirit of self-worth, protest, and self-determination that would later serve as the foundation for the abolitionist movement.

The intelligence, literary and oratory talents of some of the former slaves and quasi-free Blacks captured the interest of whites who promoted them and provided for the practical application of their abilities. Phillis Wheatley, a former slave of a Boston family, was distinguished as a Black female poetess during the era of the Revolutionary War. Her most notable works were published between 1773 and 1784. Contemporary scholars of Black literature debate whether her poems related, even implicitly, to the plight of Africans. However during her lifetime, any hint of protest in her works would have been detrimental to her welfare. In 1786, Jupiter Hammon, a former slave who became a minister and somewhat of a poet, wrote a prose piece entitled, *An Address to the Negroes of the State of New York,* which was delivered before the African Society of New York City. His poetry was religious in nature and his oratory advocated the rewards of a Black after-life and gradualism relative to slavery and oppression.

In time, learned and articulate quasi-free Blacks applied their limited opportunities and abilities to register protest and to submit petitions decrying inequality and slavery throughout the new independent American republic. James Forten of Philadelphia was born free in 1766. He became a highly successful businessman as a sailmaker. In 1797 he joined several other Blacks in the city of Philadelphia in a petition to Congress against the slave trade. He was, also, one of the signers in 1800 of a petition requesting Congress to alter the Fugitive Slave Act of 1793. Forten was opposed to emigration or back-to-Africa schemes. Paul Cuffe of Massachusetts was a Black shipbuilder and owner. In 1811, he went to Africa to investigate the possibility of resettling free Blacks to Africa. Prince Hall was a preacher who participated in the presentation of a number of petitions to end slavery be-

tween 1773 and 1788. Hall is recognized as the founding father of Black Freemasonry in America, having obtained a charter from Masons in England to establish the first African Lodge. He lobbied for the establishment of schools for Black children in Boston. Yet, Hall supported plans for Black emigration to Africa. He might be called one of the earliest advocates of Black nationalism.[15]

The scientific and literary achievements of Benjamin Banneker are testimony of the intellectual equality of African people during the period following the Revolutionary War. Banneker was born in Maryland of a free white woman and a slave father. He was fortunate to have received an education at a school conducted for white children but to which a few Blacks were admitted. He developed into a mathematician, astronomer, and an inventor. He devised an almanac which was published annually from 1792 to 1802. His abilities and achievements became known to Thomas Jefferson who recommended him to serve with the surveying commission to lay out the boundary lines and streets for the District of Columbia.

The period following the American War for Independence and up to the War of 1812 marked the beginning of the independent and separate establishment of the Black Church. The first Northern Black independent church effort occurred in Philadelphia. Separate Black churches and independent African religious denominations were established as a result of the hostile and derogatory treatment Blacks experienced when they attempted to worship in the same edifice with whites. Richard Allen was an active worshipper with the white St. George's Methodist Church of Philadelphia. One Sunday Allen and two of his companions were pulled from their knees while praying and ordered to move to the balcony. Allen and one of his companions, Absalom Jones, left St. George's and subsequently founded the Free African Society of Philadelphia. Through this organization, Richard Allen founded the Be-thel African Methodist Episcopal Church in Philadelphia in 1794. Branches of the Bethel model were established in Maryland, Dela-ware and New Jersey. The African Methodist Episcopal Church (AME) gradually developed into a national Black religious denomination. Hostility from whites also prompted the founding in Philadelphia of the African Methodist Episcopal Zion Church denomina-tion in 1796. About 1809, separate Black Baptist churches were organized in Boston, New York and Philadelphia.

Southern Blacks rarely, if ever, had the opportunity to worship with whites. Never-theless, separate Black Baptist churches in the South were organized during and after the Revolutionary War period. The first southern African Baptist church of record was formed at Silver Bluff on the South Carolina side of the Savannah River about twelve miles from Augusta, Georgia. After the treaty ending the war was signed, this congregation evolved into the first African Baptist Church of Augusta. During the same period George Liele, a slave, started a Black Baptist church in Savannah. However, after the war he left for Jamaica. Another slave, Andrew Bryan continued Liele's efforts and in January of 1788 the First Baptist Church of Savannah was founded. Blacks continued to form their own separate churches in the North and South during this period. Whites began to forbid the formation of Black churches in the South, especially, after the Vesey slave upris-ing of 1822.[16]

The light of hope for the end of human bondage and oppression that had dimly begun to shine at the end of the Revolutionary War, was soon to be extinguished as the era of the American Industrial Revolution ap-proached following the War of 1812.

***"King Cotton" and the Revival of Slavery in the South.*** The eminent Black historian Benjamin Quarles writes that, "Cotton was a powerful stimulant to slavery; the two seemed to have been made for each other."[17] It is known that the cotton gin, invented by Eli Whitney in 1793, increased the convenience and profitability of producing cotton in the South. The technological breakthrough in the process of separating the cotton fiber from the seed of the plant, in effect, caused the demand for cotton to increase at an ac-celerated rate. Only a relative few thousand bales of cotton was produced in the South before the use of the cotton gin, however, production rose in excess of a half-million bales following the War of 1812. Cotton cre-ated a need for unlimited cheap or free labor as in the cases of sugar, tobacco, rice and in-digo. Cotton promoted the resurgence and in-tensification of slavery.

However, the historians James Dormon and Robert Jones cast doubt upon the popular belief that slavery would have eventually de-clined if the cotton gin had not been in-vented. They contend that slavery had be-come institutionalized in the hearts and minds of white southerners and that the economy of the south was inextricably tied to slavery. Furthermore, white people's belief in the natural inferiority of Africans, the long history of racial slavery in the Americas, and the prevailing ideology of white supremacy would have made any effort to abolish slavery improbable barring the intervention of some revolutionary phenomenon.[18]

The War of 1812 was waged essentially to satisfy the westward expansionist designs of the new American republic. The soil and cli-mate of the south and southwest regions in-cluding Louisiana, Alabama, Mississippi, and Georgia were extremely favorable to produc-ing cotton. Consequently, the plantation sys-tem increasingly extended into these territo-ries. The acquisition and availability of more land necessitated the demand for an unlim-ited supply of Black slave labor.

Historically, materialism, ethnocentrism and greed have been inextricably connected with the practice of slavery. But the proclivity towards and passion for human enslavement possessed by white Europeans and Americans transcended the rationale for goods and markets. Southern more so than Northern whites, manifested a mean and xenophobic attitude towards Blacks that defied explanation. Their anti-African posture was, undoubtedly, psychologically and psychopathically motivated. This perhaps is the only way to explain how whites could be so inure and emotionally immune to the inhumane treatment they inflicted upon Blacks under the plantation system of the South.

The most vile violation of the African's humanity was the slavemasters's practice of slavebreeding. Because of the 1807 Congressional ban on the importation of slaves, the population of slaves began to decrease. This created a shortage of slave labor, although some scholars estimate that over a quarter of a million slaves were smuggled into the country 50 years after the restrictive law was passed. Nevertheless, the unlimited and profitable demand for Black slaves popularized the practice of domestic slave breeding. The practice often involved the slavemasters sexual promiscuity with slave women, the encouraging of Black "studs" to copulate with a number of female slaves, and a reward and punishment system for slave women who produced offspring or did not. The breeding and marketing of slaves became almost as profitable as the producing and selling of cotton. Since the cotton kingdom developed in the lower southern states, Virginia, Kentucky, Maryland, Tennessee and North Carolina supplied the lower states with thousands of slaves annually.

Saunders Reddings described vividly and compassionately how the slave traders gathered their human cargoes and marched them overland to the deep South:

The slave gangs of men, women and children slunk along in a double line. The man-

acles that fastened the left wrist of one to the right wrist of another chafed the flesh. Running through a link in the gyves and binding the whole gang together was the coffle chain with links of iron as thick as a man's finger. The sun was hot, or the wind was raw and piercing; the roads were rutted. At night the gang rested; at dawn the march began.[19]

Most towns had slave markets, auction blocks and pens. No distinction was made of men, women, mother, father, husband, wife or children. They were all sold indiscriminately, jointly or individually with profit being the only factor. Some were especially traded as concubines and studs. Illegal importing, breeding and kidnapping of slaves was a major economic enterprise. The relative small number of "free" slaves were often kidnapped, sold and reenslaved. Slave codes which were designed for the purpose of denigrating and controlling Blacks during the pre-Revolutionary War period were reinforced and new ones were enacted in the South. The slaves had no rights. Their treatment and fate depended solely upon the merciless whims and desires of the slavemasters or the dreaded slave drivers. They could be lashed, maimed, tortured or killed at the will of their tormentors and at anytime. A slave's day from twilight to dusk was filled with the strenuous tasks of hoeing, digging, plowing, planting, chopping, picking, fixing, cleaning, lifting or whatever work that might be required to maintain the plantation. Slaves could be worked eighteen to nineteen hours per day, and as Professor Reddings stated, "There was no law that said they could not be worked to death".[20]

Slaves generally lived in one room huts or shacks that were windowless, with dirt floors and cracks in the walls. They were not insulated from the rain, wind or snow. The smoke from heating and cooking was suffocating. They slept usually on pallets of rags and two or more families shared a cabin or hut. Slaves

# Administrator's Sale

OF

# SLAVES

BY virtue of an order of the County Court within and for the County of Clay, in the State of Missouri, made on the eighth day of February, A. D., 1859, the undersigned as Administrator of the estate of William Duncan, deceased, with the last will and testament of said deceased annexed, will offer for sale at public vendue to the highest bidder, at the court house door, in the city of Liberty, in said county of Clay, on MONDAY THE 25TH DAY OF APRIL, A. D. 1859, whilst the circuit court of said county of Clay is in session, the following named and described ten negro slaves for life belonging to the estate of said deceased, viz: A man named BILL, aged 53 years; a man named GEORGE, aged about 20 years; a man named JOHNSON, aged about 18 years, a boy named BILLY, aged about 13 years; a boy named JOHN, aged about 8 years; a boy named JAMES, aged about 5 years; a woman named AMANDA, aged about 34 years; a girl named BETTY, aged about 12 years; a girl named CYRENE, aged about 4 years, and a girl named ALICE, aged about 2 years, upon the following TERMS, to-wit: Upon a credit of 12 months, the purchaser or purchasers to give bond with approved personal security for the payment of the purchase money—the above named slaves are sold for the purpose of making division of the same among the parties in interest.

### THEODORE DUNCAN, Adm'r.

March 25th, 1859.

*Loaned by Rtfry B. Withers Liberty Mo 9/12/30*

Figure 2  Slave Auction Notice.

customarily made their own crude furniture and utensils. Their diets consisted mostly of salt pork, corn meal, molasses and dried beans. Black autobiographers record that the food was sometimes sufficient in bulk but totally unbalanced and not nutritious enough to sustain the slave's physical endurance and health. Sickness and death from epidemics of yellow fever, tuberculosis, cholera, malaria and other diseases were a constant plight of the slave quarters. Of course, the lot of slaves invariably depended upon the humaneness or cruelty of the slavemaster.[21]

During the Civil Rights Movement and students' revolt of the late twentieth century,

many references and analogies were made of Malcom X's characterization and description of the "house negro" and the "field negro". The house slave or servant worked and often lived in the home of the slavemaster and slavemistress. The position of the house slave was viewed by some a being a privileged and elite one. The house slave ate the same food or leftovers as the slavemaster and wore the used and discarded clothes of the plantation owner's family. The house slave's duties included housekeeping, cooking, gardening, caring for the slave master's and mistress' infants or children, and serving the general and intimate needs of their owners. The house slave was usually spared of the arduous back-breaking work in the fields and generally was not in a position to be the object of the torture and brutality accorded the field slave. On the other hand, the field slave was beaten and suffered immensely from morning to night. He or she lived in a hut or shack, wore inadequate clothing and ate the lowest quality of food. In Malcolm X's words, "The Negro in the field caught hell".

While Malcolm X submitted a sharp contrast in the treatment of the house slave and the field slave, John Blassingame's work implies that the degree of cruelty inflicted upon both was the same and differed only in nature and type. The house slave was always available and functioned always under the watchful eyes of the masters and mistresses satisfying their every vengeful use or sadistic desire. The female house slaves were the ones who were often sexually exploited for breeding purposes or for pleasure. The millions of mixed blooded Africans or mulattoes attest to the plight of the house slave. Nevertheless, one might conclude that the house slave would tend to be more loyal to their owners. The field negro or slave hated the master. The sociological dichotomy of the house slave and field slave are reflected in contemporary Black life and relationships.[22]

In spite of the inhumane, oppressive and, generally, merciless aspects of slavery, the anomaly of the "free" or quasi-free Black existed. Shortly before the Civil War the population of so-called nonslave Blacks in America numbered more than 450,000. Almost half of this number lived in the South. The term free is qualified because no Black was actually free in the North or South. While the technically nonslave Black of the South was not owned by an individual slavemaster he was, in essence, the property of and subject to the will of every white person of the community, town or state. In most southern states, the quasi-free African was required to carry a pass to certify his or her nonslave

status. Generally, free Blacks were not allowed to vote, hold public office or permitted to testify against a white person in courts of law. They were subject to curfew, forbidden the right of assembly, and could be virtually re-enslaved upon the slightest infraction of a law or ordinance. Anyone having a skin color of a dark hue was imposed with the burden of proving there nonslave status. However, the degrees of freedom enjoyed by a free Black varied from state to state and from region or particular circumstance to the other.

The free Black population of the South grew and developed from 1790 to 1860 because of several factors. Hundreds of free Blacks earned their freedom as a result of their participation in the American War for Independence. Some slave owners out of conscience or because of their inability to maintain slaves simply set them free. Often Blacks would run away to escape bondage and some were able to purchase their freedom. A definitive study by Ira Berlin, *Slaves Without Masters*,[23] implies that more than fifty percent of all free Blacks were mulattoes, the "illegitimate" offspring of white men and Black women. A small percentage were the result of the offspring of Black fathers and Indian or white women.

In spite of their unequal status and restricted position, some free Blacks acquired property and became relatively wealthy. It is known that some became themselves slaveholders. However, historians seem to agree that many of these better-off free Blacks purchased their loved ones, relatives or friends from the grips of white slavery. The presence and growth of free Blacks caused uneasiness among Southern whites. There was always the problem of differentiating the mulatto free Black from Whites. Many white-skinned Blacks passed the color line into white society. The matter of what percentage of white blood constituted a white or black person was an issue decided upon by each state. The social foundation of American intergroup relations has always been based on race and color. Consequently, it was necessary to maintain distinct racial lines for the perpetuation of racism and racist ideology.

The quasi-free and slave African were perceived as being inferior or less than equal to whites whether in the free states of the North or the slave states of the South. Any discernible Black trait or traceable drop of African blood barred a person from being a member of the white race. Yet, the form of racial slavery related to color introduced by Europeans affected the survival and base instincts of Africans as well. Color-class divisions and conflict of interests developed between free and slave Blacks which often served as a deterrent to unified resistance to the slave system. Ira Berlin writes a descriptive and plausible account of the tenuous and suspicious relationship that sometimes existed between the slave and the free Black. Whites who created the schism between free or mulatto Blacks and the bondservants, exploited the divisions in order to maintain control over the slaves. The free Black was encouraged by whites to inform on the slaves for privileges or economic rewards and house slaves often informed on the field slaves to demonstrate their loyalty to the slavemaster.[24]

The deliberate creation of color-class differences among Africans by whites caused some Blacks to falter in their concept of self-identity and collective sense of responsibility for the freedom of their race. Three major slave uprisings between 1800 and 1831 failed because house slaves or mulattoes betrayed the confidence of the leaders of the revolts. These betrayals resulted in disastrous consequences, but were not typical of all the relationships between the nonslave and slave Black populations.

**Slave Resistance, Rebellion, and White Fears.** Slavery failed to provoke the moral consciousness of whites, partly, because they conveniently adopted the rationale that

Blacks were fatalistically inferior, unintelligent, docile and child-like by nature. Therefore, it is not surprising that as late as the early twentieth century some White scholars promoted the unfounded theory that Africans accepted their subjugated plight and endured brutality, pain and suffering with geniality and passiveness. Blacks have always rejected the asinine notion that the whole race of African people had a proclivity towards masochism. Conversely, it is equally unintelligent to assume that all members of the Caucasian race were afflicted with sadism.

However, one of the most comprehensive and seminal works refuting the concept of the "docile slave" was written by the white scholar Herbert Aptheker. In *American Negro Slave Revolts*, Aptheker reveals recorded evidence of not only 250 Black slave revolts or insurrections, but also treats various other tactics of individual slave resistance. Slaves were known to have attempted and often succeeded at escape, sabotage, feigned illness, strike or refusal to work, self-mutilation, poison or assassination of slavemasters and arson.[25] The inference by historian, Stanley M. Elkins, that the intellect and will to rebel resided only in the nonslave literate Black is stereotypically suspect and unproven.[26] Whites, generally, have accorded to those non-whites who have been more socialized or "civilized" in the Eurocentric tradition a greater recognition of intelligence. However, the fact that the more freer and educated Blacks initiated rebellions and fomented resistance to slavery affirms the concern and compassion that the better-off class of African Americans have always maintained for their less fortunate brothers and sisters.

To enumerate many of the recorded slave revolts or to treat any single incident at great length would be impractical in this survey study. The intent is to dispel the myth of the docility of the African slave and to allow one to imagine what might have been the outcomes if more Black unity and cohesiveness had prevailed. The strategy of divide and conquer historically mastered by White and European people contributed then, and is effective today, towards thwarting the freedom goals and objectives of African peoples.

One of the earliest recorded slave rebellions took place in 1739 at Stono, South Carolina when more than twenty slaves seized some firearms, killed their guards and all other whites who got in their way. They marched, burned buildings and chanted freedom songs on their way to Florida where they had hoped to escape. They were eventually met and attacked by a detachment of militia. Some were killed and others were dispersed, later captured and killed. It should be noted that several slave revolts occurred during the period between 1739 and 1790 in the Atlantic states including New York and New Jersey. Virginia had a high disproportionate number of revolts.

In 1800 Gabriel Prosser and an accomplice leader by the name of Jack Bowler began a conspiracy to revolt near Richmond, Virginia. They secretly acquired and stored an arsenal of firearms and bullets, and fashioned crude swords and bayonets. On the day the revolution was to take place, over a thousand slaves rendezvoused outside the city of Richmond with the intent of attack. Gabriel Prosser failed not only because the rebellion had been betrayed by two house slaves, but fate intervened in the form of a massive thunderstorm with torrential rain showers. The storm destroyed a key bridge structure and made passages impossible. The conspirators were forced to disband and, subsequently, the militia was dispatched and scores of them were rounded up and executed. Gabriel escaped immediate capture but, again, he was betrayed by two members of his own race while trying to escape on a boat. He and other rebels were hanged.

Denmark Vesey was reported to have a literate slave and expert carpenter who purchased his freedom with money he won from a lottery. He was a respected member of the free Black community of Charleston, South Carolina and was known for his anti-slavery and human-equality sentiment and oratory. He was impressed with the successful Black revolution of Haiti and planned and took a long period to develop his own conspiracy to revolt. It was one of the most meticulously planned, organized and threatening rebellion of African slaves. An error in judgement occurred when an attempt was made to recruit a house slave to the cause. The house "negro" informed Whites of the conspiracy before it even fully materialized. Nevertheless, hundreds of the Black conspirators were arrested, tried and executed including Denmark Vesey. In effect, the Denmark Vesey conspiracy caused whites to be on guard and to fear the inevitable events of future rebellions. Black church organizations and religious practices were forbidden or carefully scrutinized thereafter.

The most famous slave revolt of the nineteenth century was led and executed by Nat Turner. Indeed, it involved the greatest number of participants and was perhaps the most bloodiest in terms of the large number of both whites and blacks killed. Nat Turner learned early to read and write and, undoubtedly, inherited his strong will and resoluteness from his father and mother. His father escaped to the North while Nat was still a boy and his mother would rather have killed her infant son than to see him sold into slavery. Nat was highly religious and became a Baptist preacher. He claimed to have had Divine visions of slave insurrections and freedom. He planned the revolt with extreme secrecy having learned of how other attempts had been betrayed. On the day of the uprising white farmers, slaveholders and any white who got in the way were systematically killed. As the revolution progressed it began to meet with armed confrontation from whites. The militia was called upon and with its overwhelming fire power and numbers the revolt was destroyed. Mass executions, mutilations and horrid tortures followed the insurrection. Turner eluded his pursuers for over two months but was eventually captured, convicted and hanged. Before he was executed, he was able to dictate his *Confessions* of the conspiracy. Nat Turner inspired the spirit of revolution among African peoples.[27]

The African American slave experience will continue to be a fertile field of scholarly research and speculation. However only Blacks, who were and still are affected socially, psychologically and politically from slavery, may have a true grasp and feeling for its dehumanizing consequences. White control of the plantation system required that they create and promote class divisions among the slaves. In spite of this strategy, most of the significant slave revolts were precipitated by the so-called free Blacks which in essence proved that they were not really free. While there were some house slaves and near-white Blacks who betrayed attempts for freedom and were loyal to their white masters, there had to have been much cooperation and complicity on the part of others in planning and organizing the revolts that did occur. The Black preacher, church groups and various religious advocates against human inequality and oppression were major proponents in many slave uprisings.

The social dynamics that existed among Africans during the era of slavery are manifested and functions in African American society of the twentieth century. Like the "free" Blacks of the slave period fought for the liberation of all Africans, the middle-class or educated (not so free) African Americans of today carry on the struggle for freedom and uplift of the Black masses. Courageous and freedom-minded Black ministers and the Black church of the twentieth century continue to protest against racism and are at the forefront of Civil Rights Movements. It may not be plausible to expect those who have benefited from slavery to lionize Gabriel Prosser, Denmark Vesey and Nat Turner of

the eighteenth and nineteenth centuries or Marcus Garvey and Malcolm X of the twentieth century. They should be celebrated as great persons among all justice and freedom loving people, but certainly they are heros of African Americans.

### Rising Abolitionism: Causes and Effects.

The axiomatic saying that, "if someone has to *let* you be free, you may never be free," can relate to the indispensable underlying role Africans played to free themselves from the bonds of slavery. Because the power of government and law was in the hands of whites, much of the literature treating the abolition of slavery in America deals with the political machinations of the executive, legislative and judicial branches in either opposing or abetting the anti-slavery movements. While many traditional and revisionist historians have underplayed the importance of African abolitionist involvement, Black people have always been the foremost instigators for their own freedom. Acknowledging Black Americans' role toward their own liberation, white historian Herbert Aptheker writes:

> Slavery was the unique experience of black people in the United States. . . . They alone endured it, survived it, and combated it. They were the first and most lasting Abolitionists. Their conspiracies and insurrections, individual struggles, systematic flights, maroon communities, efforts to buy freedom, cultural solidity, creation of antislavery organizations and publications—all preceded the black-white united efforts.[28]

It would be inaccurate to say that all Europeans or Whites supported and encouraged slavery. Individuals and groups of various ethnic origins and nationalities have always opposed slavery in America and, subsequently, they were known as abolitionists. Abolitionist oriented individuals and organizations even emerged in Britain, the country that virtually originated the "unique" concept and practice of slavery, and benefited most from its earlier perpetration.

Anti-slavery sentiment and activity had somewhat subsided after the Revolutionary War since citizens of the Northern states had essentially appeased their consciouses by making slavery, theoretically, unconstitutional. However following the War of 1812, slavery became even more essential towards the development of the cotton economy of the South. Southern plantations and businesses required a revival and extension of slavery— not its reduction or abolition. Therefore, the interest and disposition of the South were diametrically opposed to those of the North. This caused a contentious and politically divisive relationship to develop between the "free" states and the slave states. The South was adamant in maintaining slavery and rationalized the enslavement of Blacks because it perceived them to be of an inferior race.

Clearly, the South enjoyed a trade and commercial advantage over the North due to its free or slave labor and lower tariffs. As new territories and states developed in the West, it was economically important that these new states be designated as free or slave which in effect would determine the North or South balance of power in the government. The issue of slavery or freedom for Blacks determined whether or not the South would secede from the Union. To circumvent the threat of secession, efforts and compromises were made to maintain a balance of non-slave and slave states and territories. The Ordinance of 1787 had abolished slavery in the territory north of the Ohio and east of the Mississippi rivers which included the future states of Ohio, Illinois, Indiana, Michigan, Wisconsin, and Minnesota. Alabama, Mississippi, Louisiana, Florida, Texas, Arkansas Tennessee and Kentucky had been admitted as slave states which in total equalized the number of "free" and slave states. The threat of disequilibrium occurred when the Missouri territory petitioned for admission to the

Union as a slave state. A member of the House of Representatives, James Tallmadge proposed an amendment that would prohibit slavery in the state of Missouri. The amendment did not pass and the Congress moved to admit Maine as a "free" state along with Missouri as a slave state in order to preserve equilibrium between North and South. This became known as the Missouri Compromise.

Several compromises were made in 1850 designed to preserve harmony and balance between the North and South. The one that stirred anti-slavery sentiment the most was perhaps the Fugitive Slave Act. The Fugitive Slave Law allowed slave owners to pursue and reclaim alleged slaves or fugitives without due process; the alleged slave was not permitted to testify in his or her own behalf; and heavy penalties were imposed on anyone aiding the fugitive or assisting in escape. Northerners questioned the constitutionality of this Act on the grounds that it undertook to suspend the writ of *habeas corpus*.[29]

Another event that provoked constitutional controversy and anti-slavery protest was the decision rendered by the Supreme Court in the Dred Scott case of 1857. Dred Scott was a slave who originally lived in a slave territory, but was taken by his master to a free state where he lived for a number of years. Scott returned with his master to the slave state of Missouri and eventually saved enough money to purchase his freedom. His owner refused him permission and through a benefactor lawyer, Scott sued his owner on the basis that he had lived in a free state and territory and upon his return to the slave state of Missouri he was entitled to his freedom. A lower court ruled in Dred Scott's favor but the decision was reversed by the Missouri Supreme Court. The case was appealed all the way to the United State Supreme Court. Chief Justice Roger B. Taney, a southerner, declared in essence that Blacks were not and could not become citizens of the United States being members of an inferior race. Thus, Blacks were not eligible to bring suit in the courts.[30]

The Missouri Compromise, Fugitive Slave Law, and Dred Scott decision served to arouse and intensify anti-slavery sentiment and abolitionist activity. The morally unconscionable and inhumane South did not quell the spirit of resistance and drive for freedom by Blacks. Slave insurrections, mass runaways, and other acts of defiance instilled fear, desperation and doubt in the minds of southern whites for their untenable posture towards human bondage. Not only did Southern recalcitrance sow the seeds that blossomed into the Civil War, but the period of abolitionism caused the emergence of some of the most righteous, eloquent, courageous and daring men and women of both races in the history of mankind.

In the absence of military might, the most potent weapons of the defenseless and powerless are the pen, oratory and moral suasion. Armed with one or a combination of these three forces or methods of protest, abolitionists petitioned and lobbied state and federal legislative bodies seeking the repeal of slave trade and fugitive slave laws; formed anti-slavery societies to aid slaves in escaping; and published and disseminated anti-slavery newspapers and underground publications. Some of the most renown Black abolitionists from 1829 until the eve of the Civil War included men such as David Walker, Henry Highland Garnet, and Frederick Douglass. Harriet Tubman and Sojourner Truth were outstanding among Black female abolitionists.

In Chapter I, it was discussed at length how Black philosophy and political ideology developed out of the abolitionist movement or era. In David Walker's, *An Appeal to the Coloured Citizens of the World*, the genesis of Black Cultural Nationalism and Pan-Africanism are reflected. Henry Highland Garnet was one of the first African Americans to embrace the concept of—freedom by any means necessary, including violent

revolution. The charismatic leader Malcom X was destined to echo Garnet's theme during the mid-twentieth century. However, it was Frederick Douglass' integrationist/assimilationist philosophy and goals that dominated the political ideology of most Blacks until the mid 1960s.

Frederick Douglass was perhaps the most famous eloquent Black orator of the abolitionist period. His assimilationist ideology did not cause the acid and invective quality of his speeches to be diminished. If he was an integrationist, then, certainly he was a *militant* one as evidenced by the following excerpt from a speech he delivered August 4, 1857:

> If there is no struggle there is no progress. Those who profess to favor freedom and yet deprecate agitation, are men who want crops without plowing up the ground, they want rain without thunder and lightning. They want the ocean without the awful roar of its many waters. This struggle may be a moral one, or it may be a physical one, and it may be both moral and physical, but it must be a struggle. Power concedes nothing without a demand. It never did and it never will. Find out just what any people will quietly submit to and you have found out the exact measure of injustice and wrong which will be imposed upon them, and these will continue till they are resisted with either words or blows, or with both. The limits of tyrants are prescribed by the endurance of those whom they oppress. . . . If we ever get free from the oppressions and wrongs heaped upon us, we must pay for their removal . . . by suffering, by sacrifice, and if needs be, by our lives and the lives of others.[31]

One of the most effective activities by abolitionists that eroded the institution of slavery was the escape or runaway of thousands of slaves through the Underground Railroad. The Underground Railroad is an abstraction rather than a literal term used to describe the various secretive means and methods used by abolitionists to assist fugitive slaves in escaping to free states and Canada.

Hundreds of persons, White and Black, were involved in this surreptitious activity. However, prominent among Blacks was a woman, Harriet Tubman. Harriet Tubman escaped from slavery and, subsequently, was instrumental in forming a network of secret way stations to aid in the escape of other slaves. She led at least 19 missions into the South to free hundreds of Blacks from the shackles of slavery. After 1860, Tubman became active in anti-slavery meetings and also participated in the women's rights movement.

Sojourner Truth was the most prominent Black female orator of the abolitionist period. She was a self-styled preacher who felt that she had a Divine mission to travel (sojourn) and spread the (truth) about slavery. She was born a slave around 1797 but was freed by the New York State Emancipation Act of 1827. Truth was very active in the Underground Railroad and in the anti-slavery movement. Although it was not customary that women spoke at public meeting during this period, Sojourner Truth is noted, historically, for a speech she was reluctantly permitted to make at the second National Woman's Suffrage Convention, held in Akron, Ohio in 1852. The speech has been titled, "And ain't I a Woman?

The press always loomed as a major force and tool of the abolitionists. Of the hundreds of white abolitionists, William Lloyd Garrison stands out as one who used publications and the press effectively in the anti-slavery movement. Garrison founded the *Liberator*, a highly inflammatory anti-slavery newspaper, which was published from 1831 to 1865. In 1827 two educated Blacks, John Russwurm and Samuel E. Cornish, founded *Freedom's Journal*, the first journal edited by and for Blacks in America. Although *Freedom's Journal* was not totally an abolitionist newspaper, it gave Africans their own independent expression of the Black experience. Frederick

Douglass used the press to attack all aspects of slavery and in December 1847 launched his own newspaper, the *North Star*, later titled *Frederick Douglass' Paper*. Subsequently, he initiated the *Douglass' Monthly* which was published from 1859 to 1863.[32]

Although there were numerous White abolitionists, few risked death and gave their life for the cause of ending slavery as John Brown. John Brown demonstrated his passionate opposition to slavery through militant and violent acts of aggression against the white establishment. He designed and executed a scheme to recruit and arm slaves, establish guerilla forces in the mountains, and fire upon or defeat any government militia attacking them. He conferred with Black abolitionists such as Frederick Douglass and Harriet Tubman but they declined based on the likelihood that the plan would not succeed. Nevertheless, Brown, and a small contingent of followers including three of his sons and five Blacks assaulted Harper Ferry, a Federal armory in October of 1859. The group succeeded in capturing the facility and holding out until he was defeated by Federal troops. John Brown and the rest of the survivors of the coup were tried and hanged. However, Brown became a martyr and the political and psychological implications of his feat exacerbated North and South tensions.

Increasing national and international anti-slavery sentiment, slave runaways and insurrections, conflicting North and South economic and social interests, and the rising tide of abolitionist activities made slavery the paramount political issues of the government. The fragile balance between free and slave states, and the ramifications of the issues of slavery caused the South to increase its threats of secession. Slavery was to become the overriding issue and political dilemma for the newly elected 16th President of the United States, Abraham Lincoln.

*Abraham Lincoln, Civil War and the Emancipation.* Abraham Lincoln was a moral and political enigma. Historians can only guess or surmise the degree of moral consciousness that he held towards slavery. Most would agree that he was politically astute and that his moral attitude towards Blacks and slavery vacillated in proportion to what was politically expedient. Prior to assuming the presidency he was reported to have made several anti-slavery statements and he also opposed the expansion of slavery into the new territories. Yet, the pattern of his political and social decisions towards Blacks during the Civil War was ambiguous to the extent that his true feelings will never be known. However, the political disarray and factionalism of the Democrats over the slavery issue assured his election as the moderate Republican president in 1860.

Lincoln was the political heir of the turmoil and tension created by the North and South conflict over slavery that his predecessor James Buchanan could not resolve. The North had gained the balance of power with the admission of the western territories Oregon, California and Minnesota as free states. The South's economy was based on cotton and slave labor, and it was imperative that slavery be maintained in contradiction to the North's anti-slavery sentiment. Secession of the South became imminent. South Carolina was the first southern "cotton" state to secede and was followed by Mississippi, Alabama, Georgia, Florida, Louisiana, and eventually, Texas. Delegates from the secessionist states convened in Montgomery, Alabama and formed a new government—and the Confederacy was born. The Confederacy had seized federal forts and properties with the exception of Fort Sumter, and South Carolinians fired on a federal vessel entering the port of Charleston. When an attempt was made by Lincoln to supply provisions for Fort Sumter the Confederacy demanded federal troops to evacuate the facility. The troops re-

fused and were fired upon by the Confederate forces. Fort Sumter returned the fire but the overwhelming firepower and advantage of the Confederacy forced the surrender of Fort Sumter. Thus, on April 14, 1861 the Civil War started.

Lincoln had taken a precautionary stance in his inaugural address and indicated that he would not intervene with force to prevent secession unless the Confederacy provoked and initiated attack or violence first. However, after the war had begun he acted with military efficiency in requiring the government of the Northern states to muster militia and recruit volunteers to defeat the Southern insurgency. As both sides prepared for battles, North Carolina, Arkansas, Virginia and Tennessee soon joined the Confederacy. The border states of Maryland, Kentucky and Missouri remained quasi if not fully loyal and under the control of the Union. The war was to be a long, bloody and costly undertaking for both the Union and the Confederacy, and fought solely for the cause or the matter of enslavement of Africans. The argument that the war was fought to preserve the Union is irrelevant since the preservation of the Union and slavery were inextricably tied together.

Blacks regarded the war as a godsend and thousands "free" and slave, sought to join the ranks of the Union with hopes of earning gratitude from the North and freedom from Southern slavery and oppression. But at the beginning of the Civil War, Blacks were forbidden from joining the Union army. This posture of the Union War Department soon changed as military manpower shortages occurred throughout the North. The decision to use Black troops was motivated because white volunteer enlistment declined and general conscription had not been authorized. Consequently, the Militia Act of 1862 was passed which authorized the use of Black troops in instances where states could not meet their voluntary quota. The Militia Act of 1862 was ineffective towards recruiting and maintaining

Photo 8 Black Troops, Union Army. Courtesy of National Archives.

adequate military personnel levels. In March 1863, a national Conscription Act was passed that lacked a racial clause which indicated that Lincoln planned to use all sources of manpower available. A loophole in the Militia Act of 1862 provided the opportunity for the War Department to pay Black soldiers less than Whites although they had, upon enlistment, been promised equal pay. This injustice prevailed until the protest of Black soldiers, supported by a few white sympathizers and coupled with the need to recruit more Africans, caused the enactment of the Army Appropriation Act of 1864 which equalized military pay.[33]

Almost 400,000 Blacks served in the Union army of which about one-half this number were considered as combat troops and the others were assigned duties in military service units. Africans also performed service in the Union navy. Service in the Union military offered Blacks the opportunity to achieve freedom not only for themselves but also to fight for the abolition of the institution of slavery. Nevertheless, service in the Union army for Blacks was not without racism, pain and suffering inflicted by white officers and institutionalized within the Union army itself. Joseph T. Glatthaar relates in his book, Forged in Battle, how Black soldiers were discriminated against in promotion and appointment as officers; slurred as being inferior and incompetent, denied and abused in terms of medical care and treatment; issued poorer quality of weapons and equipment; subjected to various forms of punishment, brutality; and acts of racism. The degree of racism varied with each particular unit or region.[34]

In spite of deep humiliation and racism, Black Union troops served with valor and distinction. The Black military experience in the Confederacy was a different story. Slaves were used to grow, harvest and serve food for the Confederate army. Some were hired out to the army to work in labor gangs and on military construction projects. There are some accounts that Southern "freedmen" served with the Confederate army. The South never fully approved of arming Blacks, free or slave, in the Civil War. When battle losses and dire manpower shortages eventually forced the South to sanction the use of slaves to combat Union forces it was too late. The defeat of the Confederacy was imminent and the North had won.[35]

Slavery was advantageous to the South in its war effort. Therefore, Lincoln sought to abolish slavery where it benefited the Confederacy. As mentioned above, slavery was inextricably connected to the war and with the objective of preserving the Union. Consequently, as early as August 1861, Lincoln began making selective and strategic plans that would have emancipatory effect on slaves. Congress passed a Confiscation Law which allowed the Union army to confiscate the property of rebels, including slaves, that were used for insurrection purposes. The Fugitive Slave Law which required federal authorities to return runaway slaves to their southern masters was also nullified. In July 1862 a second Confiscation Law was passed providing for the seizure of the property of the rebels and the emancipation of slaves only in those states which had seceded from the Union. After it became evident that the Union forces were winning, Lincoln issued a preliminary emancipation proclamation on September 22, 1862 which was scheduled to become final and effective on January 1, 1863. The proclamation effected only those states which were still at War with the Union.

The true moral conviction of Abraham Lincoln towards slavery and Blacks will never be known. Lincoln was assassinated April 14, 1865. Much historical controversy has resulted in the attempt by some scholars to speculate or to interpret the speeches, actions and attitude of Lincoln relative to the African's freedom and equality. Some believe that the epithet, "Great Emancipator," attributed to Lincoln is a misnomer considering his racial attitudes and support of emigrationist schemes to relocate Blacks back to Africa, Haiti or Panama. Historian LaWanda Cox offers one of the strongest defenses of Lincoln's procedures and policies regarding Black emancipation. She suggests that freedom for Blacks was foremost in Lincoln's mind but that he was equally concerned about having a constitutional base for emancipation, one that would withstand judicial scrutiny. Cox believes that ". . . the [Lincoln] criticism reflects late twentieth-century conscience more accurately than mid-nineteenth century realities."[36]

Lincoln's ambiguous and ambivalent statements and actions on the issue of Black freedom were indicative of the political self-preservation nature of politicians. Most politicians tend to react positively or negatively to an issue based upon factors which might enhance their popular image or preserve their political office. Lincoln was not unlike his predecessor Thomas Jefferson on the question of slavery. Jefferson's *real* feelings on the question of slavery were obscured with contradictions. One might compare the inconsistencies of Jefferson and Lincoln on Blacks with twentieth century President Lyndon Baines Johnson. Johnson built his career as a state politician and U.S. senator opposing the freedom and civil rights of Blacks. He was elected to serve as Vice President during the Presidency of John F. Kennedy. Upon the assassination of Kennedy in 1963, Johnson became president. After assuming the presidency, Lyndon B. Johnson reversed his opposition towards the equality of Blacks and preceded to use the influence and authority of his office to have enacted the most significant Civil Rights legislation in the history of America.

*African Americans and the Rise and Fall of Reconstruction.* Reconstruction was meant to be a program designed to rebuild the physical properties of the South; to restore whatever good relations that might have existed between white Southerners and Northerners before the Civil War; and to resolve the two-century old issue of slavery and human inequality. Eventually, it succeeded in rebuilding the political and economic structures of the South and in achieving at least a working relationship between the Union victors and the old Confederacy. Reconstruction never succeeded at revolutionizing the collective hearts, minds and attitudes of white Southerners toward Africans.

Lincoln had proposed some fundamental plans for reconstruction before his death and his successor, Andrew Johnson, sought to interpret and follow through with Lincoln's ideas. The South had been devastated both in lives and property. It lost over two-billion dollars in slave-assets once Emancipation was declared and effected. In spite of the suffering and devastation the South experienced as a result of the war, white Southerners were not repentant of their stance on Africans and slavery. They vengefully opposed all laws and attempts to bring about the equality of Blacks. What developed was the agelong geopolitical schism of Northern Republicans and Southern Democrats. The Republican North ranged, traditionally, from moderate to liberal on issues relating to Black freedom and equality. In addition, Republicans viewed the enfranchising of Blacks as a means to increase their numbers and influence in the South.

Neither the Emancipation Proclamation or the Civil War resolved, completely, the African freedom and equality issue. However,

three bills known as the Reconstruction Amendments were enacted to achieve this purpose. The Thirteenth Amendment of 1865 abolished slavery; the Fourteenth, ratified in 1868, conferred upon Blacks the rights of citizenship; and the Fifteenth, passed in 1870, extended voting rights to former slaves. Southern state delegations had not only initially rejected these Reconstruction Amendments, but had begun to enact laws or "Black Codes" which in effect, reduced Africans to a form of unequal, inferior and second-class citizenship even after Emancipation. The Black Codes amounted to legally "sanitized" versions of the old slave codes. They were designed to resubjugate Blacks to virtual slave or indentured servant status. The codes limited Blacks to mostly agricultural forms of employment, restricted their areas of residence and permitted them only segregated and unequal educational opportunity. However, as Professor Quarles has pointed out, the Black Codes differed slightly from the slave codes in that they generally allowed Blacks the right to own property, to make and to enforce contracts, to sue and be sued in cases involving other Blacks, and to have legal intra-racial marriages.[37]

The treatment of the supposedly emancipated Africans by the Southerners was so unjust and severe that it prompted the Republican dominated Congress to investigate and to propose bills that would grant relief to Africans and assure their civil rights. The Congress proposed an extension of the activities of the Freedman's Bureau. The Freedman's Bureau was an agency of the War Department established March 1865 to assist former slaves and impoverished whites in employment, health programs, legal aid in labor or wages contract disputes, and in the development of schools. Secondly, the Congress proposed a Civil Rights bill which essentially was to become the Fourteenth Amendment. President Johnson vetoed both of these bills basically on the grounds that the bills provided more than the former slaves deserved and was capable of handling. The Republican Congress easily overrode the President's veto and went on to pass the Fourteenth Amendment on June 13, 1866, pending its ratification by the states. In order to force Southerners to comply with the Civil Rights measures the Reconstruction Act of March 2, 1867 was enacted. This Act specified that the defiant former states of the Confederacy were to be divided into five military districts with each one governed by a major general. The generals were to prepare the states for readmission to the Union by having each one to have a constitutional convention with delegates having been elected by voters. No state would be admitted until it ratified the Fourteenth Amendment.

Following the ratification of the Fourteenth and Fifteenth Amendments and during the brief period of Reconstruction, many African Americans were elected or appointed to serve in various political or public offices. Under the auspices and enforcement of civil rights by the federal government, Blacks served as senators, legislators and in a number of lesser state and federal public offices. Hiram R. Revels and Blanche K. Bruce, two Blacks from Mississippi, served in the United State Senate and fourteen others sat in the House of Representatives. Contrary to racist myths and stereotypes, most African American officials competently and diligently executed the duties of their offices. "It should be added that the few [Blacks] who served in high offices were mostly men of ability and integrity . . ." writes white historians J.G. Randall and David Donald.[38]

Reconstruction was an ideal that was destined to fail because African Americans, exslaves, were not allowed sufficient time to gain collective political competence and equal citizenship status with whites. Ulysses Grant succeeded Andrew Johnson as president of the United States. During the early era of the Grant Administration, the country experienced a period of territorial and diplomatic expansionism, and industrial and technological growth and development. However, Grant's tenure of office was marred with corruption and scandals which was attributed mostly to his inept ability or unfitness for the office of the president. Even before the end of his second term of office, Southern Democrats and their Northern counterparts had gained basic control of the legislature. Radical or liberal Republicans who had championed and safeguarded Black Reconstruction in the South begun to lose moderate Republican support. An economic depression plagued the second-half of the Grant term and the attention of the country turned from the problems of the South and Blacks to urgent matters of the national debt, currency and tariffs—property rights above human rights.

Radical Republicans and carpetbaggers sought to increase their political influence in the south through voting fraud and other high pressure and unethical schemes. It was natural that Blacks would vote Republican in large numbers. African Americans being new to the rights and privileges of enfranchisement were often politically naive and were exploited by the Republicans and carpetbaggers. White Democrats, fearful of the rise and threat of Black Republicanism in the South, resorted to intimidation and terror to discourage Blacks from participating in the political process in favor of the Republicans. Terrorist organizations like the Ku Klux Klan and other white secret societies perpetrated violence, arson, murder and other acts designed to instill fear in Blacks and suppress their participation in Republican politics. White racist Democrats soon reigned supreme in all the Southern states. The Republican tide that had swept in relief from oppression and reconstruction for Africans had waned.

The final death knell for Reconstruction occurred when Rutherford B. Hayes was elected President in 1876. His election was made possible because of a series of compromises and pledges he had made to end Southern racial reformism in order to reconcile the interests of the North and South. He recalled the remaining Federal troops and enforcement officers of Reconstruction from the South. The U.S. Supreme Court became indifferent and hostile towards the equal citizenship rights that the Reconstruction Amendments had supposedly bestowed upon Africans. Its rulings were unfavorable to Blacks in a number of Reconstruction cases brought before it, including the provision of the Fifteenth Amendment which guaranteed all citizens the right to vote. The Federal government had forsaken the ex-slaves by withdrawing its enforcement of Civil Rights and safeguards of Black freedom. In essence, Reconstruction had ended with the fate of African Americans left once again to the merciless and racist oppression of Southern whites. The scenario of Black and White relations from 1865 to 1877 is reflective of what would occur in the twentieth century from 1960 through 1993—social revolution, reconstruction and decline.

# FROM "NEO-SLAVERY" TO BLACK PROTEST AND SOCIAL PHILOSOPHY

*Renewal and Intensification of Oppression and Violence.* Following the end of Reconstruction, African Americans began to experience a modified or revised form of racial subjugation that might best be described as "neo-slavery". This type of slavery differed from traditional American slavery only to the extent that Blacks were no longer the chattel property of whites and that constitutionally and theoretically—but not in practice—they were proposed to be free and equal. African Americans, especially in the South, were stripped of almost every vestige of citizenship rights and denied justice, due process and

protection of the law as prescribed by the Constitution.

The eminent Black scholar W.E.B. DuBois described the fate and condition of Africans in the South after the fall of Reconstruction as a step back towards slavery. DuBois accounts for the reversion by emphasizing the economic necessity of southern whites to maintain Blacks under their subjugation because the former slaves were still the major asset of the South after Emancipation. The Civil War had destroyed the economic foundations of the South and it could not rebuild without exploiting the labor of Africans and denying their humanity.[39] However, economics alone cannot explain or rationalize the viperous hate whites possessed for Blacks or for their obsession of holding African people into perpetual servitude. The psychological dimensions of the Southern white attitude and treatment of Blacks have never been fully studied or analyzed.

The former Confederate states defied the Fourteenth Amendment which provided equal citizenship rights for Blacks, and the Fifteenth Amendment which granted all citizens the right to vote. The Civil Rights Act of 1875 entitling Africans to equal and full enjoyment of public facilities and conveyances was also ignored. Instead, the southern states almost jointly and in succession began to pass "Jim Crow" laws designed to legally circumvent and to nullify the Constitution or any other federal laws that were enacted to protect the citizenship status of Blacks. Jim Crow more aptly described those laws and statues that were passed to legally segregate Blacks from Whites in every facet of southern life including education, transportation, neighborhoods and housing. Through white mob violence, terrorist group activities, and lynchings Blacks were discouraged from asserting their rights of citizenship.

The most blatant affront to Constitutional law was the unscrupulous and cruel practices that were used to discourage and to deny

Black people the right to vote. Mississippi with a majority Black population in 1890 took the lead in eliminating Black voters. Each voter was compelled to pay a poll tax of two dollars and one could not vote if one had been convicted of certain misdemeanors. Strict and ridiculous literary competencies were required of Blacks as a condition for being allowed to caste a ballot. The "grand-father clause" was originated and adopted in Louisiana in 1898 to restrict Black voter participation. It granted the voting "franchise to any person who, although lacking the requisite education and property, had been eligible to vote on January 1, 1866, or who was the son or grandson of a person eligible to vote on that date."[40] All of the former Confederate states had contrived "legally" and effectively in depriving Blacks of the right to vote by the first decade of the twentieth century. White Southern Democrats dominated the politics of the South.

Successive U.S. Presidents, Rutherford B. Hayes, James A. Garfield, Chester A. Arthur, Grover Cleveland and Benjamin Harrison (from 1885 to 1893) either ignored or failed to enforce the Constitutional measures that were intended to ensure the equal citizenship rights of African people. The United States Supreme Court, through its distorted interpretations of the Fourteenth Amendment, consistently rendered decisions favorable to the racist and segregationist designs of White southerners. Southern businessmen and property owners benefited the industrial and commercial interests of Northern Democrats and, thus, Northern whites chose to ignore the neo-slavery developments of the South.

The emergence of the Populist Party of 1891 served briefly to garner the support of poor whites and Blacks in opposition to both the Democrat and Republican parties. However, this experiment failed when all the political camps began to exploit and intimidate Blacks in competition for their votes.

White Southerners recognized the threat of Black political participation and moved swiftly toward complete disfranchisement of Africans. White Supremacy, Jim Crowism, terror, violence, lynching and murder intensified toward Blacks in the South and reared in the North as well. Segregation, race-purity, discrimination and African inferiority—based upon so-called Biblical and scientific rationales—became the doctrines of Southern politics. Jim Crow practices ranged from the extreme to the ridiculous, from segregated rest-rooms to separate Bibles in the courtroom.[41] A new form of slavery and virulent era of racism had begun.

**Black Migration, Education, Protest and Social Philosophy.** There was little hope for change of the oppressive plight of African Americans in the North or South at the end of the nineteenth century. Although segregation was not as rampart or extreme in the North, economic discrimination in terms of employment opportunity, housing and social services for Blacks were equally appalling. If there was any vestige of hope left it was found in the Constitution and federal Civil Rights Act which in words or theory guaranteed the freedom, justice and equality for all citizens. However, much of this hope faded when in 1896 the United States Supreme Court upheld a Louisiana law that required segregated facilities for Blacks and Whites. The Court ruled in the case of a Black man, Homer A. Plessy, who had been ejected from a *white only* railway car, that the Louisiana "Jim Crow" policy of separate but equal was legal. With this one sweeping decision of *Plessy vs. Ferguson*, the U.S. Supreme Court gave constitutional approval to Jim Crowism or segregation. This "separate but equal" ruling was to negatively affect the social, economic and political life of African Americans for the next 68 years, long into the twentieth century.

Photo 9 Segregation Scene. Courtesy of The Library of Congress.

In essence, the Court ruled that separate but equal public facilities or accommodations did not violate the Fourteenth Amendment. Superficially, the decision appeared just considering the *equal* mandate of the Court. Indeed, if Black public schools, housing and other accommodations or facilities had been made equal and on par with whites much of the race conflict and injustice would have subsided. But the equitable separation of the races never occurred. Public facilities, accommodations, assets, services and other provisions for Blacks were always, demonstrably, inferior or second-class to Whites. The inequitable practice of the "separate but equal" doctrine worsened the oppressive educational and economic conditions of Blacks in the South. While schools for whites were modern, sufficiently staffed and equipped with the best instructional aids, Blacks attended comparatively run-down school structures with poorly prepared teachers and obsolete or inadequate educational supplies and equipment. Thus, education was the key to equitable employment opportunity. Without education Blacks were relegated to low-paying menial, labor intensive and hazardous jobs with no hope of advancement. Blacks were locked into an inextricable cycle of poverty.

In spite of the precipitous court ruling and monumental set-backs of the late nineteenth century, Blacks sought freedom not only of body, but of thought and mind. W.E.B. DuBois once wrote that:

> It is but human experience to find that the complete suppression of a race is impossible. Despite inner discouragement and submission to the oppression of others there persisted the mighty spirit, the emotional rebound that kept a vast number struggling for its rights, for self-expression, and for social uplift.[42]

The "separate but equal" doctrine was a catalyst for discontent among Black people of the South. Thousands resorted to migration as a means of escaping segregation, discrimination and poverty.

Small migratory movements of Blacks from the South to the North and West began during and shortly after the Civil War. But what historians refer to as the great "exodus" of African Americans from the South began during the early period of the twentieth century. It is unquestionable that Blacks fled the South in such large numbers because of the extreme oppression, segregation, violence and intimidation that they suffered from racist Southern white society and, particularly, plantation owners. Moreover, after the severe drought, crop failures and plague of the cotton boll weevils in 1915 and 1916, plantation owner and Black sharecropper or tenant were hard pressed to muster subsistence. Thus, hundreds of Blacks left the South simply to be able to feed their families. Professor Quarles writes that the earlier migratory movement of Blacks to the West—Oklahoma, Kansas, Texas, Nebraska, and Iowa—from 1879 to 1890 was stymied because of extreme cold and hardships. "Some of the migrants were thus able to weather the storm, eventually finding jobs or obtaining public lands. But others returned to the South or struck out in new directions."[43]

By far, the greatest movement of Blacks was northward between 1890 and 1920. Although figures from different sources vary, it can be estimated that during this period more than a million black Southerners left the South to live in the large urban centers of the North. Florette Henri reported that "by 1920, almost 40 percent of the Black population in the North was concentrated in the eight cities of Chicago, Detroit, New York, Cleveland, Cincinnati, Columbus, Philadelphia, and Pittsburgh."[44] The obvious reasons for the massive exodus of Blacks from the South were to escape the incidences of Jim Crow, racial violence and lynchings. Yet, other reasons were related to social and economic betterment. The Industrial Revolution created jobs that paid nominally higher wages than could ever be obtained in the South. Furthermore, the absence of overt and extreme segregation in public conveyances, schools, facilities and accommodations of the North enabled the African American migrants to regain a sense of human dignity and self-respect. However, even in the Metropolitan areas of the North Blacks were discriminated against in union memberships, certain employment opportunities and in housing.

The exodus of Blacks from the South created economic problems for white Southerners. Exploitation, injustice and brutality suffered at the hands of Whites caused Africans to flee the South. Yet, the economy of the southern states was based upon Black cheap labor and the peonage system. Consequently, southern officials attempted to restrict and prevent the tide of Black migration to the North and West. Professor Hodges relates how Blacks were intimidated and forced back on farms, refused railway and bus tickets, arrested as vagrants and even beaten in order to check their exodus.[45] White Southerners have always had a paradoxical and ironic relationship with Black people. They have, historically, mistreated and enslaved Africans. They have refused to live equitably and harmoniously with Blacks. And yet, their economic and political survival is tied inextricably with Blacks.

Migration to the North did not end the racism, discrimination, suffering and violence for African Americans. What Blacks experienced were differences in the nature, degree, types and intensity of racist treatment and hardships. The large influx of Blacks to northern cities and towns was destined to create conflict and arouse prejudice and resentment among northern Whites. The problem of providing housing, employment, health and social services for the tides of migrants was an overriding concern and issue for urban officials and politicians. Mostly un-

skilled and uneducated, Blacks were forced to live in deteriorating sections of cities and live overcrowded in hovels and ghetto structures. Conditions of squalor and deprivation caused widespread disease and deaths. Thousands died from tuberculosis, pneumonia and venereal disease. Health agencies were hard pressed to provide care for both indigenous residents and migrants. Black infant mortality rates were disproportionately high.

Structural unemployment, dislocation and impoverished conditions contributed toward problems of crime, alcohol, drugs and other forms of deviance in the ghetto. Many Northerners viewed the migrant Blacks as criminally prone and as social misfits in disregard of their historical and sociological circumstances. Blacks had to compete with floods of European immigrants for all kinds of industrial, commercial, skilled and unskilled jobs. This created inter-ethnic or interracial conflict that resulted in several race riots during the period from 1900 to 1920. All of these factors made the transition from the South to the North a matter of a dilemma for Blacks. Yet, few chose to return to the South. Overall their life-chances, educational opportunities and possibilities for social justice were somewhat better in the North. Furthermore, the lynching of African Americans throughout the United States increased dramatically from 1890 to 1920 with most of the incidences occurring in the South.

One of the major institutions that was credited most for giving assistance and for sustaining the spirit of perseverance of migrant African Americans to the North was the Black church. W.E.B. DuBois noted in his classic work, *The Souls of Black Folk,* that, "the Negro Church is the social center of Negro life in the United States, and the most characteristic expression of African character."[46] Thus, the church served as the social and spiritual link to the southern homeland the Black migrants had left behind. On the other hand, the migrants inspired within the

Northern churches a deepening sense of solidarity and community. With the increased memberships, the Black churches sponsored various programs to care for the sick, feed the hungry, and to find housing and employment.

The first decade of the twentieth century was marked not only with Black migrations, but with mob violence, race riots, and lynchings in the North and South. It was inevitable that Blacks, especially those of the North, would seek to organize to protest and to petition the government for protection and relief. Theodore Roosevelt had ascended to the American Presidency in 1901 and most politicians had turned a deaf ear to the plight of Blacks. The National Association for the Advancement of Colored People (NAACP) was organized in 1909 with W.E.B. DuBois as one of its charter members. Its purpose was to work towards the ending of segregation and the lynching of Blacks, fight for equal education and, generally, to have the provisions of the Fourteenth and Fifteenth Amendments enforced. In 1911 the National Urban League (NUL) was founded as a result of a merger of three older organizations. Its main objective was to help to facilitate the entry of Black migrant workers into the industrialized job markets of the Northern urban centers.

The beginning of Black protest and self-uplift in the twentieth century began with the founding of such organizations as the Niagara Movement, the National Association for the Advancement of Colored People, the National Urban League, and various other African American lodges and societies. The establishment of Black churches and educational institutions the latter part of the nineteenth century served as the foundation not only for these organizations, but for the Civil Rights Movements of the entire twentieth century. After the Civil War and during the Reconstruction period, African American church denominations were instrumental in establishing schools and colleges especially for

the Black population. White religious and philanthropic organizations of the North assisted these Black independent institutions and also established additional schools and colleges for African Americans. During the late nineteenth century, major white liberal universities of the North had begun to admit and graduate several select African Americans.

Because of the increased educational opportunities of the late 1800s and early 1900s and in spite of general repression and oppression, learned and talented African Americans made outstanding contributions to business and industry as inventors and entrepreneurs. In the arts and humanities, they began to create and express Black culture in literature, poetry, art, and music. Jan Matzeliger (1852–89) invented a shoe lasting machine that revolutionized the shoe making industry and made shoe lasting by hand obsolete. Elijah McCoy (1845–1929) patented more than fifty inventions related to the mechanical lubrication of rail locomotives. Matzeliger and McCoy were only two among hundreds of African American inventors from the seventeenth to the twentieth century. Some were able to have their inventions patented and other were denied.[47] Charles Waddell Chestnutt (1858–1932) and Zora Neale Hurston (1903–1960), novelists; Paul Laurence Dunbar (1872–1906) and Claude McKay (1890–1948), poets; Henry O. Tanner (1859–1937) and William Harper (1873–1910), artists; Joseph (King) Oliver (1885–1938), musician; and, W.C. Handy (1873–1958), composer, were among the many notable exponents of African American culture during this period. There was literally an explosion of Black cultural arts and letters during the Harlem Renaissance, a period which began at the height of the exodus of Blacks from the South before and during World War I—and lasted for more than two decades. More on the Harlem Renaissance will be discussed in the chapter on African American Cultural Arts and Creativity.

Education dispels ignorance, bolsters courage and gives insight into the social phenomena of inter-human relationships. Frederick Douglass the, generally self-educated, eloquent and fiery Black leader during and throughout the abolitionist, Emancipation and Reconstruction periods, indisputably, articulated the major social philosophy of African Americans. Douglass championed and fought for the assimilationist goals of social, political, economic and educational equality of Blacks and Whites. It was an ironic turn of fate that Frederick Douglass died in 1895 the year before the U.S. Supreme Court rendered its infamous *Plessy vs. Ferguson* (separate but equal) decision which legitimized racial apartheid in the United States in 1896. Douglass' death left a temporary void in the philosophical direction of African Americans. But a new cadre of Black educated elites was already forming who would challenge, modify or extend the social philosophy of Frederick Douglass.

The demise of Douglass cleared the way for the ascendancy of Booker T. Washington to the top realm of African American leadership. Washington, educated at Hampton Institute in Virginia, had assumed the principalship of a school established by white southern philanthropists for Blacks in Alabama which was later to become Tuskegee Institute. Washington espoused a social philosophy that was in many ways diametrically opposed to that of Frederick Douglass. Yet, there were certain aspects of his ideology for Black liberation that appeared logical, feasible and practical in race relationships during his time, especially, in view of the Supreme Court's "separate but equal" ruling as the law of the land.

Washington seemed to endorse Jim Crowism and segregation, conceded the political disfranchisement of African Americans and discouraged their fight for equality and civil rights. He proposed that Blacks should strive to master the crafts and vocational trades and to forsake aspirations to excel in the professional and liberal arts fields. He exhorted Blacks to emulate or adopt white Victorian principles of manners and cleanliness, and advocated self-help and self-improvement. Washington encouraged and promoted Black independent entrepreneurship. With this type of social philosophy for African Americans, it is not surprising why Booker T. Washington won the hearts, minds and influence of Whites throughtout the United States. Washington was invited to address The Atlanta Exposition of 1895. The following excerpts from his speech reveal, essentially, his race-social philosophy of the time. He spoke with much humility and eloquence stating that:

. . . In all things that are purely social we can be as separate as the fingers, yet one as the hand in all things essential to mutual progress.

On the issue of racial and social equality, he stated:

. . . The wisest among my race understand that the agitation of questions of social equality is the extremist folly, and that progress in the enjoyment of all the privileges that will come to us must be the result of severe and constant struggle rather than of artificial forcing.

A fair analysis of the full context of Washington's address beyond his obvious condescension to white interests and sensitivities might reveal a few practical and logical approaches toward Black survival and development under the conditions of that period of time. Some contemporary Black social theorists detect implications of Black nationalism in Booker T. Washington's philosophy. Others view Washington as an "uncle Tom" who pawned the best interests of African Americans in order to ensure his white appointed role as the leader of the black race. Succeeding his Atlanta Exposition address, Washington was highly recognized and praised by Presidents Theodore Roosevelt and William Howard Taft. Several white industrialists and philanthropists gave him financial aid and support for Tuskegee Institute.

Booker T. Washington did not escape detraction from some of his African American peers or fellow educated elites. Foremost among those who opposed his social philosophy and disagreed with the "accommodationist" theme of his Atlanta speech were W.E.B. DuBois and William Monroe Trotter. DuBois and Trotter were graduates of Harvard University and contrary to Washington's philosophy, they advocated a liberal instead of vocational education for Blacks, sought to repeal segregationist laws, petitioned to halt lynching, and demanded that the government enforce the constitutional provisions of equal citizenship and voting rights. Leading educated Black women who fought against lynching and segregation were Ida B. Wells Barnett and Mary Church Terrell. These and other of Washington's detractors promoted the continuation of Frederick Douglass' integrationist ideals.

Booker T. Washington and his social philosophy had some support among African Americans but by far he was lauded and praised mostly by Whites, many who were avowed racists and haters of African people. The adulation that whites had for Washington did not effect or diminish the lynching, mob violence, mutilations, and terror that they perpetrated upon African Americans during his reign of leadership. In fact, race relations worsened and over 3000 Black men and women were lynched by the time of his death in 1915. By the time W.E.B. DuBois, William Monroe Trotter and twenty or more Black professional men met near Buffalo, New York to organize the Niagara movement, the Black masses had begun to turn away

from accommodation, submission to racism, and white oppression.[48]

***World War I, Segregation, Riots and Black Nationalism.*** African Americans endured some of the most abusive, inhumane and violent treatment from whites during and after the span of World War I. The war also coincided with the peak trend of Black migration from the South to the North and the African American's new spirit of resiliency and resolve to struggle. When the United States decided to enter the War of Europe in March 1917, thousands of Blacks rushed to volunteer but they were initially rebuffed. The attitude and disposition of the federal government relative to Black enlistment in World War I were consistent with the precedents of the Revolutionary War, War of 1812, and the Civil War. Nevertheless, after the passage of the Selective Service Act requiring all able-bodied citizens between the ages of 21 to 31 to register, Blacks were accepted. Of the more than two-million African Americans who registered during the draft period, approximately 370,000 served. A high disproportionate rate of Blacks served but most were assigned to segregated labor and support military units.[49]

On the outbreak of the War in Europe in 1914, Blacks were too preoccupied with fighting and protesting the mass of murders, lynching and mob violence in the United States to form a collective opinion of the world conflict. In 1917, more than one hundred Blacks were killed and millions of dollars in property damage occurred in the Black community of East Saint Louis, Illinois as a result of a race riot and white mob violence. Racial violence erupted wherever and whenever large numbers of Blacks entered the large cities. However, it is assumed that most Blacks supported the war and opted for the opportunity, once again, to win the right of full citizenship and to become equal participants in the American democracy. W.E.B.

DuBois even urged Blacks to put aside their grievances with white America and "close ranks" during the war effort. William Monroe Trotter dissented from this point of view and continued to demand equal rights and the integration of the armed services.

The enlistment and service of Blacks in the military did not lessen the hostility of white civilians towards African American soldiers. In fact, racial tensions and violence heightened in towns and cities where Black troops were stationed. Black soldiers were greeted with contempt from whites, strictly segregated and denied admission to theaters, restaurants and other public facilities. Clashes between white civilian authorities and Black soldiers occurred frequently. The most notable of such incidences resulted in the Houston riot of the summer of 1917. The riot started when a Black soldier intervened when a white policeman assaulted a Black woman. The police then arrested and jailed the woman and soldier. When members of the Black soldiers unit inquired about the incident they were struck and shot at. Rumors quickly developed that Black soldiers were being brutalized or murdered by the police. That night, over one hundred Black soldiers broke into their armory and took ammunition and arms and marched into the city. Several whites including five policemen, and two blacks were killed. White federal troops and Texas militia eventually disarmed the Black soldiers. One-hundred and fifty-six men were court martialed for mutiny. Of the 63 that were tried, 41 received life sentences, four received shorter sentences, five were acquitted, but 13 were hanged before any appeal could be mounted. The Army had hastened to make examples of the insurrectionists.

Black soldiers suffered humiliation and insults not only in the United States but also while stationed overseas. They were discouraged and prohibited from socializing with white European women and were taunted and called "niggers" and "coons". The NAACP

was at the forefront in protesting and petitioning the government to investigate and relieve the plight of Blacks in the military. Officials of the NAACP were instrumental in having a school established for the development of Black commissioned officers. At least 1400 were commissioned and served during the War, although the top field grade officers were usually white in the segregated units. Ironically, Black leaders and organizations had appealed for more Black soldiers to be assigned combat or front-line service. Manpower demands, as in the case of previous wars, compelled the formation of various Black combat units and regiments. In spite of the racist and bigoted treatment accorded African American soldiers—which would have dampened the esprit de corps of the most avid patriot—Black companies and regiments served with gallantry and distinction. Historian Lerone Bennett writes that:

> Three of these regiments—the 369th, the 371st and the 372nd—received the Croix de Guerre for valor and the fourth covered itself with distinction in battles in Argonne Forest. The 369th . . . was the first allied unit to reach the Rhine. Although the 369th was under fire for 191 days, it never lost a foot of ground, a trench or a soldier through capture. No less courageous was the 370th . . . which was commanded almost entirely by black officers and which fought the last battle of the war.[50]

If Black soldiers and citizens expected gratitude or redemption from racial bigotry and oppression as a result of their service and patriotism after the war, their expectations were soon dispelled. The cessation and slow-down of wartime industries resulted in mass lay-offs and unemployment. Migratory problems, racial tensions, and African Americans' intolerance to racism, especially after their contributions and sacrifices during the war, brought on new conflicts, riots and resistance. After the war and during the summer of

Photo 10 Marcus Garvey's Militia. Courtesy of The Studio Museum in Harlem Archives, James Van Der Zee Collection. Used with permission.

1919, a secession or series of riots erupted in Chicago, Washington, Omaha, Knoxville, Charleston, and Longview, Texas. Whites as well as Blacks were killed which indicated that passivity to white violence was a thing of the past. A large segment of the Black population had adopted a kill or be killed and self-defense ideology.[51]

Succeeding the period which some historians refer to as the "red summer of 1919," there came to fore in America a Black man from Jamaica by the name of Marcus Garvey. Garvey was destined to become the leader of the first mass Black ideological movement in the history of African Americans. His emergence as a charismatic leader who promoted Black pride, revelled in the ancient history of Africa, advocated Black self-help, and self-determination was fortuitous, but timely for African Americans. Blacks were disillusioned with the post-war period after witnessing a re-

surgence of white hate, discrimination, violence and terrorist organizations. The formal appeals, moral suasion and patient strivings of Black intellectuals during this time were insufficient to placate the Black masses. They needed and found in Marcus Garvey a savior or a Moses that could lead them to liberation and instill within them a new feeling of self-esteem. Garvey's philosophy, work, movement, rise and decline have been discussed in Chapter I. The essence of Garvey's ideology might be described as Black Nationalism. His philosophy influenced Black thought not only during the 1920s, but was revived during the 1960s and prevails among a significant segment of the Black population up to the present. More discussion of Marcus Garvey and his contributions to the liberation struggles of Blacks will be made in the succeeding chapters on African American politics and economics.

*The Decades of Enlightenment, Depression and the "New Deal".* The period between 1920 and 1940 was pivotal towards the gradual upswing in the fate and fortune of African Americans. The first two decades of the twentieth century were ones of disillusionment and demoralization relative to Blacks in America. Consequently, psychological and socio-political change and relief were inevitable barring the complete destruction of the Black psyche. African American creativity in the arts, literature and music blossomed and flourished from the mid 1920s to 1940 marking a movement described earlier as the Harlem Renaissance. Although writers and historians attribute the nucleus of the new Black cultural movement to New York's Harlem district, the contributors, activities and effects of the period encompassed all of Black America. Few would deny that it was Marcus Garvey's philosophy and crusade of African pride, self-esteem and self-determination that inspired and nurtured Black cultural, social and economic industry during this era.

Few Black historians have attempted to connect or relate the corresponding social and ideological changes that were also occurring among some white Americans during the 1920s through the 1930s period. White historian John M. Blum and co-authors of the work, *The National Experience*, acknowledge that during this period there developed among a significant segment of the white population a mood of nonconformity and dissent. Some had begun to reject materialism and the corporate ethos and embraced progressive ideals of literature, art and intellectualism. For whites, it was the era of Sigmund Freud and his theories of Freudian psychology relating to sex and human nature. White American novelists Ernest Hemingway and William Faulkner and poet T.S. Eliot made their debut and literary contributions to the broader society. Thus, the weariness of the post-war period coupled with the social pathology in race relations existent in the country produced a form of rebellion and "radicalism" even in white society. An exemplification of this phenomenon is revealed in the following quote from *The National Experience*:

> One symbol of their protest was jazz, with its sensuality, its spontaneity, its atavistic rhythms, and with the sinuous and intimate dancing it inspired. Jazz was ungenteel, even un-Caucasian, above all uninhibited. It expressed not only protest and art of a kind but also a controversial change in sexual mores.[52]

There is no way to prove any relationship between the liberated spirit of oppressed Blacks during the Harlem Renaissance and the radicalism which developed among some white Americans. However, it is more than speculative to say that the burst of artistic talent, literary genius, and scholarship demonstrated by Blacks caused whites to view them with a different perspective. As a result, several political gains accrued to Blacks during this period.

A contributing factor towards African American cultural and intellectual development was the boost in the national economy after the recessionary period following World War I. The nation came close to full employment during the presidential terms of Warren G. Harding and Calvin Coolidge due to industrial mechanization, the proliferation of factories and the implementation of the mass-production concept of manufacturing. Although Blacks functioned at the low or menial level of the labor force, their job opportunities and incomes improved in relation to the general economy. White trade and labor unions were particularly discriminatory toward the mass of Black migrants and veterans of the war. This caused Blacks to attempt to form their own trade and worker unions. One of the most successful Black unions was the Brotherhood of Sleeping Car Porters and Maids organized by A. Philip Randolph in 1925.

Business prosperity from 1920 to 1929 did not stem the tides of injustice, racism and discrimination towards African Americans. Racial hostilities and conflicts were common throughout the country and, invariably, lynching continued in the South. The Harlem Renaissance was a movement of social protest transformed and represented in the literature, art and music of African Americans. In protest, Marcus Garvey, the father of modern Black Nationalism emerged; Carter G. Woodson, historian, scholar and the founder of Afro-American History Celebration was extolled; and jazz, the music created by Black people was born. During this period the NAACP became the major protestor and legal protector of Black rights.

National business prosperity continued until 1929 and political parties vied for pre-eminence and control at local, state and federal levels. Migrating Blacks from the South not only caused a surge in the population of the North but effected the politics of the region. In spite of the betrayal of Blacks by Republicans after Reconstruction, most African Americans perceived Republicanism as being the party of Abraham Lincoln, Emancipation and civil rights. Once liberated from the racist Democratic stronghold of the South, Blacks tended to vote Republican in the North. White northern Democrats found it necessary to attempt to attract African Americans to the Democratic Party in order to remain politically competitive with popular Republicanism of the North. This they did by offering small political amenities and appointments to Blacks. The Republicans and Democrats were not the only political parties interested in Black voters. The Socialist and Communist parties also sought the political alliance of African Americans. However, neither the socialists or communists were successful in attracting even a significant number of African Americans to their ranks. The labor-class ideologies of socialists and communists have never gained acceptance or seemed relevant to the race-specific plight and problems of Black people in America.

African Americans had begun to demonstrate an unprecedented proclivity towards political independence during the latter 1920s. This was revealed in the national election of 1928 when Alfred E. Smith ran as a Democrat against the Republican, Herbert Hoover, for President of the United States. Hoover espoused the capitalistic virtues of individualism, *laissez faire*, corporation rights and business prosperity. Herbert Hoover was indisputably conservative and implicitly White Supremacist. While Al Smith may not have been classified as a liberal, as governor of New York he advocated public assistance programs and civil liberties. Furthermore, he was Catholic. The Democrats did not win the election but Blacks voted for the Democratic Party in, surprisingly, large numbers. This proved that the Republicans could no longer depend upon the automatic support of African Americans. The end of the 1920s would usher in a new era of Black politics and witness a dramatic change in the nation's political orientation.

Herbert Hoover rode the crest of the nation's economic prosperity months after his election of 1928. No one could have predicted the abrupt economic crash that occurred near the end of 1929 and lasted well into the decade of the 1930s. Economists attributed some of the major causes of the Great Depression to speculation fever, dubious and manipulative stock market schemes, technological displacement of workers, sagging farm prices and unsound monetary policies of the banking system. Regardless of the various causes of the economic crash, the unemployment rate soared to more than 30 per cent and did not fall below 15 per cent during the entire decade of the 1930s. The Great Depression resulted in financial loss and impoverishment for millions. The impact was particularly acute for Blacks who traditionally ranged at the bottom of the economic ladder. Various policies designed to end the depression failed throughout the Hoover Administration.

By the end of President Hoover's term of office in 1933, the nation was ready for change and for a leader with imaginative ideas of how to resolve the myriad of economic woes and problems. It was virtually presupposed that a Democrat would succeed Hoover since the four years of economic adversity were generally attributed to the Republican administration. The Democrats nominated and were successful in having Franklin Delano Roosevelt, an astute northern politician, elected for president in 1932. For the first time since Reconstruction, African Americans voted in significant numbers in support of the Democratic candidates. There was an aspect of political irony related to Black support of the Democrats. The stronghold of the Democratic Party was located in the South where racial inequality, segregation and discrimination flourished. Consequently, a vote for the Democratic Party could have meant a vote for Jim Crowism. Nevertheless, Blacks and Whites wanted a change from the status quo of depression and poverty.

Franklin D. Roosevelt assumed office and began to vigorously put into effect his campaign proposal of a "New Deal" for the American society. Almost immediately, the Congress passed more than fifteen bills proposed by Roosevelt which would rectify the fallacies and shortcoming of the banking and financial system; grant assistance and relief to farmers and agriculture; decrease the unemployment rate; establish guidelines and policies for labor and wages; and provide a national plan for social security for all Americans. Of particular benefit to poor whites and blacks were New Deal programs such as the Works Progress Administration (WPA), Civilian Conservation Corps (CCC), and the National Youth Administration which were designed to put people to work. Much of the New Deal programs were based upon the Keynesian economic theory of compensatory government spending for economic recovery.[53]

Roosevelt's New Deal legislations were not enacted specifically to help African Americans but they were passed to save the nation as a whole from economic disaster. Roosevelt was mostly reserved and publicly noncommittal on civil rights for fear of offending some whites or losing Southern support for his New Deal policies. Yet, Blacks helped to reelect Roosevelt in 1936, 1940 and 1944. Perhaps the most significant early progress African Americans made *towards* citizenship and equal rights was during the four terms presidency of Franklin Roosevelt. Roosevelt revived the practice of appointing a cadre of highly qualified African Americans as his consultants or advisors on matters of race relations and civil rights. This group was known as the president's "Black Cabinet." It should always be pointed out that the President's wife, Eleanor Roosevelt, was a staunch advocate and activist for the rights and equality of African Americans. She befriended and valued the advice of Mary McLeod Bethune, renown Black educator and the only African American woman in the President's Black Cabinet. The New Deal Administration brought about several Civil Rights gains in federal employment practices and influenced several changes in social and economic practices affecting Blacks. World War II would further increase economic expansion and improve the plight of African Americans.

*World War II and Strides Toward Racial Progress.* American wars have always affected the role, status and progress of African Americans. From the Revolutionary War of 1775 to the Vietnam War of the 1960s, Whites have found it difficult to reconcile fighting for the American creed of "freedom and justice for all" with their unjust and oppressive treatment of Black Americans. While the nation wrestled with the paradox of its moral creed and conscious Blacks, through their loyalty and zeal for military service, have made some social and economic gains during and after each American war. More than any other war, World War II was more catalytic or causative in advancing the equality of citizenship for African Americans.

The outbreak of World War II obviated the need for the compensatory government spending measures of President Roosevelt's New Deal programs to stimulate the national economy. European demands for munitions to resist the invasions of Nazis Germany had caused the massive development of the defense industries long before America entered the War in December of 1941. Employment in the United States increased dramatically, and the average white American worker once again was privileged to receive the benefit of increased wages and salaries. However, the new prosperity brought on by the war did not, initially, apply to African Americans. Blacks were deliberately discriminated against and excluded from employment with defense industry firms. Industrial centers where thousands of qualified African Americans existed, whites were recruited to fill the employment needs.

The abject injustice of discriminating against African Americans in the defense industry invoked strong protest on the part of Black leaders including many liberal Whites. Blacks began to protest and picket racist defense plants and firms throughout the country. The most successive protest movement was organized by A. Philip Randolph. Randolph threatened a March on Washington involving thousands of Blacks if the Roosevelt Administration did not investigate and end the discriminatory hiring practices. A few days before the march was to take place, Roosevelt conceded to meet with Randolph and other Black leaders. As a result, the President agreed to establish the Fair Employ-

ment Practices Commission (FEPC). The success of the Randolph organization, no doubt, inspired the young Black leader, James Farmer, to organize the Congress of Racial Equality (CORE) to join with the efforts of the National Urban League and the NAACP to fight racism and discrimination. This period of the War was the genesis of the modern Black non-violent protest movements which would function and prevail throughout the twentieth century.

The exclusionary and discriminatory treatment Black civilians experienced with the defense industries were no less deplorable than the racism and Jim Crowism that Black volunteers and draftees confronted with the War Department and the armed forces. At the beginning of World War II, there were less than 20,000 African Americans in the armed services. It was the policy of the War Department to enlist Blacks only in proportion to their number in the general population. They were systematically excluded from the Marine Corps, Army Air Corps and other essential corps of the Army. Blacks in the military were relegated to serve in segregated, labor-intensive and menial support units. Even though the Selective Service Act of 1940 contained a nondiscrimination clause, the official position of the War Department read:

> The policy of the War Department is not to intermingle colored and white enlisted personnel in the same regimental organizations. This policy has been proved satisfactory over a long period of years and to make changes would produce situations destructive to morale and detrimental to preparations for national defense.[54]

Due to protest from Black leaders, manpower shortages and as the war progressed, the War Department and the Roosevelt Administration relaxed some of its racial policies.

Soon officers candidate schools were established and whites and blacks trained together.

African American army officers received commissions in relatively small numbers. A school for training Black pilots was established at Tuskegee Institute on July 19, 1941. Approximately 600 Blacks received their wings by the end of the war. The heroic conduct of a Black messman, Dorie Miller, stationed on the U.S.S. Arizona during the Japanese attack on Pearl Harbor December 7, 1941, influenced the Navy to change its racial policy of enlisting Blacks only to serve as cooks. Before the end of the war a relatively few African Americans were commissioned as naval officers. With few experimental exceptions, the policy of racial segregation in the armed forces remained intact throughout the duration of the war. In 1945, white and black units were briefly integrated for an assault against the Germans. Before the end of the war, more than 700,000 African Americans served in the different branches of the armed forces. About a half-million of them saw service overseas in various combat units and fighting capacities.[55]

Black military units and individual African American service men and women served in World War II, generally, with honor and distinction. They did so in spite of the discriminatory treatment accorded to them by their white counterparts in arms, and the contempt and hostility they suffered from white civilians. Wherever Black troops were based racial incidents and clashes with the civilian populace seemed inevitable because of white bigotry and Jim Crowism. During the war years, violent race riots erupted in Detroit, Los Angeles and New York. Social injustices, beating and lynchings continued in the South and race relations grew tense in the North. From a progressive perspective, African Americans learned to fight back politically, legally and physically during and after World War II.

World War II was, unequivocally, beneficial towards the advancement of black Americans for a number of reasons. First, Black men proved that they were not cowards and were capable of mastering weapons of war, engaging in warfare, and killing as well as whites. Second, African American civilian and armed service personnel obtained vocational, technical and scientific training and skills in defense industries and in military occupations more than ever before. This enabled millions of them to become more employable and economically self-sufficient. A third positive factor which might be attributed to the war was that there emerged during the 1940s a generation or cadre of Black intellectuals, professionals and leaders who became visible and recognized by the white establishment or policymakers.

The new vanguard of Blacks that had begun to develop during the Harlem Renaissance and through World War II were more politically sophisticated and daring. Using the political strategy of bloc voting in the North and in the South where they could vote, Blacks were able to negotiate civil rights considerations between the Democratic or Republican parties. Moreover, the indirect and direct economic and social gains which accrued to African Americans during the Roosevelt Administration caused them to shift their traditional political loyalty from the Republican to the Democratic Party. Blacks would vote eighty to ninety percent Democratic throughout most of the twentieth century. Roosevelt replaced Lincoln as the symbolical political benefactor of African Americans.

Franklin D. Roosevelt died April 12, only a few months before the Japanese surrendered and the war ended on August 15, 1945. Harry S. Truman, the Vice President, became the 33rd president of the United States. Truman, a native of Missouri and oddly enough, had a penchant for fairness. This was greatly evidenced when he adopted for his election slogan in 1948, a "Fair Deal" for America, which replaced Roosevelt's "New Deal" policies and programs. Truman was the first president to publicly and actively promote a comprehensive program of Civil Rights legislation, policies and programs. In 1946, he appointed a special Commission on Civil Rights to make recommendations on ways of protecting the civil rights of Americans. The commission in its report of 1947 entitled, *To Secure These Rights,* made sweeping proposals in the areas of discrimination in employment, antilynching, antipoll-tax and segregation. Truman presented much of the Committee's recommendations in the form of legislation to Congress which it repeatedly failed to pass.

Truman's call during the election year 1948 for antilynching, antipoll-tax, antitransportation-segregation and fair employment practices (FEPC) legislation caused Southerners to defect from the Democratic Party and form the Dixiecrat Party in opposition to civil rights. Despite the lack of Southern democratic support, Truman narrowly won reelection. His election was significantly aided by the Northern Black vote. Truman was not successful in having any of his civil rights measures passed by both houses of the Congress. However, he contributed much to social justice, desegregation and civil rights for African American through his issuance of Executive Orders.

Harry S. Truman issued Executive Order 9981 on July 26, 1948 which called for the end of segregation in the armed forces of the United States. Desegregation of the armed forces was the first major institutional step towards challenging the civilian law of "separate but equal" which had prevailed since 1896. Although Truman's order did not immediately effect equity and solve all of the racial problems of the armed services, in time, the military complied and proved the economic efficacy, logic, fairness and practicality of integration. The Executive Order also influenced a softening of many southerners resistance to absolute segregation because in the military, Blacks were routinely placed in positions of authority over Whites. It is important to note, too, that on the same date

that Truman pronounced the military desegregation order he issued Executive Order 9980 which barred discrimination in federal employment and work done under Government contract.

Several factors or events occurred during the 1950s that increased the momentum of civil rights for African Americans. The NAACP, having grown confident because of its influence and successes during the 1930s and 1940s, was incessant in its court challenges against racial segregation. The Korean War (1950–1953) served as positive proof of the workability of racial desegregation and, thus, accelerated the process of integration in the armed services. Furthermore, desegregation in the Federal Civil Service and with Defense contractors proceeded at a moderate rate. Because of President Truman's unrelenting efforts to achieve fair and equal treatment for Black Americans and the NAACP's successful tactics of legal challenge and moral suasion, the number of white sympathizers for racial justice increased—even in the South. However, the most essential and effective factor was the gradual ideological change of the U.S. Supreme Court and its series of decisions in opposition to racial discrimination.

The most monumental action against racial segregation occurred on May 17, 1954 when the U.S. Supreme Court ruled in the case of *Brown v. Board of Education of Topeka* ruled that public school segregation was unconstitutional. Thurgood Marshall, Special Counsel for the NAACP, had argued that segregation was inherently unconstitutional and that it stigmatized an entire race and thereby denied it equal protection of the laws as guaranteed by the Fourteenth Amendment. Chief Justice Earl Warren and a majority of the Court agreed. Thus after 58 years, the "separate but equal" decision of the *Plessy v. Ferguson* case of 1896 had been reversed.

Southern response and opposition to the Supreme Court's ruling was discussed briefly in Chapter 2 in relation to the genesis of the

Photo 11  Segregation Protest March. Courtesy of National Archives.

African American studies idea. However, the magnitude of White Southern resistance and defiance to the desegregation ruling requires further treatment. The traditional segregationist states varied in their adoption of one of the following responses or stances: 1) reluctant conformance, 2) tokenistic and symbolic compliance, and 3) outright defiance.

Gradual voluntary desegregation occurred primarily in the border States of Delaware, Maryland, West Virginia, Kentucky, Missouri, Oklahoma and in addition, the District of Columbia. Desegregation in a few school districts in Texas and Arkansas occurred briefly until State politicians could mount formal opposition. Upper Southern States such as

Virginia and Tennessee adopted a pattern of gradual token integration just sufficient enough to suggest minimal compliance with the law. More than one-hundred southern U.S. senators and congressmen signed a document termed the "Southern Manifesto," which declared the 1954 Supreme Court decision a violation of the Constitution. In essence, according to a report of the U.S. Commission on Civil Rights, defiance

> . . . included the adoption of resolutions which purportedly nullified the Court's decision and "interposed" the States' authority between the Federal Government and the people; called for the impeachment of Supreme Court Justices; and provided for the closing of schools if that became the only alternative to desegregation.[56]

Violent and armed confrontations between community residents, state or federal militia occurred at public schools in various southern states where Black students and their parents attempted to test or comply with the Supreme Court's ruling.

The Ku Klux Klan and other hate groups were regenerated to bolster the desegregation resistance movement. Mob violence and riots erupted in Clinton, Tennessee and in several small towns in Kentucky requiring the National Guard to assure the safety of African American children attempting to enter the previously all-white schools. One of the most famous incidents happened in Arkansas when the Governor, Orval Faubus, defied the Little Rock school board's concession to integrate Central High School in September of 1957. Faubus used the National Guard to prevent Black students from entering the school. President Dwight D. Eisenhower requested that Faubus withdraw the National Guard. However, when the Black students returned the next day they were blocked by screaming and vehement whites. Eisenhower then federalized the National Guard and ordered 1,000 paratroopers to Little Rock to escort the

Black students. Prince Edwards County in Virginia closed its public schools and provided tuition grants for white children to attend private schools. The Court ordered the county to reopen the schools. Gradualism, legal schemes and procedural delays were used to thwart the Courts order to desegregate "with all deliberate speed."

African Americans were not only denied admission at public elementary and secondary schools, but also to state colleges and universities. The most notable cases marked by turbulence, civilian or state resistance, NAACP litigation and federal marshalls involved: the University of Alabama and Black student, Autherine Lucy—1956; the University of Mississippi and Black student, James Meredith—1962; and the University of Georgia, and Black students, Charlayne Hunter and Hamilton Holmes—1960. The NAACP and its Legal Defense and Educational Fund represented African Americans in virtually all of the school desegregation cases. Public school, college and university desegregation has been vastly implemented in the United States but it is yet to be fully and optimally completed as of 1992.

President Dwight D. Eisenhower, former General and Supreme Commander of Allied Forces in Europe, governed the country during the crucial beginning and crux of the modern Civil Rights Movement. He was politically enigmatic in comparison with traditional politicians. Eisenhower had a penchant for moderation and "military" orderliness in his approach to political issues, management and delegation of authority. While he never expressed his own view or position of the merits of the Supreme Court's school desegregation ruling of 1954, his Administration did propose new civil rights legislation both terms of his tenure in office. On April 29, 1957, Congress passed the first civil rights bill for Blacks since the Reconstruction bill of 1875. The legislation was enacted mostly to protect the voting rights of African

Americans. The Act created a Federal Civil Rights Commission to make recommendations to Government in the areas of voting, education and education.

# THE CIVIL RIGHTS MOVEMENT—1955 THROUGH THE 1980s

*The Struggles and Politics of Non-Violent Protest.* After the historic desegregation decision by the U.S. Supreme Court, Blacks intensified their struggle for full Constitutional rights, and citizenship. However Whites, especially those in the deep South, were equally determined to see that the equal rights and protection African Americans sought under the Constitution would not be achieved. It is debatable as to which specific racial event marked the beginning of the mass Civil Rights Movement of the twentieth century. Many believe that it was initiated with the boycott of the segregated city transit system of Montgomery, Alabama by thousands of Blacks in December of 1955. If mass action of the Civil Rights Movement began with the Montgomery bus boycott, the collective national spirit and mood for Black rebellion started with the brutal lynchings of Blacks which took place in Mississippi earlier during the year of 1955. The most notorious was the kidnapping and murdering of a Black fourteen-year-old boy, Emmett Till for having allegedly whistled at a white woman in Money, Mississippi August 28, 1955. Till's body was found in the Tallahatchie River, beaten, shot to death and mutilated. Two white defendants were acquitted for the murder by an all-white, all-male jury in spite of clear evidence of their guilt. This incident gained international attention and fired the moral indignation of not only Blacks, but many Whites. The mood and mold for African American rebellion nation-wide had been set.

In December of 1955 the widely-heralded Montgomery Bus Boycott was organized and initiated by thousands of Blacks when Rosa Parks, a Black woman and member of the NAACP, refused to yield her seat to a white man when the public bus filled with Caucasians as the segregationist law required. Her subsequent arrest caused the 381-day boycott which lasted until the federal courts ruled that segregation on public transportation was illegal. The success and inspiration generated by the Montgomery Bus Boycott encouraged African Americans to launch similar civil rights tests and feats all over the country. The boycott received national and international media coverage and propelled into world focus Dr. Martin Luther King, Jr. who was elected to head the Montgomery protest movement. King, who received the Ph.D. in systematic theology from Boston University, became one of the major charismatic figures and leaders of the Civil Rights Movement. Without a doubt, Martin Luther King, Jr. was the founder and leading exponent of the philosophy of non-violent social protest in America. King was assassinated April 4, 1968, but he remains one of the most martyrized figures of the Civil Rights Movement of the twentieth century.

The *Brown v. Board of Education of Topeka desegregation decision* and the Montgomery Bus Boycott served as catalysts for the myriad of school segregation cases, challenges and violent incidents of the 1950s. If it can be established that the Eisenhower Administration spanned the beginning and crux of the Civil Rights Movement, then President John F. Kennedy inherited the explosive and climatic periods of its dramatic course. As pointed out in the preceding Chapter, the southern Black student "sit-in" movement of 1960 had successfully challenged segregation in public accommodations. The student organization, SNCC, was provoking resistance and terrorism from Whites in its "Freedom Rides" and voter registration efforts. By the time

Kennedy was inaugurated president in 1961, the issue of racial oppression and the struggle of African Americans for human equality in America had become a significant political factor in the court of world opinion. Contradictions of the freedom and justice creed of the United States was a source of embarrassment to many white politicians and intellectuals. Therefore, it was prudent that Kennedy include civil rights in his "New Frontier" Democratic platform. It was improbable that the Democrats could have won the election without Northern Black bloc voting which was further strengthened by the increasing number of Black registered voters in the South. African Americans had begun to vote overwhelmingly democratic ever since the Roosevelt era.

Kennedy did not move immediately to propose new civil rights legislation. However, in 1962 a Constitutional Amendment making the poll tax illegal was passed, and executive action was taken to improve the plight of Blacks in the areas of voting rights, employment, education and public transportation. What Kennedy did more than any previous president was to publicly and emphatically denounce racial injustice in America routinely in his speeches in the North and South.

The period from 1963 to 1965 was one of the most momentous eras of the Civil Rights Movement. During the Spring of 1963, Martin Luther King, Jr. and other Black leaders staged a protest rally and march in Birmingham, and led a series of other mass demonstrations in the South demanding equal rights and access in employment, housing and public accommodations. Thousands of demonstrators were arrested, including King. On June 12, Medgar Evers, a field secretary for the NAACP in Mississippi, was assassinated in front of his home by a white segregationist. The largest mass organized rally demanding freedom and justice for all citizens was the monumental "March on Washington for Jobs and Freedom" staged in Washington, D.C. on August 28, 1963. Nearly a quarter of a million Blacks and Whites, peacefully, marched from the Washington Monument to the Lincoln Memorial. It was at this event that Martin Luther King, Jr. delivered his most famous, "I Have a Dream" speech. However, less than a month after the March on Washington, September 15, a Black church was bombed and four young girls were killed in Birmingham, Alabama.

Prior to and during these events of 1963, President Kennedy had submitted to Congress a more comprehensive and effective civil rights bill. The bill provided for the Government to file suit to desegregate public accommodations and to assure African Americans equal educational and employment opportunity. The bill was debated, modified, negotiated and delayed by and between both houses of Congress. It would not pass during the Kennedy Administration. President John F. Kennedy was assassinated on November 22, 1963.

Many historians are reticent in acknowledging the creditable civil rights record and achievements of President Lyndon Baines Johnson. Paradoxically Johnson, a Southerner, made civil rights for Blacks one of his major concerns after Kennedy's assassination. He pushed through the Congress the most far-reaching civil rights legislation in the history of the United States. On June 10, 1964, the strong Civil Rights Bill proposed initially by President Kennedy was passed by Congress. The Voting Rights Bill which eliminated all devious policies and barriers for Black registration and voting, especially in the South, was passed on August 6, 1965. It is doubtful that these bills and other civil rights measures would have passed without the political astuteness and southern influence of Lyndon B. Johnson. In addition, Johnson continued the Kennedy practice of appointing African Americans to high-level judicial, governmental and ambassadorial

Photo 12  Thurgood Marshall. Courtesy of National Archives.

positions. His most notable appointment was that of Thurgood Marshall, the first Black to become a Justice of the U.S. Supreme Court.

There were few White voluntary concessions on civil rights during the 1960s. The advances that were made resulted from the struggles, sufferings and sacrifices of the blood and lives of, mostly, Black people. The progress of African Americans occurred amid a background of white racist reprisals and acts of violence. The few white activists were not spared from their wrath. The bodies of three civil rights workers, two white and one black, were discovered murdered in August of 1964. Eighteen white segregationists were charged with conspiracy to deprive the victims of their civil rights. In 1965 a white minister, James Reeb, was killed in Selma, Alabama and a white woman, Viola Liuzzo, was killed after the mass Selma-to-Montgomery March. A few other whites were killed or wounded while participating in civil rights demonstrations. More than 50 race riots, numerous church burnings, and hundreds of other acts of racial violence occurred in cities throughout the United States during the 1960s.[57]

Prominent Black leaders and their respective organizations during the Civil Rights Movements of the 1960s were Martin Luther King, Jr. (SCLC); Roy Wilkins (NAACP); James Farmer and Floyd B. McKissick (CORE); Stokely Carmichael and H. "Rap" Brown (SNCC); and Whitney Young of the National Urban League (NUL). For the most part, these leaders embraced the integrationist objectives and assimilationist ideal of nineteenth century Black philosopher, Frederick Douglass. Contending for leadership and for a different ideological bent for the Black masses during this period was the dynamic and charismatic Islamic minister, Malcolm X.

The ideological scheme and message to Black people that Malcolm X espoused were significantly antithetical to that of Martin Luther King, Jr. and to most of the other leaders of the Civil Rights Movement. Malcolm X caste whites in satanic images, opposed integration, stressed self-help, promoted Pan-Africanism, and urged Blacks to achieve liberation "by any means necessary,"[58] not excluding violence. Malcolm X's philosophy represented, partly, a revival of Marcus Garvey's ideology. It appealed to the rising number of Black students and to many older African Americans who had grown weary and cynical of the gradual and peaceful approaches of the traditional leaders. Malcolm X was assassinated on February 21, 1965 as a result of his defection from the Muslim organization of Elijah Muhammad. The philosophy and exhortations of Malcolm X influenced the politics and civil rights activities of many African Americans throughout the late 1960s and the 1970s.

***Black Power and the New Politics of Liberation.*** By 1970, the diligent and sacrificial efforts of SNCC and the other civil rights organizations toward Black voter education and registration had begun to reap significant political dividends nationwide for African Americans. Increased African American voter participation was made possible through the momentous Voting Rights Act of 1965, which was extended and amended by Congress in 1970, 1975, 1982 and 1991. The increase in the number of African Americans elected to the U.S. House of Representatives, mostly from predominantly Black districts, led to the formation of the Congressional Black Caucus (CBC). The number of Black elected officials increased from 280 in 1965 to 1,469 in 1970 constituting less than one-half of one percent of elected officials. However, in 1980 the number increased to 4,912 which represented approximately one percent of the 490,200 elective offices in the United States. The largest increases were in the South where Black voter registration had previously been obstructed or denied.[59]

Photo 13  Martin L. King Jr. and Malcolm X. Courtesy of The Library of Congress.

The Civil Rights Movement of the sixties resulted in an increase of the Black middle class from 13 percent in 1960 to 27 percent in 1970. Though there was a relative decrease in the number of middle class African Americans after 1975, by 1984 the rate increased to 39 percent. Improvement in the economic condition of African Americans could be attributed to the civil rights laws of 1964 and, specifically, to Title VII, which required and end to discrimination in employment and job advancement policies based on race, sex or national origin. Title VII and Affirmation Action programs contributed greatly to the increase of the Black middle class and to its occupational diversity.[60] Moreover, the Federal Job Corps, federal and private supported job training programs further increased the economic status of millions of Black Americans. Tokenistic hiring of Black in untraditional executive and administrative positions in corporations, state and federal agencies, and at predominantly white colleges and universities increased until the mid 1970s. In addition, the Vietnam War effected the employment rate and opportunities for Blacks until it ended in 1973. In general, the decade of the seventies was a milestone of economic progress for African Americans. However, it was not without racial conflicts, racism and sociopolitical setbacks. Improvement in the condition of Blacks provoked resentment and reprisals by many Whites.

On the other hand, the Black Power, Black Nationalist and Black Pride ideologies which were revived during the Black student movements of the late sixties, especially after the King assassination, fortified the spirit of resistance and rebellion of millions of African Americans. The young generations and even the newly emerged Black middle class began to revel in their African heritage and many adopted African customs, dress and names. Several groups such as the Black Panther Party based in Oakland, California, was openly critical of the oppressive nature of the

capitalistic system and of social injustice and police brutality. A significant number of Blacks serving in the armed forces during the Vietnam War were politically influenced by Black Nationalistic ideology and the philosophies of Marcus Garvey and Malcom X which sparked many racial incidents in combat and garrison units.

The new Black ideology and its motivations were bound to provoke clashes with white authorities and African American communities across the nation. As Blacks began to *demand* justice, rights, and cultural awareness, violent incidents and riots erupted in the Los Angeles" Watts community, Newark, Cleveland, Detroit and many other cities. White perceived Black "radicals" of the Black Panther Party, civil rights student and community activists were routinely harassed and arrested by the police. Huey Newton, George Jackson, Joanne Chesimard, Fred Hampton, Bobby Seale, Eldridge Cleaver of the Black Panthers; The Reverend Ben Chavis of North Carolina; and Angela Davis, communist professor of U.C.L.A. are only some of the most prominent Blacks who were incarcerated on various questionable charges.

African American students demonstrating for social justice, academic equality or Black Studies at Jackson State College, Southern University and South Carolina State College resulted in the death of several and hundreds were arrested. Black Nationalist ideology had fostered a degree of rebellion and crime in the ghetto as well as civil disobedience among the Black middle class. For the first time race, racialism and racism were not the only factors which motivated Whites to brutalize and imprison Blacks. African Americans were now being incarcerated and held as political prisoners.

Out of a backdrop of national disunity, disorder and White backlash, it was easy for Republican Richard Nixon to defeat the Democratic candidate Hubert Humphrey in the 1968 presidential election. Nixon rode to

power by appealing to white Southern Democrats. He promised to restore law and
order, resist "forced-integration" and school
bussing, and to eliminate or reduce welfare
and social programs. In the 1972 election,
Nixon captured forty-nine of the fifty states
and for the first time, the South voted overwhelmingly for a Republican president.

President Nixon did not disappoint his
Southern constituency and other white conservative supporters. During his first term of
office when opportunity existed, Nixon
changed the ideological make-up of federal
courts by appointing to vacant judgeships
arch white conservatives. The social and legal
philosophy of the U.S. Supreme Court was
drastically altered with the confirmation of
Nixon conservative appointees Harry Blackmun, Lewis F. Powell, and William Rhenquist. The conservative federal jurist, Warren
Burger, succeeded retiring Earl Warren as
Chief Justice of the Supreme Court. The social and economic gains that African Americans had made as a result of the Civil Rights
Movement began to erode during the Nixon
Administration. In spite of Nixon's popularity
for having secured a cease-fire agreement of
the Vietnam War and effected U.S. troop
withdrawal, he was forced to resign before the
end of his second term because of the Watergate "break-in scandal. When Nixon resigned
on August 9, 1973, Vice President Gerald R.
Ford completed the remaining term of his office. Ford's brief term in office was haunted
with the suspicion that he had made a prear-
ranged deal to grant a presidential pardon to
Nixon for any crimes he may have committed
in the Watergate fiasco. Furthermore, Gerald
Ford inherited an ailing national economy
with a soaring unemployment rate. Ford was
unable to win the 1976 election on his own
merit. He was defeated by the Democrat
Jimmy Carter from Georgia, who became the
first president from the deep South since before the Civil War.

President Jimmy Carter halted the obvious
reversal of progress that Blacks and other racial minorities had made during the Civil
Rights Movement. He promoted Title VII
and Affirmative Action programs, enforced
the Voting Rights Act and other civil rights
statues, and appointed African Americans to
high federal and Cabinet posts. Carter is particularly recognized for having appointed
more Blacks, Hispanics and women to federal
judgeships than any of his predecessors. However, no vacancies on the U.S. Supreme
Court occurred during his four-year term in
office. Carter's positive attention to civil
rights was in recognition of the decisive
Black bloc vote which he garnered during the
1976 election. He profited politically from
the millions of African Americans who became voters as a result of the work of civil
rights organizations and the Voting Right
Act, especially in the South. Jimmy Carter
lost his bid for reelection in 1980 to Ronald
Reagan, a Republican from California, due to
a number of economic and foreign policy failures attributed to him by the American public.

Ronald Reagan revived and advanced the
anti-Black and anti-civil rights policies that
had begun to be popular with the Republican
administration of former President Richard
M. Nixon. Reagan Republicanism represented
the interests of rich conservative Whites, corporations, White ethnic immigrants and the
millions of White Southerners who defected
from the Democratic Party. Reagan's constituents were fed up with the array of civil
rights statues and equal opportunity and affirmative action programs which were
designed to remedy the historical affects of
slavery and racism suffered by African Americans. He moved swiftly to discredit or dis-
mantle federally funded poverty, job training
and affirmative action programs. The Reagan
Administration viewed as "reverse discrimination" the goals and timetables of Affirmative
Action programs. He appointed arch conservatives to head The Equal Opportunity

Commission (EEOC) and the United States Civil Rights Commission (USCRC) who in turn, reduced sharply or invalidated thousands of discrimination suits filed against employers.[61]

Ronald Reagan continued the Nixon strategy of naming to lower federal courts, and to the U.S. Supreme court "strict" conservative justices. In 1981, Reagan was able to make his first appointment to the Supreme Court, Sandra Day O'Connor, conservative and the first woman to be confirmed for the highest court. When conservative Chief Justice Warren E. Burger retired he was able to have William H. Rhenquist, a sitting member of the Court, confirmed to become the Chief Justice. When vacancies developed on the Supreme Court, Reagan nominated conservative justices whose judicial records demonstrated their disdain for civil rights and anti-discrimination laws. The Senate rejected at least two of his appointees but he succeeded in naming to the Supreme Court and gaining the confirmation of conservative justices Antonin Scalia and Anthony M. Kennedy. Before the end of his second term in office, Reagan had tilted the balance of the Supreme Court and numerous other federal courts of appeal towards conservatism and anti-civil rights ideology.

White racists and hate groups were emboldened by Reagan's anti-civil rights posture. Racial attacks and harassment against Blacks and other minorities increased dramatically during his second term in office. Racial incidents and bigotry spread on major college campuses and recruitment of African American faculty and students at these institutions in the affirmative action tradition decreased. The Reagan Administration produced sharp cuts in minority financial aid. Consequently, the number of Black academic professionals, physicians and lawyers declined. Not only academe but, also, the corporate world was effected by the neoconservative stance of the Reagan Administration and fewer African Americans advanced beyond mid-level management positions. Although there was a growing Black middle class from the 1960s to the 1980s, the black-white salary gap widened. Advances in racial integration in schools and housing were minimal during the Reagan years.[62]

The regressive and mean civil rights policies of the Reagan Administration galvanized and increased the political participation and activism of African Americans. Blacks developed the potential political strength to influence at least 220 electoral votes or elect almost twenty percent of Democratic convention delegates in the national election. The number of large city Black mayors and elected officials increased. Of historic significance, was the candidacy and run of Jesse Jackson for the President of the United States as a Democrat. Jackson, a Black charismatic and articulate Baptist minister, made a strong showing among Black and minority voters nationwide. His second attempt for election to the office of President was even more impressive in 1988. This time he attracted a significant number of White votes in various states. In the Super Tuesday primary of March 8, Jackson was victorious in five Deep South states and came in second in eight other southern and border states by garnering 28 percent of the popular vote.[63]

George Bush was elected President in 1988, thus, continuing the Republicans' mold of conservatism. Bush gained the support of Reagan supporters and easily beat the weak liberal-labelled Democratic candidate, Michael Dukakis. The racial attitude of George Bush was revealed early when he used the law-and-order race issue to appeal to white conservatives during his campaign. Willie Horton, a Black prison inmate who had committed violent crimes while on prison furlough, was shown repeatedly in Bush's television political advertisements. Nevertheless, Bush was more politically astute and compromising in his relations with African Americans.

In contrast to Reagan, George Bush appointed and nominated several eminently qualified African Americans to relatively important positions within his administration. Among his most significant Black appointments were, Louis Sullivan as Secretary of Health and Human Services, and General Colin Powell, as Chairman of the Joint Chiefs of Staff in the Department of Defense. However, the latent anti-civil rights attitude of George Bush surfaced in his appointment of justices to the Supreme Court. When moderate Justice William Brennan, Jr. announced his retirement on July 20, 1990, Bush nominated Judge David Souter of the U.S. Court of Appeals for the First Circuit in Boston as Brennan's replacement. Judge Souter was a confirmed white conservative. However, he was a virtually unknown and obscure judge from New Hampshire, and had rendered no controversial civil rights or racial opinions during his judicial career. Souter was confirmed as a Supreme Court Justice on October 8.

The African American Supreme Court Justice, Thurgood Marshall, announced his retirement the summer of 1991. George Bush named Clarence Thomas, also an African American but a conservative, to replace Marshall's seat on the highest court. Thomas' nomination sparked national controversy because of his unenthusiastic prosecution of discrimination cases filed while he was the Chairman of the Equal Employment Opportunity Commission (EEOC), and his indifference to affirmative action and Women's Rights issues. Blacks were divided in their support of the Thomas nomination. However, conservative Republicans staunchly supported the Clarence Thomas nomination and defended him against serious improprieties which were alleged against him by an African American woman. In spite of the controversy, in October 1991 the Senate confirmed Thomas as the 106th justice of the Supreme Court by one of the narrowest margins in American history.

In the decade leading up to the twenty-first century or the year 2000, the struggle for liberty, justice and equality for African Americans has not ended. As late as 1992, it was necessary for the Congress to pass another Civil Rights Act to overturn six 1989 Supreme Court rulings that had seriously weakened the protections against employment discrimination provided by Title VII of the Civil Rights Act of 1964.

## · QUESTIONS AND EXERCISES ·

1. All races and cultures have made scientific, technical and aesthetic contributions to world development and human progress. What are some of the early contributions Africa and African people have given the world?

2. Study and discuss medieval (476 A.D. to 1450 A.D.) contacts of Europeans and Africans. If race and color were not significant prejudicial factors during this period, when and why did they develop?

3. What common factors contributed most to the rise and decline of the ancient West African empires of Ghana, Mali, and Songhay?

4. What were the Europeans' social, political and economic motivations for initiating slavery and the Atlanta Slave Trade?

5. Develop a paper analyzing the changing attitudes of White Americans toward slavery before and after the Revolutionary War, and leading to and after the Civil War.

6. Explain the political and economic factors which prevailed in the South and North that caused the failure of Reconstruction.

7. Study Abraham Lincoln's attitude toward Blacks. Should he truly be remembered as the "Great Emancipator"?

8. After each American war Blacks have made significant social, political and economic gains. What are some of the gains made after World War I, World War II, the Korean Conflict, and the Vietnam War?

9. Discuss the progress or lack of progress African Americans have made since the Civil Rights Movement of the 1960s to the present.

---

# · NOTES AND REFERENCES ·

1. Joseph E. Harris, *Africans and Their History*, (New York: New American Library, Mentor Book 1972) 26–33.

2. See Chancellor Williams, *The Destruction of Black Civilization*, (Chicago: Third World Press 1974) 62–100.

3. African scholars may not be in agreement as to which successive mansa to attribute certain conquests and achievements. cf. John G. Jackson, *Introduction to African Studies*, (New York: Carol Publishing Group 1990 (1970) Robert W. July, *A History of African People*, (New York: Charles Scribner's Sons 1970); and Chancellor Williams, *The Destruction of Black Civilization*, (Chicago: Third World Press 1974).

4. St. Clair Drake, *Black Folk Here and There*, Vol 2 (Los Angeles: Center for Afro-American Studies, University of California 1990) 77–100.

5. See John Henrik Clarke's "Introduction" in Jackson, *Introduction to African Civilizations*. pp. 3–35.

6. Oliver Ransford, *The Slave Trade* (London: John Murray (Publishers) Ltd. 1971) p. 40.

7. Drake, *Black Folk Here and There*. Chapter 7.

8. Patrick Richardson, *Empire and Slavery* (London: Longmans, Green and Co. Ltd. 1968) 3–21.

9. John M. Blum et al., *The National Experience*, 2nd ed. (New York: Harcourt, Brace & World, Inc. 1968) 53–55.

10. Ransford, *The Slave Trade*. 96–120.

11. A detailed account of the market mechanisms of colonial America's slavery is given by Patrick Richardson in his *Empire and Slavery*, 14–34. Important in this discussion is the economic factors influencing the status and treatment of slaves.

12. See Warren L. Young, *Minorities and the Military* (Westport, CN: Greenwood Press 1982). 192–93.

13. John Hope Franklin, *From Slavery to Freedom* (New York: Alfred A. Knopf 1967) 130–40.

14. The term Negro in reference to Black Americans ceased in popular and academic usage after 1968. John Hope Franklin's book,

*From Slavery to Freedom,* was published in (1947) 1967.

15. See also, Gary B. Nash, Race and Revolution (Madison, WI: Madison House 1990) 57–87.

16. Charles H. Wesley, *In Freedom's Footsteps* (Cornwell's Heights, PA: International Library of Afro-American Life and History (1967) 1976. 113–115.

17. Benjamin Quarles, *The Negro in the Making of America* (New York: The Macmillan Co. 1969, Collier Books 1970). p. 63.

18. James H. Dormon and Robert R. Jones, *The Afro-American Experience* (New York: John Wiley & Sons, Inc. 1974) 126–127.

19. Saunders Redding, *They Came in Chains* (Philadelphia: J.B. Lippincott Company 1950) 1969. p. 70.

20. Ibid., p. 56.

21. See John W. Blassingame, *The Slave Community* (New York: Oxford University Press 1979).

22. cf., *Malcolm X Speaks* (New York: Grove Press, First Evergreen Black Cat edition 1966) 10–17 with John W. Blassingame, *The Slave Community. 250–257.*

23. Ira Berlin, *Slaves Without Masters* (New York: Vintage Books 1976).

24. Ibid. pp. 250–82. Berlin not only relates the occasional divisions between nonslave and slave Blacks, but also gives a balanced account of their mutual support and cooperation.

25. Herbert Aptheker, *American Negro Slave Revolts* (New York: Columbia University Press 1943).

26. See Stanley M. Elkins, *Slavery,* (Chicago: The University of Chicago Press 1959). 138–39.

27. For more on Slave Revolts see Harvey Wish, "American Slave Insurrections Before 1861," *Journal of Negro History,* XXII (July 1937) 229–320, also Philip S. Foner, *History*

*of Black Americans* (Westport CT: Greenwood Press 1983) 131–162.

28. Herbert Aptheker, *Abolitionism* (Boston: Twayne Publishers 1989. p. xiii.

29. Inference of the Fugitive Slave Act of 1850 relative to 20th century Supreme Court philosophy and debate is discussed in Ena L. Farley, "The Fugitive Slave Law of 1850 Revisited," *The Western Journal of Black Studies.* (Summer 1979) 110–115.

30. A more detailed background and analysis of the Dred Scott case is given in J.G. Randall and David Donald, *The Civil War and Reconstruction* (Boston: D.C. Heath and Company 1961) 108–113.

31. From a speech Douglass delivered at the West India Emancipation at Canandaigua, NY. From Philip S. Foner, *The Life and Writings of Frederick Douglass* (New York: International Publishers 1975 (1950). 437.

32. For a history of Black periodicals and newspapers, see Walter C. Daniels, *Black Journals of the United States* (Westport CT: Greenwood Press 1982).

33. Warren L. Young, *Minorities and the Military* (Westport CT: Greenwood Press 1982) 195–199. See also Joseph T. Glatthaar, *Forged in Battle* (New York: Meridian 1991).

34. Glatthaar, *Forged in Battle. 169–206.*

35. Young, *Minorities and the Military. 198–99.*

36. See LaWanda Cox, *Lincoln and Black Freedom* (Columbia, SC: University of South Carolina Press 1981). 11–12, 30.

37. Quarles, *The Negro in the Making of America. 130–131.*

38. Randall and Donald, *The Civil War and Reconstruction. 622–623.*

39. W.E.B. DuBois, *Black Reconstruction in America 1860–1880* (New York: Atheneum Publishers 1971 (1935). 670–71.

40. *Freedom to be Free.* A Report to the President by the U.S. Committee on Civil

Rights (Washington, D.C.: Government Printing Office 1963) 57.

41. See C. Vann Woodard, *The Strange Career of Jim Crow* (New York: Oxford University Press 1966) for an interesting account of Jim Crowism in the South.

42. W.E.B. DuBois, *Black Reconstruction in America 1860–1880,* 702.

43. Benjamin Quarles, *The Negro in the Making of America,* 159.

44. See Florette Henri, *Black Migration* (Garden City NY: Anchor Books 1976) p. 69. (also chapter 2)

45. Norman E. W. Hodges, *Black History* (New York: Monarch Press 1971) 145–46.

46. See W.E.B. DuBois, *The Souls of Black Folk* (New York: Signet Classics 1969) 210–25 for a "poetic" description of the nature of the Black church.

47. For a detailed and pictorial account of Black inventors and their problems with the patent process see Portia P. James, *The Real McCoy* (Washington, DC: Smithsonian Institution Press 1989)

48. Lerone Bennett, Jr., *Before the Mayflower,* 336–339.

49. See L. D. Reddick, "The Negro Policy of the U.S. Army," *Journal of Negro History,* 34-1 (1949).

50. Lerone Bennett, Jr. *Before the Mayflower,* 347–48.

51. Only a cursory account of the many race riots that occurred from 1916 to 1920 can be reported in this survey work. For more study see: Mary Frances Berry, *Black Resistance White Law* (New York: Appleton-Century-Crofts 1971) 139–173.

52. John M. Blum and others, *The National Experience,* p. 651.

53. A review of fundamental economics might be necessary for one to understand the technical aspects of how the New Deal programs effected economic recovery. The book by Richard G. Lipsey and Peter O. Steiner, *Economics,* 6th ed. (New York: Harper & Row 1981) is recommended.

54. U.S. Commission on Civil Rights Report, *Freedom to be Free* (Washington, D.C.: GPO 1963) 114–115.

55. See John Hope Franklin, *From Slavery to Freedom,* ch. 29; Benjamin Quarles, *The Negro in the Making of America,* ch. 9; L.D. Reddick, "The Negro Policy of the U.S. Army," *Journal of Negro History,* 34/1; R. Dalfiume, *Desegregation of the U.S. Armed Forces* (Kansas City: University of Missouri Press, 1969)

56. U.S. Commission on Civil Rights Report, *Freedom to be Free,* 152–153.

57. Two of the most detailed and concise chronologies of Black notable events and of the Civil Rights Movement are Alton Hornsby, Jr., *The Black Almanac* (Woodbury, NY: Barron's Educational Series, Inc. 1973) and Lerone Bennett, Jr., *Before the Mayflower,* 557–607.

58. Malcolm X, *By Any Means Necessary,* ed. G. Breitman (New York: Pathfinder Press, Inc. 1970.

59. *Focus* (Washington, D.C.: Joint Center for Political Studies 1980) December. p. 6.

60. See Bart Landry, "The New Middle Class (Part I)," *Focus* (Washington, D.C.: Joint Center for Political Studies 1987) September. pp. 5–7.

61. See C. Calvin Smith, "The Civil Rights Legacy of Ronald Reagan," *The Western Journal of Black Studies* 14 (Summer 1990): 102–114.

62. See *Business Week,* March 14, 1988, 63–69, also, *Newsweek,* March 7, 1988, 18–45.

63. *Political Trendletter,* Joint Center for Political Studies, March 1988.

# Chapter 4

## Sociological Perspectives of African Americans

### AFRICAN AMERICAN SOCIETY AND CULTURE

*Sociology and African Americans.* The concept of sociology originated in Europe and developed out of a morass of social and political upheavals which characterized European societies of the eighteenth and nineteenth centuries. The decline of feudalism and church authority of the Middle Ages gave rise to race posturing, religious persecutions and class conflicts. In 1839 a French philosopher, Auguste Comte (1798–1857), conceived or coined the term sociology and intended it to form the basis of a science to study human order and relational harmony. In fact as some contemporary sociologists assert, Comte "was a strong believer in what nowadays would be called law and order."[1] The French scholar, Emile Durkheim (1858–1917) and German sociologist, Max Weber

(1864–1920), were among the early major contributors to the field of sociology. The point of this historical reference is to establish the fact that sociology as social theory was founded and derived from a European and not an African worldview.

Sociology, generally defined, is the study of relationships, values, beliefs and organizational structures of societal groups. The prefix *socio* meaning society combined with *logy* which infers study or science, translates sociology as being a study of society. The classical European sociologists or philosophers studied values, beliefs, behaviors and organizational propensities in order to learn how to control and to establish order within the society. Both Comte and Durkheim were concerned with discovering and effecting humanistic codes of values and morality outside the realm and dogma of conventional religion or church. Durkheim saw the school system as

an alternative institution for instilling normative values and beliefs. Max Weber related
human values and behavior to economics and
linked the "Protestant ethic" to the development of capitalism. Weber is noted, too, for
his conceptualization of the term "ideal type"
which creates certain typical ideal patterns of
social or nonsocial behavior for purposes of
comparison. In the execution of his theories,
Weber championed the notion of objective
social science.[2]

Historically, Western European sociological theory has significantly affected the social, political and economic plight of African
Americans and Africans. Although the study
of sociology originated out of the revolutions,
religious feuds and class conflicts of Europe, it
was inevitably influenced by the African or
Atlantic Slave Trade which flourished from
the sixteenth well into the nineteenth century. The subjugation of Africans by Europeans and the racial oppression of Blacks in the
Americas were not dealt with explicitly by
the classical sociologists. But how could such
pathological conduct relative to values, morals, behavior and human relationships escape
their sociological consideration?

Sociology began to take root in the
United States at the height of racial segregation, violence and oppression near the end of
the nineteenth and the beginning of the
twentieth centuries. Early American sociologists such as William G. Sumner, George
Herbert Mead, Robert Park and several others
were influenced to some extent by the classical social theory of Europe. The order theories of Comte, social Darwinism of Spencer,
secular humanism of Durkheim, the ideal
type theory and scientific objectivism of
Weber were taught at various American universities and often applied toward the analysis
and disposition of the African American
plight. Thus, it resulted in a white European
created and imposed solution for the deposed
and oppressed condition of Africans. Blacks
were particularly affected and influenced by

the work and "empiricist tradition" of the sociology faculty of the University of Chicago.
Led by Robert Park, the school conducted research and field studies in urban sociology
that included racial antagonism not only related to African Americans but the growing
populations of European immigrants to the
midwest. As indicated in Chapter One, two
eminent Black sociologists were trained under
the influence of members of the "Chicago
school."

Sociology as an academic discipline has a
long tradition of popularity in the curricula of
predominantly Black colleges and among African American academic professionals and
students. Although W.E.B. DuBois was basically a historian by training, his most significant scholarly contributions were sociologically oriented. Generally, the most significant
works of African American scholars and writers have been in the areas of sociology and
history. While sociology is a popular subject
of Whites and Blacks, its basis of appeal between the two races might be different. The
apparent interest of white sociologists in
human organizations, interactions and values
has been for the purpose of theorizing and establishing social mechanisms of order, control
and equilibrium. Thus as Butler A. Jones
notes, "the early academic and public image
of sociology was reformistic and problem oriented."[3] On the other hand, many African
Americans view sociology, figuratively, as a
medium of social introspection relative to racism and racial politico-economic inequity in
American society. It is small wonder that
Black sociologists have been among those
having taken the lead in critiquing the social
system and fermenting social protest. Indeed,
Black sociologists and historians were prominent in the demand and development of African American or Black studies programs.

Even during the classical era of sociology
(1890–1930) white scholars were reluctant to
deal with the sociology of race except to
imply the inherent inferiority of Blacks and

to academically legitimize the continuation of African people in a subordinate societal position. Many white scholars favored the application of sociological theory towards the resolution of the problems of Blacks in the society. The "Chicago school" trained a few Black sociologists, notably E. Franklin Frazier and Charles S. Johnson, and used them to collect and present data relating to the social conditions of Blacks in urban and rural environments. W.E.B. DuBois was asked to research the social and political conditions of Blacks in Philadelphia in 1896. Consequently, he produced one of his most famous works, *The Philadelphia Negro.* But for the most part, Blacks were intended to be subjects of sociology and not sociologists to the extent that they would formulate theory.[4]

Many Black sociologists view sociology and its theoretical approaches from a different perspective than whites. African Americans have perceived sociology as a field that can effect theories of Black liberation and propose guidelines for social, political and economic equality. Since African Americans occupy a different or oppressed status in the society, many Black sociologists have chosen not to study or practice sociology solely from a detached or value-free stance. Progress for Black people has not occurred as a total result of scholarly objectivity, but from the subjective works and active involvement of African American scholars.

Because of the perceptual conflict in sociological inferences and objectives grounded in the different intent, experience and worldview of African and European peoples, a concept of Black Sociology developed concomitantly with the establishment of Black studies programs of the 1960s. While much of sociological theory is basic and common to all human nature, values, mores and beliefs can be different within each defined race or ethnic group. Culture and behavioral patterns based upon a people's values are more authentically conveyed and are more apt to

be correctly interpreted by members of the same race or ethnic group. Moreover, Africans or the Black race had been characterized by European and American whites as having no civilization, history or values of significance. The subjugation and colonization of Africa by the Europeans and the enslavement, segregation and oppression of Blacks in America was evidence of White belief in the inferiority of the Black race. The exponents of a Black sociology reasoned that it was detrimental to the African American self-image and self-concept to be uncritical of traditional sociology and of its terms, concepts and approaches towards the study of Black people. The fear was that certain sociological theories, paradigms or frames of reference would function to serve the interests of whites rather than those of the Black community.

Black anthropologist Dona Richards admonishes against the uncritical use of Western European social scientific theory as it relates to Black or African peoples. She writes that

> Contrary to the propaganda of academia, white social theory does not represent a universally valid and "objective" body of thought, nor a neutral tool to be used for the purpose of understanding human experience. It might be argued, instead, that it represents a particular view of the world as seen from the perspective of supposed Western European superiority, and that an image of the inferiority of African civilization is inherent in the terms, definitions, and theoretical models on which [much] white social theory is based.[5]

From the preceding discussion it is evident that there exists differences and debate relative to sociology and African Americans.

*Race, Racism, Color, Culture and the African American.* Race, racism, color and culture are factors which have determined the nature and extent of social and sociological relationships of Black people in America since their involuntary arrival in 1619. More than a century earlier, European philosophers and explorers had pronounced the native inhabitants of the African continent "inferior" in relation to the race, color and culture of Europeans. The concept of race, especially, has been and continues to be a controversial and indefinable term. In spite of the fact that there is apparently no universal agreement on the meaning of race, most anthropologists suggest that race is biologically transmitted. In socially practical terms, race refers to certain physical characteristics of people in the world or within a society with diverse populations. Otto Klineberg writes in support of this perspective that

> A race, then, may be defined as a large group of men possessing in common certain physical characteristics which are determined by heredity. The other, non-physical, qualities which have been ascribed to races are in this sense secondary, in that they do not belong to the concept or definition of race; they are not used, for example, in race classification.[6]

Klineberg's classic work, *Race Differences*, seems to reject the notion that such physiognomical qualities as mental ability, intelligence, character, morality and cultural proclivities have any relation to race.

For classification purposes, the races of mankind have been traditionally divided into three general physical-type categories: Negroid or black, Mongoloid or yellow and Caucasian or white. Consistent with the physical-difference theory of race, other racial characteristics are considered such as eye color and form, hair color and texture, shape of nose, bodily stature, and cephalic index (the maximum breadth to the maximum length of the head seen from on top, and expressed in percentage). Anthropologists caution against making any absolute racial characterizations

based on physical factors because of historical migrations, conquests and the inevitable intermingling of peoples.[7]

The issue of race was used, historically, as a pretext to conceal the ethnocentric-xenophobic beliefs and attitudes of pre-capitalist European nomadism. The concept of racial superiority, rank and differentiation gained much acclaim when Count de Gobineau, a French aristocrat, published his *Essay on the Inequality of Human Races* in 1853–1857. Gobineau's essay may have initially been inspired by the class conflicts of Europe. However, his "racial-type" theories and racist doctrines served to give further moral support for Europe's colonialization of Africa and, certainly, as a rationale for White enslavement and oppression of African Americans. Early rank-type racial theories such as Gobineau's evolved into the phenomenon of nineteenth and twentieth century American racism. Racism has and continues to be a primary sociological factor affecting the social organization and the political and economic conditions of African Americans.

Racism, unlike race, is a definitive concept. The problem of racism is not one of definition but that of proof, evidentness and visualization in all of the situations where it is practiced or may exist. Yet, racism is very much perceptible and concrete to an individual or a group subjected to its practice. Racism has been defined as a belief in the innate superiority of one's own race and as an ideology of racial privilege. However, racism goes beyond ones belief or attitude. Racism is not only a racialist dogma but it is an enforceable practice of race persecution and domination. For racism to exist, a person or race must possess the power to affect, assert or enforce disadvantages and discrimination upon another individual or population. Whites have maintained the power to enforce social, political and economic disadvantages upon Blacks ever since the first twenty landed at Jamestown in 1619.

While legislative enactments and cultural refinement have caused a significant reduction in individual acts of racism against African Americans, institutional racism has remained relatively the same—although it has become more sophisticated in practice. Institutional racism is imperceptibly embodied in the policies of social, political and economic institutions of the society and are designed to restrict access or subordinate Blacks or other racial-ethnic minority groups. In his discussion of economic forces and institutional racism, Robert B. Hill differentiates between prejudice and discrimination. Hill states that "prejudice involves negative attitudes or beliefs about racial or ethnic groups, while discrimination involves negative treatment of them."[8] Racism with all of its forms and attributes is an integral part and problem of the sociology of African Americans.

Universal antagonism between peoples of the world exists, partially, because of the general classification, division and identification of the races of mankind by color—Negroid (black), Caucasoid (white), and Mongoloid (yellow). Yet, most respected social theorists and scholars agree that "Skin color, of itself, however, has very limited scientific use as a criterion of these primary races."[9] Not only is skin color indefinite and limited in race differentiation, it has no precise value in determining intelligence, character, values, morality or culture. None the less, African Americans have probably suffered more social disadvantage and racial antagonism because of their color than any other race or group. Within the monolithic perception of race and color, color yields a decisive advantage in American society.

Negative associations with the color black or blackness were generated, partly, by white Europeans as a moral or religious rationalization for their capture, transportation and enslavement of Africans. It was economically convenient and morally consoling to translate their Biblical myths and cultural superstitions of black and blackness into a justification for Black slavery. However, one of the most recent and definitive works treating the origins of prejudice against dark-skinned people was done by Black sociologist/anthropologist St. Clair Drake. In Drake's book, *Black Folk Here and There*, he reveals no consistent symbolism or myth—religious or secular—elucidative of the European's or indeed any peoples' prejudice against the color black.[10]

Racial and cultural antagonisms between white and non-white peoples have been known to exist since the Middle Ages. Peoples who might be classified as non-white comprise approximately seventy-five percent of the world's population while whites represent a clear minority. Yet contemporarily, non-whites are generally subjected to cultural, political and economic domination by those who legitimately or opportunistically classify themselves as white. Psychiatrist Frances Cress Welsing proposed a controversial theory to explain white ethnocentric or xenophobic behavior towards non-white or colored peoples. The Cress Theory of Color-Confrontation posits that

> . . . whites are also vulnerable to their sense of numerical inadequacy. The behavioral manifestations or expressions of their sense of this inadequacy in their numbers become apparent in the drive or need to divide the massive majority of "non-whites" into fractional as well as frictional minorities. This is viewed as a key and fundamental behavioral response to their own minority status in the known universe.[11]

Welsing further suggests that white thrust towards superiority over peoples of color, the drive towards materialistic acquisition and accumulation, and quest for a technological culture and power are psychologically motivated for the maintenance of white supremacy. However the most controversial aspect of Welsing's theory is not so much that of whites' numerical inadequacy, but their genetic inadequacy of the ability to produce color. She argues that the inability to produce the skin pigments of melanin which are responsible for all skin coloration is genetic deficiency state and that whites, indeed, desire to have colored skins.

If the sociological-biological phenomenon of color has psychologically affected European Americans, it has also influenced the social relationships and intra-race social structures of African Americans. The dichotomous white-master and black-slave relationships of the era of American slavery inevitably gravitated into gross miscegenation. The sexual liberties taken by white masters upon African females resulted in the birth of thousands or perhaps millions of human beings of mixed black and white stock. Africans having visible evidence of European color and physical characteristics were termed "mulattoes" indicating a mixed breed. While light-skinned Africans were not allowed to escape the caste of the black race, privileges and benefits were usually accorded mulattos by the slavemasters that were denied dark Africans. The superior rank and economic status of whites caused blacks to equate wealth and power with white color or whiteness. Thus, a nominal but significant class structure based on color developed among African Americans during slavery and existed appreciably until the Black Power and Black Pride Movement of the 1960s.

In spite of the lack of scientific evidence that color is an absolute determinant of race, *skin color* is one of the major criterions for ranking human groups as superior or inferior in America and in Europe. Antagonistic social relations which developed from the color-hierarchy of early American life still prevail and affect the conscious or sub-conscious behavior of Blacks and Whites in their daily life experiences. The American value system is based significantly on race/skin-color and white supremacy. Historically, Black Americans have adopted coping strategies for social betterment and economic survival. Thousands of light-skinned African Americans or mulattoes "pass" for white and some have passed permanently into the white race to benefit from the privileges that whiteness allows. More significant is the fact that thousands of other mulatto African Americans could "pass" but have chosen and still choose to remain true to their African heritage and fight for a society that will be void of color discrimination. Color and race are imperatively germane to the sociology of African Americans.[12]

From an Afrocentric perspective, culture is clearly related to race although some social scientists dispute the notion that there exists an absolute correlation between race and culture. Furthermore, there is a tendency of many Euro-American social theorists to deny that African American culture is significantly different from that of the dominant white American society. Sociologist Jerry D. Rose concedes that there is "at least a rough correlation between the distribution of racial types and of cultural forms. . . ." However, he attributes the origin of such distinction to the geographic isolation of groups. He appears to suggest that when isolation is broken down cultural differentiation is diminished or dissolved.[13]

The debate relative to the correlation of culture and race exists, essentially, because of the various concepts of culture. Culture has various meanings to different groups or peoples. Culture includes more than an individual's or group's customs, language, artifacts and physical environment. History, social experience, values and beliefs are equally important in the understanding of culture because these factors constitute a people's worldview. To understand a people's culture is to understand their worldview.

African American culture is distinctive not only in terms of the contrast between African and European cultures, but also because of different and conflicting worldviews pertaining to racial experiences and race relations. Although Blacks and Whites share the same land space, their social and racial experiences are different. The African American view of America is one of historical slavery and segregation, and of contemporary discrimination and socio-economic inequality. Black beliefs and values are predicated towards the attainment of racial and social justice. Moreover, Blacks remain generally "isolated" residentially or community-wise from Whites. America is still, basically, a "segregated" black and white society. The contrast between the collective social, political and economic positions or statuses of African Americans and Whites is striking and vast. The relative positions of power and influence of Blacks and Whites have not changed. It is inconceivable that from these phenomena one could deny the existence of a distinct African American culture.

Racialism, racism and the ethnocentric ideology of color in the United States have forced upon African Americans a culture that is significantly different from that of the dominant white society. African Americans tend to reject the term or concept of "subculture" which some sociologists use to describe the culture of a minority population. The prefix *sub-* connotes a culture that is "less than" or inferior to the larger culture. Cultures should not be systematically ranked but considered relative to each other. When cultures are "ranked" according to race, the inevitable result is racism. Because of racialism, racism, discrimination and oppression, African Americans have developed a contraculture to the dominant white society. Therefore, race has a direct correlation to the culture of African Americans.

The biculturation theory does not negate the contracultural aspect of African American culture. Amuzie Chimezie supports this contention with his assertion that

It is true that Blacks participate in Euro-American culture, however, most of the participation is effected through coercion and the use of punishment if one fails to participate. Also, it is doubtful whether a majority of Blacks relate to the white part of the cultural dualism in their community with the same feeling as they do to the Black part.[14]

Of course the "punishment" that Chimezie refers to is related to the social, economic and political costs such as education and employment that African Americans would be deprived of if they failed to embrace to some extent white American culture. A study by Caroline Torrance pertaining to African Americans and the American Ethos revealed that ". . . although Blacks support the ideology of American society it is not for the same reasons as Whites, but because of high levels of Black consciousness."[15]

The Arab scholar A. Abdel-Daim speaks of four levels of culture: local, national, regional [world region] and universal.[16] However, two additional levels of culture must be considered in the differentiation and analysis of African America culture. The major differences between Black and White American cultures prevails at the neighborhood and family levels. It is at these two levels of cultural separation where even the superficial effects of integration have failed.

One can reach one's own conclusion as to whether or not Black total acculturation into American society can ever be realized after considering the assimilation variables or possibilities that Milton M. Gordon outlines in his book, *Assimilation in American Life*. Gordon lists the subprocesses or conditions which must exist before a minority racial/ethnic group might be culturally or behaviorally assimilated into a dominant society or culture as follows:

1.  Change of cultural patterns to those of host society.

2. Large-scale entrance into cliques, clubs, and institutions of host society, on primary group level.
3. Large scale intermarriage
4. Development of sense of peoplehood based on host society.
5. Absence of prejudice.
6. Absence of discrimination
7. Absence of value and power conflict.[17]

Gordon proposed that the preceding conditions should be thought of as steps or stages in the assimilation process. It must be pointed out that his assimilation variables applied to or have more relevance for the white European ethnic and immigrant populations. After well over a century of emancipation from slavery, Blacks have not made significant collective progress relative to Gordon's assimilation stages. While the acculturation of white European ethnic groups might have been delayed, race, racism, color or culture have not prevented them from becoming fully assimilated into American society on a voluntary basis. The panacea for racial problems and antagonism proposed by social psychologists as the "contact theory" or desegregation has failed in changing, profoundly, the racial status and power ratio between blacks and whites in the United States.

*Concepts and Approaches Toward a Black Sociology.* The concept of a Black sociology is based purely and simply on the factor of race difference. The premise to this assertion is that Black Africa and African peoples possess a distinct universal ethos, culture and worldview. Blacks of diaspora such as African Americans have retained sufficient elements of their African psyche and culture to make them unique in spite of slavery and oppression imposed upon them by Europeans and white Americans. Furthermore as Ronald W. Walters states, "Black life has been distinctive and separate enough to constitute its

own uniqueness, and it is on the basis of that uniqueness that the ideology and the methodology of Black social science rests."[18] Nathan Hare, the first coordinator and developer of formal Black/African American studies foresaw the need for Black scholars to develop new appropriate norms and values, new or adaptive research methodologies and new ideologies to authenticate the academic nature of the Black experience.

In simple terms, sociology is the study of human group life. This definition might be a true assessment of the field, but the theoretical findings and implications of sociological study is based upon which human group is studied and which group or people is doing the studying. There are major differences between the social experiences and cultures of African and European peoples or the black and white races which pose several questions. Considering the differences between the two races, then how valid is the sociological study of Blacks or Africans when it is based solely on the social experience, philosophy and ideology of Whites or Europeans? Should Blacks always be judged or judge themselves using Whites or Europeans as their norm, standard or behavioral norm? Is universal sociological thought limited to the exclusive theoretical constructs and worldviews of white classical and neo-classical scholars and philosophers? Is fair or balanced consideration accorded the philosophical social perspectives of scholars of African and Asian descent? Finally, is it logical that Black scholars should define and interpret their own social experience and develop new approaches or adapt traditional methodologies toward the study of African peoples? These questions are posed simply as a premise and justification for the Afrocentric orientation to sociology as it is applied to African Americans.

Robert Staples, an eminent Black sociologist, feels that many of the traditional ways of studying sociology are overwhelmingly influenced and based on white norms, mores and values. Thus, there is the tendency to glorify Whites and to patronize or demean Blacks and other non-white groups. He points out that the Chicago school of sociologists, and white sociologists in general, were concerned with focusing upon and studying only the so-called problem Black populations such as low income families, single parents, emotionally disturbed or academically non-achieving or delinquent children and youths. While some of their methodologies were acceptable, ideologies which influenced the interpretation of the research data were not. Staples criticizes traditional sociology for often attempting to function as a pure science by seeking to "objectively" study group life without much concern for the practical use of the knowledge. He postulates that Black sociology of necessity must function as an applied science having as its objective the application of sociological theory towards the liberation and development of the Black community. Staples supports the contention that in the American society, Blacks and Whites share little in common in terms of political and economic participation, social experience and culture. Consequently, the specific need for Black sociology is to study the Black experience and culture as an internal social system along with analyzing external constraints of African American life and institutions.[19]

The functionalist paradigm, conflict theory and symbolic interactionism have been the principal empirical and theoretical sociological models for the study of human or group values, behaviors and social relationships. Functionalism is a theory derived from Auguste Comte's order and morality concept of sociology objectives. Neo-classical sociologists such as Talcott Parsons and Robert Merton have contributed toward the development or modification of the functionalist approach. Functionalism assumes a normative consensus of values within societies and social institutions which constitutes an order or equilibrium state. Any individual, group or

phenomenon that disrupts or upsets the societal equilibrium is viewed as problematic and the source of the disturbance must be reordered and controlled so that order and equilibrium can be resumed. Civil law is viewed as a constructive means of readjusting society and restoring order.

Conflict theorists maintain the opposite view that conflict is normal and inevitable as competing groups fight for power, advantageous position and scarce resources. Conflicts are eliminated through the institutional suppression of the dissident or rebellious group in favor of the dominant group. The dominant group's values and ideas results in its exercise of cultural hegemony over the subordinate societies or groups. Symbolic interactionism is a social-psychological theory which emphasizes the self as a social object and entity that is changed, weakened, strengthened or otherwise affected in its interaction with others.

The brief explanations of the prevailing major sociological paradigms, functionalism, value-conflict, and symbolic interactionism, are presented in order to reveal their ideological implications. The common scheme of traditional Western sociological models is to gain knowledge of human behaviors, values, beliefs or cultures for the purpose of ranking and controlling specific segments of the society. The biological theories of Charles Darwin and the sociological ideology of Herbert Spencer (social Darwinism) are reflected in the social objectives of European and Euro-American sociology. In essence, much of the theory implicitly fosters the ideology of European dominance and superiority. By labeling Africans or the underclass as intellectually inferior, misfit, morally deficient or deviant, the rationale for colonialism and slavery was promoted and sustained.

It is interesting that the victims of slavery and racism were adjudged to be socially and psychologically deviant or pathological while the perpetrators of these inhumane practices (slavemasters and racists) were perceived as socially, morally and psychologically healthy and superior. No where in the standard literature of sociology has the proclivity to enslave and oppress or inhumane racism been described or labeled as social deviance or psychopathic psychological behavior. What becomes evident is that the definition and interpretation of social phenomena is effected by race, culture and historical consciousness.

For example, runaway and rebellious slaves were perceived as disrupters of order and deviant by most whites but these acts were viewed by Africans as positive and heroic. In the Black ghetto where the unemployment rate for young men and women averages more than thirty percent, hustling, pimping or minor drug trafficking is perceived by many ghetto dwellers as coping and survival activities. Conversely, the same behavior is viewed as deviant and contrary to maintenance of law and order by many traditional sociologists and to white society. African Americans and European Americans do not always share the same perceptions of social behavior and conduct. Without a Black sociological perspective or approach, traditional sociology might well be meaningless insofar as its benefit to the Black community.

Not all Black social theorists subscribe to the idea of the need for the development of new paradigms for the study of African Americans. Many apply traditional approaches and methodological constructs to Black life, especially, in the absence of alternatives. Those who are of Afrocentric persuasion and who matured professionally within the African American/Black Studies field after 1968 are perhaps the most insistent in developing new constructs or adapting conventional ones to the Black experience. Undoubtedly, as racial integration becomes less of a reality in American society and assimilation virtually impossible, increasingly, African Americans will seek social recourse in an African identity and culture. With the develop-

ment of such a trend, the concept of a Black sociology will become more popular in concomitance with exploratory efforts to create new or appropriate sociological approaches and methodologies for Black research.

For a case in point, sociologist and Black studies scholar Terry Kershaw criticizes the positivist and critical methodologies used in the study of the Black family or the Black experience. Particularly, he found that the impersonal, non-intuitive and objective technique of the positivist method yielded a distorted evaluation and concept of the Black family. The positivistic methodology relies on the findings of previous empirical and theoretical data; the construction of research instruments based on the researcher's common sense knowledge of social processes; and the execution of experiments, observations, surveys or interviews with value neutrality being the guiding principle. The method of positivism is ahistorical and the results often reestablishes and reinforces the status quo.

Critical methodology offers an improvement over positivism in that it requires the investigation of all intra-group strata, studies the historical development of the group, and develops a global understanding of the political and economic experiences of the social group. Furthermore, it compares conditions with understandings, critiques the present ideology, discovers immanent possibilities for action, discovers fundamental contradictions and educates in order to effect improvements. Although the two methodologies are different, for Black studies purposes Kershaw suggests a synthesis of positivist and critical approaches.[20]

Concern by Black studies scholars of traditional approaches to the study of Black life was sparked by Daniel P. Moynihan's study entitled, *The Negro Family: The Case for National Action*. Using basically the positivistic methodology and focusing only on low income African American families, Moynihan concluded that the Black family was weak

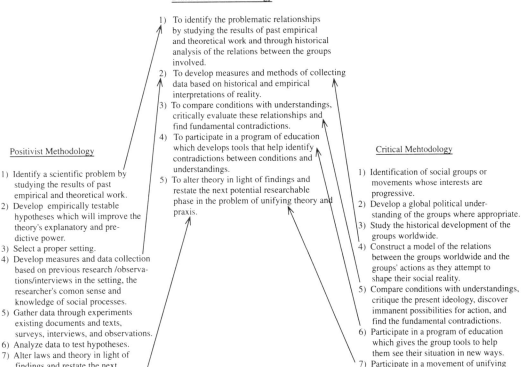

Black Studies Methodology

1) To identify the problematic relationships by studying the results of past empirical and theoretical work and through historical analysis of the relations between the groups involved.
2) To develop measures and methods of collecting data based on historical and empirical interpretations of reality.
3) To compare conditions with understandings, critically evaluate these relationships and find fundamental contradictions.
4) To participate in a program of education which develops tools that help identify contradictions between conditions and understandings.
5) To alter theory in light of findings and restate the next potential researchable phase in the problem of unifying theory and praxis.

Positivist Methodology

1) Identify a scientific problem by studying the results of past empirical and theoretical work.
2) Develop empirically testable hypotheses which will improve the theory's explanatory and predictive power.
3) Select a proper setting.
4) Develop measures and data collection based on previous research /observations/interviews in the setting, the researcher's comon sense and knowledge of social processes.
5) Gather data through experiments existing documents and texts, surveys, interviews, and observations.
6) Analyze data to test hypotheses.
7) Alter laws and theory in light of findings and restate the next researchable phase of the problem.

Critical Mehtodology

1) Identification of social groups or movements whose interests are progressive.
2) Develop a global political understanding of the groups where appropriate.
3) Study the historical development of the groups worldwide.
4) Construct a model of the relations between the groups worldwide and the groups' actions as they attempt to shape their social reality.
5) Compare conditions with understandings, critique the present ideology, discover immanent possibilities for action, and find the fundamental contradictions.
6) Participate in a program of education which gives the group tools to help them see their situation in new ways.
7) Participate in a movement of unifying theory and practice.

Steps 1, 2 and 5 of the Black Studies method are a synthesis of Positivist (P) and Critical (C) methods while steps 3 and 4 borrow directly from Critical Method.

Step 1 is a synthesis of step 1 (P) and 3 (C):  Step 2 is a synthesis of step 4 (P) and 4 (C):  Step 5 is a synthesis of Step 7 (P) and 7 (C).

Figure 3  Black Studies Synthesis Methodology. From Terry Kershaw's Black Studies Synthesis Methodology, printed by permission of the author.

and deteriorating because of female dominated households caused by the absence of the Black male. The lack of two-parent families contributed toward educational under achievement and delinquency of Black youth. Considering historical factors, all levels of Black family income and ideological values, the conclusions of Moynihan's were erroneous. In fact in comparison to past trends, the stability of the African American family had significantly improved and demonstrated much strength and adaptability.[21]

The task of developing new or revised models for researching and analyzing the Black experience is challenging in a world where White social theory and definitions dominate. The number of African American academic professionals at major research institutions are decreasing along with research grants and funds traditionally made available for studying the Black experience. Nevertheless, it is imperative that the Black social scientist be self-determining and free to develop paradigms for the study of his own people. The test of a peoples freedom depends upon their ability and courage to define, validate and legitimatize their own experience and achievements. Dennis Forsythe states that

> It is the task of Black sociology to stress the uniqueness of the Black experience and to see that knowledge collected on Blacks is used for change rather than for control.[22]

***The African American Family.*** The union of males and females for the purpose of procreation, extension of ancestral lineage and propagation of the human species is a universal phenomenon. The social laws, modes and practices which determine the genesis of the conjugal union or relationship between man and woman to perform the functions of procreation and ancestral propagation have always varied in accordance to group cultures and customs. Each basic human unit that is united and related to perform these functions is described as a "family." Since family initiations and practices may vary between different racial or ethnic cultural groups or societies, the African American family is studied from an African centered or Afrocentric perspective.

This discussion will not focus extensively on the classic and ongoing debate of some scholars as to whether or not the Black American family has retained sufficient African cultural traits to be truly distinctive from European culture. However, it is essential to emphasize that the overwhelming number of scholars of the African and African American experiences reaffirm the fact that the African American family has retained numerous cultural characteristics and practices which

are germane to the continent and peoples of Africa.[23] Even in the absence of explicit evidence, it is logical to assume that certain latent cultural traits prevail in spite of Black slavery and oppression. In fact, oppression, racism and discrimination have caused Blacks more or less to reject White or European values or culture and to rediscover and revel in their African heritage. Factors supporting this notion are revealed in the growing popularity of the wearing of African dress, the taking of African names, emulation of African value systems and the celebration of Kwanzaa by Black Americans—a practice that reemerged after the 1960s Black Power Movement. In other words, if much of African familial culture was lost during slavery, it is now being rediscovered and reconsidered after almost four centuries.

There is no doubt that European influence and domination have caused much of traditional African familial values and practices to be diminished in the lives of Black Americans. Yet, it is important towards understanding African American culture to study some of the African family structures which existed prior to the arrival of Blacks in the New World. African family structures are based upon kinship and descent systems that are significantly different from Europeans. Both matrilineal and patrilineal family systems are practiced in Africa. The matrilineal family bases and computes all of its kinships through the lineage or ancestry of the mother. Conversely, patrilineal societies determine their kinship through the father's lineage only.

In terms of marital forms, monogamy, polygamy, polygyny and polyandry are practiced depending upon which society or cultural group either form is sanctioned. Monogamy means a male or female having only one spouse and polygamy allows a person to have more than one partner in marriage. When a man has more than one spouse it is called polygyny, and when a woman is married to more than one it is known as polyandry. The African concept of an extended family differed in some aspect from the European model. The African extended family included more than the "nuclear family" comprising husband and wife and immediate blood relatives. The extended family constituted even distant lineage, ritualistically adopted kin, and multiple related family units living often within the same compound.[24]

It is important to mention the various lineage, marital union and extended family practices of Africa because of the contrast to white or European culture. The differences were a source of frustration to the African American slave. Matrilineage, patrilineage and the various marital forms were functional for each specific African society. Strict rules of behavior and conduct were observed and enforced by the community based upon the cultural norms of each society. However, European civilizations regarded patrilineage and monogamous relationships culturally superior to any other practices. Perceptual differences in the ranking of patriarchy over matriarchy is of sociological contention between white and black Americans even today.

Initially, Africans attempted to continue their African familial roles in the slave quarters of America. However, African traditional family customs were eventually forcibly eroded or modified to conform to the concepts of Christianity. Slavemasters determined the extent of Black family structures and cohesiveness. In spite of the liberties that masters took with slave women, the White church encouraged Blacks to practice Christian monogamous relationships. White ministers of the South preached against adultery and fornication between married slaves and were faced with a religious dilemma when slaves were sold and separated. Studies by Blassingame and Gutman seem to indicate that, ironically, certain White religious principles did impress upon slaves a value for two parent households or functional monogamous families. Enduring two parent relationships and households formed during slavery were recorded and reported among ex-slaves many years after Emancipation.[25] The evidence is conclusive that slavery did not totally destroy Black family culture or diminish the value of the functional benefits of the African concept of the extended family. After Emancipation became effective, the former slaves vigorously attempted to find kin that had been sold apart from their relatives, runaway or otherwise relocated.

The subject of contemporary sociological concern is the conditions of poverty, racism, racial violence, segregation and discrimination which have persisted centuries after slavery and still impact upon the Black family. Many social theorists have proposed that the African American family has been irreparably weakened and remain unstable because of historic and chronic racism and discrimination. A relatively high rate of crime, vice, juvenile delinquency, drug and alcohol abuse, and school drop outs characterize a significant segment of the Black population. Daniel P. Moynihan argued in his study, *The Negro Family: The Case for National Action*, that the reasons for the deviancy and educational under achievement of youths was that the Black family was marked by a large number of female-headed households, illegitimate births and absent fathers. In his opinion, slavery had destroyed the quality of African American family life and left it in "a tangle of pathology" which in consequence impeded the progress of Black Americans.[26]

The Moynihan study provoked national concern and reaction among black and white scholars, but two conflicting theories resulted. Rutledge Dennis terms the two competing schools of thought as the Weak-Family Theory and the Strong-Family Theory. The Weak-Family Theory concurs to some extent with Moynihan's assessment that slavery did affect Black family development, but that weakness and instability has been caused more by the social, political, economic and psychological affects of racism which have prevailed since slavery. While not discounting the affects of slavery and of contemporary racism, the Strong-family Theory proponents emphasize the survivability and adaptability of the African American family which are indicative of its strength and viability.[27]

The Weak-Family concept was rejected by a host of notable Black scholars including Andrew Billingsley, Robert B. Hill, and Robert Staples.[28] Billingsley using the case study method, Hill the empirical-quantitative approach and Staples an Afrocentric ideological basis, repudiated the "pathological" generalizations of the Black family that Moynihan reported. Strong-family theorists propose that the Black family should be evaluated within the context of its own social reality and, thus, validating Black coping strategies and African heritage. Furthermore, a look beyond the lower-upper and lower income strata of the African American population reveals a remarkable history of Black progress and achievement in spite of racism and discrimination.

Those who agree that oppressive factors have contributed toward deviance and instability of the Black family believe that strength and viability cannot be achieved until racism and discrimination have been abolished. Weak-Family theorists define the optimum family model and structure in terms of White middle-class norms. The more Black families approximate White middle-class standards the stronger and more stable they are perceived. Nathan Hare criticizes the Strong-Family school of thought because it has the effect of absolving white people of blame for their racist and oppressive role in weakening the African American family. Yet, he applauds the independent spirit and Black pride intent of the Strong-family proponents.[29]

The difference of the two Black family theories might be explained as being analo-

gous to the cliche of "viewing the glass half full or half empty." Blacks often subscribe to the social definitions of white society although their perceptions of social phenomena might differ. For instance, an Afrocentric theorist may not prefer the term "illegitimacy" to describe Black children born out of wedlock or without a formal father. Strong-family and Afrocentric theorists may view children born out of conventional wedlock as an inevitable human social occurrence resulting from imposed racial poverty and Black male unemployment. There is no such thing as an illegitimate human being with reference to birth. But here again, the dominant society determines and defines concepts of social legitimacy and illegitimacy.

As perhaps millions of White women who yearn for children hasten to take advantage of the scientific medical advances of producing human life through "test-tube" babies, surrogate motherhood, genetic engineering, and frozen human embryos, the questions of legitimacy and the absence or identity of the biological father are seldom if ever applied or considered. Furthermore, concomitantly with the White Feminist Movement unmarried female\with child has become vogue as a lifestyle for some corporate career women.

The so-called crisis in the African American family has always existed because Blacks, for the most part, have never been fully capable of carrying out the Eurocentric convention of family life because of institutionalized economic and political constraints. The massive unemployment and underemployment of Black males have contributed to the dramatic increase in black-female headed households. The Black situation is best described by Margaret Wilkerson and Jewell Gresham:

> One of the most pernicious aspects of the white patriarchal definition of an acceptable household (one headed by a male who is able to provide for his family) is that the masses of black youth and men who are

excluded from the opportunities and rewards of the economic system cannot possibly meet this requirement. Then both males and females of the subjugated class are castigated as being morally unfit because they have not held their reproductive functions in abeyance. . . . At the same time, there is the insidious notion that households headed by black women are *destined* for poverty, not because of the absence of economic means but because of the absence of the male.[30]

The causative factor of the high rate of African American families with female householders with no spouse present is, primarily, poverty. Thirty-one percent, or 9.3 million, of all Black persons were poor in 1989 and this rate has not changed significantly since 1969. Based on current economic trends, Black families are three and one-half times as

likely to be poor as White families. The case in point is that the proportion of Black families with female householders with no spouse present who were poor in 1989 was 46.5 percent. This should be correlated with the fact that in most general occupational categories, the median earnings of Black males 15 years and over are less than 70 percent of White males' earnings. Statistics show that African Americans are able to maintain conventional Eurocentric models of family life as their economic and employment opportunities improve.[31]

While poverty has been stated as the primary factor affecting the stability of Black family life, one cannot discount other causes. The materialistic bent of white Western scientific and technological culture has given rise to a myriad of moral and social maladies

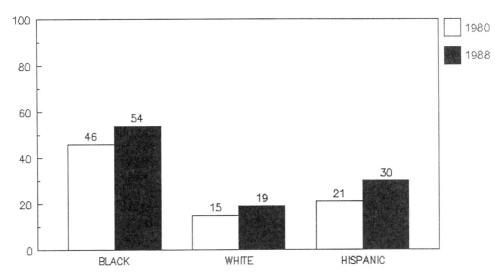

PERCENT OF CHILDREN UNDER AGE 18 WHO LIVED
WITH ONE PARENT, BY RACE AND HISPANIC ORIGIN:
1980 AND 1988

NOTE: PERSONS OF HISPANIC ORIGIN MAY BE OF ANY
        RACE
SOURCE: U.S. BUREAU OF THE CENSUS

Figure 4 Percent of Children Under Age 18 Who Lived with One Parent.

including crime, drug addition, sexual deviancy and disease, and neurotic and psychiatric pathologies which have influenced the abandonment of traditional family values. These social and moral maladies have affected Whites as well as Blacks. Although 64 percent of Black babies were born out-of-wedlock compared to 18 percent of White babies in 1988, the rate has increased faster among Whites than Blacks. The number of Blacks having babies out-of-wedlock in 1980 was 55 percent compared to 11 percent for Whites.[32]

Conventionally, the initiation and recognition of family begins with marriage between male and female. Because of the longer life expectancy of women and perhaps for other natural procreative reasons, the ratio of females is usually higher than males. For a number of reasons, the perception or reality of a Black male shortage has been of sociological concern relative to the marriage rates of African Americans. It is generally acknowledged that the comparatively short life expectancy, higher number of homicidal and accidental deaths, and incarceration of Black males have affected the marriage rate of African Americans. However, the perceived Black "male shortage" has more credibility when it is related to middle-class African Americans. The marriage sex-ratio imbalance among middle-class African Americans may not actually infer a shortage, but a lack of mutual or reciprocal acceptability between Black males and females based on educational and occupational values. Until very recently, the rate of Black females completing four or more years of college exceeded that of Black males. Thus, the shortage is reflected structurally when Black women may not choose to marry men who have less education or occupational status.[33]

In studying the African American family today, more emphasis should be placed on middle and upper middle-income class groups. Some of the focus should shift because research reveals that the quality of family life is related substantially to levels of income and education. Prior to the 1960s, the overwhelming majority of Black families could have been classified as having lower and upper lower incomes in comparison with Whites. However since the 1960s, more than a third of African American families earn $25,000 to $50,000 annually placing them statistically in the ranks of the middle income or class.[34] By concentrating more on Black middle income families will not diminish the fact that there exists vast economic and income disparities between whites and blacks. It will show, however, that the perceived weaknesses and instabilities of the Black family tend to diminish in proportion to an increase in income and educational opportunity.

Strong-family theorists view the African American family from a holistic perspective. This was particularly evident in Hill's study, The Strengths of Black Families, which revealed that Black families generally have strong work and achievement orientations, strong kinship bonds, strong religious beliefs and ties, and the ability to adapt to changing roles and functions. Hill's study destroyed the myth of the slothful Black male who was prone to desert the family. Instead he found that on the whole, Black fathers were responsible husbands and parents. Moreover, the study indicated that Black families are characterized by an equalitarian pattern in which both spouses share decision-making and the performance of household duties. The claim of "female dominance" based on the perception that wives in low-income Black families earned more than males and sustained the household was not supported by the study. In spite of White political protestations that Black families are prone towards welfare dependency, Hill found the "self-help" attitude remarkable even among low-income Blacks.[35]

Specific studies treating marital factors effecting conflict within the Black family are relatively few and the findings are speculative and inconclusive. A common fault of most literature on the subject is that Black family life is usually compared to the normative cultural values and behaviors of Whites based upon Eurocentric ideals. Family conflict and the succeeding emotional responses develop out of a cultural mode and psyche. White or European social theorists do not apply a Black or Afrocentric frame of reference to interpret, analyze or understand the internal conflict within white families. Although much social and behavioral experiences are shared between Black and White Americans, the affects of racism, discrimination, and political and economic dominance are not felt or reacted to in common. Undeniably, racism and oppression have and continue to affect the quality of Black family life. Therefore, more race specific studies relative to African American intra-family relations or conflict should precede comparative and cross-cultural investigations. White and non-white "objective" differentiations may obscure rather than clarify factors of Black family conflict.

Separations or divorces are the result of failed marital relationships and to an extent reflects deficiencies in the values and moral codes of the society. The Eurocentric and capitalistic philosophy of individual rights and moral freedom, as opposed to collective welfare and responsibility, have influenced many African Americans to abandon traditional African oriented family values. Some white social theorists devote an inordinate amount of effort studying and reporting Black family "deviance" and dysfunctions while ignoring the moral decline, racism, legitimized aberrant family structures, liberal divorce laws, sexual crimes and pathologies, drug and alcohol abuses characteristic of an increasing number of White families. Social problems and dysfunctions of the Black family are presented as if they are characteristic of Black culture and not influenced in part by white

cultural dominance, racism and economic disparity.

African American family conflicts or marital dissolutions, like any other human unions, can occur for intimate and personal reasons devoid of any external factor or stimulus. However, external socio-economic forces do intervene and affect relationships between marital partners. The social affects of racism and of economic discrimination are among the indirect or direct causes of an infinite number of Black family conflicts which often culminates into separation and divorce. The problem is that it is difficult to quantitatively determine the extent to which racism and economic discrimination per se affect the marital stability of Black families.

Nevertheless white sociologist, Reynolds Farley, found in an early study that Black men and women with the characteristics of higher social standing are more likely to maintain their marriages than Blacks with characteristics of lower status. The study showed minor differences in the prevalence of divorce but socio-economic factors were related to widowhood and desertion. Widowhood and desertion were both inversely related to socio-economic status. African Americans with low status jobs were more likely to be widowers than men with prestigious occupations. The socio-economic variables considered were education, occupation and income, of which income was the most strongly linked to marital stability. The lower the income, the more likelihood of marital separation.[36]

Robert B. Hill maintains in a more recent work that institutionalized racism and structural discrimination relatively affect the functioning of both low-income and middle-income Black families. Hill further asserts that discriminatory socio-economic policies, whether intended or unintended, have in effect undermined Black family stability. He contends "that institutional racism has contributed significantly to the erosion of the social and economic well-being of black families . . ." and ". . . that the sharp increases in unemployment, poverty and one-parent families among blacks were due, in large part, to the structurally discriminatory effects of major economic forces and policies."[37]

Various studies show that there is a positive relationship between Black spouse abuse and income level. In effect, the higher the level of family income, the lower the level of abuse reported. Black families encounter institutional economic racism and discrimination in the forms of unemployment, underemployment and underpayment in the labor force. The social trauma and stigma of being unemployed can cause mental health problems. It has been observed that increased mental hospital admissions and higher suicide rates have coincided with increased and extended periods of state or national unemployment. Historically and consistently, African American families are affected by a high unemployment rate. Underemployment and underpayment are economic variables which cause psychological and interpersonal stress. All of these factors induced by institutional racism impact profoundly on the emotional climate of Black families.[38]

This discussion has attempted to cast the African American family in a mold of Afrocentric analysis and ideology. While Daniel P. Moynihan and others of his persuasion attribute social ills, and instabilities of the Black family to factors internal to Black households and communities, this thesis has focused on the external forces of social, political and economic racism and oppression. It would be intellectually naive to deny that dysfunctions and inadequacies of Black family life do not exist. Still, it is even more illogical that the Black family should assume total responsibility for its debilitated condition (blame the victim) and, thereby, absolve white Americans of 400 years of subjugation and oppression of African Americans.

There is no need to debate the validity of the Weak-Family theory or the Strong-Family theory. What is needed is a reconciliation and synthesis of both schools of thought. The African American family is both weak and strong. It is weak because Black people as a whole are politically and economically powerless and subject mostly to the will of the dominant white society. The strength of the Black family is evident in its survival after centuries of slavery. Each generation of African American families are stronger, more achieved and more influential than the preceding ones.

*The African American Male and Female: Consensus and Conflict.* The sociology of African Americans cannot be fully comprehended without studying the separate and unique social development and role perceptions of the Black male and female. Only by analyzing the historical social relationships and the prevailing politico-psychological issues contributing to problems or conflicts between Black males and females can the strength of the African American family be fully appreciated. In general, the American society subscribes to gender specific socialization of males and females relative to roles of masculinity and femininity. But beyond this social reality, Black males and females have been and continue to experience different modes of socialization because of the effects of slavery, racism, discrimination and the competing force of White cultural hegemony.

Historically, the treatment, purpose and role of Black men and women were set apart starting with their forced voyage to the New World on slave vessels. The men and boys were shackled and chained in holes below deck while some of the slave women and girls were allowed to roam on deck. They were considered too weak to attempt to disrupt or escape. Invariably, others were subjected to sexual molestation by the ship's crew. During slavery in America, the female slave had

greater economic value than the male because of her reproductive ability and use as a
sex object for the slavemaster. Young slave
girls were used as breeders, concubines or
prostitutes depending upon their evaluation
by their white masters. Differential slave male
and female roles were based on the economics interests of the master. It was the masters
who determined how much care slave women
received during pregnancy and the treatment
or attention that was given to slave children.
The Black slave woman was forcibly at the
disposal of her owner and only incidentally a
daughter, wife, or mother.[39]
   In slavery, the Black male was virtually
emasculated. He had no more respect or
rights than a child. He had to seek permission from the master to court or marry a slave
women. He could not protect his girl friend,
daughter, wife or mother from the sexual
abuse or use of the slavemaster without being
whipped or killed himself. The slave woman
has been known to offer herself to the master
in order to spare her Black man from suffering and death. Often, the Black father was
separated from his slave mate and their children. Historians do record that some masters
did regard the sanctity of Black slave families
and marital unions.[40] The socialization and
sex role differentiations experienced during
slavery have effected to some extent the contemporary relationships between Black males
and females.
   In relation to post-slavery and contemporary society, Black males and females are still
effected both similarly and differently by the
gender role-socialization practices of the
dominant White society. The socializing effect of White American culture on African
Americans is compounded by racism and discrimination. Various social theorists suggest
that race, racism and discrimination are significant factors which contribute toward the
differential socialization of the African
American male and female. Moreover, because of racism Black males and females are

socialized differently than White males and
females in terms of the gender-role expectations of American society. Differences in
White/Black gender role-expectations are believed to effect Black male/female conflict.
   Sociologist Clyde W. Franklin, while not
denying the reality of the socialization effects
of racism upon African American life and behavior, proposed in an earlier thesis that
white racism is a conditional rather than a
causal variable in producing and perpetuating
Black male/female conflict. In his opinion,
white racism alone was an inadequate and illogical explanation for the cause of Black
male/female conflict.[41] Yet, it is implicit in a
subsequent essay by Franklin that Black male
and White male differential perceptions of
masculinity and the "acting out" of masculine
roles could be causative factors contributing
to Black male/female conflict. The socialization of Black males into "white" definitions
of masculinity including power, dominance,
competitiveness, aggressiveness, non-emotion-
alism and non-feelingness could have conflic-
tive effects in Black male/female relationships.[42]
   According to sociologist K. Sue Jewell, a
major part of Black male/female conflict may
be attributed to the "definitions" assigned to
white and black Americans through the
media. Traditionally, positive definitions and
images are assigned to White males and females and negative ones are portrayed of
Black males and females. White supremacy is
the basis upon which both positive and negative definitions are developed.[43] For example,
White males are generally depicted as being
in authority, competent, courageous and fully
in charge and protective of their families.
Black men are usually portrayed as being sub-
missive, subservient, dependent, coward or
simple. White women are seen with attrac-
tive bodies, subordinate and supportive of the
white male, and taking care of the house and
children. On the other hand, Black women
are shown as being dominant, physically large

and threatening, and more competent and self-sufficient than the Black male. These false definitions and images caused many Black males and females to aspire for the White "ideal" and to negate each other. Television programs such as *The Jeffersons, Good Times, What's Happening, and Gimmie a Break* are but a few that were characteristic of the images and definitions described.

The politico-psychological intent of the negative characterizations of the Black male and female through media imagery was to reflect upon the master, male and female slave relationships which existed during the ante bellum period. The imagery of the domineering Black woman and emasculated Black male was a source of friction between Black males and females during the Black Power Movement of the 1960s. Black males viewed their protest and rebellious activities as a sign that they had finally regained their manhood that was lost during slavery. Consequently, some expected Black women to assume subordinate roles that would be simply supportive of the males' struggle. Thus, many African Americans had internalized the stereotypical and negative definitions which were depicted by white society and this adversely affected Black male/female relationships during the Black Power Movement.[44] The media continues to be a socialization factor perpetuating definitions of white supremacy, racial stereotypes and mythical sex roles and imagery. Jewell implies that conflict between sexes and races are inevitable if the negative definitions are internalized rather than rejected.

One of the most divisive issues that threaten the harmony of African American male and female relationships is the imputation of matriarchy as a characteristic of the Black family. It has been clearly stated in this chapter that the matrilineal and patrilineal forms of family relationships were normal accepted practices of African society. However, Europeans have always regarded matriarchal societies as being culturally inferior. The de-

meaning of matriarchal cultures is unjustified from a universal perspective. The noted African scholar, Cheikh Anta Diop, insists that matriarchy "is not the distinctive trait of any particular people but has controlled at a given time the social organization of all the peoples of the earth."[45]

The matter of matriarchy generated little or no concern in the Black community until Daniel P. Moynihan used the term to describe the large number of Black female-headed, low-income families in urban areas. Unfortunately, African Americans have since broadened the concept to imply on a relational basis feminine domination. Many African American men, sensitive to the historical emasculated role of Black males in slavery and during the oppressive Jim Crow era of the South, began to lean ideologically toward Eurocentric "paternalism" which is unrelated to African patriarchy. The Western and white American concept of patriarchy or paternalism translates as masculine imperialism and feminine passivity. African patrilineal and matrilineal family systems did not function to establish male or female superiority or inferiority, but as social laws governing ancestral inheritance and descent.

The matriarchal issue sparked interest in a reexamination of sex roles in African American marital relationships. Differential historical and economic factors reduce the significance of comparing Black with White sex roles and attitudes. Nevertheless, African Americans are inevitably influenced in some degree by White social paradigms. Therefore, attempts have been made to fit the analysis of Black marital sex roles into the conventional sociological classifications of traditional, contemporary or modern, and egalitarian. The traditional arrangement differentiates marital or mate responsibilities on a sexual basis. In a marriage, the husband has the primary responsibility for financially supporting the family while the wife has the basic responsibility for maintaining the home and child rearing. Contemporary or modern sex-role proponents reject the notion of as-cribing any responsibilities or activities on a sexual basis. The egalitarian philosophy de-veloped from the socio-economic necessity of both husband and wife or man and woman having to work to support the home or household. Egalitarian relationships acknowl-edge that the profession or occupation of both partners are of equal importance and practices shared responsibility in the manage-ment and execution of home or household duties.

It has always been of socio-economic ne-cessity for both spouses of Black marriages to be employed in order to support the family long before it became popular or necessary among Whites. Therefore, it is not surprising that a study by the Institute for Urban Affairs and Research found that more than eighty percent of Blacks polled support the egalitar-ian division of family tasks. The study revealed that most African Americans believe that both spouses should be employed, but in spite of dual employment, eighty-five percent agreed that motherhood is the most fulfilling experience a woman can have.[46]

While egalitarianism has proven to be a functional adaptation in African American marital relationships, certain sex ideologies and socio-political motives of the Feminist Movement have produced Black male/female conflict. It was evident from the beginning that the bases, grievances and objectives of the Feminist Movement were not totally compatible with the plight of Black women. In the first place, the contemporary Feminist Movement was initially founded by white women and based upon their grievances ad-dressed to the White male dominated society. Secondly, the White Feminist Movement was primarily concerned with sexism, but Black women were faced with the social reality of being oppressed on the basis of sex and race. In response to this reality, Black Feminist or-ganizations were soon organized to deal with

the unique problems and issues of Black women which included sexism and racism.

While the Feminist Movement and its ide-ology produced division between Black and White women, it also generated divisiveness and dissension among Black men and women. The crux of the division was based simply on the priority of racism or sexism. Since both Black men and Black women are oppressed by white society on the basis of race, separate efforts toward liberating either the Black man or woman were argued to be counter-produc-tive to the crusade to free the entire Black family—men, women and children. Black women questioned other Black women on the logic and feasibility of forming alliances with the white Feminist Movement since White women have historically discriminated against Black women and men on the basis of skin color.

Many African American men view both Black feminists and White feminists threaten-ing to their own liberation struggles, man-hood or masculinity. They opposed the femi-nist ideology of "unisexualization" defined as efforts to erase gender identity and biocul-tural distinctions between male and female. Particularly in the area of employment oppor-tunity, Black feminists were accused of work-ing unwittingly with White feminists against the interest of Black men. Hare writes that, "almost to the exact extent that the white fe-male has entered the labor force the black male has been pushed out of it, with obvious consequences for black sexual and family re-lationships . . . plus the white female's prox-imity and intimate relationship to the white male foreordained her privileged access to the necessarily limited new jobs."[47]

Although most Black feminists seem to agree that they are not oppressed significantly by Black men economically and politically, Black women still share many of the concerns of the Feminist Movement. Some of the com-mon concerns usually expressed are sex dis-crimination in employment, government and private support for day-care centers, improved health-care facilities for women, and inexpensive abortions for any women who choose them. Furthermore, some argue that it is categorically different to be Black and a woman in America than it is to be Black and male. African Americans generally support many of the objectives of Black feminists. However, much strain and conflict continues between Black males and females relative to the sex/race implications of feminist movements and organizations. If African Americans as a race are to ever achieve equality in American society, Black males and females will have to organize with rather than against each other. One thing is clear, Black feminism is essentially different from White feminism in both context and motive. The difference of the two movements is the key to the eventual resolution of the conflict between African American males and females.

In relative figures and terms, the incidence of interracial dating and marriage is minimal between Blacks and Whites. In fact, the overwhelming majority of U.S. marriages remain racially endogamous, each person remaining loyal to his or her own race.[48] Nevertheless, the incidence of interracial dating and marriages is a source of social and emotional controversy between African American males and females. There has never been widespread acceptance of the practice of having sexual contact outside of one's race, clan or society. Even during slavery when miscegenation involving White man/Black woman was regarded as routine, the practice invoked political, moral and religious controversy.

The rate of interracial marriages has varied intermittently in relation to political and economic factors. In a recent study, Clarence Spigner found that Black/White interracial marriages involving Black husband/White wife decreased from 1980 to 1987 based on U.S. Census data. However, there was a slight increase in Black wife/White husband marriages during the same period.[49] Few recent studies relate the socio-political, psychological and economic factors that give rise to Black/White interracial relationships. However, an impressive review of literature on the subject was done by Delores P. Aldridge in her essay entitled, *Interracial Marriages: Empirical and Theoretical Considerations*.[50] The point of this discussion is to reveal that very often Black/White interracial relationships are a source of conflict and dissension between Black males and females.

Some of the resentment of Black women of Black men marrying or dating White women stems from the perceived shortage of available Black males especially among the middle-income strata. Black woman/White man biracial relationships are less frequent than Black man/White female unions. However, a slight increase in Black woman/White man marriages has been noted during the past decade. Many Black men are pained to see Black women take white male spouses the same as Black women are when Black men choose White women. Both may interpret these biracial unions as a personal rejection of their racial worth. Traditionally, it has been the case of middle and upper-income Black males marrying lower class White women and, conversely, high income Black females choosing lower status White men. In other words, higher status Blacks tend to marry Whites who are down the social and income ladder while Whites marry Blacks who are their social and income superiors. However, in recent years such unions are becoming more socio-economically equal.[51]

One can logically assume that both unity and conflict patterns exist universally between men and women. The nature of the issues and social circumstances which bind or divide males and females are determined by societal codes which are either egalitarian or inequitable in regards to sex, race and culture. Maulana Karenga asserts that Black male/female relationships are affected more by societal rather than personal factors.

Karenga posits that the causative factors are inherent in the three major American value systems: capitalism, racism and sexism.[52]

Since the 1960s, scholars and politicians have developed a monadic or gender specific approach towards studying or analyzing the African American community. This approach has led to the separate categorization of socio-economic problems affecting Black males and females. Consequently, there is an abundance of literature publicizing the distinct and sometimes competing socioeconomic conditions of the Black male and female. This practice alone has promoted a kind of intra-community political division between Black men and women. Moreover, it has aided the dominant white society well in its masterful ability to divide and control a specific group, race or Third World nation. Criticism of this approach is not to deny that racism and its attendant properties have not often differentially affected the Black male and female. But it must be emphasized that much of the negative statistical analyses and implications can and has been manipulated and distorted by some politicians and the media to the detriment of all African Americans.

Of particular concern, is the proliferation of news and\or information focusing on the Black male's proclivity towards crime and juvenile delinquency; homicidal or "fratricidal" rate; unemployment; school drop-out rate or ineducability; drug proneness; violence; family irresponsibility; and a host of other social dysfunctions. These social problems of Black males do exist, but they apply to much less than one-half of the total African American male population in the United States. Characteristic of a preponderance of sociological studies, focus is too often directed on the lower income or more disadvantaged strata of populations. It is not that the problems and conditions of the Black underclass should be ignored but academic and political integrity demand a more balanced perspective.

The negative statistics and conditions of the African American male gained such enormous attention that in 1991 a group of Black and White political leaders and scholars joined to establish the 21st Century Commission on African American Males, for the purpose of assisting Congress in developing a national policy for addressing the crisis facing Black men. Clearly, this was a noble undertaking by well intentioned leaders. However, it is illogical to assume that the social dysfunctions and plight of the Black male occur within a vacuum without also adversely affecting Black females and children. By concentrating on and imputing the problem only to the Black male, it tends to veil the inequitable and unjust status of all Black Americans. Indeed, the African American male probably should not be the focus of attention but instead the Congress itself. For it has been, historically, the racially biased and conservative policies of the White dominated Congress that have created unequal social and economic opportunities for all African Americans.

White politicians and media are often inclined to give the impression that Black males are primarily responsible for America's awesome drug culture, crime rate and moral deterioration. In reality, the moral decline of the country as a whole began with slavery continuing through the so-called sexual revolution to the contemporary billion-dollar saving and loans bank and junk-bond financial crimes. Yet, the social deviance and dysfunctions of the Black male and some of the other racial minorities are, deceptively, the focal point of television news and documentaries, and of the campaign rhetoric of conservative and liberal political office seekers. Sociologist Jewelle Taylor Gibbs states one case in point when she clarifies the Black male drug myth:

This stereotype grossly misrepresents the actual incidence of drug use by black youth, and it illustrates the hypocrisy of a society that views substance abuse by blacks and whites differently. Film and television generally depict the drug problem as having a black face, but according to figures from the National Institute of Drug Abuse, whites account for 80 percent and blacks for 20 percent of overall illicit drug use. While "crack" has been widely publicized as an inner-city problem, cocaine was popularized in the 1970s as a white middle-class recreational drug, glamorized by Hollywood celebrities and purchased by Wall Street stock brokers and suburban yuppies.[53]

It is evident that it is more politically expedient and beneficial to focus on Black males as the source and crux of the drug crisis. Not only drugs, but all of the nation's other social maladies result from the pre-eminence accorded to the capitalistic, materialistic, moral-relativistic and racist values of the broader society. The Black male problem is a product of these values.

# AFRICAN AMERICAN SOCIAL INSTITUTIONS

**African American Religion and the Black Church.** Religion of some nature, form or practice is virtually a universal phenomenon. However, the definition of the term *religion* is less generic because it is culturally determined. And like numerous terms or words of European origin, religion loses some of its conventional meaning in translation from a Eurocentric to an African or Afrocentric frame of reference. This becomes apparent when one studies John S. Mbiti's, *African Religions and Philosophy*. For Africans, the whole of existence is a religious phenomenon and all natural organic and inorganic creations have religious meanings. Religion is manifest in the material and the spiritual, in song and music, and libation and festivity. The spiritual conception of God is instinctive.[54] African Americans are reputed to be immensely religious because of their African culture and background.

E. Franklin Frazier rejected the notion that Black Americans have retained their African religion and religious practices, contending that the African religious traditions were destroyed with slavery and oppression in America. He asserted that the slaves and subsequent freedmen became totally influenced by the white Christian religion.[55] Frazier's theory or assumptions were not supported by the majority of historians and religious scholars. Contemporary scholars, especially Black theologians, concede that there were some discontinuities due to slavery and the influence of white Christian practices but that the continuities far outweigh the elements of African religious culture which were lost.

Few if any Africans were converted to Christianity before their arrival in the New World. As slaves, they could not worship their God or gods, speak their languages or practice any of their native rituals except clandestinely. They were either persuaded or forced to accept Christianity. Through Christianity, Africans were counseled to be passive, obedient and patient and told that their reward for succeeding in these virtues would be eternal life or heaven. Religion as imposed by the Europeans and Americans was not intended so much as to save the "heathens," but as a medium for instilling the ideal of docility in the minds of the slaves to discourage rebellion. The purpose for which Christianity may have been intended was only partially effective because Africans could never reconcile the religious teachings of love, compassion and righteousness with their plight of suffering and oppression.

Therefore, African American religion was born out of the contradictions of slavery and it developed as a spiritual means to protest racism and to achieve independence from White authority. An account of the origin and development of Black separate or independent religion and church has been given in the preceding chapter on African American history. A summary will suffice here for the purposes of reflection and continuity. It was discussed that in the North, Blacks worshiped in many White churches on a segregated basis.

The first recorded movement by Blacks to form their own independent church began in 1787 when Richard Allen, Absalom Jones and other Black worshippers walked out of St. George's Methodist Church in Philadelphia when they were ordered from their knees to move to the balcony. This incident eventually led to the founding of the African

Methodist Episcopal Church (AME), one of the major Black religious denominations existing today. The establishment of the AME Church was followed by the organization of the African Methodist Episcopal Zion Church denomination in 1796 and several independent Black Baptist churches were founded in major Northern cities after 1809. About the same time, separate churches had begun to be organized in the South by quasi-free Blacks. These Black churches or groups were subjected to strict surveillance by the slavemasters for obvious reasons.

African American religion and churches were founded on the principles of protest and liberation. Early Black ministers were at the forefront of abolitionist movements and contributed to the oratorical denouncement of

Photo 14 The Black Church. Courtesy of The Library of Congress.

slavery. The major slave revolts were conceived and led by Black ministers and church leaders. Gabriel Prosser who planned the Virginia uprising of 1800 was a devout Methodist, Denmark Vesey, author of the most elaborate slave revolt in South Carolina in 1822, was also a Methodist leader. The largest slave revolt in American history was organized by Nat Turner, a Baptist minister of Virginia. The tradition of Black ministers and church leaders functioning as activists in liberation struggles began in the seventeenth century and continues into the twentieth century. Many of the prominent leaders of the Civil Rights Movement of the 1960s were ministers including Martin Luther King Jr., Malcolm X and Jesse Jackson. These and other ministers were supported by thousands of their church members and followers. Black religious denominations will hardly deny that they are not only religious, but political and economic institutions serving the interests of African Americans. Black religion has adapted to conform to the needs of its Black constituents. The most pressing needs of African Americans are freedom, equality of opportunity and social justice.

The terms Black religion and Black church implies more than race/color differentiation from White religion and church. The authentic Black church has traditionally been significantly different from White religion in role, objectives, form and manner of worship, and in practice. Although the Black churches which seceded from the white Methodist and Baptist denominations borrowed much of the evangelical and ecclesiastical practices from white churches, African Americans soon developed their own styles and orders of service.[56] Theologians Gayraud S. Wilmore and James H. Cone refer to the term "Black Church" as that institution or group of Christian denominations owned and operated, at least at the local level, by people of African descent. Wilmore and Cone offer another definition of Black Church that is more or

less ideological in nature. It relates to the "cultural and attitudinal factors and values descriptive of those who claim membership in such a church."[57]

In any event, Black or African American religion and church is more than a fusion of European and African religious cultures and values. The explicit political orientation and objectives of many Black churches make them different from White religious institutions. But beyond their historical political tradition, the authentic Black church differs from the conventional White church in emotional expression, devotional activity, and in musical or choral style and performance. Contemporarily, and as in slavery, the more removed from White institutional influence the more distinctive are African American religious and church characteristics. The musical and worship styles of Black Americans are closely linked to African ritualistic and festive traditions.[58] Fused with Christian practices of European origin, a distinctive style of Black religious service emerged. However, some scholars suggest that the contemporary style of African American ministers was first established by slave preachers. Ethnomusicologist Portia K. Maultsby characterizes the dramatic and intense style of early Black preachers as

1) the use of vocal inflections, which produced a type of musical tone or chant, and facilitated the dramatic and climatic style of preaching; 2) The use of repetition for highlighting phrases of text; 3) the use of rhythmic devices for stress and pacing; and 4) the use of call-responses structures to stimulate "spontaneous" congregational responses.[59]

Maultsby relates Black spirituals, and the modern free-style collective musical and individual lyrical improvisations of African American gospel music, to West African influences based on current research, authentic sound recordings and live performances.[60]

Emergent out of the throes and struggles of the Civil Rights, Black Power and Black Studies movements of the late 1960s the concept of a Black Theology developed. The concept developed when a group of "radical" Black clergy met to formulate a supporting statement of the use and ideology of the term "Black Power" after moderate Black leaders had rejected the slogan. The group of Black clergy were members of the National Committee of Negro Churchmen (NCNC), later changed to the National Conference of Black Christians (NCBC). The ideological and institutional bases of Black Theology "was to build an alternative to the liberal and neo-orthodox theologies of the American religious establishment."[61] Thus as James H. Cone states, "black preachers and civil rights activists of the 1960s initiated the development of a black theology that rejected racism and affirmed the black struggle for liberation as consistent with the gospel of Jesus."[62]

Black theology was created as a distinctive religious movement, essentially, for the purpose of relating to the oppressed masses of Blacks and to comfort them in their struggles against racism and discrimination. Excerpts from a statement by the National Committee of Black Churchmen issued June 13, 1969 reads: "Black theology is a theology of liberation. . . . It is the affirmation of black humanity that emancipates black people from white racism, thus providing authentic freedom for both white and black people. . . . [63] While Black theology is not enthusiatically endorsed by many Black liberals and integrationists, it is a growing movement and a respected approach to racial and ethnic theology.

Concepts and ideologies may change but the basic structures of social institutions usually remain constant. The purposes and functions of the Black Church are virtually unchanged since the Revolutionary War and on into the twentieth century. Historically, it has been an institution which has provided

mental and emotional escape from oppression for African Americans. The Black church's social, cultural and political functions have been summarized, but more need to be stated relative to its economic contributions toward the betterment of the Black community.

Since the Reconstruction era, many African American religious denominations and churches have provided mutual aid or insurance societies to cope with the crises of sickness, death and burial of its members. In large urban areas, beginning mostly with the Great Migrations of the early twentieth century, Black religious organizations and denominational units have established child care centers, low-income housing, credit unions and various other socio-economic auxiliaries. The Church's founding of several Black educational institutions was mentioned in the previous chapter.

Either independently or in association with White religious denominations, private enterprise or the federal government, African American churches have engaged in numerous economic development projects in the Black community. With the strength and support of the Black church, national organizations for the improvement of the economic condition of Blacks were founded during the 1960s and 1970s. Notably, the Rev. Martin Luther King, Jr. initiated Operation Breadbasket in Atlanta as a selective buying organization aimed towards getting Blacks hired by white businesses. Rev. Jesse Jackson is recognized for having started People United to Save Humanity (PUSH). The PUSH organization negotiated multimillion dollar contracts for construction and/or employment of Blacks with major corporations. Opportunities Industrialization Centers (OIC) was founded by the Rev. Leon Sullivan of Zion Baptist Church of Philadelphia to train young unemployed Blacks for jobs which were being advertised in the daily newspapers. All of these organizations were developed with the backing of African American churches. Black church members availed themselves when picketing or boycotting were required to pressure discriminatory firms and businesses to employ Blacks.[64]

African American religious denominations and churches are the sustaining force of Black communities throughout the United States. The foresightedness of the early Black Church in establishing schools and colleges has provided for the education and training of thousands of Black teachers, doctors, lawyers, scientists, engineers and other professionals. Collectively, African American religious denominations and churches are probably the wealthiest of all Black owned social institutions even if one only considers their massive holding in real estate. The Black minister has been compared with the traditional African tribal chief or clan leader. W.E.B. DuBois wrote in his classic work, *The Souls of Black Folk* that, "The Negro Church of to-day is the social centre of Negro life in the United States, and the most characteristic expression of African character."[65]

*African Americans and the Institution of Education.* The institution of education transmits the culture, values and standard of living of a society. The American institution of education as it relates to Blacks may be divided into two distinct historical and functional eras. The first era relates to how Blacks were affected by the educational system after the U.S. Supreme Court's *Plessy vs. Ferguson* (separate-but-equal) decision of 1896. The second period began with the Court's *Brown vs. Board of Education* (desegregation) decision of 1954. It could be claimed that another era prior to 1896 existed which affected the freedmen's educational rights. This was before the Court invalidated the Civil Rights Act of 1875 with its unfavorable "state rights" case rulings of 1883. But for contemporary and practical reasons, only the separate-but-equal and the desegregation eras will be discussed here.

The *Plessy vs. Ferguson* decision gave judicial and constitutional sanction to the separating of Blacks from Whites in public conveyances and accommodations which was broadly interpreted to include all public facilities and institutions including schools. Before the ruling, Blacks were already subject to separation throughout the country on the whim or discretion of Whites. However, in the South a wall of separation or racial apartheid followed. The Court did not explicitly label Blacks as inferior, for although it legalized the separation of the races, it specifically indicated that facilities or accommodations must be made equal.

In all probability, much of the racial problems, tensions and even violence that have characterized American society would have been averted, indeed, if facilities and institutions for Blacks and Whites had been made equal. Instead, public schools and facilities between Blacks and Whites became even more disparate and deplorable. It is difficult to accept the popular belief that all African Americans were simply anxious to have close association with their oppressors after they had been so inhumanly treated during slavery and even after emancipation. For the most part, Blacks wanted to develop their race economically and socially by means of having equal opportunity and access to the best schools and educational facilities.

There is a relative paucity of literature that treats in the same context the dual aspirations of both Blacks and Whites to be separated from each other. One is certainly to be misled to believe that all African Americans have been obsessed with the desire to socially mingle or to assimilate with Whites. History reveals that between 1880 to 1920 a multiplicity of Blacks of various socio-economic statuses advocated Black and African separate self-development, self-determination and self-sufficiency.[66] Marcus Garvey revived the separate development ideology after 1920 and it was widely embraced during the 1960s and to the present—long after the desegregation order of 1954. It is not profane to hypothesize or imagine what kind of progress African Americans might have achieved under separate-but-*EQUAL* educational development in America. Neither the race problem nor the issue of Black independent schools has subsided in the United States.

What did develop under the dual but *UNEQUAL* education system were generations of educationally ill-prepared and academically handicapped African Americans. Critics of the separate-but-equal policy appeared to argue that it was separateness not inequality that resulted in poor educational achievement for Blacks and began championing legal initiatives to achieve school desegregation. Hardly any fair-minded and intelligent educator, parent or child would support the Black deficient and unequal school system which remained legal for 58 years. However within the abyss of racism and social separation which prevailed, a significant socio-psychological benefit did accrue to Black children under the system. Under separation, the school was truly an institution located in the African American community, attendant with Black professional educator role models and influenced by other Black cultural and social institutions. The school, although comparatively inadequate and unequal, was a product of the African American community and it responded to the needs of the community as much as the white racist society would allow. Implicit in this benefit are the factors of race-culture maintenance and self-concept effect which would later raise political questions during the 1960s.

In 1954, the U.S. Supreme Court reversed the 58 year-old separate-but-equal decision of 1896 by its ruling in the *Brown vs. Board of Education* Case. The Court essentially concluded "that in the field of public education the doctrine of separate but equal has no place. Separate educational facilities are inherently unequal." The ruling meant that

segregation in all state schools was unconstitutional. The Court further decreed that desegregation was to proceed with "all deliberate speed." Subsequently, school authorities were ordered to submit plans for desegregation, and the federal courts would decide if the plans were in compliance with the decision of 1954.

The 1954 school desegregation decision introduced the second era of institutionalized education relative to African Americans. The problem with the term or process of desegregation was that it raised many complex legal and political questions, in addition to the rejection and violent resentment it incited in the South. Some of the pertinent issues raised and questions asked included: The Court used the term desegregation. Is desegregation the same as integration? What are the legal implications of *de facto* vs. *de jure* segregation? (De facto, basically, means unintentional or non-governmentally influenced segregation resulting from the conventional policy of building schools to serve specific neighborhoods regardless of race. On the other hand, de jure segregation occurs where public officials deliberately conspire or manipulate to maintain or assure the existence of segregation. For example, school districts could deliberately "gerrymander" school districts or attendance border lines). If intentional segregation was proven which race should be bussed or transported? Did the quality of the school matter? Was it to be automatically assumed that given equally trained faculty and like facilities that Blacks would have higher educational achievement just by simply being among White students and teachers? What would be the positive and/or negative benefits of desegregation to White students or to Black students?

The preceding questions are only a few among many that were generated by the desegregation ruling by the Court. In response to the first question, social theorists like to differentiate between the terms desegregation and integration. Desegregation implies the mere physical mixing of persons without regard to race, color or socio-economic status. It can be a rather mechanical process in the execution of ones civil rights. Integration is a subjective, psychological and attitudinal social process. True integration is achieved only when two or more races or groups develop mutual respect for each other. A degree of cultural assimilation, interaction and inter-personal relationships must exist including inter-mixing and mutual acceptance into each race's or group's social and family institutions.[67] In other words, desegregation is a preliminary stage towards the societal goal of equitable integration. In relation to education, neither optimum desegregation nor integration have been achieved for Blacks on a national scale in American society.

De facto and de jure segregation are facts of life within the American institution of education. Intent is the key legal factor but it is very difficult to prove. While the practices are not as blatant or easily observable as they were during the 1950s and 1960s, tacit racial "segregation" in education of one form or the other continues. Segregation has been transformed into institutional racism and, thus, produces the same result.

The effects of school desegregation attempts have not all been positive for African Americans. The reason is that African Americans have borne most of the burdens and hardships of desegregation. It is they who have witnessed the closure of schools in their community; suffered the unpleasantness of having their children bussed into an often hostile White neighborhood school; and observed the loss or demotion of Black principals, teachers and staff. Numerous studies have been made assessing and measuring the educational advantages of desegregation for Black students. The results of these studies have proven to be conditional or inconclusive. While the perceived social benefits of desegregation and integration to African

Americans have been evaluated, few if any studies have been done to measure the social costs of desegregation and integration to the Black community. Based on the evidence of a continuing Black/White race problem, and the widening educational, economic and political disparities between the two races, it is obvious that integration has not been the panacea for America's social ills.

The implementation of desegregation and integration policies and practices has been almost totally within the scope and authority of the dominant white society. Consequently, care has been taken by the White power structure to assure that the degree of desegregation that has been realized in the society will not negatively affect, substantially, the educational, social or economic interests of Whites. For desegregation and integration to truly succeed, both races must share, equitably, the social costs as well as the benefits.

Besides the social theory that contact in the classroom between Black and White students will promote better race relations and cultural understanding, it was purported that the academic achievement of Blacks would automatically improve simply by studying in an interracial environment. Sociologist James S. Coleman whose 1960 seminal study was used to support school desegregation, later reversed his conclusion that African American students unqualifiedly learn better in integrated classrooms. Coleman confessed that desegregation had proven to be much more complicated than many had realized. Furthermore, he rejected the belief that an all-Black school is inherently inferior and stated that "there have been and there are all-black schools that are excellent schools by any standard."[68]

The political emotionalism of desegregation and integration beclouds the fact that school desegregation is only one measure towards resolving the American race issue. By promoting only school desegregation (social contact) hoping that it will lead to integration (social acceptance), is an attempt to place the burden of achieving racial equity and harmony squarely on the shoulders of White and Black youth while acquitting the empowered older generations of historical and political responsibility. The lower educational achievement of African Americans is not caused by their lack of social mixing with Whites, but because of unequal and inadequate funding and staffing of predominantly Black schools.

Culture and the value one places on one's own culture are significant factors that can affect educational achievement. Culture legitimizes a person's identity and behavior and as a result enhances their self-respect. In recent years, cultural diversity has been proposed as a concept to be adopted towards the improvement of race relations. However, desegregation and integration poses a social dilemma. Cultural diversity requires cultural specificity of education. Integration has the effect of eliminating cultural and racial boundaries while cultural diversity seeks to maintain them. America boasts of its cultural and racial heterogeneity but practices White cultural hegemony. Thus, the educational institution may have a greater interest or efficacy in educating the non-White student out of his or her culture than it has in improving the student's learning ability and knowledge. It may be difficult for a Black student to have a positive self-race concept when only White culture is projected as the epitome of human development.

The most common complaints or grievances registered by Black students matriculated at predominantly white schools and universities are that they experience a sense of loss of their racial identity and a feeling of cultural alienation. Without the concern of the educational institution for cultural diversity, predominantly White academic environments can intensify the Black student's struggle for scholastic achievement and psychological survival.[69] Their plight is further exacerbated by the customary lack of Black teachers and professional role models.

After more than 30 years succeeding the U.S. Supreme Court's desegregation ruling, African American educational attainment beyond high school appears to be declining. College entry by Black high school graduates has experienced a marked decline since 1977. Several reasons may account for the diminishing enrollment of young Blacks into colleges and universities. Primarily, the economic or income status of African Americans has worsened in comparison to Whites. The situation is compounded by the troubled American economy and structural changes in the labor force. Secondly, educational grants have been curtailed and financial aid and other types of student assistance have decreased or become more restrictive since the early 1970s. Some reports indicate that the decline might be attributed to lower competitive achievement test performance. Other studies suggest that the educational aspirations and goals of Black students have changed significantly in recent years.[70]

Decline in African American educational attainment because of economic and financial reasons are more easily understood. The reasons attributed to achievement test performances and to educational goals and aspirations are more socio-politically and psychologically related and, possibly, may transcend those that are purely economic. Of course, there are economic implications associated with school facilities disparity and socially environmental factors arising from low-income school districts and neighborhoods. However, Black and other minority group social scientists have long contended that achievement or standardized tests are, in part, based on white middle-class norms, values and experiences and, thus, are culturally biased. Other socio-political and psychological reasons relate to the desegregation and integration factors previously discussed.

For a brief span after the Civil Rights Movement of the 1960s, professional and occupational employment opportunities for Blacks increased and broadened relative to types and rank or status of positions. There were good reasons then for Black high school graduates to aspire for higher educational attainment because they could see the economic rewards of having a college education. White resistance to Affirmative Action and Equal Opportunity programs, which were chiefly responsible for improved employment opportunity for Blacks, caused this trend to be checked. Although it is imperative that one must have a college education in order to receive a high income, Blacks are questioning the costs and sacrifices of obtaining an academic degree considering the relative benefits of vocational and technical training. This is certainly a causative factor in spite of the comparative historical employment levels many African Americans have achieved in the public, corporate and academic fields. These gains have been mostly individual or symbolic. Collectively, the relative employment opportunity for African Americans as a race, in comparison to Whites, have remained virtually unchanged.

A discouraging aspect related to Black college enrollment is the decline of more than 20 percent in the number of Blacks entering graduate school. The percentage of Master's degrees awarded to Blacks decreased from 6.7 percent in 1976–1977 to 5.8 percent in 1980–1981 although the percentage completing doctoral degrees remained stable. The number of African Americans receiving Ph.D.s increased from 3.8 percent in 1976–1977 to 3.9 percent in 1980–1981 of the totals awarded.[71] The decline in Black graduate degree professionals will have a severe effect on the desired goal of achieving greater Black economic independence and self-determination. In the past, a disproportionate number of Blacks held degrees in the liberal arts and humanities but there are signs that this is changing. If collective Black self-reliance and self-determination is to ever be achieved, science and technology must begin to assume a higher priority in the Black community.

The eminent African American educator and philosopher Carter G. Woodson once admonished that "the education of any people should begin with the people themselves."[72] In the spirit of Woodson's exhortation, the historic predominately Black colleges have been committed to this ideal ever since their inception and establishment during and after the Civil War. Lincoln University in Pennsylvania, founded in 1854, and Wilberforce University in Ohio, founded in 1856, are cited as the first Black colleges in the United States. However, other less successful institutions were initiated prior to Lincoln and Wilberforce universities in 1839, 1842, 1849 and 1851.[73] The majority of these colleges and universities are located in the South. In spite of their threatened existence because of the politics of integration, nearly one-hundred of these colleges still exist.

Statistics available in 1980 revealed that 90 Black colleges graduated as many Blacks as 1,500 White colleges, in spite of the fact that only 30 percent of all African American students attended a predominantly Black college. Because few Blacks matriculated at White universities prior to the desegregation decision of 1954, Black colleges account for more than 80 percent of all African American college graduates.[74] Even today and despite the increasing number of African Americans enrolling at predominantly White colleges and universities, historic Black institutions still account for a large share of Blacks receiving bachelor's degrees in the biological, physical and technical sciences; and in engineering and mathematics.[75]

**The Institution of Sports and African Americans.** The institution of sports or athletic competition is socially and economically important in the United States and, specifically, to the sociology of Black Americans. Although Blacks have always participated in recreational sports of some degree among themselves, competitive sports did not emerge as a significant activity until after Emancipation and the establishment of Black colleges and universities. Segregation restricted Blacks from participating in major league baseball during the 1880s. Consequently, Blacks begun to organize their own teams and leagues in 1884. Records reveal that in the North Blacks and Whites often played openly against each other in baseball. The color-line in professional football did not occur until after World War II, and basketball was minimally desegregated in 1951 with the signing of Chuck Cooper by the Boston Celtics. In April 1947, Jackie Robinson broke the modern color barrier in major league baseball. The first known Black boxer, Tom Molineaux, dates back to 1810. However, with the beginning of the twentieth century, Blacks in boxing became of major interest and activity in American sports.[76]

Following the U.S. Supreme Court's school desegregation decision of 1954, historic Black colleges and universities provided the opportunity for African American athletes to participate in American sports on a much broader scale. Initially, there was reluctant but gradual acceptance of Black athletes on white school teams. But soon after the dexterity and skill of African American players were recognized and acclaimed, they were allowed and recruited to participate in intercollegiate sports at white colleges and universities in large numbers. Blacks who competed successfully on white teams had to be, demonstrably and unequivocally, better or superior in athletic ability and performance than their white teammates.

The drawing power and winning capabilities of Black athletes greatly increased their economic value in the five sports areas of basketball, football, baseball, boxing and track. Particularly in football and basketball,

the fan attraction and star playing ability of Black athletes are essential to the financial maintenance of major White college and university athletic budgets, alumni support and general student recruitment. Competition and rivalry in the recruitment of star Black athletes during and after the 1960s have induced corrupt academic practices which are designed to attract and to retain star Black student athletes at almost any cost.

Thus, the academic objectives and welfare of the Black and sometimes White student athlete becomes of secondary importance to the economic interests of the educational institution. In too many instances, traditional academic requirements and standards are "bent" in order to recruit or to retain high-risk Black student athletes. On behalf of coaches, special adjustments relating to class attendance and course selections may be allowed the Black student athlete. "Mickey-mouse" and non-degree tract courses are often advised for the Black student to facilitate his arduous practice schedule and to make up for days absent because of off-campus games. As late as the 1990s, several major college athletic programs were fined or suspended for paying "out-of-pocket" money or providing gifts to satisfy the needs of some Black athletes. In addition, the Black athlete often unwittingly participates is his own exploitation because of the lure and prospect of becoming a famous and wealthy professional sports figure. The sports institution, its practices and effects, has become a social issue and of sociological concern to African Americans.

The problems of sports for African Americans are: 1) There is a disproportionate number of Black athletes participating. The percentage of Blacks in collegiate and professional sports is higher that the 12 percent they represent in the total population. 2) The massive media promotion and attention given sports highlighting the performances of star Black athletes may have conflicting and counter-beneficial affects on many African American youth. Many Black youth are socialized into believing that sports are a viable and lucrative career option, when in fact, they have better odds of becoming a doctor, lawyer, or teacher than succeeding as a professional sports player. 3) Since Black athletes are more than likely to be exploited and academically short-changed and few ever make it to the professional ranks, the African American community suffers a loss in competent professional human resources. Of the number of Blacks awarded collegiate athletic scholarships, less that 30 percent ever graduate from college.[77]

The disproportionate ratio of participation, success, skill and ability of Black athletes has caused numerous "race-oriented" explanations to be proposed by Blacks and Whites. A number of sportscasters and scholars have put forth the theory that Blacks are natural athletes because of their physiological and physical characteristics. Such a theory implies that Blacks are genetically superior to Whites, at least, in athletics. Others have fostered the claim that Blacks are more proficient at "reactive activities" and that Whites excel in those sports requiring "self-paced activity." In recent years the number of so-called "scientific" explanations for Black alleged superiority in athletics have proliferated. However, an examination of much of the literature reveals no convincing evidence of anthropometric, physiological or anatomical differences between Blacks and Whites that inherently or permanently would cause either to be superior or inferior in athletic performance outside of long practice and dedicated training.[78]

However, the fostering of popular racial conceptions relative to sports without fully exploring the most logical non-racial explanations have had negative social, educational and political affects on African Americans. Indeed, most sports sociologists concur that the reasons for the success and disproportionate participation of Blacks in sports are social,

economic and cultural rather than any other factors. More important is the fact that African Americans have gained prominence and success in only about six of the major sports activities—basketball, football, baseball, boxing, track and field. Blacks are conspicuously absent or barely represented in golf, tennis, hockey, soccer, skiing and a host of other competitive sports in America. Gary A. Sailes and other sports sociologists have noted that, generally, Black communities lack the facilities, equipment, peer-models, instruction or programs to participate in these sports and, consequently, they gravitate toward those athletic activities that require minimal facilities, conveniences and costs.[79]

In his essay, *On the Issue of Race in Contemporary American Sports*, Harry Edwards implies that racism is the reason why some White Americans are willing and eager to concede that African Americans are superior athletically, while at the same time such genetically claimed attribute is not accorded people of African descent in any other sphere of human talent and ability. The implication may be, regardless of how subtle, that Blacks are superbly talented for certain athletic achievements but lack the intellect to excel in various other sports activities or even in such positions as quarterback in football and pitcher in baseball. Indeed, in addition to economic constraints, institutional racism in high revenue sports such as golf, hockey and tennis serves to inhibit and discourage many African Americans from participation.[80]

Few social theorists recommend that African American youth be discouraged from sports participation. Many of those who have successfully managed athletic and academic careers have made significant and enduring contributions toward the development and uplift of the Black community. Certainly, African American youth should have the option or opportunity to pursue a career in sports in addition to having access to the scientific, medical, legal, academic, technical or vocational professions. The problem is that the capitalistic ethic and profit making priorities of the sports industry have caused an inordinate number of Black athletes to be exploited at the expense of the overall betterment of the African American community. While sports have provided thousands of under privileged Blacks the opportunity to attend college, it has ruined the career chances of an equal number because of racism and through the false socialization of many Blacks into believing that athletics are their exclusive domain of ability and achievement.

Sports is not the social-equalizing and apolitical institution it is purported to be. The integration or interracial contact which is apparent from the bleachers and as seen by television viewers at home is limited mostly to the playing field. Sports has not provided for the collective upward social mobility of African Americans. There exists an interrelatedness of sports and society. Underneath the media-hype, cheering and gladiatorial atmosphere of sports events lies the social maladies of racism, discrimination and inequality which afflict the broader society.

# SOCIO-ECONOMIC STRATA OF AFRICAN AMERICANS

*Blacks and the Dialectics of Class.* Class is difficult to define in cogent and precise terms in relation to human rankings or hierarchical stratifications. The classical debate of Karl Mark and Max Weber over the economic, social or political determinants of class may not be wholly useful in analyzing the few strata which exist within the Black community. Class, like so many social terms of European origin, loses some of its generic intent when viewed from an African or Afrocentric frame of reference. Thus, culture and cultural experiences influence concepts and perspectives of class. The constant and conditional factors of

race, racism and color in the United States which affect African Americans, complicates and obscures conventional concepts of class.

Black capitalists and millionaires are not fully exempt from the denigratory status which White racism imposes upon them. On the other hand, there are certain persons and professional or occupational groups that may be rated median or high-class in the Black community who would not merit the slightest status from White society. Bart Landry's, *The New Black Middle Class,* is an excellent book which delineates and differentiates the old and new Black middle and upper class from that of White society.[81] Landry, using Whites as the standard, reveals that middle class is not the same between the two races.

However, from an Afrocentric point of view, Black social organization must not always be studied or analyzed on a comparison basis with White society. Sociological literature is replete with Black-White comparative ratios and statistics relative to the social and economic progress of both races. Since equitable Black/White integration in American society is remote and assimilation is at most a fantasy, at some point Black people must establish their own graduations of status and standards of reference. The standards and goals of African Americans may surpass Whites in some areas and in others may fall realistically below. Class, status and progress for African Americans cannot be measured or evaluated solely on the bases of White standards.[82] Economic, educational, professional or occupational achievements may be given different cultural related weights and values by Blacks in contrast to Whites. Moreover, in a racist society, class is effected by more than income, education and occupation.

One of the most comprehensive works treating the concept of class was written by Oliver C. Cox, and African American sociologist. In, *Caste, Class & Race,* Cox supported the thesis that the capitalistic virtue of individualism is the basis of social class.

The legacy of an accumulation of successes and material wealth by individuals and individual families is the ideal which the so-cial-class system is based upon. African Americans to some extent are, inevitably, in-fluenced by capitalist goals and ideology. However, what is evident in Cox's differen-tiation of social class and political class is that Blacks, in opposition to racism, collec-tively form a political class structure regard-less of social class divisions. This is paradoxi-cal to the theory that political class and social class are distinct phenomena.[83] In other words, class consolidation exists in the political struggle against White racism and oppression but ordinarily solidarity may not be characteristic of Black social classes.

Contemporary sociologist William Julius Wilson theorizes that there is increasing potential for conflict between African Ameri-can social classes because of economic differ-entials. Wilson posits that the Equal Employ-ment Opportunity acts and Affirmative Action programs resulting from the Civil Rights Movement of the 1960s created an economic gulf between those Blacks who were educated and prepared to avail them-selves of the new opportunities and those who were unprepared and unskilled and who could not. Following the 1960s there was an unprecedented rise in the numbers of African Americans holding white-collar jobs and positions that previously had been denied to them. A few millions of Blacks were em-ployed as mid-level corporate and govern-ment managers, academic and technical pro-fessionals, supervisors, clerks and salespersons with incomes ranging well above the middle-income range of $20,000. This change in the racial constituency of the labor force created a new Black economic class that were less af-fected by race and racism. Thus, Wilson enti-tled his book, *The Declining Significance of Race*.[84]

The problem in accepting Wilson's theory as wholly valid lies in the fact that the economic status or advancement of African Americans has never exempted them from the insidious and socially regressive affects of racism. Racism is responsible for the creation of the massive Black underclass and it is ra-cism which restricts their opportunity for economic elevation. Furthermore, the "economic class" of Blacks that Wilson pur-ports that is immune from racism is also re-stricted in economic ascent because of their race. Thus, the disadvantage of race or of being Black has neither been diminished nor eliminated but middle income and low in-come Blacks are affected by racism in differ-ent ways. The Black common laborer may have to endure derogatory treatment and ra-cial epithets from a White foreman and, in a relative manner, the Black corporate mid-manager or clerical assistant is racially or cul-turally ostracized and denied a much deserved promotion. The Black underclass youth may have difficulty in getting a college education and, relatively, the Black college graduate is likely to be underemployed or unemployed.

During slavery, the relative higher economic privilege and status of free Blacks and mulattoes did not diminish the factor of their race. They were not deemed or treated equal to Whites but simply functioned in a different realm of racism. Their economic class did not alter their political class or caste which is true in the case of Black-White race relations today. The socio-economic class of African Americans is less significant than their political state of existence. Blacks as a political class are viewed the same in Amer-ica regardless of their social class distinctions.

Intra-racial stratification based on color exists among African Americans to some ex-tent as a result or carry-over from miscegena-tion during slavery. Although the skin-color factor within the Black community has virtu-ally disappeared, integration re-introduced it during the late twentieth century because Whites still favor employing and relating to African Americans of mulatto or light-skinned appearance. A recent study assessing the role of skin-color differences in the Black community revealed that a small degree of the formerly widespread class stratification still exists. Lighter-skin African Americans tend to have made higher educational and occupational achievements. Yet, the study found that, "while color stratification and differences persist in the Afro-American community, they make little difference in terms of the attitudinal configuration of Afro-American society and politics."[85]

The concept of class in America probably evolved from the rank and order, post-medieval industrial revolution era of Europe and developed under the politico-economic ideology of capitalism. Under capitalism, the bases of social class are somewhat, indistinguishably, related to wealth, income, education and occupation. Because of racism in the United States, the social class of Blacks are less definable than their economic or political class. Class, from an Afrocentric perspective, must not be void of spiritual, moral and ethical values in consideration of definition. Otherwise, Blacks will continue to be oppressed by the more wealthy and educated social class.

*The Black "Middle Class".* It should be noted from the previous discussion that the term middle-class in reference to African Americans should be qualified in comparison with the same concept as it relates to White society. The vast differences in Black-White economic wealth, political power, social equity and privilege requires differential use and application of the concept of middle-class unless income is the only criteria. Even then, less than one-third of all Black households earn a middle-class income of $35,000 or more, compared with about 70 percent of all White households. Furthermore, Black families are lacking, comparatively, in capital or financial equity in terms of stock and bond holdings. A Census Bureau study in 1984

found that the median Black household net worth was less than $3,500, about one-eleventh of the White median. On the whole, African Americans have little accumulated wealth because of their late entry and still small impression in the economic mainstream of the country.[86] Even with income rivaling some of their White counter parts, the credentials and capabilities of Blacks are secondary to their race and color— often within but certainly outside of the workplace.

The segment of the African American population which Landry describes as the "new" Black middle-class started to develop after the U.S. Supreme Court's *Brown vs. Board of Education* school desegregation in 1954 and mushroomed during the 1960s. Generally, they are the first generation middle-class representing the sons and daughters of factory, farm and domestic workers of the segregation and separate-but-equal eras. Growth of the Black middle-class had begun to wane less than two decades from its inception. There is no attempt here to minimize the tremendous economic progress of African Americans since the 1960s. On the other hand to presume that parity or equity of economic opportunity and access exists would be fallacious.

In regards to the theory that race is declining as a significant factor relative to Black social and economic progress depends on one's scope and analysis of the entire race problem. Race may not be significant on an individual, case-by-case Black-White situation. Some Blacks and Whites choose not to see race as an issue based on their personal experience. Individually, African Americans have made miraculous gains in income and position in American society. But from a collective perspective, even an unlearned observer can see that the basic economic-political power imbalance between Whites and Blacks have not virtually changed since Reconstruction. If institutional racism is not a major contributing factor towards the imbalance, then social theorists have yet to offer another logical explanation.

The perception or claim that the Black middle-class is indifferent to the plight of the Black underclass is most inaccurate. Historically, it has been the Black economically and politically advantaged who have been at the forefront in petitioning and protesting for the uplift of the Black masses. Although notable betrayals and divisions between Blacks during slavery have been recorded, in most of the insurrection attempts there was cooperation between the free Black and the slave. The Civil Rights Movement of the twentieth century is a prime example of solidarity between all African American social strata for the purpose of achieving freedom, justice and equality.

The Black middle-class is a dynamic socially mobile group striving to lift itself out of the depths of historical oppression and poverty. Beyond economic aspirations and accumulations, the Black middle-class is differentiated from the lower class by a pattern of behavior expressed in stable family and social organizational relationships. This segment of the Black community is concerned with "front" and "respectability," and has a drive for "getting ahead."[87] The contemporary Black middle-class is marked more by their social and civic responsibility, especially, in relation to the advancement of the race. Since the late 1960s, a growing number of the members of the Black middle-class are reviving and reveling in their African history and culture along with many Black Cultural Nationalists who are widely represented in the lower income groups. Generally, it is conceded that Black politico-historical commonality and survival are paramount to socioeconomic divisions.

**The Black Poor and Underclass.** It is the custom to refer to those people who are economically disadvantaged and impoverished

as the low-class. The term low-class connotes more than economic destitution, it also implies social deviance or moral corruption. Therefore, it must be emphasized that in spite of popular conception, Blacks who are positioned at the bottom of the economic ladder are not necessarily moral degenerates or criminals. Consistent with the prevailing racist ethos of the country, low character, low morals, low intelligence, crime proneness, drugs, shiftlessness, laziness and lack of ambition are traits which are generally ascribed to the Black poor. Low income does not automatically make one a criminal or a social deviant. If it is concluded that poor and low-income persons are inevitably prone to vice and criminality, then sociologists may find it difficult to explain the large number of white-collar crimes, drug enterprising activities, and moral corruption increasingly associated with wealthy people, high-income corporate officials, and the socially prominent.

In recent years, there has been an attempt made to further stratify the Black poor who are commonly categorized as members of the lower class. A sub-stratum of the low-class has been termed the "underclass" by some contemporary social theorists. Although Gunnar Myrdal is credited for having alluded to the term in the 1960s, it increased in popular usage with the publication of *The Black Underclass* by Douglas G. Glasgow. Glasgow describes the underclass as the hundreds of thousands of destitute Black men and women confined in economic poverty and social decay, who are unskilled, jobless and detached from the mainstream of society primarily because of institutional racism. In Glasgow's opinion, the underclass is distinguished from the lower class basically by its lack of social mobility.[88]

Wilson asserts that the Black lower class is a heterogeneous grouping and that the underclass is a more impoverished segment of the lower class. Underclass Black families are likely to be headed by females and the community is marked by large numbers of "adult males with no fixed address—who live mainly on the streets, roaming from one place of shelter to another."[89] Some social theorists apply the concept of underclass to all American poor or disadvantaged ethnic groups. However, Garry L. Rolison argues that underclass means more than just being poor and that, furthermore in America, it is based more on racial rather than ethnic identification. Simply poor ethnic groups possess the potential for assimilation into the dominant society. The physical difference of racial groups such as Blacks are immutable and, thus, prohibits their attainment of dominant-group membership. Consequently, Rolison defines the underclass as

> . . . that subgroup of the propertyless engaged in capitalist social relations who are denied the exchange of their labor power as an interactive function of their subordinate class position and racial membership. As a result, members of the underclass are simultaneously underemployed and tend to belong to an unprivileged racial group.[90]

Whether one agrees with Rolison's contention or not there are sharp differences in the social affects and outcomes of ethnic versus race discrimination. Ethnic groups have entered the society and have become a part of the mainstream with comparative minimal difficulty while African Americans as a whole remain economically differentiated and socially unassimilated.

The Black underclass are found mostly in impoverished and physically deteriorating urban areas. They represent a highly disproportionate number of the nation's school dropouts, welfare recipients, drug abusers, juvenile delinquents, and adult crime. These are not inherent behavioral characteristics, but because of their social and economic environment and circumstance they are forced to endure a life of hopelessness, despair and moral decay. The plight of the Black urban

underclass is worsened or compounded because of the flight of White city-dwellers and entrepreneurs to the suburbs, thus, taking with them the tax base needed to maintain the metropolis. Wilson is correct when he points out that it is not only the flight of Whites but that it is the attendant exodus of middle-class and working low-income Blacks from the cities which negatively affects the plight of the underclass. The underclass is left without role models and with weakened social institutions such as churches, schools and other social organizations when middle-class and working Blacks leave the community pursuing Whites for jobs in the suburbs.[91]

The major distinguishing characteristic of lower class Blacks and the underclass is that of social mobility. For lower class Blacks, poverty may be a transitory condition. But the underclass is locked into a situation where they lack adequate schooling, skills and training to obtain meaningful and long-term employment. Unemployed and socially isolated, Black youth develop and adopt illegitimate economic means of subsistence and survival. They may rely on drugs as a livelihood or as an escape from harsh reality.

In spite of the conditions of the ghetto or the underclass community, according to the 1990 Census the birth rate and fertility of Blacks is somewhat greater than that of Whites. A significant part of the underclass community exists on welfare and on Aid to Families with Dependent Children (AFDC). This fact alone has caused white politicians and legislators to reduce welfare payments and to deny cities the needed federal program to fight poverty in the Black community. Yet, billions of both Black and White tax dollars are expended for the support of the awesome and wasteful military defense budget.

Robert Blauner and other social theorists have described the communities of the lower class and underclass Blacks as being analogous to colonies under a colonial system of oppression and exploitation. Ghetto residents have little or no power to improve their economic lot. They exist as a cheap source of labor and nearly all of the economic institutions in their communities are owned and controlled by Whites outside the ghetto. Blacks are kept in a state of dependency and subject to the deliberate suppression by the white power structure including its law enforcement and judicial agencies. Although colonialism is defined as one country having economic and political dominance over another foreign nation, the term "internal" or "domestic colonialism" has been used to describe the African America experience in the United States. The ghetto is simply a domestic colony rendered powerless under capitalist exploitation and racist ideology and controlled by powers external to itself.[92]

## DEVIANCE, RACISM, LAW, JUSTICE AND AFRICAN AMERICANS

*Sociological Approaches to Black Deviance: A Critique.* This discussion of crime, delinquency, law and justice in relation to Black people in America is based partly upon the domestic colonialism model mentioned above by Robert Blauner. However, in function, the classical treatise of Frantz Fanon and the contemporary analogy of Robert Staples are more germane to the understanding of the nexus of race, racism, crime, law and justice in the United States.[93] In addition to these writers, numerous African American scholars have subscribed to the colonial analogy in explanation of much of Black social disorder, crime and delinquency in urban America.

Deviance in sociological theory means the violation of societal order or a behavior that is contrary to established norms. Acts or behaviors such as theft, murder, burglary, rape and arson are considered as deviant by universal human standards. But deviance can be construed to mean difference in the way one dresses or wears one's hair, speaks, walks or manifest one's culture providing these behaviors are contrary to the norms of the dominant society. When Europeans began their exploitation of Africa during the sixteenth century they perceived Black Africans to be different and conveniently labelled them as deviant because they defied in appearance, conduct and culture the European standard of human order. Slaves were perceived by whites as deviant simply because of their race, culture and subjugated status. Thus, an entire people can be labelled and treated as a deviant class.

Classical and neo-classical Euro-American sociologists have attempted to "scientifically" study the incidence of group or class deviance in terms of value and culture conflicts based upon socio-psychological differentiations and attributes. The colonial model for viewing deviance diminishes the importance of social and psychological analyses and interposes politics and economics as the primary causative factors of social disorder in the Black community. Social psychology is more relevant when focus is reversed from Blacks, the oppressed deviants, and redirected towards the normative oppressive standards of Whites.

The term racism, as an ascriptive variable in functionalist and value conflict theories, is conspicuously absent from Euro-American sociological literature. Yet, the writings of Black social theorists are replete with terms and concepts of race and racism. Racism is more than a sociological phenomenon, it is a political means of class domination and social control. Therefore, the colonial analogy for studying deviance correlates the political order and politico-economic objectives of the dominant White society with Black deviance and social disorder. In other words, the politics and economics of racism is both causally and conditionally related to much of Black deviance and social disorder. The dominant political order through statues and constitutional edicts, discriminatory economic policy and institutional racism fosters the social disorganization of Blacks so that it may legally, judicially and forcefully exert social control and dominance.

Euro-American traditional sociology is inordinately purposed for the study and analysis of the racial-ethnic, foreign born and, particularly, the poor rural and urban Blacks in the United States. These groups are forced to live in social isolation or segregation in colonies which serve the political, economic and even psychological interests of the dominant society. Under conditions of poverty, unemployment, educational deprivation and/or environmental congestion caused by institutional racism—delinquency, vice and crime inevitably develops within the colony. Applying the theory of Social Darwinism to the situation, the domestically colonized are ascribed as socially pathological. Their morals and values are ruled to be in conflict with the interests of the dominant society.

Thus, the "natives" of the colony are determined as unfit and undeserving of concern or for governmental policies directed toward alleviating their inopportune plight. Although Frantz Fanon was speaking of conventional colonialism as it related to the Third World, his perception of how the settler (oppressor) views the values and morals of the natives (the oppressed class) is relevant to the internal or domestic colonial analogy:

It is not enough for the settler to delimit physically, that is to say with the help of the army and the police force, the place of the native. As if to show the totalitarian character of colonial exploitation the settler paints the native as a sort of quintessence of evil. Native society is not simply described as a society lacking in values. It is not enough for the colonist to affirm that those values have disappeared from, or still better never existed in, the colonial world. The native is declared insensible to ethics; he represents not only the absence of values,

but also the negation of values. He is, let us dare to admit, the enemy of values, and in this sense he is the absolute evil.[94]

Poverty induced and racist influenced dysfunctional behaviors, values and morals of the domestic colony have led to the scientific stereotyping of Blacks as a deviant race or class. Sociological and psychological theories are used to explain race inspired social phenomena which are, to a great extent, politically and economically caused and promoted by the dominant society.

Robert Staples states that "race is a political identity because it defines the way in which an individual is to be treated by the political state and the conditions of one's oppression . . . thus what is "good or "bad," "criminal" or "legitimate" behavior is always defined in terms favorable to the ruling class."[95] From the news media and from White law-and-order politicians, one cannot help but form the opinion that African Americans are the major cause and perpetrators of crime in the United States. Blacks appear to be the most criminally prone because of the definition given to criminal acts, decision as to the magnitude of punishment, and importance accorded to various crimes as determined by the dominant white society. Statistics report only the number of criminal offenders which are arrested, prosecuted or incarcerated. They do not show the thousands of other cases, mostly non-Black, where no arrests were made and the thousands of other instances where convictions were overturned because of the race, prominence and wealth of the defendant.[96]

While statistics show that Blacks commit a higher disproportionate rate of homicide, robbery, assault, retail drug and other street crimes, less attention is given and few statistics are available on multi-million dollar white-collar and governmental crimes perpetrated mostly by middle-class and upper-class white individuals. For instance, billions of dollars are criminally gained or lost annually as a result of white-collar crimes occurring in the financial and governmental sectors of the economy. The impact of these crimes affect all tax-payers and will effect the economic condition of future generations.[97] Blacks are hardly ever involved in the billion-dollar import and export wholesale drug trade, gang-land killings, extortion and other vice activities of the organized crime world. Nevertheless, historical focus has been away from these highly profitable crimes which whites dominate. In fact, these types of crimes are glamorized and often made into movies for further profit.

In applying traditional sociological paradigms to the study of Black deviance, one must recognize that such approaches are fully intended to protect and not reflect upon the fundamental interests of those in power. The colonial model posits that there exists definite relationships between race, racism and crime in the Black community. It further postulates that Black social, cultural and psychological characteristics are less relevant as causes of deviance or crime in the urban ghetto than the deleterious affects of White political oppression and economic exploitation.[98]

*Blacks and the Law Enforcement and Justice Systems.* The historical and constant revelation has been that African Americans constitute from 40 to 50 percent of the men and women incarcerated in state and federal prisons in the United States. The significance of this percentage of the inmate population is that in 1988, Blacks represented only 12.3 percent of the nation's population. African Americans accounted for more than three-million of over seven-million persons that were arrested in 1987. Of this figure, more than half were arrested for murder and rape. The homicide rate among Black males is disproportionately higher than the national average. In major metropolitan areas, Blacks are more likely to be involved in almost 50 percent of the arrests related to narcotics. These figures relating to Blacks the justice system and various crimes are compiled annually by the U.S. Bureau of Justice Statistics and other state and municipal police and crime agencies. Offhand, the conclusion that one may draw from this data is that Blacks commit almost 50 percent of the crime in America based upon arrest and imprisonment rates.

In no way are all the crimes committed in the nation limited to those few common categories of which official records are maintained. The crimes which are customarily recorded or reported are those committed by persons of certain lower socio-economic strata of which Blacks and a few other racial-ethnic minority groups are highly represented. Street crimes and crimes of passion or emotion such as murder, homicide, assault, burglary, rape and controlled substance selling or dealing are the few types of felonies which are widely acknowledged as crimes against society. Besides the myriad of white-collar crimes perpetrated each year, more than a hundred others such as kidnapping, felonious impersonation, perverted sex felonies, white slavery, blackmail, counterfeiting, sabotage, forgery, treason, and assassination are not included in national crime statistics. These crimes are less likely to be committed by African Americans.

Law enforcement, arrests, prosecutions and convictions are within the discretionary powers of the ruling class. If one is White, wealthy, prominent or politically influential the possibility of being arrested, convicted and incarcerated for a serious crime is slight. Most studies seem to support the thesis that race and class are determining factors in judicial dispositions and court sentencing. However, a few other research findings are not as conclusive. In the case of juvenile offenders, Robert Perry questions the methodology of the studies which reject the notion of a race and class bias in judicial dispositions.[99] A study conducted in 1986 by two University of

Washington sociologists, Robert Crutchfield and George Bridges found that Blacks are nine times more likely than whites to go to prison in the state of Washington and are jailed eleven times as often as whites in the state of Idaho. The authors of the study wrote, "It is safe to conclude that race is a factor in legal decisions, and minorities receive substantially different treatment than whites throughout the legal process."[100] Joan Petersilia concluded in a study that "blacks and Hispanics are less likely to be given probation, more likely to receive prison sentences, more likely to receive longer sentences, and more likely to serve longer time."[101]

Ever since slavery, the law enforcement and judicial systems have seldom been the vigilant protector or legal benefactor of African Americans. The discretionary powers of the police and the judicial edicts of the courts have generally favored Whites in cases where both Blacks and Whites were involved. In the dispensation of capital punishment, Blacks are more than three times as likely to receive the death penalty than Whites. Blacks comprise 12.3 percent of the population but of the 1,901 persons on death row in 1987, over 40 percent were African Americans. The political orientation of the court system is reflected in the racially biased nature of its sentencing. Black defendants charged with killing Whites are 4.3 times as likely to receive the death penalty as White defendants charged with killing Blacks. Black defendants charged with killing Whites are sentenced to death seven times more often than Whites who kill Blacks. Race is consistently a factor in criminal processing.[102]

The police have maintained a 400 year old tradition of repression and violence among African Americans. Their chief function is to protect the property and rights of the dominant society and to suppress individual or group rebellions against oppression in the Black community. Rather than to provide service and protection to the African American community, the police function primarily to protect the White community from Blacks. They are the gendarmes of the functionalist ideology of social control and law-and-order in relation to racial-ethnic minorities in the United States. Few, if any, African Americans would disagree with this assessment.

The police, as a law enforcement institution, has a reputation for disregarding the human and constitutional rights of Black citizens and denying them of equitable process under the law. During the height of the Civil Rights Movement between 1950 and 1973, more than 6000 people were killed by the police—45 percent were Black. For every White person killed by the police, 22 Blacks are killed. There are more than 40,000 police departments in the nation with over a million officers. Less than 20 percent of all police persons are Black. Police are entrusted with an awesome amount of power and legalized discretion of life and death over people they may suspect or pursue. Many are inadequately educated and prepared to render the kind of professional and social services necessary to foster good relations between diverse groups in a racially antagonistic society.[103]

Overt racism has declined in recent years because of Black community vigilance and legal protests. Studies have shown that a significant reduction in police brutality occurs in cities having Black mayors and city managers, but still the problem continues.

# · QUESTIONS AND EXERCISES ·

1. What are the major contentions some Black social theorists maintain of traditional Eurocentric sociology? Discuss the concept of Black sociology.

2. While some Euro-American scholars tend to minimize the importance of race, color and culture definitions, why do these factors persist as major social problems in American society?

3. Conceding that the culture, racial status and experience of Blacks are different from that of Whites, should the same research paradigms and evaluative criteria be applied to both races?

4. State the difference in the meanings of desegregation and integration. Apply Milton M. Gordon's assimilation variables to these two concepts of race relations.

5. Critique Daniel P. Moynihan's study *The Negro Family: The Case for National Action* in relation to the counter-arguments it provoked among Black social theorists.

6. Discuss and compare perceived differences in the early socialization of Black males and females with those of White males and females.

7. Why are Blacks portrayed in the media as the major drug traffickers and users when statistics show that Whites are the principal importers, entrepreneurs and abusers of drugs?

8. Why has the Black church historically served as the most constructive social institution of African Americans?

9. Write a substantive paper analyzing and critiquing the concepts of **race, culture, color** and **class.**

# · NOTES AND REFERENCES ·

1. Peter L. Berger and Brigitte Berger, *Sociology* (New York: Basic Books, Inc. 1972) 21–22.

2. See Ruth A. Wallace and Alison Wolf, *Contemporary Sociological Theory* (Englewood Cliffs NJ: Prentice Hall 1991) 18–25, 140 and Max Weber, *Basic Concepts in Sociology.* Translated by H.P. Secher (Westport CT: Greenwood Press 1976)

3. Butler A. Jones, "The Tradition of Sociology Teaching in Black Colleges," in *Black Sociologists,* ed. by James E. Blackwell and Morris Janowitz (Chicago: The Univeristy of Chicago Press 1974). 122–123.

4. See Rhett S. Jones, "Black Sociology: 1890–1917," *Black Academy Review* (Winter 1971) vols. 2, nos. 1–4. pp. 43–67.

5. Dona Richards, "The Ideology of European Dominance," *The Western Journal of Black Studies* (Winter 1979) v.3/4. 244.

6. Otto Klineberg, *Race Differences* (New York: Harper & Brothers Publishers 1935) p.18.

7. See Ruth Benedict, *Race: Science and Politics* (New York: The Viking Press 1945) 22–38.

8. Robert B. Hill, "Economic Forces, Structural Discrimination and Black Family Instability," in *Black Families* edited by Harold E. Cheatham and James B. Stewart (New Brunswick: Transaction Publishers 1990) p. 89.

9. Benedict, *Race: Science and Politics*, p. 26.

10. See St. Clair Drake, *Black Folk Here and There* (Los Angeles: Center for Afro American Studies, University of California 1990) Vol. 2, 1–76.

11. Frances Cress Welsing, "The Cress Theory of Color-Confrontation," *The Black Scholar* (May 1974) p. 38.

12. For further study of the history and problems of mulatto Africans see "White by Day . . . Negro by Night," *Ebony* (November 1975) 80–83. and Alvin F. Poussaint, "The Problems of Light-Skinned Blacks," *Ebony* (February 1975) 85–91.

13. Jerry D. Rose, *Introduction to Sociology* (Chicago: Rand McNally College Publishing Co. 1980) 74–75.

14. Amuzie Chimezie, "Theories of Black Culture," *The Western Journal of Black Studies* (Winter 1983) vol. 7(4). 218–219.

15. Caroline Torrance, "Blacks and the American Ethos: A Reevaluation of Existing Theories," *Journal of Black Studies* (September 1990) Vol. 21(1) 82–83.

16. A. Abdel-Daim, "The Dialectics ot Culture: Arab and American Relations," *The Western Journal of Black Studies* (Spring 1979) Vol. 3(1). p. 3.

17. Milton M. Gordon, *Assimilation in American Life* (New York: Oxford University Press 1964) p. 71.

18. Ronald W. Walters, "Toward a Definition of Black Social Science," in *The Death of White Sociology*, ed. by Joyce A. Ladner (New York: Vintage Books 1973) p. 197.

19. Robert Staples' perspectives on Black sociology were obtained through an exchange of letters and telephone conversations. Also see Robert Staples, *Introduction to Black Sociology* (New York: McGraw Hill 1976).

20. See Terry Kershaw, "The Emerging Paradigm in Black Studies," *The Western Journal of Black Studies* (Spring 1989) v. 13(1), 45–51.

21. Daniel C. Thompson, *Sociology of the Black Experience* (Westport CT: Greenwood Press 1974) 79–80.

22. Dennis Forsythe, "Radical Sociology and Blacks," in *The Death of White Sociology*, ed. by Joyce A. Ladner (New York: Vintage Books 1973) p. 233.

23. W.E.B. DuBoise, Carter G. Woodson, Melville Herskovits and John W. Blassingame are among those who write of the African continuities evident in African American family life. These authors are referenced variously in this book.

24. For an in depth study of the African family see, Niara Sudarkasa, "African and Afro-American Family Structure: A Comparison," *The Black Scholar* (November/December 1980) 37–60; and Cheikh Anta Diop, *The Cultural Unity of Black Africa* (Chicago: Third World Press 1978).

25. See John W. Blassingame, *The Slave Community* (New York: Oxford University Press 1979) 149–191; and Herbert G. Gutman, *The Black Family in Slavery and Freedom 1750–1925* (Vintage Books 1977) 3–44.

26. See Daniel P. Moynihan, "The Negro Family: The Case for National Action," (Washington, D.C.: U.S. Department of Labor 1965)

27. Rutledge M. Dennis, "Theories of the Black Family: The Weak-Family and Strong-Family Schools as Competing Ideologies," *The Journal of Afro-American Issues* (Summer/Fall 1976) 315–328.

28. See Andrew Billingsley, *Black Families in White America* (Englewood Cliffs NJ: Prentice-Hall 1968); Robert B. Hill, *The Strength of Black Families* (New York: Emerson Hall

Publishers 1972); and Robert Staples, *Introduction to Black Sociology* (New York: McGraw-Hill 1976).

29. See Nathan Hare, "What Black Intellectuals Misunderstood About the Black Family," *Black World* (March 5–14.

30. Margaret B. Wilkerson and Jewell H. Gresham, "The Racialization of Poverty," *The Nation* (July 24/31, 1989) 126–132.

31. U.S. Department of Commerce, Bureau of the Census. *The Black Population in the United States 1990 and 1989.* Series P-20, No. 448.

32. Statistics cited from William P. O'Hare et al., "African Americans in the 1990s," *Population Bulletin,* Vol. 46, No. 1 (Washington, D.C.: Population Reference Bureau, Inc. July 1991).

33. See Jewelle T. Gibbs, "Developing Intervention Models for Black Families: Linking Theory and Research," in *Black Families,* edited by Harold E. Cheatham & James B. Stewart (New Brunswick: Transaction Publishers 1990). 330–331.

34. Cover Story, "The Black Middle Class," *Business Week* (March 14, 1988) 62–70.

35. Synopsis of the study of Robert B. Hill, "A Positive Look at Black Families," *Manpower* (January 1972) 24–27.

36. Reynolds Farley, "Trends in Marital Status Among Negroes," in *The Family Life of Black People,* edited by Charles V. Willie (Columbus OH: Merrill Publishing Co. 1970) 172–183.

37. Robert B. Hill, "Economic Forces, Structural Discrimination and Black Family Instability," in *Black Families,* edited by Harold E. Cheatham & James B. Stewart (New Brunswick: Transaction Publishers 1990) 87–105.

38. See Odell Uzzell and Wilma Peebles-Wilkins, "Black Spouse Abuse: A Focus on Relational Factors and Intervention Strategies," *The Western Journal of Black Studies*

(Spring 1989). 13(1) and Gloria Jones Johnson, "Underemployment, Underpayment, and Psychosocial Stress Among Working Black men," *The Western Journal of Black Studies,* (Summer 1989). 13(2).

39. Blassingame, *The Slave Community,* 149–191, and Kenneth M. Stampp, *The Peculiar Institution* (New York: Vintage Books 1956).

40. Ibid.

41. See Clyde W. Franklin, "Black Male-White Male Perceptual Conflict," *The Western Journal of Black Studies* (Spring 1982) v. 6(1). 2–9.

42. See Clyde W. Franklin, "Black Male-White Male Perceptual Conflict," *The Western Journal of Black Studies* (Spring 1982) v.6(1). 2–9.

43. K. Sue Jewell, "Black Male/Female Conflict: Internalization of Negative Definitions Transmitted through Imagery," *The Western Journal of Black Studies* (Spring 1983) v. 7(1). 43–55.

44. See Michele Wallace, *Black Macho and the Myth of the Superwoman* (New York: The Dial Press 1978) 3–33.

45. Diop, *The Cultural Unity of Africa,* p. 14.

46. Shirley J. Hatchett and Alida D. Quick, "Correlates of Sex Role Attitudes Among Black Men and Women: Data from a National Survey of Black Americans," *Urban Research Review,* Howard University Institute for Urban Affairs and Research, 1983. Vol. 9, No. 2.

47. Nathan Hare and Julia Hare, *The Endangered Black Family* (San Francisco: Black Think Tank 1984) p. 25.

48. See Clarence Spigner, "Black/White Interracial Marriages: A Brief Overview of U.S. Census Data, 1980–1987," *The Western Journal of Black Studies* (Winter 1990) v. 14(4) 214–216.

49. Ibid., p. 214.

50. See Delores P. Aldridge, "Interracial Marriages: Theoretical Considerations," *Journal of Black Studies*, (March 1978) v. 8(3).

51. For an empirical investigation of Black/White dating and sexual contacts see Robert Staples, *The World of Black Singles* (Westport CT: Greenwood Press 1981) 137–163.

52. Maulana Karenga, *Introduction to Black Studies* (Inglewood CA: Kawaida Publications 1982) p. 218.

53. Jewelle Taylor Gibbs, "Called Anything But a Child of God," *Focus*, Joint Center for Political and Economic Studies (December 1991) v. 19(12).

54. See John S. Mbiti, *African Religious and Philosophy* (Garden City NY: Anchor Books 1970).

55. E. Franklin Frazier, *The Negro Church in American* (New York: Schocken Books 1966, 1964) 1–19.

56. Gayraud Wilmore, Jr., "The Case for a New Church Style," in *The Black Experience in Religion*, edited by C. Eric Lincoln (New York: Anchor Books 1974) 34–44.

57. Gayraud S. Wilmore and James H. Cone, *Black Theology* (Maryknoll NY: Orbis Books 1979) p. 241.

58. See Melville J. Herskovits, *The Myth of the Negro Past* (Boston: Beacon Press 1958) 207–260.

59. Portia K. Maultsby, "The Use and Performance of Hymnody, Spirituals, and Gospels in the Black Church," *The Western Journal of Black Studies* (Fall 1983) v. 7(3) p. 164.

60. See Portia K. Maultsby, "Influences and Retentions of West African Musical Concepts in U.S. Black Music," *The Western Journal of Black Studies* (Fall 1979) v.3(3). 197–212.

61. Wilmore and Cone, *Black Theology*, p. 18.

62. James H. Cone, *For My People* (Maryknoll, NY: (Orbis Books 1991) p. 18.

63. Ibid., p. 53.

64. See Gil B. Lloyd, "The Black Church and Economic Development," *The Western Journal of Black Studies* (December 1977) v. 1(4) 273.

65. W.E.B. DuBois, *The Souls of Black Folk* (New York: The New American Library 1969) p. 213.

66. See Sylvia M. Jacobs, The African Nexus (Westport CT: Greenwood Press 1981).

67. See Kenneth B. Clark, "Desegregation: The Role of the Social Sciences," *Teachers College Record*, (October 1960) 16–17.

68. Cited from, *The Adams Report: A Desegregation Update*, Institute for Services to Education, Inc., Washington, D.C. (September 1978) p. 3.

69. Winifred O. Stone, "The Black Student on the Predominantly White Campus," *Journal of Afro-American Issues* (Winter 1977) v.5(1) 4–18.

70. Gerald D. Jones and Robin M. Williams, Jr., eds. *A Common Destiny* (Washington, D.C.: National Academy Press 1989) 337–344.

71. Ibid., p. 345.

72. Carter G. Woodson, *Mis-education of the Negro* (Washington, D.C.: The Associated Publishers, Inc. 1933) p. 32.

73. For a historical account of predominantly Black colleges see, Alton Hornsby, Jr., "Historical Overview of Black Colleges," *The Western Journal of Black Studies* (Fall 1978) v. 2(3) 162–166.

74. Tony Brown, "You Owe Your Children a Black College," *The Black Collegian* (August/September 1980) 36–37.

75. Jones and Williams, *A Common Destiny*, 345–346.

76. Harry A. Ploski and James Williams, eds., *The Negro Almanac* (New York: John Wiley & Sons 1983) 905–922.

77. See Harry Edwards, "The Black Athletes: 20th Century Gladiators for White America," *Psychology Today*, (November 1973) 43–52, also, Harry Edwards, "On the Issue of Race in Contemporary American Sports," *The Western Journal of Black Studies*, (Fall 1982) v. 6.(3). 138–147.

78. See Earl Smith, "The Genetically Superior Athlete: Myth or Reality," in *Black Studies: Theory, Method and Cultural Perspectives*, edited by Talmadge Anderson (Pullman, WA: Washington State University Press 1990) 120–131.

79. Gary A. Sailes, "A Socioeconomic Explanation of Black Sports Participation Patterns," *The Western Journal of Black Studies* (Winter 1987) v. 11(4) 164–167.

80. Edwards, "On the Issue of Race in Contemporary American Sports," p. 141.

81. Bart Landry, *The New Black Middle Class* (Berkeley: The University of California Press 1987).

82. Ibid., Landry's book validates the distinctiveness of Black and White class structures through comparison.

83. See Oliver C. Cox, *Caste, Class & Race* (New York: Doubleday & Co. 1948. Reprint, Modern Reader 1970) 148–150, 154–162.

84. William Julius Wilson, *The Declining Significance of Race*, 2nd ed. (Chicago: The University of Chicago Press 1978, 1980) 19–23, 120–121.

85. Richard Seltzer and Robert C. Smith, "Color Differences in the Afro-American Community and the Differences they Make," *Journal of Black Studies* (March 1991 v. 21(3). 284–285.

86. See "The Black Middle Class," *Business Week* (March 14, 1988) 62–70, and "Between Two Worlds," *Time* (March 13, 1989) p. 58.

87. Although some of the characteristics have been transformed since the 1960s, for an excellent study of the Black middle-class

see, St. Clair Drake and Horace R. Cayton, *Black Metropolis*, II (New York: Harper Torchbooks 1962) 658–715.

88. Douglas G. Glasgow, *The Black Underclass* (San Francisco: Jossey-Bass, Inc. Publishers 1980. Reprint. Vintage Books 1981) vii–ix, 7–11.

89. Wilson, *The Declining Significance of Race*, pp. 158–157.

90. Garry L. Rolison, "An Exploration of the Term Underclass as it Relates to African-Americans," *Journal of Black Studies* (March 1991) v. 21(3), 296–297.

91. See William J. Wilson, "The Ghetto Underclass and the Social Transformation of the Inner City," *The Black Scholar* (May/June 1988) v. 19(3) p. 13. Also, "The American Underclass," *Time*, August 29, 1977. 14–27.

92. See Robert Blauner, "Internal Colonialism and Ghetto Revolt," *Social Problems*, v. 16, 393–408.

93. See Frantz Fanon, *Wretched of the Earth* (New York: Grove Press, Inc. 1963) 249–310; and Robert Staples, "White Racism, Black Crime, and American Justice: An Application of the Colonial Model to Explain Crime and Race," *Phylon* (June 1975) v. 36(2). 14–22.

94. Fanon, *The Wretched of the Earth*, p. 41.

95. Staples, "White Racism, Black Crime, and American Justice: An Application of the Colonial Model to Explain Crime and Race," p. 14.

96. See Patrick C. Coggins, "Status of Crime Among Black American Men: Current Status, Causal Factors, Prevention and Treatment Strategies," *Journal of Research on Minority Affairs*, v. 1(1) 76–89.

97. For example note the multi-million dollar savings & loan bank frauds, insider trading, junk bond manipulations and illicit leverage buy-out schemes and crimes of the 1980s and early 1990s.

98. Staples, *Introduction to Black Sociology*, 240–241.

99. See Robert Perry, "Differential Dispositions of Black and White Juveniles: A Critical Assessment of Methodology," *The Western Journal of Black Studies* (Winter 1985) v. 9(4). 189–197.

100. Lonnie Rosenwald, "Minorities More Likely to Go to Jail," *Spokane Chronicle*, Monday, 17 Feb. 1986.

101. Joan Petersilia, "Racial Disparities in the Criminal Justice System: Executive Summary of Rand Institute, 1983," in *The Criminal Justice System and Blacks*, edited by Daniel Georges-Abeyie (New York: Clark Boardman Co. Ltd. 1984) 241.

102. See E. Yvonne Moss, et al., "African Americans and the Administration of Justice," *Trotter Institute Review* (Fall 1991) v. 5(3) 6–10.

103. Compare H. Bruce Pierce, "Towards Police Brutality Reduction," *The Black Scholar* (May/June 1980) v. 17(3) 49–52 and Damu Smith, "The Upsurge of Police Repression," *The Black Scholar* (Jan–Feb 1981) v. 12(1) 35–55.

# Chapter 5

# Black Psychology and Psychological Concepts

## AMERICAN AND AFRICAN AMERICAN PSYCHOLOGY

*A Synopsis of Psychology and Race.* There is an inevitable link between psychology and race in any situation where peoples of distinct cultures and races attempt to relate, interact or interpret the behaviors of each other. Indeed, psychology is the study or process of assessing human behavior and mental acts. Race, culture and class often serve as correlative variants. Like sociology, American psychology developed from the classical European thought and philosophy of the eighteenth and nineteenth centuries. Some of the early philosophical contributors to modern psychology include Wilhelm Wundt, Hermann Ebbinhaus, Carl Stumpf and Sigmund Freud of Germany; William McDougall, Francis Galton, British; and Edward B. Titchener, British/American. The field was heavily influenced by Germans. However, the philosophies and race implications of British Charles Darwin, Francis Galton and Herbert Spencer are particularly significant relative to Black or African peoples. Thus, White American psychology is European race-specific in terms of its philosophical origin and behavioral foundation. It may not be always wholly relevant or applicable in the analysis or treatment of Blacks or African Americans.

A review of much of the introductory literature will reveal that psychology is defined in many ways depending, mostly, on the method of approach or the orientation of its many branches of study. Since psychology deals with the infiniteness of the human mind and behavior, it is characterized by much divisiveness and theoretical fragmentation.[1]

Euro-American psychology has a close historical relationship with the field of anthropology which is one of the reasons that much of the early study was focused on the physical and cultural characteristics of the nonWhite or so-called nonliterate races of mankind. Physical or anatomical differences in the cranial capacity of the skull was once used to determine the extent of civilization or intelligence of a people. During the early twentieth century, American psychologists took particular interest in conducting tests designed to differentiate between whites and the intelligence of "primitive" people, Blacks, certain Asian groups, Native Americans and Pygmies.[2] Building upon the "survival of the fittest" philosophy of Charles Darwin; the social Darwinist concepts of Herbert Spencer; and the race-difference implications and the eugenics concepts of Francis Galton—James M. Cattell, an American functionalist psychologist, developed and nurtured the idea of mental testing and measurements. American psychology seems to have been influenced more by philosophers and psychologists in the vein of Darwin and Galton than by Wundt.[3]

Historically, a significant number of White American psychologists or behavioral scientists have taken an interest in race research related to Black people. Even during the mid-twentieth century, it was implicitly and explicitly argued in some studies that Blacks were mentally and intellectually inferior. These studies were based upon flawed culturally-biased methodology and white supremacist models and served to fuel the racial antagonism which ensued after the 1954 school desegregation decision by the U.S. Supreme Court.

The genetic and heredity theory of Black intellectual inferiority was revived by Arthur R. Jensen in an article which appeared in the *Harvard Educational Review* in 1969. Prior to Jensen's "IQ and Scholastic Achievement" thesis, A. Kardiner and L. Ovesey's psychiatric study of Blacks had suggested that historical racism, environmental influences and dysfunctional compensatory behavior rather than heredity accounted for Black intellectual deficiency.[4] The perceived mental deficiency of African Americans were disquieting, but not as much as the fact that the findings were made by White behavioral theorists and were racially biased. Invariably, such studies were based on White middle-class cultural norms. Blacks or Africans have been constantly scrutinized and studied by European people who have historically debased and "scientifically" adjudged them to be intellectually inferior.

While Europe is accepted as the natural continuum and foundation of White culture and behavioral patterns, Africa is usually dismissed by White behavioral theorists as being irrelevant to the psyche and behavior of Black Americans. The colonial and anthropological approaches of traditional psychology toward the study of African Americans amount to a form of scientific racism and are being challenged by an increasing number of contemporary Black psychologists. Unless one accepts the theory of a uniform universal race and culture, then psychology has to be, to a great extent, race-culture specific. The psychological research done and results obtained by Black behavioral scientists have already proven to be quite different in approach and concept to that practiced by outsiders to the Black or African American experience.[5]

The conception of race is psychological. Racism is indicative of a psychopathic personality or a mental disorder. Race is ingrained in the social fabric of American society. Race is a constant social issue which affects the subconscious and unconscious thoughts of Blacks and Whites whenever and wherever the two races interact or relate. Because of race and racism, many African Americans either consciously or subconsciously experience self-alienation, a sense of powerlessness, social isolation, cultural obfuscation and hopelessness. On the other hand, the following statement by Frances Cress

Welsing may describe the White conscious or subconscious in relation to race:

> All major and minor behavior-energy crystallization or behavior-units in the global white collective—no matter how simple or complex, old or new, short-or long-lived must conform, in the final analysis, to the basic behavior-energy equation of white over non-white (or white power over non-white powerlessness).[6]

White supremacy and race-awareness are significant psychological factors in the genetic survival of the white race regardless of whether they are consciously or subconsciousness manifested. This is so because Whites constitute a world numerical racial minority in comparison to Black, Brown, red and yellow peoples. The (Cress) Welsing Theory holds that white racism is a motivational psychological state. The numerical and "color inadequacy of whiteness necessitates a social structure based on white superiority."[7] A paucity of literature exists on the psychology of race. However, implications of psychology and race are reflected in much of the literature germane to the field of African American studies. The Cress Theory, although controversial, did originate from a Black psychological perspective.

*Definition and Development of Black Psychology.* The purpose of the preceding discussion was to emphasize the race/culture specific nature of the term and concept of psychology. African Americans may not wholly defer to European definitions and conceptions relative to the study of human behavior and mental activity. In contrast to a psychology founded solely upon a Western (Caucasian, Occidental, White) or Eastern (Mongoloid, Oriental, Yellow) race and culture, the psychology of African Americans is more related to the Black (Negroid or African) race and culture.[8] John S. Mbiti makes the point that the behavior of Africans is based primarily upon religious, spiritual (spirits), ancestral and mystical beliefs germane to the history and culture of Africa. In other words, Africans have their own ontology or concept of universal reality. Consequently, African people behave and are motivated by what they believe, and what they believe is based on what they experience.[9]

Afrocentric oriented psychologists argue that the African American experience is sufficiently different from that of White Americans to warrant its own branch of study. Slavery, racism and degrees of acculturation have not obliterated certain African ontological beliefs and foundations. Furthermore, racism, discrimination, oppression and cultural obfuscation have created more than ever the need for different psychological approaches toward the analysis of Black behavior and mentality. While many white psychologists have concentrated on measuring mental or intellectual disparities between certain races or ethnic groups, contemporary Black psychologists seem more concerned with differentiating between race-ethnic social realities or worldviews.

The origin of the concept of psychology in this discussion is important only in relation to the race or culture it is intended to apply. In the European tradition, the concept is said to have originated as early as the fourth and fifth centuries B.C. with the thoughts and philosophies of Plato, Aristole, and other Greek scholars. Wilhelm Wundt is credited to have started the first psychological laboratory in Leipzig, Germany in 1879.[10] Proponents of African (Black) psychological foundation traces its beginnings back to the ancient Kemet (African-Egyptian) civilization around 3200 B.C.[11]

The contemporary organized concept of Black psychology began during the late 1960s almost concomitantly with the idea for a Black sociology, and during the nationwide quest and demand for Black/African American Studies departments and programs. The

Civil Rights, Black Power and Black Studies movements of the 1960s generated the optimum social, political and educational environments for the creation of racially and culturally unique fields of academic inquiry. It was natural that the struggle for social justice, political and economic freedom include also the long suppressed desire of Black Americans for intellectual liberation.

The modern field of Black or African psychology developed out of the formation of the Association of Black Psychologists (ABP) in 1968. During this era, a number of other African American professional organizations were formed apart from the traditional White academic associations. Particularly, the ABP group of psychologists began to discover that the application of Eurocentric normative behavioral values and patterns to Black experience norms often yielded less than reliable findings and implications. The reason being that Black (African) behavioral norms and ethos may differ significantly from White (European) behavior patterns, mental motivations and cultural values upon which traditional psychology is founded. Blacks have not been served well in the psychological problems areas of education, self-concept and personality development, intra-group conflict, child and family relations, mental health therapy and counseling with conventional unadjusted European models.[12]

Joseph L. White and Thomas A. Parham describe in their book, *The Psychology of Blacks*, that "Black psychology and the psychology of Blackness reflect an attempt to build a conceptual model that organizes, explains, and leads to understanding the psychosocial behavior of African-Americans based on the primary dimensions of an African-American world view."[13] In defining and numerating the objectives of Black psychology, most of its proponents tend to broaden its perspective by not totally dismissing the utility and value of traditional psychology. For example Adelbert H. Jenkins writes that

"there are existing viewpoints in contemporary Western psychology that can also be used to make a fuller and fairer assessment of the Afro-American."[14] Cook and Kono allude to Black psychology as existing as "the third great psychological-philosophical tradition" leading the way towards a more equalitarian or "universal psychology" embracing "a theory of the human psyche which is broad enough to include the characteristic elements of mind in all cultures . . . not merely Black culture."[15] Some African American psychologists see Black psychology as a reactive response to White psychology while others assert that Black (African) psychology is reactive, proactive and inventive.

It is obvious from the various positions or views taken by Black psychologists that there exist somewhat distinct schools of psychological thought relative to the study of African Americans. Maulana Karenga has characterized the African American schools of thought as traditional, reformist and radical. The traditional school seems to support and apply conventional Eurocentric paradigms and norms toward the analysis of Black behavior. The reformists attempt to make adaptive changes in conventional psychological thought to conform to the Black American experience with little regard for African foundations. Radical or revolutionary theorists argue that the African ethos is the primary normative basis for the analysis of African American personality and behavior. Independent of European psychological theory, radical theorists employ and include African religion, philosophy, spiritualism, ritualism, concept of time, and worldview as the foundation of Black psychology.[16]

The Afrocentrist psychologist or social theorist maintains that there exists oppositional racial-cultural psychological proclivities between Blacks/Africans and Whites/Europeans. Joseph A. Baldwin postulates that African Americans and White Americans function psychologically under distinct "cosmologies." These cosmological systems, "therefore, represent fundamentally different ontological systems and cultural definitions, which reflect their distinct approaches to conceptualizing, organizing and experiencing reality."[17] For example, the racial-cultural ethos of the European American is characterized by its quest for control and mastery over nature, survival of the fittest ethic, future orientation, individualism, materialism, artificiality, intervention and aggression, white supremacy and racism.[18] In an oppositional sense, the African American cosmology is said to be oriented towards achieving harmony and unity with nature, collectivism, egalitarianism, spiritualism and ritualism.[19]

In their seminal work, *Roots of Soul*, psychologists Alfred B. Pasteur and Ivory L. Toldson also hold to the theory that the Black/African and the White/European minds perceive and interpret universal phenomena somewhat differently and, thus, their expressive behavior and value systems are in sharp contrast. The expressive difference of Blacks are explained as being the result of the hemispheric specialization of the right side of the brain. The right hemisphere is postulated to be the seat of creative and artistic capacities which accounts for the cultural predilection of Blacks for a form of rhythm, motion and language or rhetoric which is distinct from the ordered, structured, and control-oriented expressive behavior of Whites. Pasteur and Toldson observe further that the impact of Black expressiveness upon the white world has been an altering one—bringing it closer in feeling and sensibility, in rhythm and motion to that of Africa.[20] Implications of the psychology of cultural expressiveness relative to Blacks is treated extensively in Molefi K. Asante's book, *The Afrocentric Idea*. Asante expounds on the psychological aspects of

rhythm and styling in the language delivery or rhetoric of Black Americans.[21]

African ethos and philosophies cannot be excluded from the development of Black psychological theory. In stating the foundation for Black psychology, Wade W. Nobles wrote:

> Black Psychology must concern itself with the question of "rhythm." It must discuss at some great length, "the oral tradition." It must unfold the mysteries of the spiritual energy now known as "soul." It must explain the notion of "extended self" and the "natural" orientation of African peoples to insure the "survival of the tribe." Briefly, it must examine the elements and dimensions of the experiential communalities of African peoples.[22]

Indeed, fields of study are the products of the culture or cultures from which they are derived. Difference in historical experiences effect any paradigms or approaches toward the study of a particular ethnic group or race of people.

The traditional Euro-American disciplines of today have taken many decades and perhaps centuries to develop into their present stage of intellectual respectability and academic practicality. Black psychology as well as other emerging fields in African American Studies will have to develop new or modified methodological and theoretical scientific guidelines in order to achieve academic credibility. Conflicting ideologies and competing paradigms will occur and are "healthy" towards the refinement of a developing discipline. Considering the morass of repressive social and political conditions out of which African American studies evolved during the 1960s, the progress and development of Black psychology, sociology, history and the various other fields of study constituting African American studies have been phenomenal.

# PSYCHOLOGICAL DIMENSIONS OF OPPRESSION

**Behavioral Affects of Slavery and Racism.** Much has been written and observed relative to the social and behavioral patterns of African Americans that is attributed to the experiences of historical slavery and contemporary racism. It would be virtually impossible for a people to endure more than 300 years of enslavement and not be psychologically affected, and the affects not be culturally transmitted to some extent generations after the overt slave era has ended. Moreover, it should not be difficult to understand how the mental, emotional, personality, social behaviors and values of Blacks may still be consciously, subconsciously or unconsciously affected from slavery, since Emancipation was proclaimed only about 130 years ago. Legalized segregation, the core of racist ideology and racism ceased in America less than 40 years ago with the U.S. Supreme Court's desegregation decision of 1954. With the continuance of individual and institutional racism in the society, African Americans still experience various aspects of the psychology of oppression.

Slavery has to be understood as an oppressive form of physical and psychological torture in order to grasp the magnitude of its horrendous and indelible affects. In fact, slavery was an enduring form of torture of the minds, bodies and souls of Africans. Peter Suedfeld's study, *Psychology and Torture*, is particularly relevant to the slave experience. Blacks were tortured basically for the same five reasons Suedfeld listed as rationales for torturing prisoners of war—information, incrimination, indoctrination, intimidation and isolation.[23] They were tortured to force the revelation of information of revolts and to incriminate and betray fellow slaves. Torture was used to indoctrinate the slave with the

values and wishes of the slaveholders and to force the abandonment of their African beliefs and practices. Torture and beating were standard methods of intimidation employed for the purpose of deterring rebellion and evoking a spirit of docility. Isolation was a form of torture in itself. Unapproved and unwarranted congregating were met with punishment.

The acts and rationales of slave oppression and torture are enumerated and described for the purpose of providing insight of the probable psychological affects they might have had upon African Americans. Slaves were brainwashed, afflicted with self-rejection and alienation, made to fear their captors (whites), and developed a dependency on the slavemasters or white society. Some of these attitudes and dispositions have been passed on and are reflected in the behavior of many African Americans. The discussion relates to the treatment of prisoners of war in order to point out the concern that military psychiatrists and the American public in general have for war veterans who have been subjected to oppression and torture. The Korean and Vietnam Wars are prime examples. Presenting prisoner of war veterans' experiences as being similar to that of ex-slaves is not an extreme analogy. Extreme cruelty and inhumane acts of oppression inflicted by one group upon another, psychologically, affects both the victims and the victimizers.

Psychologists and sociologists are not in agreement as to the degree or significance of the effects of slavery on contemporary African Americans. However, clinical psychologists Na'im Akbar and Bobby E. Wright are prominent among Black behavioral scientists who have supported the theory that the impact of slavery has a continuing influence on the psychology of African Americans. Akbar argues that certain African American individual behaviors are influenced by collective factors which are historically remote.[24] From a psycho-historical perspective, he describes some of the destructive attitudes affecting the psyche of many African Americans today which may have had their origins in the slavery situation. These dispositions and attitudes are related to property, work, leadership, "clowning," personal inferiority, community division, family instability, and color consciousness.[25] It must also be acknowledged that slavery had the effect of developing some strengths as well as causing certain weaknesses in the African character.

According to Akbar, the master's fine house, exquisite clothes and luxurious material possessions created mixed attitudes in the minds of the enslaved Blacks. On one hand, it caused the slave to resent property and property ownership. The slave developed an unconscious delight in destroying or vandalizing property. The opposite affect was that property and material goods caused the African slave to be unnaturally attracted to expensive flashy clothes or goods which resulted in a tendency towards conspicuous consumption. This theory is similar to the psychological implications Frantz Fanon indicated which existed between the colonizer and the colonized in, *The Wretched of the Earth*.[26] In fact, much of the psychological affects of slavery are analogous to Fanon's behavioral concepts of colonialism in the Third World.

Many of African Americans' attitude toward work might be attributed to the slave experience. Slaves worked with no compensation for their labors. Consequently, work was viewed as punishment and the slaves developed a hatred for work.

The leadership crisis and lack of unity in the Black community may have had its attitudinal origins in slavery. Any emerging leaders of the slave community were eliminated or co-opted to serve the interests of the slavemasters. Therefore out of fear, there developed a hesitancy towards strong Black leadership, but also, the communities would suspect their leaders. Politically costly and numerous divisions of the Black community may have

roots in the stratification of the field versus the house slaves. Social divisions of the quasi-free Negro and mulatto during slavery were designed for the purposes of dividing and conquering by the masters. Even though it has virtually disappeared as a divisive factor in the Black community, intra-racial color consciousness was learned from Whites and emulated by African Americans during and after slavery. Many white slavemasters would elevate and educate their Black offspring conceived through rape or miscegenation. The psychological affects of color prejudice have had attitudinal and personality influences on African Americans.[27]

Many of the psychological affects of slavery on the stability of the Black family have been discussed in the previous chapters. Behavioral or personality traits such as self-rejection, personal inferiority and acquiescence to white domination are slave acquired characteristics according to Akbar's, *Chains and Images of Psychological Slavery*. Perhaps the most controversial slavery acquired trait which Akbar mentions is that of "clowning." He implies that the over representation of African Americans in the entertainment and sports fields developed from the opportunity which some slaves had to serve as jester, clown or fool for the entertainment of the master. Reference is made also to the majority of film and media roles, comedy based, which Blacks have been allowed to participate.

The essence of the works of Na'im Akbar, the clinical psychologist and Franz Fanon, the psychiatrist, is that both slavery and colonialism causes the victims to internalize certain destructive behavioral traits or characteristics which contribute to their continuing oppression long after freedom or decolonization has been achieved. All psychologists may not concur that the historical affects of slavery and oppression presently influence African American behavior and status. However, it is imperative that Black psychology consider all historical variables which have impacted upon the life experience of Black or African people in its academic and therapeutic purposes and objectives.

Even if Black behavioral affects from slavery are minimized or discounted, the thesis that African Americans are afflicted with various psychological dimensions of oppression resulting from the racism of post-slavery is generally supported by most Black psychologists. The psychological affects of racism or racial oppression have not only caused social dysfunctioning, aberrant behavior and cultural alienation, but have in the past and continue to impact upon the mental health of African Americans.[28] Racism is the abstract component of physical racial slavery. Although the physical bondage of slavery has ended, racism maintains Blacks in a state of psychological oppression and bondage.

*Psychotherapy, Mental Health and African Americans.* In 1968 the National Advisory Commission on Civil Disorders reported that the United States was headed toward the permanent establishment of two societies, one predominantly white and the other largely Black.[29] More than twenty years later, 1989, a study approved by the National Research Council revealed that racial separation in American life has remained relatively the same.[30] Thus, it is obvious that African Americans have maintained, basically, a social and cultural distinction apart from European Americans since the landing of the first 20 Africans at Jamestown in 1619. Consequently, a major contention of Black psychotherapists is that orthodox Western psychology and clinical approaches are not usually adapted to accommodate the distinct behavioral styles, personality and mental functioning of African people.

In spite of the significant difference in cultural origins, ethos, behavior and personal values between Blacks and Whites, psychologist K. Alan Wesson argues that the White psychotherapist

> . . . use the Anglo-American standards as tools for comparison, judgment, and measurement of the black man and his society. With the apparent differences in mind, it is totally inappropriate for the white to judge and evaluate the black using these (his own) white standards. . . . An assumption made here is that black behavior is no different from white behavior, which certainly is not true. . . . The white assumption has taken the view that blacks are merely white men with black skins. . . .[31]

Own-race diagnosis and psychotherapy are essential elements to be considered in the treatment of mental health problems of African Americans. Recognition of the fact that European paradigms may not be totally applicable in defining and diagnosing African or Black American mental disorders has led to the development of Black mental health models. Among the prominent Afrocentrist mental health theorists are: Daudi Ajani ya Azibo, Joseph A. Baldwin, and Wade W. Nobles.[32]

Azibo, Baldwin and Nobles posit that effective therapy for African Americans must begin with a knowledge of African (Black) psychology, philosophy, culture and personality theory. African mental health models involve dimensions of spirituality in concurrence with mental and emotional factors in psychotherapy. Thus, the European psychologist's knowledge, methodologies and behavioristic perceptions may be inadequate for dealing with the African psyche. The overriding assumption is that diagnosis and therapy are more accurately and effectively provided when the clinician and client have the same racial identity and that their culture, history and values are more in common. However, an African definitional system or standard is established in order to measure and determine the subject's degree of disorientation or deviance from the African as opposed to the

European norm. Black personality research proposes to learn how and why does a high level of African/Black consciousness enhances the psychological functioning of African Americans. It is known that a positive concept of one's self is a first step towards good mental health.

Research studies do not accurately or reliably measure the extent that racism and discrimination have upon the mental health of African Americans. Individuals differ in their ability to cope or to tolerate racial bigotry, denigration and persecution. While it may be difficult to quantify in biological terms the impact that racism has upon an individual or group, it is undeniable that racial oppression negatively affects the psychological or mental health of Blacks. Beyond the negative behavioral and personality affects discussed in the previous topic, racism and racial antagonism cause African Americans to suffer an undue amount of depression, stress, anger and hypertension. Unsuccessful adaptation and coping strategies for these maladies can lead to serious social and biological dysfunctions.[33]

Depression is generally perceived as being manifested by a dejected emotional attitude or mood resulting from feelings of inadequacy, helplessness, hopelessness, loss or loneliness. Stress may be described as a physiological/emotional response to an act or threat to ones physical well being. According to various literature on the subject, depression might be caused by numerous psychological, biological or even genetic factors. Therefore, it is not intended to give the impression that racism is the only or primary cause of depression and stress of African Americans. One may logically assume, however, that injurious treatment or unpleasant experiences resulting from exposure to racism or racist conditions and acts may contribute toward the symptoms which characterize depression or stress.

No racially identifiable African American person can consciously, subconsciously or un-

consciously escape some degree of the affects of racism and racial subjugation in the United States. Encountering the affects and influences of racism or race-consciousness is a daily, indeed, hourly experience of Black people whether they are in the workplace, the school, the market, the bank or on the street. A Black person sees himself or herself functioning at a negative disparate level in almost every social, political and economic sphere of the American society. Black Americans are confronted and subjected almost totally to White authority figures in employment, education, commercial and financial institutions, social and government institutions, law enforcement and judicial systems and in the media. Race and color more than any other factors, determines the collective quality of life, achievement potential, health, and life-chances of African Americans. From this social reality of Black life, it is inevitable that some symptoms of depression and stress develop. Furthermore, Black/African psychology seems to suggest that there are certain forms of depression and stress disorders peculiar to African Americans as the result of their distinct social reality.

Some psychotherapists report that when their Black clients are asked to give descriptions of themselves many allude to their feelings of worthlessness. The Black clients seem to struggle to maintain a sense of positive self-regard in the face of oppressive circumstances. However, some managed to develop successful coping mechanisms which enabled them to respond defensively to their feelings of anxiety, fear, and anger generated from a hostile or overbearing environment. African Americans may push themselves harder to succeed and to overcome the stereotypes of being Black. The tremendous effort that is required to do this is awesome and may in itself be a contributor and/or cause of the high incidence of depression, stress, anger or hypertension in Black people.[34]

Two Black psychiatrists, William H. Grier and Price M. Cobbs, wrote a book during the height of the Civil Rights Movement in 1968 entitled, *Black Rage*. In a chapter dealing with the mental illness and treatment of Black Americans, the writers give a narrative description of the psychological "Black Norm." In essence, they speak of the natural tendency of Blacks to be wary and internally rebellious against a social system that is set against them. They develop a profound distrust of their white fellow citizens and exercise eternal and unrelenting vigilance to protect themselves from humiliation, mistreatment or physical hurt. Consequently, Grier and Cobbs state that they develop "a sadness and intimacy with misery which has become a characteristic of black Americans. It is a *cultural depression* and a *cultural masochism*."[35]

Black anger often stems from the perception of having been treated unfairly or discriminated against which can cause frustration and generate aggression. The Black Norm attitude described by Grier and Cobbs can be attributed to the African American experience of having been reduced or relegated to insignificant and "minority" roles in the school, workplace, community or society as a whole. Psychotherapist Betty Davis writes that

> As a consequence of racial roles in society, it is normal for Blacks to express anger as a healthy response to oppression and racism, better known as sublimation. Psychotherapists must begin to recognize and accept this anger as a healthy cultural response and assist Black clients to fund constructive outlets for these feelings, instead of labeling them pathological. The clients' responses to stressors and/or behaviors through self-actualization may be a valuable means of support in working through the reactions to feelings of anger or aggression.[36]

It is apparent from the professional opinions and writings of Black psychologists and psychotherapists that race problems and racism are an integral aspect of the Black psyche and, thus, should not be excluded as relevant psychological variables in the diagnosis and treatment of depression, stress, anger or hypertension in African Americans.

Hypertension is one of the major health problems of Blacks in the United States. Hypertension can be caused by physical, physiological and/or psychosocial factors. However, research relating to the etiology of hypertension from psychosocial conditions is inconclusive. It is believed that the enhanced risk of hypertension among Blacks is attributed to a combination of psychological, biological, socioeconomic, sociocultural and ecological factors. While depression, subjective and chronic stresses, anger and anxiety are known to be contributors, socioeconomic factors (inadequate and inappropriate diet, poverty) and chemical dependency (alcohol, tobacco, drugs) are equally suspected.[37] The psychosocial experiences and socioeconomic conditions of Blacks are different from those of Whites because of racism and various psychological dimensions of oppression. This differential factor may be responsible for the higher incidence of hypertension among the African American population.

Racial oppression has been shown to have direct and indirect effects in causing the symptoms of depression and stress in both the middle and lower income strata of African Americans. The economic and political barriers to social mobility are prime contributors to Black stress and depression. Discrimination and prejudice based on race impede the employment and job advancement of African Americans which can contribute to various symptoms related to mental disorders.[38] Even on the job, African Americans may experience feelings of social isolation, race related anxiety, and cultural alienation. Blacks often have to adopt white "normative" or protective coping behaviors in order not to jeopardize their employment, especially, in major

American corporations.[39] Similar psychological related experiences are reported by Blacks in the academic and governmental fields of employment.

Working conditions or exploitative working situations can have the effect of lowering self-esteem and may create psychological tensions which contribute to the symptoms of stress, anxiety and depression.[40] Because of these negative race related psychosocial experiences, Blacks are at a disproportionate risk for mental health disorders.

## PSYCHOLOGY OF BLACK IDENTITY, PERSONALITY AND SELF-CONCEPT

*Racial and Ideological Identity.* One of the most destructive psychological consequences of slavery was the loss or obfuscation of the African's distinct human identity. During slavery, every effort was made by the oppressor to obliterate, diminish or disregard the African's individual self-concept and collective identity as a people. This was an essential step towards the dehumanization of the slave. During and since slavery, Black people have continually struggled to reassert and enhance their racial designation and to reestablish their cultural identity. The process has been fraught with various psychological difficulties and ideological conflicts among the African ex-slaves. Black people have had to wrestle with their different perceived self-identifications created during slavery on the one hand and their attributed identifications by Whites on the other.

Identification is defined by some behavioral theorists as a psychological phenomenon that serves to increase feelings of worth and importance by identifying with, or taking on the characteristics, values, or cultural attributes of some person or group that is well received by others.[41] Identification is psychologically essential for the ego development and maintenance of the individual or group. A person normally has a related individual and collective identity. However, sometimes individual and collective identities are in conflict. A person may choose or prefer an identification that is consistent with his or her social reality or one which allows escape from reality.

The identification dilemma of Blacks in America has been and continues to be one that is caused by psychological and ideological conflicts of perceptual racial identification and acceptance. In other words, Blacks have always deliberated over whether to seek the acceptance of and identification with Whites or to adopt and declare a Black or African identity distinct from that of European Americans. Race related assimilationist, integrationist, cultural nationalist, and separatist ideologies continue to be divisive elements effecting the thought and philosophy of Black Americans. In response to ideological differences, the collective identification or race label of Blacks in America has changed or a popular identity has existed concurrently with others variously during the course of American history. The changes referred to are Black self-identifications and not attributed identifications.

The racial identification changes have been influenced by corresponding changes in the political, economic, social and cultural outlooks and conditions of Black people which in turn, has altered their psychological inclinations and ideological perspectives.[42] Since slavery to the present, the various names Blacks have adopted for racial identification include: African, Ethiopian, Colored, Negro, Afro-American, African American and Black.

Beverly H. Wright posits that, historically, changes in the collective identification of Blacks have been directly related to their external or internal locus of control of events and circumstances effecting their condition.

Blacks are externally oriented when they feel that they are powerless to influence social and political events effecting their condition. When Blacks feel that they can effect or change social and political events they become more internally oriented. For example, during the "Colored Era" Blacks felt powerless to effect white hostility and oppression. The "Negro Era" was one in which Blacks began to exert moral suasion, court appeals, and peaceful protest. It was an era that produced hope and a weakening of the external forces which stifled their courage and initiative. Thus, they became more internally motivated. The "Black Era" commencing in the 1960s represented a period of open defiance, rebellion, retaliatory violence and a demand for Black Power.[43] It was an era of self-defining irrespective of attributed racial identifications. During the Black Era, Blacks have had more internal influence over their condition than at any other era in American history.

Sterling Stuckey found that the term Negro was once strongly associated with *slave*, especially, in the South. Negro was more often pronounced demeaningly as *nigra* or *nigger* by southern Whites. Stuckey also informs that the terms *colored* and *brown* were preferred by many of the light-skinned Africans of mix-race ancestry who formed much of the free Black population.[44] Historically, as well as today, the term African reflects a pride in being a member of the black race. The term African was used in the titles of many Black organizations which originated during and shortly after the slave era. Yet, there were those Blacks of the assimilationist and integrationist persuasion who adamantly opposed the title of any Black organization which would indicate a clue of its racial origin or constituency.[45]

Much of the variability of Black racial identification has been related to the collective political consciousness of Blacks during different stages of American social and economic development. However, underlying any ideological rationale is the psychological factor of Black self-concept. The terms African American and Black gained popular usage only after millions of Black Americans had begun to develop attitudes of "self-love," and a strong Black or African consciousness.

Prior to the Civil Rights and Black Power Movements of the 1960s, it might be postulated that most Blacks possessed weak African- centered psychological orientations. Consistent with the Frederick Douglass' assimilationist philosophy and aspirations, a significant segment of the Black population tended to view with disdain any identity symbol that would jeopardize their acceptance by Whites or would be contrary to Eurocentric values and standards. This mental attitude has been described or alluded to by Leahcim T. Semaj, Na'im Akbar and other Afrocentric psychologists as an anti-self disorder or alien race preference disorientation.[46] However, it should be noted that part of the reason why many Black Americans avoided identification with Africa was because of the traditional European and American negative depiction of continental Africans in the media as cannibals, savages and primitive barbarians.

A study of students by Josephine Moraa Moikobu attempted to reveal the nature, character, and extent of Black American and African identification. Moikobu revealed that Black Americans and Africans relate on a common basis according to specific *internal* and *external dimensions* of identity. Internal dimensions of identity apply to those internal or inherent attributes that come about through genetic constitution of which the individual has no control such as color and ancestry. External dimensions of identity are those based on external political, social, and economic forces including certain cultural phenomena. For example, Black Americans expressed their internal dimensions of identity with Africans in terms of their mutual color (Blackness), common race and ancestry. They saw as external dimensions of identity

Whites as a common oppressor, similar suffering from racism and a unified stance against the notion of White supremacy. Black Africans saw as internal dimensions of identity the commonality of Blackness and like exposures to White prejudices and racism. They listed as external dimensions of identity with Black Americans their mutual struggle for political and economic power, common views toward colonization and international affairs, and African behaviors. Since Black Americans are "citizens" of the United States and, differentially, Africans are members of African "independent" states, the two peoples have less commonality of external dimensions of identity.[47]

Recent national polls indicate that Black Americans prefer the racial identification of "Black" by a significant margin. A study conducted among Black students at a California university and an Arizona University supported previous surveys that Black is the more contemporary and socially acceptable race label compared with Black American, Afro-American, and Black Afro-American and others. Those preferring Black American wished to express ethnic pride as well as a degree of patriotism since "my people built this country." Those selecting Afro-American wished to emphasize their African ancestry arguing that "our roots are not in America."[48] The student survey may have limited use since it was not stated whether the terms African and African American were listed on the questionnaire.

Since the 1960s, Blacks have been more inclined to accept or acknowledge an African identification. After more than three hundred years of rejection and denial of equal opportunity, the reclamation of African heritage and values may be therapeutic for the psychological functioning of Blacks in America. Until Blacks are accorded equal rights, justice and opportunity, they may increasingly repudiate Eurocentric values and ideology and embrace an African ethos and identification.

The African American have always had to endure the mental travail of "double-consciousness" . . . feeling the "twoness,—an American, A [Black]; two souls, two thoughts . . . two unreconciled strivings; two warring ideals in one dark body, whose dogged strength alone keeps it from being torn asunder" as was eloquently described by W.E.B. DuBois.[49]

*African/Black Ordered and Disordered Personality.* Like so many abstract psychological words and concepts, there is not a consensus of a specific definition of the term personality. Personality has various meanings and implications depending upon the objectives of the clinician or impressions one gains from observing the behavioral characteristics of another person. It appears from an analysis of much literature that behavioral scientists lean toward the belief that the essence of an individual's personality emanates from the depths of the inner-self, transcending mere observable traits. Personality may be differentially defined based on Eurocentric or Afrocentric worldviews and perspectives.

However, the definition stated by Gordon Allport that, "personality is the dynamic organization within the individual of those psychophysical systems that determine his characteristic behavior and thought,"[50] serves as a partial bridge between Afrocentric and Eurocentric concepts. While Eurocentric behavioral scientists concur that culture and personality are closely related, Afrocentric psychologists stress the interrelatedness of race and culture relative to the African or Black personality. From the framework of Black personality theory, one's psychological experience is inextricably related to race. Joseph A. Baldwin asserts that biological and psychological phenomena are interrelated and interdependent as defined by the natural order, such that psychological experience derives from a biological basis. Thus, each biogenetic (racial) type has its own distinct set of psychological and behavioral traits or dispositions.[51]

The unique environment, institutions, values, socio-economic and political experiences, and African ethos influence Black Americans to behave within a prescribed set of functional psychological norms. Race and culture are powerful forces that contribute to Black personality development and normal psychological functioning. However, racism and White cultural hegemony can have dysfunctional affects upon African self-consciousness and cause the development of a disordered Black personality. Therefore, basic to the principles and practice of Black psychology are the definition and delineation of behavioral traits and attitudinal characteristics which constitute a normal African/Black personality.

Irene Atwell and Daudi Ajani ya Azibo conceptualize that Africans/Blacks have normal or correct personalities when they have beliefs, values, attitudes and behaviors that are African oriented; recognize themselves as African and Black; prioritize the interests, survival and proactive development of Africans/Blacks; and support a standard of conduct that neutralizes people and things that are anti-African.[52] The objective of this Black normalcy concept is not meant to be ethnocentric or anti-others, but to recognize the potential of psychological dysfunctioning which often results from an anti-self personality. Pro-self or pro-own group does not necessarily translate into being anti-others.

The question of personality disorder arises when an African/Black denies his or her own race and culture and adopts behaviors and attitudes that embrace and extol the alien or oppressor group to the detriment and destruction of his or her own self or group. Atwell and Azibo conclude that an African/Black so afflicted manifests an orientation to reality that does not promote the maintenance of his or her race, but promotes instead the interests and designs of the non-African group whose

cognitive elements are operative in his/her psyche—including those that are anti-Black or African. Therefore, they explain that the correct African/Black personality orientation constitutes genetic Blackness plus psychological Blackness or the conscious manifestation of African-centered psychological and behavioral functioning in genetically Black persons.[53] From the various explanatory descriptions of the psychological functioning of Blacks, it becomes evident that Africanity which forms the basis of the normative Black personality might be manifested in conscious as well as in subconscious, preconscious and unconscious states. While alien socialization might effect certain conscious behaviors, those which exist in the individual and collective unconscious are psychologically indelible.

Since mental health may be determined by ones correct or normal psychological and behavioral functioning, Azibo has constructed a nosology of African personality disorder referred to hereafter as The Azibo Nosology. The Azibo Nosology is a diagnostic system or guide for an Africentric representation of personality. It makes three prefatory points to be taken in consideration for mental order or mental disorder of Blacks. First, it explicates the nature of the relationship between personality order and personality disorder. Secondly, it advances the criticality of the Self in personality or mental order and disorder. Thirdly, in spite of the risk of being criticized for its moral emphasis, the nosology promotes and contends that values are fundamentally inherent in the diagnostic process.[54] The nosology lists and diagrams eighteen disorders peculiar to the African/Black personality. The Azibo Nosology represents a compilation of personality disorder theories from a host of Black behavioral theorists including those of Azibo. (See figure 5)

While it is not possible to discuss all of the eighteen disorders in this survey work, attention will be given to a few which are

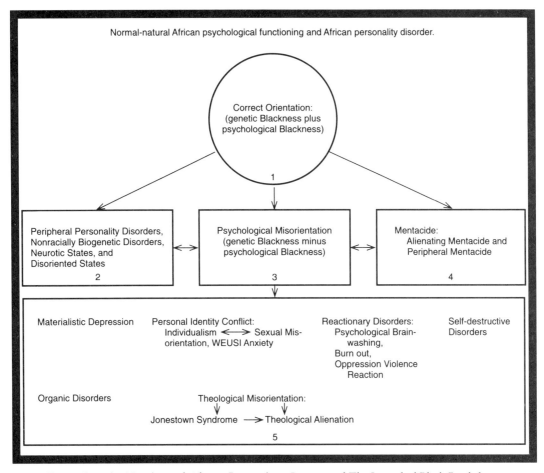

Figure 5  Azibo Nosology of African Personality. Courtesy of *The Journal of Black Psychology*.

perhaps more notable and lucid. For example, psychological misorientation, mentacide, alien-self disorder, anti-self disorder, psychological brainwashing, oppression violence, and self-destructive disorders have been alluded to in previous discussions. These are almost self explanatory.

Psychological misorientation means that the individual functions without an African-centered belief system of which alien values and concepts exist at the expense of psychological Blackness. Mentacide has the affect of rendering the Black/African psyche void. Instead the vacuum is filled with un-

natural and unwarranted acceptance, admiration and allegiance to European, Arab or any other alien group regardless of the denigratory opinion these groups may have toward Africans or the injustice and inhumanity Blacks suffer at their hands. Mentacide has been figuratively described as the rape or murder of a person's mind.[55]

The alien-self disordered Black persons tend to view themselves and world phenomena totally from a Eurocentric or alien perspective preferring intimate social and personal relationships with an alien group rather than with their own. An individual with an anti-self disorder is willing and is often chosen by the alien group to work against the survival of his own people. Racism and the psychology of oppression are instrumental toward the development of alien-self and anti-self personality disorders.[56]

Psychological brainwashing results in the development of a mental disorder that impels the individual to inform or collaborate with the alien group. The individual may even extol the merits of being oppressed and indulge in self-blame. Oppression violence is a reaction to an oppressive milieu or environment. The individual may engage in unpremeditated violent acts, directed at in-group or out-group members. These types of behaviors are analogous to the mental disorders Franz Fanon observed during the Third World liberation movement which related to colonialism.[57] Self-destructive personality disorders are evidenced by deviant behaviors such as drug and alcohol abuse, suicide, fratricide or Black on Black crime. It include all those behaviors that are destructive not only to the individual but to the collective Black society.[58]

The Azibo Nosology does not maintain that European-centered psychology is totally inoperative in the diagnosis of Blacks. However, the African-centered, Azibo Nosology is applicable to many of the personality disorders peculiar to Africans/Blacks. Throughout the emerging field of Black/African psychology, new or alternate Afrocentric psychotherapy models are being developed. Some will subsume existing methodologies and others may counterpoise Eurocentric psychological paradigms.

A fundamental thesis of Black psychology is that the normative or healthy psychological functioning of the African American depends significantly on the extent that the individual has developed or manifests a positive African/Black self-consciousness. Based on the assumption that slavery and racism have severely diminished, diffused or otherwise negatively affected the African American cultural consciousness, several models have been presented to describe the process of conversion from a weak to an affirmative or strong Black identity and personality. The most notable of such models is the one proposed by W.E. Cross. Cross outlined five descriptive stages of change from a Negro (weak) to a strong Black state of being. Stages of the process are: 1) pre-encounter, 2) encounter, 3) immersion-emersion, 4) internalization, and 5) internalization—commitment.[59]

Cross' pre-encounter stage is descriptive of an African American who is completely devoid of a Black frame of reference. The individual thinks, acts, behaves White/European or other alien group, devalues anything African/Black, and denies his or her own Blackness. The encounter stage occurs when the individual first encounters a personal racist incident or experiences first-hand the humiliating and denigrating effects of racism. Such an experience can shock the person into discovering the reality and scope of racial distinctiveness and antagonism that permeates American society. Consequently, the individual becomes uncomfortable with a White or race-neutral ideology and began to explore and reassess his or her Black identity. Upon discovering or rediscovering an African or Black identity, the person becomes immersed into Black culture and begins to adopt African/Black cultural symbols, dress and lifestyle. The person emerges or withdraws from a white or alien ethos and begins to assume the characteristics of a Black identity and personality. Internalization is the stage at which the person has become culturally, socially and psychologically confident with his or her new Black identity. Anti-white or alien group feelings may tend to diminish. From the Black/African internalization state, the persons may then advance to an internalization—commitment level of consciousness. At this stage, the individual is not only culturally secure, but becomes politically committed towards the eradication of racial injustice and inequality.[60]

The field of Black psychology has been virtually handicapped because of the lack of reliable instruments to study or measure the efficacy of African American psychological functioning and the behavioral aspects of personality and identity. However, in 1985 Joseph A. Baldwin and Yvonne R. Bell developed an instrument descriptively entitled, *The African Self-Consciousness Scale: An Africentric Personality Questionnaire*. The Africentric Personality Questionnaire is an appropriate scale to measure the authentic cultural reality of African Americans. The African Self-Consciousness Scale aptly addresses the cross-cultural nature of the Black experience in American society.[61] (See figure 6).

**A Discussion of Black Self-Concept Theory.** Ever since the late 1930s, the matter of African American/Black self-concept or self-esteem has been a popular issue of academic concern. For various reasons, it is assumed that the slave experience and the subjugated post-slavery experience of Blacks have afflicted them with attitudes and dispositions of self-derogation. The Black Power and Black Pride movements of the 1960s ushered in an era of psychological reversal of many of the previous held perceptions African Americans may have held of themselves. Yet, some behavioral and social theorists argue that vestiges of negative Black self-concepts still afflict the psyche of many African Americans.

Black self-concept is a term specifically used to define or refer to an African American's perception of his or her own worthiness. In general, self-concept is how one characterizes or perceives one's self in relation to others at any specific time and under certain societal or global conditions. Black self-concept is related to all of the psychological elements of Black identity and personality previously discussed. Therefore, what is termed as the Black self-concept may also be

described as a conscious, preconscious, subconscious or unconscious psychological phenomenon. From an analysis of the various studies, it is evident that various concepts and definitions of Black self-concept exist.

Research on the Black self-concept is fraught with many criticisms. First, many of the studies may be perceived as unidimensional because color-awareness has been used as the primary determinant of Black positive or negative self-concept. Self-evaluation might be based on several factors including color. Secondly, white people are always used as the model race of comparison. Indeed, much of the research on the Black self-concept has been initiated by White investigators.[62] Thirdly, the preponderance of subjects have been pre-school, primary, and high school children or adolescents.

From 1939 to 1973 alone, over one-hundred studies and re-studies related to the measurement or determination of the Black self-concept have been conducted. Many more empirical studies have been executed up to the present date. The findings have been as varied and inconclusive as the myriad of methodologies and techniques employed in the research testing. While a few of these studies tend to refute the negative Black self-concept theory, most reveal that for various reasons, the color white (and implicitly White people) are held in higher esteem by Black children than their own color and race.[63]

Interest in Black self-concept research and theory became a popular academic pursuit after 1939 when Black psychologists Kenneth B. Clark and Mamie P. Clark developed the black and white "dolls test" to determine children's racial awareness and preferences.[64] In successive studies by the Clarks and by others, it was speculated that Black children's choice of white dolls was indicative of their individual and group self-hatred. Criticism of the Clarks' methodology led to numerous variations. Other tests have included not only

# THE BALDWIN AND BELL AFRICAN SELF-CONSCIOUSNESS SCALE

Instructions: The following statements reflect some beliefs, opinions, and attitudes of Black people. Read each statement carefully and give your honest feelings about the beliefs and attitudes expressed. Indicate the extent to which you agree by using the following scale:

| 1 ——— 2 | 3 ——— 4 | 5 ——— 6 | 7 ——— 8 |
|---|---|---|---|
| Strongly disagree | Disagree | Agree | Strongly agree |

Circle the number closest to your own feelings. Note that the higher the number you choose for the statement, the more you agree with that statement; and conversely, the lower the number you choose, the more you disagree with that statement. Also, there is no right or wrong answer, only the answer that best expresses your present feelings about the statement. Please respond to all of the statements (do not omit any).

1. I don't necessarily feel like I am also being mistreated in a situation where I see another Black person being mistreated.
2. Black people should have their own independent schools which consider their African heritage and values an important part of the curriculum.
3. Blacks who trust whites in general are basically very intelligent people.
4. Blacks who are committed and prepared to uplift the (Black) race by any means necessary (including violence) are more intelligent than Blacks who are not this committed and prepared.
5. Blacks in America should try harder to be American rather than practicing activities that link them up with their African cultural heritage.
6. Regardless of their interests, educational background and social achievements, I would prefer to associate with Black people than with non-Blacks.
7. It is not such a good idea for Black students to be required to learn an African language.
8. It is not within the best interest of Blacks to depend on whites for anything, no matter how religious and decent they (the whites) purport to be.
9. Blacks who place the highest value on Black life (over that of other people) are reverse racists and generally evil people.
10. Black children should be taught that they are African people at an early age.
11. White people, generally speaking, are not opposed to self-determination for Black people.
12. As a good index of self-respect, Blacks in America should consider adopting traditional African names for themselves.
13. A white/European or Caucasian image of God and the "holy family" (among others considered closest God) are not such bad things for Blacks to worship.
14. Blacks born in the United States are Black or African first, rather than American or just plain people.
15. Black people who talk in a relatively loud manner, show a lot of emotions and feelings, and express themselves with a lot of movement and body motion are less intelligent than Blacks who do not behave this way.
16. Racial consciousness and cultural awareness based on traditional African values are necessary to the development of Black marriages and families that can contribute to the liberation and enhancement of Black people in America.
17. In dealing with other Blacks, I consider myself quite different and unique from most of them.
18. Blacks should form loving relationships with and marry only other Blacks.
19. I have difficulty identifying with the culture of African people.
20. It is intelligent for Blacks in America to organize to educate and liberate themselves from white-American domination.

Figure 6  Baldwin and Bell African Self-Consciousness Scale. From *The Western Journal of Black Studies*, (Summer 1985) 9(2); Washington State University Press. Reprinted by permission.

## The African Self-Consciousness Scale (continued)

21. There is no such thing as African culture among Blacks in America.
22. It is good for Black husbands and wives to help each other develop racial consciousness and cultural awareness in themselves and their children.
23. Africa is not the ancestral homeland of all Black people throughout the world.
24. It is good for Blacks in America to wear traditional African-type clothing and hair styles if they desire to do so.
25. I feel little sense of commitment to Black people who are not close friends or relatives.
26. All Black students in Africa and America should be expected to study African culture and history as it occurs throughout the world.
27. Black children should be taught to love all races of people, even those races who do harm to them.
28. Blacks in America who view Africa as their homeland are more intelligent than those who view America as their homeland.
29. If I saw Black children fighting, I would leave them to settle it alone.
30. White people, generally speaking, do not respect Black life.
31. Blacks in America should view Blacks from other countries (e.g., Ghana, Nigeria, and other countries in Africa) as foreigners rather than as their brothers and sisters.
32. When a Black person uses the terms "Self, Me, and I," his/her reference should encompass all Black people rather than simply him/herself.
33. Religion is dangerous for Black people when it directs and inspires them to become self-determining and independent of the white community.
34. Black parents should encourage their children to respect all Black people, good and bad, and punish them when they don't show respect.
35. Blacks who celebrate Kwanzaa and practice the "Nguzo Saba" (the Black Value System), both symbolizing African traditions, don't necessarily have better sense than Blacks who celebrate Easter, Christmas, and the Fourth of July.
36. African culture is better for humanity than European culture.
37. Black people's concern for self-knowledge (knowledge of one's history, philosophy, culture, etc.) and self (collective )-determination makes them treat white people badly.
38. The success of an individual Black person is not as important as the survival of all Black people.
39. If a good/worthwhile education could be obtained at all schools (both Black and white), I would prefer for my child to attend a racially integrated school.
40. It is good for Black people to refer to each other as brother and sister because such a practice is consistent with our African heritage.
41. It is not necessary to require Black/African Studies courses in predominantly Black schools.
42. Being involved in wholesome group activities with other Blacks lifts my spirits more so than being involved in individual oriented activities.

Figure 6—*Cont.*

dolls, but assorted methodologies using photographs, movies, crayons, colored pictures, etc. No attempt will be made here to discuss the voluminous studies of the Black self-concept. However, some recent studies seem to infer that many Black children, even 30 years after the Civil Rights and Black Power Movements, have color preferences for white people rather than for people of their own race. It is important to note that Sharon-ann Gopaul-Mc.Nicol stated in her study that Black "parents may be implicitly guiding their children's experience" when they "buy only white dolls for their children."[65]

Logically, one may assume that the inclination for some Black children to prefer and admire white dolls or people more than black dolls and their own race is a behavioral trait that is, in part, acquired from their African American parents. The cultural and social values of children are initially and profoundly influenced through parental relationships and the home environment. Consequently, Black self-concept studies have been grossly misguided. It would be far more progressive for African American adults to be subjected to Black/African consciousness tests and studies than Black children. The psychological models and instruments developed by Azibo and Baldwin are useful in evaluating the self-consciousness of African American adults and children. Children who originate from strong African/Black centered households are bound to reflect some of the same characteristics in the choices they make in their daily lives.

One must realize that attitudes and beliefs of White supremacy are basically learned by White children from their parents and adult role models. Because of their religious and spiritual nature, Black parents tend to teach their children egalitarian values and to love everybody. Certainly, there is a religious variable that may influence children's social values and racial behaviors. Then too, the insidious institutional racism that prevails in the public school system and schools cannot be ruled out as a major negative socialization factor effecting the self-concept of Black children. The educational subject matter, perspectives, and pictures included in textbooks are white and European oriented. For the most part, American authority figures, folklore symbols and media models are White.

Thus, a tremendous amount of research is not necessary to determine if and why Black children may be prone to prefer and to identity with Whites. The causes of such behavior are well known. White cultural hegemony and institutional racism are powerful forces that can have a debilitating affect on the self-concept of children and adult African Americans. Consequently, doll tests and similar color-choice experiments should be discontinued because they are of little value in treating the root causes of Black low self-esteem. The motive and implications of these white/black dolls color awareness tests seems to reinforce the ethnocentrism of whites and focuses unwarranted attention on the myth of white superiority.

*Psychology of the Media and Blacks.* One of the most powerful phenomena influencing the mind, thought, and behavior of American people is the mass media. The media in the context of this discussion means all audio or visual materials or devices that influences the mind. Whether or not it pervades as billboard, print, film or broadcast media, it is designed to persuade, socialize and to control the minds of people who observe, listen or view the messages it imparts on every facet of human life. The media has minimal, if any, restraints in the United States and it serves basically as its own arbiter of the psychological, cultural, social and political messages it conveys. Historically, the media has been an influential force in the field of race relations and it has served as a formidable antagonist to the social progress of African Americans. Whites dominate and control the mass media.

Of the various types of media, Blacks have been adversely affected most by the television and film industries. When television began to emerge as the most popular medium of the American public during the late 1940s, African Americans, regardless of their socio-economic strata, made whatever sacrifices necessary to acquire this intriguing electronic box and to view the fun and paradisiacal fantasies of the White world. Blacks did not initially appear on television except as menial and subservient characters such as buffoons, butlers, doorman, porters, valets and waiters. There were sporadic and short-term appearances of Blacks in a few programs in the North, but in the South Blacks were not shown except as deviants and criminals on news casts. The brief duration of *The Nat King Cole Show* (1956) and talented Black performers on the *Ed Sullivan Show* (1948–1971) were among the few exceptions.[66]

During the early 1960s, African Americans continued to be restricted to roles characterized as "Black parts" although a few made occasional appearances in regular network series. The quantity of Black characters did not increase until the 1970s when they began to star in a number of comedy shows. Whites have always tolerated and appreciated Blacks in the roles of comedians, athletes and entertainers (singers and dancers). On the whole, the general stereotypical images and roles of Blacks on television have continued since the 1970s, although a few became hosts and cohosts of various programs during the 1980s. Blacks are seldom cast in strong character roles and their life and experience are usually unidimensionally portrayed. A relative decline in the presence of Blacks in television and film was observed in the early 1990s.

Perhaps the most positive contribution that television has made to the progress of African Americans was its explicit coverage during the 1960s of the Civil Rights Movement including the Montgomery Bus Boycott. The major networks showed to the world and

in vivid detail the brutality that was being inflicted upon Blacks by Whites as they struggled for freedom and justice. The media may not ever be prone to demonstrate this type of balance and integrity again. Since the 1960s, the media has reverted to the politico-psychological devastation of the Black psyche by portraying and attributing negative definitions to African American life.

The white dominated media has the power to create images and assign definitions to certain non-white groups within the society. Positive images are assigned to Whites and negative images are ascribed to Blacks. Images are the vehicles for creating definitions. Thus, Blacks may define themselves based upon the media or television images they have internalized. If negative images are transmitted and internalized, self-destructive or alien-self behavior patterns may develop. John Henrik Clarke once wrote that

> Because what we see about ourselves often influences what we do about ourselves, the role of image and the control of the mind is more important now in a media-saturated society than ever before in history. . . . The image before the African child of today, both in Africa, the United States and throughout the world, is a clear indication of what they will be as adults and what they will think as adults.[67]

People in the American society rely substantially on visual media images for forming their social, political and economic opinions. The negative images of Blacks which Whites internalize can perpetuate the myth of Black inferiority and white supremacy.

Not only are the media's distortions and stereotypes of Black social reality disturbing, but the conspicuous absence or non-portrayal of African Americans is equally appalling. The subliminal message conveyed by the absence of African American models and actors from the media is that Blacks are a nonentity in American society. Nearly 100 percent of

U.S. households own at least one television set. More than ninety-eight percent of the characters or models in television are White. Yet, Blacks watch television on the average of 24 hours a week while Whites watch television on an average of only 17 hours a week. This could mean that African/Black people are internalizing European/American culture and values at a faster rate than white people. The potential negative psychological affects to Black identity, personality and self-concept are quite obvious. There is almost an inseparable relationship between the media and culture.

If one is non-white, the media is effective at alienating one from one's own race. For example, Blacks who downplay their racial identity and lack own-race commitment are lauded, consulted, and frequently featured. Conversely, Blacks who demonstrate a pro-Black bias and a strong commitment for struggle are ignored or discredited. This is a politico-psychological aspect of the mass media.[68]

Seldom do Black women appear in the commercials and advertisements of the print or broadcast media. More often in group scenes of commercials and advertisements, one symbolic Black fleetingly appears but hardly ever more than one. One wonders if the media has adopted a quota system. Tony Brown, an eminent Black journalist explains that

> What you're looking at is more of the unconscious racism which assumes that blacks should never be in the majority. So as long as advertisers can create a world in which blacks are always in the minority, it seems to keep white people safe, or give them a false sense of security. . . . And since two-thirds of the world is not white, they're only fooling themselves.[69]

Often when more than one Black is portrayed it is in a stigma-oriented commercial. It appears that a disproportionate number of Black models promote personal care products.[70]

There are no Black heroes or super figures featured in film or television series. Only sports and entertainment personalities are acclaimed and showered with adoration. Unless the issue is on race or race relations, rarely are Black scientists, economists, politicians or other professional authority figures portrayed or consulted in the media. The African American's image in the media and on television is restricted to Whites' conception of Black life and culture. While African Americans are represented and highly achieved in almost all professional and occupational fields the media, for racial and psycho-political reasons, has historically failed to project a balanced perspective of the Black experience.

# · QUESTIONS AND EXERCISES ·

1. Why has psychology been a fertile field to foster racism and to perpetuate racist myths than perhaps any other discipline?

2. Define Black psychology and discuss its educational implications and dimensions.

3. What does "psychology of oppression" mean relative to the African American experience in the United States?

4. How have racism and discrimination based on color and race, perceivably, impacted

upon the mental health of African Americans?

5. What is meant by Black/African ordered or disordered personality?

6. Review the full context of Professor Daudi Ajani ya Azibo's article, "African-centered Theses on Mental Health and a Nosology of Black/African Personality Disorder," published in the *Journal of Black Psychology* (Spring 1989) 15 (2). Discuss its methodological construct and implications relative to the normal psychological functioning of African Americans.

7. Germane to the healthy functioning of Blacks are the problems of self-consciousness and pro-Black/anti-Black racial identification. Study and discuss the Joseph A. Baldwin and Yvonne R. Bell *Africentric Personality Questionnaire* presented in this chapter. If applicable, substitute for your race or ethnic group.

8. Explain how the media, especially television and film, contribute psychologically to negative socialization, stereotyping and personality disordering of African Americans and other racial-ethnic minority groups.

## ▪ NOTES AND REFERENCES ▪

1. See Duane P. Schultz and Sydney Ellen Schultz, *A History of Modern Psychology*, 4th ed. (San Diego: Harcourt Brace Jovanovich 1987) p. 4.

2. Robert V. Guthrie, *Even the Rat was White* (New York: Harper and Row 1976) 29–46.

3. Schultz and Schultz, *A History of Modern Psychology*, 150–151.

4. See Arthur R. Jensen, "How Much Can We Boost IQ and Scholastic Achievement?" *Harvard Educational Review* (Winter 1969) 39: 1–123; and A. Kardiner and L. Ovesey, *The Mark of Oppression* (New York: Norton 1951)

5. For a review of many essays by Black psychologists and behavioral scientists on the psychology of African Americans see, Reginald L. Jones, ed., *Black Psychology* (New York: Harper & Row 1972)

6. Frances Cress Welsing, *The Isis Papers* (Chicago: Third World Press 1991) p. 44.

7. Ibid., p. 9.

8. See Norman D. Cook and Sumiko Kono, "Black Psychology: The Third Great Tradition," *The Journal of Black Psychology* (February 1977) v. 3(2) 18–28.

9. John S. Mbiti, *African Religions and Philosophy* (Garden City, NY: Anchor Books 1970) 5, 20–21.

10. Schultz and Schultz, *A History of Modern Psychology*, 1–2.

11. Daudi Ajani ya Azibo, "African Psychology in Historical Perspective and Related Commentary," (Draft of chapter of book sent for use October 1991) Temple Unviersity. p. 4.

12. See Gerald G. Jackson, "The Origin and Development of Black Psychology: Implications for Black Studies and Human Behavior," *Studia Africana* (Fall 1979) v. 1.(3). 270–286.

13. Joseph L. White and Thomas A. Parham, *The Psychology of Blacks* (Englewood Cliffs, NJ: Prentice Hall 1990) p. 23.

14. Adelbert H. Jenkins, *The Psychology of the Afro-American* (New York: Pergamon Press 1982) p. xvi.

15. Cook and Kono, "Black Psychology: The Third Great Tradition," pp. 18–19.

16. Maulana Karenga, *Introduction to Black Studies* (Inglewood CA: Kawaida Publications 1982) 326–351.

17. Joseph A. Baldwin, "Psychological Aspects of European Cosmology in American Society," *The Western Journal of Black Studies* (Winter 1985) v. 9(4) p. 216.

18. Ibid., 217–272.

19. See Dona Richards, "The Implications of African-American Spirituality," in *African Culture*, edited by M. K. Asante and K. W. Asante (Westport CT: Greenwood Press 1985).

20. Alfred B. Pasteur and Ivory L. Toldson, *Roots of Soul* (Garden City, NY: Anchor Press/Doubleday 1982) 4–26.

21. See Molefi Kete Asante, *The Afrocentric Idea* (Philadelphia: Temple University Press 1987).

22. Wade W. Nobles, "African Philosophy: Foundations for Black Psychology," in *Black Psychology*, edited by Reginald L. Jones (New York: Harper & Row 1972) p. 31.

23. Peter Suedfeld, *Psychology and Torture* (New York: Hemisphere Publishing Co. 1990) 2–3.

24. Na'im Akbar, *Chains and Images of Psychological Slavery* (Jersey City: New Mind Productions 1984). Akbar has described certain continuing effects of slavery in the first of two essays comprising the book.

25. Ibid., 9–40.

26. See Franz Fanon, *The Wretched of the Earth* (New York: Grove Press 1963).

27. For a study of color prejudice among Blacks see Ozzie L. Edwards, "Skin Color as a Variable in Racial Attitudes of Black Urban-ites," *Journal of Black Studies* (June 1972) v. 3(4), 473–483.

28. Joycelyn Landrum-Brown, "Black Mental Health and Racial Oppression," in *Handbook of Mental Health and Mental Disorders Among Black Americans*, edited by Dorothy S. Ruiz (New York: Greenwood Press 1990) 113.

29. President's National Advisory Commission on Civil Disorders, 1968. *Report of the National Advisory Commision on Civil Disorders*. Washington, D.C.: U.S. Government Printing Office.

30. Gerald D. Jaynes and Robin M. Williams, Jr., editors, *A Common Destiny* (Washington, D.C.: National Academy Press 1989) 103.

31. K. Alan Wesson, "The Black Man's Burden: The White Clinician," *The Black Scholar* (July–August 1975) 13–14.

32. See Daudi Ajani ya Azibo, "Treatment and training Implications of the Advances in African Personality Theory," *The Western Journal of Black Studies* (Spring 1990) 53–62; Joseph A. Baldwin, "African Self-Consciousness and the Mental Health of African Americans," *Journal of Black Studies*, 15(2) 177–194; and Wade W. Nobles, "Black People in White Insanity: An Issue for Black Community Health," *Journal of Afro American Issues*, 1976, (4) 21–27.

33. For a comprehensive study of Black mental and physical health issues see, Reginald L. Jones, ed., *Black Adult Development and Aging* (Berkeley: Cobb & Henry Publishers 1989).

34. Betty Davis, "Factors to Consider in Effective Treatment in Interracial Therapy," *The Western Journal of Black Studies* (Summer 1979) v. 3(2), 135.

35. Willaim H. Grier and Price M. Cobbs, *Black Rage* (New York: Basic Books 1968) Bantam edition 1969. 149.

36. Betty Davis, "Anger as a Factor and an Invisible Barrier in the Treatment of Black

Clients," *The Western Journal of Black Studies* (Spring 1980) v. 4(1). 29–30.

37. H. F. Myers, N. B. Anderson and T. L. Strickland, "A Biobehavioral Perspective on Stress and Hypertension in Black Adults," in *Black Adult Development and Aging*, edited by Reginald L. Jones (Berkeley: Cobb & Henry 1989) 311–336.

38. Harold W. Neighbors and Suzan Lumpkin, "The Epidemiology of Mental Disorder in the Black Population," in *Handbook of Mental Disorder Among Black Americans*, edited by Dorothy S. Ruiz (New York: Greenwood Press 1990) 55–68.

39. Talmadge Anderson and William M. Harris, "A Socio-Historical and Contemporary Study of African Americans in U.S. Corporations," *The Western Journal of Black Studies*, (Fall 1990) v. 14(3). 174–181.

40. See George Kaluger and Charles M. Unkovic, *Psychology and Sociology* (Saint Louis: The C. V. Mosby Co. 1969) 179–210.

41. Kaluger and Unkovic, *Psychology and Sociology*, 199.

42. See Robert Staples, *Introduction to Black Sociology* (New York: McGraw-Hill 1976) 286–294.

43. Beverly Hendrix Wright, "Ideological Changes and Black Identity during Civil Rights Movements," *The Western Journal of Black Studies* (Fall 1981) v. 5(3). 186–197.

44. Sterling Stuckey, *Slave Culture* (New York: Oxford University Press 1987) 198–199.

45. Ibid., 202–209.

46. See Leachcim T. Semaj, "The Black Self, Identity, and Models for a Psychology of Black Liberation," *The Western Journal of Black Studies* (Fall 1981) v. 5(3).

47. Josephine Moraa Moikobu, *Blood and Flesh: Black American and African Identification* (Westport Ct: Greenwood Press 1981) 91–96.

48. Michael L. Hecht and Sidney Ribeau, "Sociocultural Roots of Ethnic Identity,"

*Journal of Black Studies* (June 1991) 21(4). 501–513.

49. W.E.B. DuBois, *Souls of Black Folk* (New York: New American Library 1969) 45.

50. Gordon W. Allport, *Pattern and Growth in Personality* (Ft. Worth: Holt, Rinehart and Winston 1961) 28.

51. Joseph A. Baldwin, "Notes on an Africentric Theory of Black Personality," *The Western Journal of Black Studies* (Fall 1981) v. 5(3) 173–174.

52. Irene Atwell and Daudi Ajani ya Azibo, "Diagnosing Personality Disorder in Africans (Blacks) Using the Azibo Nosology: Two Case Studies," *The Journal of Black Psychology (Spring 1991)* (Spring 1991) 17(2) p. 3.

53. Ibid., 3–4.

54. See Daudi Ajani ya Azibo, "African-centered Theses on Mental Health and a Nosology of Black/African Personality Disorder," *The Journal of Black Psychology* (Spring 1989) 15(2) 173–214.

55. For further explication of psychological misorientation see J. A. Baldwin, "African Self-Consciousness and the Mental Health of African Americans," *Journal of Black Studies,* 15(2) 177–194, also see Bobby E. Wright, 1979. "Mentacide: The Ultimate Threat to the Black Race." Paper presented at the Atlanta Summit on Afrikan Psychology. September.

56. Semaj, "The Black Self, Identity and Models for a Psychology of Black Liberation," p. 159, also, Na'im Akbar, "Mental Disorder Among African-Americans," *Black Books Bulletin* (January 1981) 7(2) 18–25.

57. Fanon, *The Wretched of the Earth* 285–310.

58. Akbar, "Mental Disorder Among African Americans," 18–25.

59. W. E. Cross, "The Negro to Black Conversion Experience: Towards a Psychology of Black Liberation," *Black World* (June 1971) 20(9), 13–27.

60. Ibid.

61. Joseph A. Baldwin and Yvonne R. Bell, "The African Self-Consciousness Scale: An Africentric Personality Questionnaire," *The Western Journal of Black Studies* (Summer 1985) v. 9(2) 61–68.

62. Vivian V. Gordon, *The Self-Concept of Black Americans* (Washington D.C.: University Press of America 1977) 72–73.

63. Gordon, *The Self-Concept of Black Americans,* 26–55. (Gordon outlines and summarizes the results of more than 100 studies from 1939 to 1973.)

64. K. B. Clark and M. P. Clark, "The Development of Consciousness of Self and the Emergence of Racial Identification in Negro Preschool Children," *Journal of Social Psychology* (1939) 10, 591–599.

65. Sharon-ann Gopaul-Mc.Nicol, "Racial Identification and Racial Preference on Black Preschool Children in New York and Trinidad," *The Journal of Black Psychology* (February 1988) 14(2) 67.

66. George H. Hill and Sylvia S. Hill, *Blacks on Television* (Metuchen, NJ: The Scarecrow Press 1985) 1–7.

67. John Henrik Clarke, *African World Revolution* (Trenton, NJ: Africa World Press, Inc. 1991) 329–330.

68. Sonja Peterson-Lewis and Afesa Adams, "Televisions Model of the Quest for African Consciousness: A Comparison with Cross' Empirical Model of Psychological Nigrescence," *The Journal of Black Psychology* (Spring 1990) 16(2) 55–72.

69. Tony Brown, "Racism on TV" *Detroit Free Press* (December 27, 1979) 149(237) p. 1.

70. See Richard A. Davis, "Television Commercials and the Management of Spoiled Identity," *The Western Journal of Black Studies* (Summer 1987) v. 11(2) 59–63.

# Chapter 6

# Politics and African Americans

## AN OVERVIEW OF BLACK POLITICAL EXPERIENCE

*Political Science and the Nature of Black Politics.* Political science, like the other areas of human study, is culturally and geographically conceived, defined and developed. From a Eurocentric worldview, it has been stated that politics dates back to the ancient Greeks (500 to 300 B.C.). Furthermore, it is postulated by some Euro-American scholars that "Plato may be called the father of political theory and Aristotle the parent of political science, at least in the West."[1] Within the same view, political science is broadly defined as a study of the principles and organization of the government of states. Thus, politics is the practical and functional exercise of policy-making and rule of the state or government.

The problem or argument is not so much with the definition of politics or political science as it may be with the claim that any one race or country is responsible for its concept or theoretical origin. As indicated in the preceding chapter on Black history, various recorded Egyptian (Ethiopian) civilizations existed in North Africa as early as 6000 to 4000 B.C. The sophisticated West African states of Ghana, Mali and Songhay thrived and declined within the periods of 700 to 1600 A.D. Certainly, these African civilizations and states were developed under sound culture-specific political principles, methods and organizations of government.

The point is that Europeans were not the sole initiators of the concept, practice or study of politics. African people did not wait in darkness for hundreds of centuries for Europeans or Asians to conceive of political science or any of the other human studies discussed in this text. The evolvement or development of all concrete or abstract phenomenon by various human societies has resulted from some form of study, regardless of methodology. Therefore, concepts of function, application and practice of political ideas or ideologies may differ according to cultural-racial values and experiences.

African American or Black politics represents a case in point. Politics infers an individual or group who participates in the formulation of policy for the rule of a government or state. Historically, because of slavery, segregation and overt oppression Blacks have been excluded from *conventional* participation in the political affairs of state. Even presently, it is questionable as to the extent that African Americans, through conventional politics, can affect governmental policy considering their comparative lack of power and representation. The politics of Black Americans have been devoted to the objective of eliminating their disfranchisement and inequity based on race. Black politics is predicated upon the abolition of racism and White oppression. On the other hand, and historically, it has been the purpose of white politics to minimize or deny Blacks political participation in order to sustain white political rule.

In many ways, Black politics is diametrically opposed to the political functions and objectives of white society. The meaning and exercise of Black politics are often different from those of whites even though both races participate in the same political process. Black politics functions as a sub-system effecting the white controlled political system, electorally or otherwise, in matters pertaining to racial equality and justice. Thus, as one political writer has stated Black politics "is not solely the electoral process but the total process of articulating black needs and of eliciting white response."[2] Hanes Walton, an eminent Black political scientist, also contends that Black politics cannot be studied exclusively from an electoral angle. Black

voting or electoral participation is only one political activity among many that constitutes Black politics. Some of the most effective Black political activities have included strikes, boycotting, demonstrations, civil disobedience, and marches.[3] Historically, Blacks have used these various strategies and techniques to influence the enactment of public policy to alleviate racial segregation, oppression and discrimination. Until the passage of the landmark Voting Rights Act of 1965, non-electoral or unconventional politics were the primary activities employed by Blacks to achieve their political objectives.

The Voting Rights Act of 1965, including several extensions and modifications up to the year 1991, has given rise to the belief that African Americans have advanced from protest politics to electoral politics. Considering the contemporary politically powerless state of Blacks, such an assumption might be premature. The fact is that for reasons of racial inequality, Blacks have different political goals and objectives than Whites. It has to be proven that social, economic and political equality can be achieved by Blacks through their participation in traditional electoral politics before one can be sure that protest politics are completely terminated.

**Black Political Ideologies.** If Black politics are presented as being distinct in conception and function, then it is logical to assume that there exist differences in the ideological orientation of African Americans. Some have argued that beyond rhetoric and symbolism a viable Black political ideology has not been developed or at least sustained since slavery. The implication is that Blacks have conformed to or adopted the political ideologies of white or European people.[4] Those who dismiss the significance of Black ideology are prone to view it only from a functional or practical basis. However, ideology for the purpose of this discussion is meant to include the various classifications of ideas, beliefs, theories, thoughts or philosophies Blacks have manifested over the years toward the liberation of their race. Just because African Americans have not possessed the power, means and resources to effectuate or realize certain ideologies does not mean an absence of Black political ideology. Black political ideologies have been derived from the consciousness of Black people's circumstances and the state of their existence.

The political ideology of White Americans is based on their beliefs and practices of individualism, materialism, capitalism and white supremacy.[5] While the influence and affect of the dominant White American ideology is significant, Black political ideology is effected more by race and race relations in the United States. During and after the slave era, Black political ideology and political activity have been related to race, racism and social relations. At least three distinct racial or race relations ideologies continue to loom as divisive elements in the Black community. Although many of the values and characteristics of these ideologies overlap, they might be broadly differentiated into three categories: 1) integrationism, 2) separatism, and 3) Black nationalism.

Frederick Douglass was the foremost architect and promoter of the political ideology of racial integration and assimilationist ideals during the slavery and post-slavery periods. The moral and theoretical bases for desegregation, school integration, equality of the ballot, social equality and social-mixing can be found throughout his voluminous works and writings.[6] There is little doubt that the spirit and racial philosophy of Frederick Douglass influenced the organization and political ideology of the NAACP. The NAACP became the premier Black political organization and a catalyst for Black politics in the twentieth century. The integrationist ideology of the NAACP and the Urban League is reflected in their membership. Both organizations are

interracial in character and depend to some extent on White liberals' support.

Competing with the ideology of integration is the Black political philosophy of separatism. Ever since Booker T. Washington delivered his famous "Atlanta Compromise" separatist address in 1895, separatism has appeared as a viable alternative to Black/White social and economic integration. When Washington enunciated his separatist ideology, it created one of the greatest political divisions among Blacks in the history of the African American experience. The ideology of Black separatism was diametrically opposed to the integrationist ideals of Frederick Douglass which was another factor that prompted the organization of the NAACP in 1909. (See chapter 3)

The classical version of Black separatism advocated by Booker T. Washington in 1895 is not entirely comparable to modern separatist ideology. Washington's accommodationist advice during that time was for Blacks not to agitate for social, intellectual and professional equality with Whites. Contemporary separatists exhort Blacks not only to equal Whites, but to excel them as a tribute to and redemption of their African heritage. Modern Black separatism is difficult to define because of its similarity with Black nationalism. Raymond L. Hall posits in his book, *Black Separatism in the United States*, that Black separatism is a subcategory of Black nationalism.[7] While Hall has produced an excellent work on Black separatism, his differentiation between Black separatism and nationalism lacks clarity. The reason may be that the two ideologies borrow and subsume each other. Another reason is the ambiguity of the territorial division factor.

Neither integrationism, separatism nor Black nationalism are absolute in definition and value characteristics. Each ideology has degrees of similarity with the other. For example, integrationists are zealous in their fight to desegregate public facilities and institutions. Yet, they have lobbied and mounted vigorous political campaigns to maintain the predominantly Black historical colleges and universities. Integrationists are not likely to seek significant desegregation of the Black church or Black religious denominations. Although Black nationalists may believe in all Black enterprises, they do not reject White markets and patronage.

Realizing the futility and improbability of territorial division or land separation, modern separatist ideology means a form of equitable racial co-existence with Blacks controlling the major social and economic institutions in the Black community. Self-determination and self-sufficiency are essential to the values of separatist ideology. Separatists are determined to have pride in blackness and to maintain their separate Black identity. Black separatism and nationalism are born out of the distrust of Whites to ever effect racial justice and equality.

Black nationalism is an African-oriented social movement. Contemporary Black nationalism fosters an identification with African states and the belief that the redemption of Africa is imperative for the liberation of African people in both America and Africa. Marcus Garvey was the foremost exponent of Black nationalism in America during the 1920s. In addition to his return-to-Africa theme, Garvey instilled into the consciousness of the masses of Blacks a sense of self-worth and economic independence from Whites. Yet, Garvey was an avid believer and practitioner of capitalism. Further evidence of the nexus between Black separatism and nationalism is the fact that Garvey was an admirer of Booker T. Washington.[8]

Black integrationist, separatist and nationalist political ideologies developed near the end of the nineteenth and early twentieth centuries. Although the major exponents have long since been deceased, their racial ideologies still have a profound and active effect on the contemporary politics of African Americans. Martin Luther King, Jr. revived with political fervor the integrationist-assimilationist ideologies of Frederick Douglass during the Civil Rights Movement of the 1960s. Also during the 1960s, Malcolm X was the flamboyant standard-bearer of the Black separatist-nationalist ideology. Integrationist and separatist ideologies have always conflicted and have caused much political disunity in the Black community. Martin Luther King, Jr. and Malcolm X were ideological and political adversaries during the 1960s era just as Jesse Jackson and Louis Farrakhan (the present Islamic Black nationalist leader) are today.

Nevertheless, the integration oriented Black organizations and leadership (NAACP and Urban League) are the most influential and hold the preferred attention of the White liberal Democratic establishment. African Americans seem to be inextricably tied to the Democratic Party although the reward for such loyalty is not always apparent. Black separatist-nationalist proponents have attempted to organize an independent political bloc. Harold Cruse criticized the NAACP for opposing the objectives of the first Black political convention in Gary, Indiana in 1972. The NAACP refused to support the independent political party plank. Cruse laments that, "the traditional civil rights leadership will oppose any attempt on the part of an alternate leadership to organize blacks into an independent political bloc."[9] This is a classic example of how "internal" Black political ideologies can effect external electoral participation and outcomes.

**Black Liberal and Conservative Political Philosophy.** American mainstream political philosophy is divided into two major classifications, liberal and conservative. Variant philosophies ranging to the left or right of these two classifications are generally labelled populism and libertarianism. While liberalism and conservatism may aptly describe White political thought orientations in America, Black political ideologies do not conform in all aspects to these concepts. Too little attention has been given to the notion that Blacks view liberal and conservative ideologies from different socio-political perspectives. Although the social, political and economic experiences of Black Americans are quite different, the assumption has been that Black political philosophy fits without qualification into the dominant society's liberal, conservative, populist or libertarian paradigms. Blacks are an oppressed race. It is illogical to assume that the political views of the hare are the same as those of the fox.

Historically, African Americans have identified with and supported liberal democratic politics. This would seem natural since liberalism subscribes to certain egalitarian human principles. In spite of the long staunch support Blacks have given to the liberal Democratic Party, ideological consensus has never existed between White and Black liberals. It is obvious that the goals and benefits Blacks seek from supporting liberal politics are, in part, different from those expected by Whites. The difference between Black/White perceptions of liberal and conservative are not easily discernible. The key to understanding the difference is inherent in the general definitions of liberal and conservative philosophies.

Political theorists now prefer to distinguish between classical and modern liberal philosophy. Classical liberalism strongly advocated the use of government intervention and funding to bring about solutions to all social and economic problems affecting the society. Furthermore, the government was perceived as the guarantor of egalitarian principles and programs. The popularity of this form of liberalism gained momentum during the Great Depression when Franklin D. Roosevelt managed to stem the tide of unemployment, poverty and financial disasters with a series of "New Deal" government sponsored economic

programs.[10] Although the New Deal programs were not intended or designed to address racial inequality, Blacks benefitted (under segregated programs) along with the general population. Therefore, Blacks began to associate racial uplift with liberal democratic politics.

Blacks view a liberal political philosophy as one that is conducive to fighting and reducing the social ills of racism or racial inequality. On the other hand, Whites become disdainful of liberalism when it focuses upon altering the racial status quo. White political theorists seldom if ever inject the term racism in liberal or conservative ideology. The word racism and its implications permeates the works or literature of Black political scientists. Nevertheless, through conventional and unconventional means, Blacks forced the issues of racism and civil rights upon liberal democratic politics. Under almost successive Democratic Party administrations from Franklin D. Roosevelt to Lyndon Johnson, liberalism became inseparable with civil rights. Government intervention was sought not just for economic purposes but to promote racial equality and social justice. Classical white liberals never intended for the race issue to be a major tenet of liberalism.[11]

The broadening of the scope or umbrella of liberalism to include not only Blacks but gays, feminists, and the organized interests of labor and environmental groups led to widescale abandonment of the Democratic party by Whites. In 1980, many crossed over to the conservative ranks of the Republicans. It was clear to the Democrats after the 1984 election that a new liberal ideology had to be developed in order to "save" the party. Thus, a modern or neoliberal political philosophy has emerged. Modern or neoliberalism reflects greater value-orientation and advocates a strong role of government in promoting economic growth through the development and subsidization of high technology. This philosophy represents a marked shift from social to economic liberalism.

Modern liberalism in its broadest sense differs from classical liberalism in terms of government role and function. William S. Maddox and Stuart A. Lilie state that

> Modern liberals, while still valuing private property and the market, are willing to support government intervention to promote individual welfare and to regulate the economy. At the same time liberals argue fairly consistently that in terms of one's personal activity outside the economic realm, the individual should remain free of governmental restriction.[12]

A difference in Black and White interpretation and expectation of liberalism is implicit in Maddox and Lilie's emphasis of "individual welfare." Modern Democratic and Republican liberalism now stress individual rather than group rights. Liberalism to Blacks may mean a philosophy committed to the struggle of group or racial rights and equality.

Following the climax of the Civil Rights Movement period of the mid-1970s, a small number of African American academic professionals began to articulate a "conservative" ideology which sharply contrasted with traditional Black liberal philosophy. Considering the history and role that White conservatism has played in the repression of Black justice and freedom, one may find it difficult to rationalize the existence of a Black conservative ideology. However, as in the case of liberalism, Blacks and Whites may concur on certain conservative principles but for different reasons. Before such an anomaly may be understood, one must have a general idea of the meaning of American conservatism.

Conservatism is an attitude or a philosophy which opposes change. It seeks to maintain tradition or status quo. Conservatives oppose what they see as the liberals' disregard for an objective moral order or their support of moral relativism. Conservatism places private property and economic freedom above all other freedoms. Conservatives believe in

minimal interference of government in the lives of people and business except to establish law and order and to protect property rights.[13] Maddox and Lilie suggest that "conservatism has been associated with support for all basic American values, attachment to big business, [fundamentalist] religious approaches to politics, and general closed-mindedness."[14] One of the more popular conceptions of conservatism is the belief in self-reliance or rugged-individualism. This latter characteristic has a significant appeal to Black conservatives.

Since African Americans suffer the tradition of racial discrimination and oppression, short of masochism, Black conservatives should demand change. Nevertheless, Black conservatives posit that the maximum benefit from government intervention on behalf of civil rights has already been obtained. Therefore, they believe that the traditional mono-dimensional Black liberal philosophy of civil rights agitation is outmoded and that new self-help economic policies should be developed. For the most part, Black liberals do not agree entirely with such assumption.

One of the most profound essays on Black conservatism was written by political scientist W. Avon Drake. In this work, Drake maintains that the foundation for Black conservative philosophy was laid by Booker T. Washington during the last nineteenth and early twentieth centuries. Modern proponents of Black conservative ideology include Thomas Sowell of the Hoover Institution, Walter Williams of George Mason University, and Glenn C. Loury of Harvard. Drake has perceptively summarized four key points that synthesizes the theoretical underpinnings of Black conservatism. They are:

1. the premise that racism cannot fully explain Black economic subordination;

2. the premise that political power will not ensure economic success for Blacks;

3. the argument that a free market offers the best opportunity for Black progress;

4. the assertion that Blacks hold the key to their socio-economic salvation in America.[15]

Furthermore, some Black conservatives purport that most social problems besetting Blacks are of their own making and that local, state, and government programs do little to solve them. These conservatives depreciate the value of affirmative actions programs. Black conservatives tend to soft-pedal racism, blame the victim, and let the White establishment off the hook.[16]

Black and White conservative ideologies differ in focus and theory. While Black conservatism challenges the ideological dominance of Black liberalism, it fosters naivete relative to American capitalism and racism. Black conservatives are not novel in their advocacy of self-reliance and self-determination. Marcus Garvey, Elijah Muhammad, and Malcolm X were forerunners of the Black self-help philosophy. The question that Black conservatives should consider is: If African Americans contribute more than 200 billion dollars annually to national income or (GNP) and pay billions in taxes, why should they not demand substantial returns for the development of the Black community?

*Synopsis of Black Political History.* The politics of Africans in America have been almost unidimensionally related to the issues of enfranchisement and civil rights. Early Black political activity following the American Revolution in 1783 focused upon the abolition of slavery. Since slavery, the predominance of the politics of African Americans has been devoted to the acquisition and maintenance of voting rights and all other cardinal rights of citizenship. As previously discussed, Black politics have not always been demonstrated in conventional or electoral forms but through petition protest and moral suasion.

It is recorded that early suffrage did exist for a few "free" Blacks of the South and to some extent among those in some of the Northern states. A limited number of free Blacks voted in Tennessee in 1834 and in North Carolina in 1835. Although their vote was not large, Blacks were given equal suffrage and voted in Massachusetts, Maine, New Hampshire and Vermont in 1840. New York and Rhode Island imposed certain property qualifications.[17]

Blacks who could vote in the North were active electorally or otherwise in the presidential election of Abraham Lincoln in 1860 and in his subsequent re-election campaign of 1864. Several Black Republican Clubs and suffrage organizations were formed in northern cities in support of Lincoln's party and its hoped for anti-slavery stance. Frederick Douglass campaigned and supported the election of Lincoln in 1860. Blacks did not vote in the South in 1860.[18]

In spite of periods of vacillation and dubious advocacy of Black enfranchisement by the Republican Party, the majority of Blacks tended to be supportive of the Republicans until the early twentieth century. After the passage of the Fifteenth Amendment in 1870, Black Republicans gained significant influence in the South. However, the liberalism of the Republicans on anti-slavery and Black enfranchisement issues caused the Republican Party to lose power among whites in the South after 1870. In 1876 in order to placate the South, Republican presidential candidate Rutherford B. Hayes agreed to withdraw federal Reconstruction enforcement officials in exchange for Southern electoral votes. This became known as the compromise of 1877. The purpose was to attract more whites and to save the Republican Party in the South.

The Republican Party became stigmatized as being the "nigger party" by southern Democrats. Thus, white Republicans began to purge or alienate Black Republicans and to form Lily-White political organizations. Black members of the Party were known as the Black and Tan Republicans. Attempts to form coalitions between White and Black Republicans proved to be futile. With the Compromise of 1877 having resulted in a hands-off policy by the Republican Administration, Blacks were subjected to much oppression and abuse by southern whites. Successive Republican presidents tried to bolster the Republican Party in the South by placating whites while not losing entirely the support of Blacks. By 1890, eight southern states had disfranchised all Black voters through the revision of their constitutions. This put an end to Black politics in the South. The South became a one-party region under the domain of white supremacy Democratic Party politics. The Democratic Party prevailed exclusively in the South until 1964.[19]

In American politics, Blacks have been impelled by logic and intuition to identity with and to support the political party which has accorded them, as a race, the most hope for freedom and enfranchisement. During the 1800s and even after the Rutherford B. Hayes betrayal in the Compromise of 1877, Blacks generally supported the Republican Party. They had good reasons to be loyal and dedicated to Republican politics since constitutional amendments passed on behalf of their enfranchisement, the Emancipation, and the first Civil Rights Act were promoted and passed under traditional or radical Republicanism. Blacks decreased their support of or defected from the Republican Party only after they had been alienated and rejected by Republican party leaders and standard-bearers. For a long period after 1890, Blacks had virtually lost their enthusiasm for either of the political parties. The Republicans were indif-

ferent or non-accommodating and the Democrats did not actively seek Black voters.

A noticeable shift of the majority of African Americans from the Republican to the Democratic Party occurred in 1936 after the first term of the Roosevelt New Deal era. It is Hanes Walton's and several other political scientists' contention that Blacks did not change their loyalty to the Democratic party instantaneously but instead there was a gradual transition beginning initially at the local level. Indeed, there always were some Northern Blacks who supported selective Democratic candidates, and so did a number of Southern Blacks who maintained suffrage.[20] It is evident that Blacks generally avoided association with the Democratic Party prior to 1936 because of the overt racial meanness and, particularly, the anti-Black attitudes of most white Democrats. Yet, it was the anti-Black and ultra-conservative sentiment that Republicans developed after 1877 which drove Blacks away from the Republican Party, their initial political benefactors.

There is little doubt that the contemporary loyalty of most African Americans to the Democratic party stemmed from the social and economic policies of Franklin D. Roosevelt. Successive Democratic presidents, Harry S. Truman, John F. Kennedy and Lyndon B. Johnson sponsored various measures of civil rights bills or proposals. However the fact that Dwight D. Eisenhower, the Republican president who succeeded Truman, received 40 percent of the Black vote in 1956 obscures the notion that African American party loyalty is inflexibly Democratic. It is uncertain as to whether Blacks are attracted to the political party alone or to the promise of equality and charismatic appeal of the candidate regardless of his or her party affiliation. After all, the Democratic Party is relatively new in its support of egalitarian and civil rights principles. The Republicans certainly have a much longer history of supporting the social and political equality of African

Americans. However, almost a century has passed since the Republican Party has made a *strong* national commitment to civil rights and equality for African Americans.

The Black Northern vote, political activities and influence have long been significant in national party politics and in presidential elections. It was not until the U.S. Supreme Court *(Smith v. Allwright)* decision declared the White primary system unconstitutional in 1943 did the southern states and Black voters in the South became, possibly, pivotal in presidential elections. The white primary was a system initiated in the southern states to bar Black political participation. Blacks contributed to Harry S. Truman's margin of victory in California, Illinois, and Ohio in 1948. The elimination of the white primary system sparked massive Black voter registration in the South during the 1950s.[21]

The era of Black protest which developed from the violent school desegregation rebellions, other racial atrocities, and the Montgomery Bus Boycott of the mid-1950s did more to arouse the national civic consciousness of African Americans than any other events in American history. Partly as a result of the urgency of this period, Congress passed Civil Rights Acts in 1957 and in 1960 to protect Black voting rights. It established a Commission on Civil rights as an investigative agency. Other non-electoral political tactics and activities such as the student sit-ins and freedom rides of the 1960s galvanized Black politics in the North and South. The increased electoral power and political influence of African Americans by 1960 resulted in the election of five Black U.S. Congressmen and contributed to the crucial margin of votes necessary for the successful election of President John F. Kennedy. Significant, too, in the development of the "new" Black politics was the extensive voter-registration and voter education projects conducted from 1962 to 1964 by all the major civil rights organiza-

tions including the NAACP, SNCC, and CORE.

The effect or pivotal significance of the Black vote in presidential or general elections is not conclusive. The Black bloc voting theory suggests that under certain political circumstances the African American electorate can be the decisive factor in the failed or successful election of a president in particular. Especially after the passage of the 1965 Voting Rights Act, the Black vote was expected to be strategically significant in presidential primaries and in the general election. However, this does not always prove to be the case. For example, it is questionable as to the effect Blacks had in the landslide victory of Lyndon B. Johnson in 1964. Although Johnson received 90 percent of the Black vote, his ultra-conservative Republican opponent Barry Goldwater won the electoral votes in Mississippi, Alabama, Georgia, Louisiana and South Carolina in spite of the fact that these states have large Black registered voter populations.[22] It would appear that the Black vote was not critical in the Johnson election.

In the presidential election of 1968, Democratic presidential candidate and civil rights advocate Hubert H. Humphrey lost to conservative Republican Richard M. Nixon in spite of Black support for the liberal Democratic ticket. Political scientist Ronald W. Walters attributes the reason for the ineffectiveness of the Black vote in this election was a low Black voter turnout. Walters further speculated that "the low turnout implied a boycott of the Democratic candidate by Blacks, a negative sanction in the eyes of party leaders and strategists—black and white."[23] In 1972, the Republican Richard Nixon won handily again in his re-election bid against Democratic candidate George S. McGovern. McGovern received 90 percent of the Black vote.

The year 1972 was significant in the history of Black politics although African American voters were unable to influence the presidential election. Shirley Chisholm, a Democratic member of the House of Representatives from New York was the first Black woman to announce and to run for the president of the United States. However, the Democratic convention held at Miami Beach nominated Senator George McGovern for president. Rep. Shirley Chisholm received 151.95 of the 2,000-plus ballots on the first roll call. Sixteen Blacks were elected to Congress in 1972, and Andrew Young of Atlanta was the first Black elected to Congress from the Deep South since Reconstruction.[24]

The 1976 election proved to be evidential that the Black vote could under certain political conditions be a determining factor in presidential elections. Political theorists generally acknowledge that the African American vote provided the margin of victory for President Jimmy Carter in 1976. It was essential for Carter, a Southerner, to carry the South. He could not have done this without the substantial large Black voter registration of the southern states. Conservative Republican Ronald Reagan defeated Jimmy Carter in his re-election bid of 1980. It may not be appropriate or valid to apply the Black pivotal vote theory to the 1980 presidential election. Carter's ineffective domestic economic policy and his failed foreign policy and actions taken during the Iran hostage crisis contributed to his general unpopularity. In addition, the failing economy and the accrued White back-lash from affirmative action and equal opportunity programs that were responsible for Black progress during the 1970s kindled the fires of racial antagonism and racism. Ronald Reagan appealed to the base instincts and racist attitudes of southern whites and ultra-conservatives who overwhelmingly supported his election and re-election bids for the presidency in 1980 and 1984.

Black politics of the 1980s signified an enormous decline in unconventional or protest politics and a shift to electoral participation. From July 1982 to July 1983 the number of Black elected officials nationwide increased by 8.6 percent. This was significant because the rate of increase of Black elected officials declined since the early 1970s following the upsurge resulting from the passage of the 1965 Voting Rights Act. The number of Black registered voters increased dramatically from 1980 to 1982. The African American members of Congress rose from 18 to 21, and the number of Black state legislators also increased significantly during this period.[25] It is important to note that these increases occurred during the first term of the Reagan Administration.

One of the most historic events of the 1984 campaign and election year was that the Reverend Jesse Jackson, a Black "disciple" of the 1960s Civil Rights Movement, made a very serious bid for the presidency. Jackson's political strategy was to develop a "rainbow coalition" of Blacks, Hispanics, women and other oppressed members of the American society. Jackson made extensive use of the political influence and power of the Black church in mobilizing his bid for the nomination. However, Walter F. Mondale was voted by the Democratic Party at the San Francisco National Convention to be the presidential nominee to oppose Ronald Reagan in the 1984 election. Nevertheless, Jackson ran an unprecedented campaign. More Blacks than ever participated in the convention. There were 697 Black delegates representing 17.7 of the total. Even though Jackson's candidacy for the nomination was marred with intra-racial and intra-Party controversy and disputes, Black politics were propelled to new heights in the American political arena.[26] What was even more phenomenal was Jackson's second bid for the Democratic presidential nomination in 1988.

In the 1988 Democratic primary election, Jesse Jackson received three times more White votes than he did in 1984. Jackson doubled his overall primary vote to 6.6 million

Photo 15   Shirley Chisholm. Courtesy of National Archives.

Photo 16  Jesse Jackson. Courtesy of The Library of Congress.

ballots as opposed to 3.15 million in comparable primaries in 1984. Numerically, he won 2.1 million White votes in 1988 compared with 650,000 in 1984. While he received only 5 percent of the White vote in 1984, he received 12.5 percent in 1988. Nevertheless, Jackson's candidacy remained almost grossly dependent on Black voters. He received 92 percent of all ballots cast by Blacks or approximately 4.3 million votes.[27]

For the third consecutive terms (1980, 1984, 1988), the Republicans won the presidential elections. In the general election, George Bush defeated Michael Dukakis. While nine out of every ten Blacks voted for the Democrat Michael Dukakis, it was insufficient to effect Bush's presidential victory. Still, Bush failed to equal Ronald Reagan in attracting conservative White Democrats. Blacks were caught up in the age-long dilemma of being virtually written off by the Republicans and taken for granted by the Democrats. The reverse was true during the Reconstruction era, and before the 1930s, when Blacks voted almost unanimously for Republicans and were rejected by the Democratic Party. Undoubtedly reflecting on the historical compromise of 1877, Linda F. Williams in comparing the 1984 and 1988 elections stated that

> the Democratic party has attempted to hold on to black voters, its most loyal constituency, while downplaying black influence in the party in hopes of stemming the flight of white voters.[28]

There were indications at the beginning of the 1992 campaign that the Republicans under the Bush presidency were seeking to cultivate Black voters in realization that the primary constituency of the GOP represents, generally, a socio-economic minority.

# CONCEPTS TOWARD BLACK POLITICAL EMPOWERMENT

*The Politics of Black Power.* There is a direct relationship of psychology and the political socialization of people. When Stokely Carmichael enunciated the shrill cry of "Black Power" from the back of a flat-bed truck at the rally of the Voter Registration March Against Fear in Greenwood, Mississippi in June of 1966, the affect was electrifying and disturbing to the minds of Blacks and Whites. It was a psychologically liberating experience for millions of African Americans. For over 300 years, successive generations of Black people had been socialized and conditioned into believing that it was prohibitive and impossible to associate power with blackness or Africanity. Conversely, Whites have been psychologically influenced for centuries to believe that power is an exclusive trait and right of people of European stock and ancestry.

Initially and ironically, the most vocal critics and denunciators of the term Black Power which was used to describe the aspirations and context of the Civil Rights Movement were several of the older "mentally enslaved" Black leaders who would have felt psychologically uncomfortable possessing power in the presence of white people under any circumstance.[29] These were the ardent integrationists who would surrender all claims to power as long as they could be socially merged and accepted into White society. On the other hand, Whites were not about to share political or economic power with their former slaves who they deemed to be humanly and intellectually inferior.

Because of the controversy and intense emotion that the slogan Black Power generated, the progressive and mostly youthful proponents had to divert and devote much of their effort towards defining and explaining the concept of Black power and easing the fears of "Uncle Tom" Blacks and liberal Whites. Conservative Whites fully understood the meaning of power regardless of the shade or color it was manifested. Stokely Carmichael, the leading symbol and advocate of Black Power, attributed to the term a clear and logical political meaning. In essence, Carmichael explained that the political system of America is structured and designed to render Black people socially and economically powerless. The majority of Blacks lacked adequate education and were economically deprived and propertyless. Therefore, it was imperative for Black people to have power to make or participate in making the decisions which govern their lives, and to effect social change of the American society.[30]

The aspect of Black Power ideology which evoked the most concern and dissent was the advocacy of Black self-determination. Self-determination, economic self-sufficiency, and Black pride were not new concepts proposed for the political empowerment of African Americans. Marcus Garvey and other early Black philosophers had already authored and articulated the principles of self-determination. However, integrationists perceived any ideas or actions promoting Black independence as regressive and supportive of the degrading social system of segregation. They fearfully and inaccurately contended that Black Power was synonymous with segregation. The psycho-political implications of Black apprehension for any measure of independence from whites are clear. As has already been referred to in the works of Franz Fanon, colonization or slavery politically socializes many of its subjects into accepting dependency upon the oppressor as a normative state. The "free slave" may unconsciously resist the idea of "breaking away" or functioning without the scrutiny, approval or supervision of the "master."

The politics of Black Power conflict in many ways with integration as it is currently implemented in American society. Symbolic or token representation of Blacks in the political system in the name of integration does not translate, in effect, into actual power sharing. Simple desegregation cannot achieve Black power. Token desegregation does not alter white control over matters affecting the quality of life and destiny of the Black community. Black power means an assertion of Black identity and the recognition and operation of a Black political agenda. Since America is still divided, basically, into Black and White communities, Black power advocates argue for political control or ownership of the social and economic institutions within the Black community.

Integration has been extolled as a paragon for racial equality by many. But in effect, the concept of integration has served as a political ploy for the socio-economic elevation of a relatively few system-accommodating individuals rather than for the uplift of African Americans as a whole. One might observe that integration politics have been inequitably manipulated to the extent that White Power has been further enhanced and Black Power has suffered relative diminution. Manning Marable has remarked that, "racial integration has produced the symbols of progress and the rhetoric of racial harmony without the substance of empowerment for the oppressed."[31] Thus, it appears that significant conflicts exist between Black power and integration politics. An overriding question is: Can African Americans achieve some measure of political parity or power under the existing two-party system?

The political history of African Americans reveals that they have often attempted or succeeded at establishing independent political parties or organizations in order to project and to protect their political interests. Organizing and maintaining separate or independent political organizations are consistent with Black Power ideology. One of the most important goals and accomplishments of Black Power advocates during the Civil

Rights Movement was their assistance in the establishment of Mississippi Freedom Democratic Party (MFDP) in 1964. The purpose of the MFDP was to challenge and to end the discriminatory exclusion of Blacks from the regular white controlled Democratic Party. The MFDP challenged the seating of the regular Democratic delegates at the national convention in Atlantic City but their claim was rejected. The seating of five white congressmen from Mississippi was challenged by the MFDP in 1965 on the grounds that Blacks had been excluded in the primary and general elections. The House of Representatives voted to dismiss the challenge. Subsequently the MFDP did achieve some successes in 1967 and 1968. Elements of the MFDP are still functioning in the state of Mississippi.

In 1966 SNCC organized a Black independent political party in Lowndes County, Alabama (80% Black population) for the purpose of nominating candidates for the offices of sheriff, tax assessor and members of the school board. The party was called the Lowndes County Freedom Organization (LCFO). It used as its ballot symbol the Black panther. The LCFO slate lost the election by a narrow margin because of violence on the election day. Carmichael later used the Lowndes County scenario to define and rationalize the political slogan of Black Power. With Blacks being in a position to elect sheriffs, they could put an end to police brutality. Black

Photo 17   Fannie Lou Hamer, Mississippi Freedom Democratic Party Leader.
Courtesy of The Library of Congress.

# PROJECTIONS OF THE BLACK POPULATION: 1990–2080
## (Numbers in thousands.)

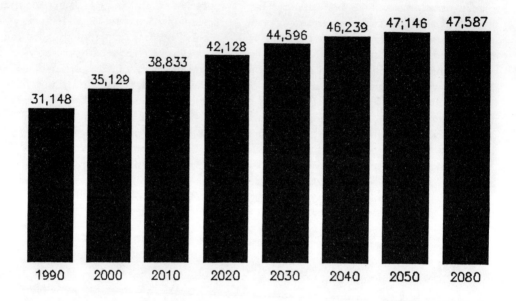

SOURCE: U.S. BUREAU OF THE CENSUS

Figure 7  Projection of the Black Population.

tax assessors could collect and channel funds for the building of better Black schools and road to serve the Black community.[32]

As indicated in the previous topic of discussion, the African American bloc vote may often serve as the pivotal factor in determining the outcome of primaries and general elections. In order to capitalize upon this reality and to enhance the political prospects of Black Power, Ronald W. Walters has stated that, "there needs to be some political organization capable of providing the option of running a candidate in the general election, or of throwing the organization's support to either one party or the other in accord with the outcome of the bargaining."[33]

The genesis of a Black organized revolt of the traditional Democrat and Republican two-party political system occurred when African Americans held the National Black Political Convention in Gary, Indiana on March 10–12, 1972. More than 10,000 Blacks, 3,000 registered delegates from 46 states, came to Gary to adopt a National Black Agenda based upon the common interests and political objectives of the masses of Black people in the United States. As one political analyst wrote, "Gary leaped past the limits and concepts of its conceivers, the

Black elected officials and the Congressional Black Caucus."[34] The Black media reported much factionalism as might be expected at any political convention. Some almost un-reconcilable differences between Black Power/Nationalists and Black elected officials precluded, at that time, the formation of a Black independent party. However, a holistic and unified African spirituality prevailed at the convention. The National Black Political Assembly was organized as the continuum of the Gary convention and has met annually in various other cities. The Black Nationalists established a Black Independent Political Party in 1980. However, a truly unified Black politi-cal party is still in the process of development.

Insofar as Black interests are concerned, the Democratic and Republican parties are becoming increasingly non-distinguishable in the 1990s. If this trend continues, it will serve to fuel the independent party initiatives smoldering in the arena of Black politics. For a Black independent political party to suc-ceed it must have the support of the regis-tered voting majority of African Americans. The purpose of such a political party may not be always to have its own slate of winning candidates, but to negotiate or bargain for benefits between the two traditional parties. The goals and objectives of Black power poli-tics are to sustain a posture of independence, develop as a pivotal-force in the electorate and, to maintain leverage in the two-party American political system. Black Power political activists ultimately seek to change the social and economic order to one that is free of racial inequality and injustice.

***Dialectics of Black Alliances and Coalitions.*** John Henrik Clarke, the eminent African historian, once stated, in essence, that Blacks are one of the most naive of people in in-stances where Black/White political alliances or coalitions have been formed.[35] In the con-text of this inference, Clarke was recounting the historical experiences of Africans (Egypt,

Ethiopia) with the Greeks and Romans more than 1600 to 2000 years ago. Other historians relate the tragic experience of the Black freedmen in their attempts to ally or coalesce with the White Populists near the end of the nineteenth century.[36] The most controversial and precarious coalition attempts and experi-ences of Blacks with other races or ethnic groups and, indeed, intra-racially have oc-curred in the twentieth century.

Maulana Karenga has suggested that the reason Blacks have failed to achieve more profitable and substantial political relation-ships with other groups is because they have not observed the basic distinction between a coalition and an alliance. Karenga exhorts that an "alliance is a long-term ongoing unity based on common interests and common basic principles whereas a coalition is a short-term working association based on specific short-term goals."[37] The basis or rationale for any political relationship between persons or groups is self-interest. Historically, it appears that African Americans have sustained ex-tended coalitions and/or alliances with other groups while their own immediate self-interests have been poorly or unequally served.

Coalition is a political strategy resorted to when one faction of individuals cannot singly achieve its goals and objectives without the support and aid of another external faction that has similar objectives or who stands to reap specific benefits as a result of mutual co-operation. Individuals or groups coalesce to achieve certain goals or benefits. The motive is self-interest. However, often in political coalitions there exist differentiated self-interests which can lead to unequal results or benefits for one of the factions. Coalition building has been a functional factor of Black politics during slavery, the abolitionist and Reconstruction periods and, even more, in the twentieth century. The common patterns or attempts of Black coalitions might be de-scribed as follows:

1. Black liberals and White liberals coalition.
2. Blacks and Jews coalition.
3. Blacks and other ethnic-racial minorities coalition.
4. Black Power, nationalist and liberal (intra-racial) coalitions.

Although the above coalitions are not inclusive, they are particularly relevant to contemporary Black politics.

The most common, debatable, and frequently assessed coalition has been the one that, variously, has existed between Black and White liberals. Whether relating to Black/White liberal coalition or to Blacks coalescing with other groups, the classical discussion of the "Myths of Coalition" in Stokely Carmichael and Charles V. Hamilton's book, *Black Power: The Politics of Liberation in America,* incisively analyzes the misconceptions of coalition. Carmichael and Hamilton posit that it is mythical and a fallacy to assume that: 1) Black interests are identical with White liberals and other reform groups; 2) powerless and insecure people can develop effective and trusting relationships with politically and economically powerful groups; and 3) coalitions can be developed and sustained on a purely moral, collegial or sentimental basis.[38]

Black liberals might be characterized as those who seek integration with Whites, but who also demand redress from Whites and the government for their unequal economic and political plight. White liberalism is egalitarian in nature, but it remains to be seen as to how far whites have ever been prepared to go towards relinquishing or sharing power with Blacks. Real or significant integration between the races has not occurred. The NAACP and the Urban League are the most prominent and effective civil rights organizations purposed to improve race relations and to redress the wrongs of racism. These organizations were initially bi-racially focused and administered. They were and still are, to some extent, partly dependent upon a few economically and politically powerful Whites for funding and support.

The NAACP and the Urban League have been responsible for forging major social, political and economic gains for Blacks. However, for more than eighty years of Black/White coalition within these organizations, Blacks have participated and functioned from a position of weakness than from strength. No one can say for sure how much the prohibitive pressures and attitudes of eminent Whites benefactors have restricted or restrained some of the more aggressive and expeditious civil right actions of these organizations. But one may observe and logically assume that in order to preserve Black/White liberal coalitions, that cautious and non-intimidating approaches towards civil rights litigation and action have been and still must be pursued. A successful and effective coalition can result only if the constituent factions are of equal strength or at least can demand equal respect. Black Power advocates disdain Black/White coalitions because of the tendency of Whites to want to control the organization.

Some political analysts argue that the primary political objectives of Blacks are no longer race-specific. This view is shared by many Black conservatives who believe that many social and economic policies transcend race or are not racially related. Thus under such a premise, race issues are impertinent in Black/White political coalitions. In electoral politics the Black candidate, especially, has to succumb in policy initiatives and rhetoric to a form of "deracialization" in order to vie successfully for office.[39]

Deracialized politics infers that the high disproportionate rates of Black poverty, unemployment, homelessness, disease, crime, and incarceration are related solely to economic variables and social dysfunctions independent of racial injustice and discrimination. Deracialized political philosophy functions with the assumption that all institutional barriers to social, political and economic equality based on race, color and culture have been eliminated. And thus, power, cannot be discerned as being inordinately possessed by any single race or ethnic group. Racism and discrimination will have become obsolete and, indeed, so will white and black politics and coalitions. Such an utopian state of race relations is yet to be consummated in American society.

Historically, Blacks and Jews have been perceived as having maintained, from time to time, a type of political or moral coalition in the area of civil rights. However, in business and economic dealings, Blacks have been known to possess anti-Semitic attitudes towards white liberal Jews. Jewish people have supported and have been highly active in Black civil rights organizations, but many African Americans feel that they have been economically exploited by the Jews.[40] Prior to the 1960s, Jewish researchers virtually dominated or controlled the scholarship on African Americans. The factors that incline Blacks and Jews to coalesce politically are their similar histories of suffering and persecution. Blacks point to their long-suffering of slavery and Jews, their experience of the Holocaust. Beyond this vestige of moral sentiment, Blacks and Jews have little in common.

C. Eric Lincoln perceptively notes that Jews are persecuted primarily because of their religion and Blacks because of their race and color. Jews can be Jewish or otherwise, but Blacks cannot change their race or color. Lincoln writes that "being white, individual Jews have behaved more or less like other whites, and that they have been neither better nor worse than other whites with whom they are associated."[41]

A new era of Black-Jewish strained relations begun during the late 1970s when Jewish leaders demanded the resignation of the Black Ambassador Andrew Young when he supposedly made contact with members of the Palestine Liberation Organization. During the same period the Jewish community opposed the Affirmative Action interests of African Americans. Jewish intellectuals gave credence to White claims relative to the impropriety of "reverse discrimination" and "quotas" to remedy historical discrimination of Black Americans. Blacks are also concerned about the trade and military alliance Israel has maintained with the oppressive and racist regimes of South Africa. The following statement sums up the political implications of Black-Jewish coalitions:

> Their is no question that individual Jews and Jewish organizations and their leaders have worked as part of a liberal coalition with Blacks and organized labor to form a powerful political force for social and economic reform in the United States. It is also clear that Jewish organizations and leadership have done so when it is in their perceived interest to do so as do we. It is reasonable to believe that they will continue to work with Blacks when they believe that it is in their interest to be allied with Blacks and their aspirations.[42]

Irreparable breaches developed in Black-Jewish relations during the 1984 and 1988 presidential elections involving the Rev. Jesse Jackson and the Muslim leader, Minister Louis Farrakhan. It is predicted that in the future and, certainly throughout the 1990s, each group will independently use whatever power and influence it has to pursue its own political objectives.

America is populated with various racial-ethnic groups who are negatively affected socially, politically, and economically because of their minority status. Efforts to form national political coalitions and alliances in the past have proved largely ineffective because each group experiences discrimination, exploitation, racism or alienation in different ways. Differences in cultural, social and economic objectives of Blacks, Hispanic, Asian and Indian (Native) Americans have often been divisive ones. Yet, there have been times when these differences have been bridged briefly enough to effect certain mutual political gains. Black coalition with other racial-ethnic minority groups has been less than effective because of intra-class unity structures within each of these groups. Although Jesse Jackson based his political campaigns of 1984 and 1988 on what he termed as a Rainbow Coalition, there has been little or no evidence to show how solidly he attracted other minority racial and ethnic voters.

The concepts of race and ethnicity can be confusing if one is attempting to stratify the diverse population groups in the United States. Obviously, racially defined minorities are not perceived the same as ethnically defined minorities. In this book, African American and Black are meant to refer to descendants and all immigrants from Africa and the Caribbean of black stock. Hispanic may refer to those persons who trace their heritage to Spanish speaking countries who might be white or mixed of race and color. The Asian classification includes peoples of Japanese, Chinese, Korean, Pilipino, non-native Indians, Vietnamese and other Asian and Pacific Islanders. When White or white American is mentioned it has meant those persons of European descent who consider themselves non-Hispanic.[43]

For political purposes, the term minority generally applies only to groups physically distinctive from the European-American majority in the United States. A minority status in America usually implies a group with a history of discrimination and social stratification, while ethnicity refers to a national identity and distinctive culture and language.[44] Defining and stratifying these groups are important to Black politics and the prospect of coalition initiatives. If the current Hispanic and Asian immigration and birth rates continue to increase at the present rate, in a

half-century or more (2050 or 2080) non-Hispanic whites will comprise less than half of the total U.S. population. Each racial minority or ethnic group has its own legitimate self-interests which may not be conducive to coalition, but can result in intergroup conflict of a kind greater than with the present White majority. Blacks can no longer assume "automatic" coalitions with other racial-ethnic groups without carefully assessing mutual interests and common goals.

The viability of Black politics in the 21st century may not depend so much on coalescing with external groups, but on alleviating the ideological schism between Black liberals and Black Power/Nationalists. Factionalism and opposing ideologies have always existed in Black politics. During slavery the political coping strategy of the house slave was different from that of the field slave. In the early nineteenth century, Blacks were torn between emigrationist and anti-emigrationist political resolutions to American oppression. African Americans have always been divided relative to the issue of racial integration or on the degree of functional separation between blacks and whites.

The remarkable occurrence was the volatile coalition that existed between the NAACP, SCLC, and Urban League, and the members of SNCC and CORE for the purpose of pressuring for the passage of the Civil Rights Act of 1964. Intra-racial political organizational unity was also demonstrated for the support of the Voting Rights Act of 1965. SNCC and CORE were distinctively opposed to the conventional politics and appeasement philosophy of the other traditional civil rights organizations. Some political analysts believe that strategic and tactical harmony between the five or six major Black political organizations began to wane soon after the great March on Washington in 1963. In any event, the coalition disintegrated in June 1966 when Stokely Carmichael (SNCC) and Floyd McKissick (CORE) espoused and promoted the political ideology of Black Power. The traditional civil rights organizations such as the NAACP, SCLC and Urban League retreated from this bold and radical Black political posture.[45]

Black Power politics ushered in a revival of Black pride, independence, self-determination and protest ideology which conflicted diametrically with those elder and traditionally oriented Blacks who sought to pursue conventional legal processes to obtain racial equality. However, one of the most antagonistic issues preventing the coalition of Black liberal and Black Power/Nationalist factions is the emphasis or de-emphasis of racial integration. The conflicting political tenets of Black liberal, conservative, and Black Power factions will have to be mediated or resolved before an effective and viable coalition may be maintained. If conciliation is possible, it may pave the way for the formation of a viable Black independent political party.

*Black Political Leadership.* A Black political leader is one who commands respect and has earned the gratitude of a progressive strata or faction of African people. Black political leadership is not and never has been limited to electoral politics. Throughout the history of the Black experience in America, the primary need and role for Black leaders have been to champion the freedom of African people and to deliver them out of the inhumane circumstance of White racism and oppression. While the philosophy, approach, and method of each true leader may have varied, his or her objective remained constant. Those persons who have historically or who presently stand ready to risk their personal well-being in order to press for the liberty and uplift of Black people are the ones who measure up to the criteria of true Black political leadership. Based on this standard, a student of Black history would have to study the writings, oratory, and works of a hundred or more eminent Black figures from the 1600s to the present 1990s to determine the number of Black political leaders that have existed and the ones who qualify as Black leaders today.

The typology of Black leadership has been a popular area of study, especially, during and succeeding the 1960s. Social scientists have analyzed the racial ideology of Black leaders, revealed how they acquire leadership status, studied their various styles and unique appeals, and attempted to quantify the level of support and confidence that they have earned among Blacks. The quality of Black leadership has been measured in terms of the degrees of loyalty the leader exhibits towards the White oppressor race as opposed devotion to that which is in the best interest of the Black community. Politically, a Black leader is despised or esteemed on the basis of the rights and resources he or she can demand or negotiate, and obtain from the white dominated system for the uplift and benefit of the Black community. The difficult problem Black leaders are confronted with is whether or not they can be politically cooperative with Whites and still be competitive enough to forge social and economic benefits for their Black constituency. All eminent Black spokespersons are not truly Black leaders.

Historically and contemporarily, many African Americans who have been viewed, designated or promoted as Black leaders might more appropriately be described as simply racial diplomats, charismatic spokesmen or as ceremonial agents of non-black interests. Many so-called Black "leaders" are not stewards of the Black community but are creations of the news media. These persons are often selected and promoted by white politicians or serve as representatives of political organizations whose purposes and commitments are inconsistent with the welfare and best interests of African Americans.

A study by Daniel C. Thompson from 1940 to 1960 characterized three patterns of race relations leadership: (White) Segregationist—(Black) Uncle Tom, (White) Moderate—(Black) Racial Diplomat, and (White) Liberal—(Black) Race Man.[46] Since Thompson's study was completed prior to the social revolution that occurred in the later 1960s, his perceptions and descriptions of Black leadership patterns have undergone some change. First, his description of the Uncle Tom tended to fuse the racial ideology of the white segregationist with the Black renegade or the Black acceptor of the racial status quo. While the definition of a White segregationist has not changed, a Black who espouses a self-determination and separatist ideology (not the same as segregationist) is not perceived as an Uncle Tom. The difference in segregation and separation is that the former is involuntary and enforced by Whites and the latter is voluntary on the part of Blacks. After 1966, Black Power advocates began to reassess the attributes of inequitable integration. Furthermore, it is an issue of scholarly debate today as to whether or not Booker T. Washington was an Uncle Tom or a proponent of Black separatist/nationalist ideology.

The White moderate that Thompson described is a leader who is either ambivalent or lukewarm to the segregation-integration controversy. The moderate fosters the gradual approach to racial equality. The Black racial diplomat attempts to minimize race and naively embraces and articulates a "color-blind" approach to racism in America. The White liberal possesses an egalitarian racial philosophy and tacitly supports the moral basis of integration. On the other hand the Black race man described by Thompson probably would fit the profile of Black Power/Nationalist leaders today. Thompson's study was designed to study the leadership typology of Blacks in New Orleans. In labeling the types of Black leaders, he compared their patterns of race relations leadership with those of Whites.[47]

Chuck Stone, former assistant to the dynamic African American Congressman Adam Clayton Powell, characterized Negro politicians who exploited Blacks with their favored status among Whites as "Uncle Toms" and "ceremonial negro leaders."[48] Stone's characterization of these two types of leaders revealed that: neither poses as a threat to the white power structure; neither is willing to disturb the infrastructure of the societal order or to "rock the boat;" both hold their positions of leadership at the whim and on the terms of Whites; and neither is prepared to utilize their influence to energize or to organize the masses of Blacks for an assault on racism. The differences are that the ceremonial negro leader tries "to keep his or her political tracks covered in the [Black] community" and often gives the impression or puts up the facade of challenging "the periphery of the white power structure." However, the Uncle Tom has little involvement with the Black community and functions basically out of "naked fear" of white people.[49]

While some contemporary Black political leaders conform to the above descriptions, recent indications are that Black leadership that is solely anointed and legitimated by Whites can not so easily deliver the votes and "souls" of the Black community to the white power structure. Although the ballot has increased the number of Black public officials, low-income Blacks and the Black underclass have experienced relatively little change in their condition. Despite the great surge in the number of Black elected officials, the Black leadership still lacks real power to effect social change.

The Democratic and Republican parties are becoming similar in their rejection of government intervention and funding for the remedy of social problems and racial inequities. The Black electorate is a significant factor in American politics but African Americans are, seemingly, wed to the Democratic Party. Yet, they have not used the power of their electoral leverage to produce social and economic gains to enhance the collective condition of African Americans.

Black political leaders who have little identity or familiarity with Black issues and concerns become alienated from the African American community. Fair minded or at least politically wise White candidates may often have an equal opportunity of appealing to the Black electorate. However, a new Black political leader is emerging in the political arena. The centuries old preoccupation of Black leaders with the attainment of integration, and their traditional advocacy for social programs which perpetuate Black dependency may be out of line with the developing ideology of Black self-determination and self-economic initiative. In the future more and more Black leaders will be demanding a return of their billions of tax-dollars towards the building and development of their own Black communities.

Conventional institutionalized Black politics started after the passage of the Voting Right Act of 1965 when a few Blacks were elected to the U.S. House of Representatives from predominantly Black districts. In 1971, the thirteen Black members of the U.S. House of Representatives formed the Congressional Black Caucus (CBC). As of January 1990, African American United States Congresspersons numbered 24 out of the House of Representatives' total of 435. All of the Black Representatives are Democrats with the exception of one. Initially, the CBC depicted itself as a unified bloc of legislators representing the national Black community. The function of the CBC has broadened to address a wide range of national concerns through legislative processes. Nevertheless, it has remained devoted to improving the condition of Blacks and minorities and to fighting racism.[50]

There has been an appreciable annual increase nationwide of Black elected officials at the federal, state, regional, county and municipal levels since 1965. For example, the Joint Center for Political Studies reported that the number of Black elected officials increased from 4,912 in 1980 to 7,370 in 1990. However, this total represents less than two percent of total elective offices in the United States. For Blacks candidates to attain more and higher elective offices they will have to attract more non-Black votes. The trend towards Black candidates attracting more White voters was evident in the 1988 elections. The question is, as Black candidates improve in their ability to gain white voters, will it effect their political efficacy towards the African American community?

A discussion and analysis of Black leadership is not complete without including the role of the church in producing the practical majority of Black leaders. In the African American experience, religion has never been separated from politics. This is the primary reason why most of the struggles for freedom, justice, and civil rights ever since the eighteenth century to the present have taken place in the Black church and was led by Black ministers.[51] The numbers of Black ministers who have played a role in liberation and civil rights struggles are too numerous to treat here. However, it is important to mention Henry Highland Garnet (1815–1882), a contemporary of Frederick Douglass in the early anti-slavery crusades. Garnet was a pastor as well as a political activist. Many of the slave insurrections were planned and executed by ministers of which Denmark Vesey (1767–1822) was one of the most renown. Vesey, a methodist minister, used the church as a base for planning one of the most famous slave revolts. A few of the most prominent ministers or religious leaders who were political activists during the 1960s include Congressman Adam Clayton Powell, Martin Luther King, Jr., Malcolm X, and Jesse Jackson.

Thus, it is not surprising that after the passage of the Voting Rights Act, a large number of Black elected officials are ministers.

It would be erroneous to assume that all Black ministers have been active advocates and supporters of the freedom and uplift of the Black masses. Many have been suppressors of African American resistance movements and used as pawns to promote the political interests of the white establishment. The Black preacher, unquestionably, wields much influence over millions of Blacks. However, one study found that the role and behavior of Black ministers are geared toward the congregation's expectations and, therefore, effect the kind of apathetic, active or very active political leadership a particular minister might exhibit. For example a conservative minister may emphasize only spiritual leadership within the church devoid of any political activism. A moderate minister may not initiate political activism but will respond to the congregation's willingness to act on specific social and political issues. The liberal minister was found to be one that initiates political activism.[52] Regardless of these variations, African American ministers have been primary motivators of Black political activism and the mainstay of Black leadership.

# THE BLACK ELECTORATE AND BLACK ELECTED OFFICIALS

*African American Voter Patterns and Characteristics.* Before the passage of the Voting Rights Act of 1965, it was generally understood that in the South the lack of Black political participation was often the result of fear of whites and various forms of intimidation. The political machines, Black civic and political organizations of the urban North generated a significant Black electorate. However, the traditional parties and their political bosses were the recipients of the benefit of the Black electorate while African Americans received comparatively few rewards for their political participation.

Since 1965 and the phenomenal increase in Black voter registrants, political scientists have sought to analyze Black voter behaviors and the characteristics of the Black electorate. In the South, particularly after the fear of violence, intimidation, and voter discrimination has subsided, much non-political participation and apparent apathy still exist among African Americans. Compared to the number of eligible Black voters and those who actually vote, this lack of political participation is not merely regional but national in scope and concern. The perception has been that voting among African Americans has been exercised more by the better educated, lower middle and upper income groups than among the larger lower income-classes. Considering the various demographic factors such as age, income, education and occupation, it is not conclusive in all cases which are the primary determinants of Black voting or non-voting behavior.

In one study, it was found that extensive non-voting among Blacks could not be attributed to fear. Moreover, Black voting could not be specifically related to higher levels of education, income, and occupation. Of these three factors, income appeared to have the greater association although it was not shown to be the case in all elections. The efforts of Black political and civic organizations have the greater effect in the motivation of the Black electorate.[53] In general, it might be concluded that social pressures within the Black community in concomitance with regional political, social, and economic histories significantly affect Black electoral participation and voter turn-out.

In addition to demographic or socioeconomic factors, political scientists also advance the political efficacy theory to explain the degrees of interest and participation of

# PERCENT REPORTED REGISTERED BY RACE AND HISPANIC ORIGIN: NOVEMBER 1984 AND 1988

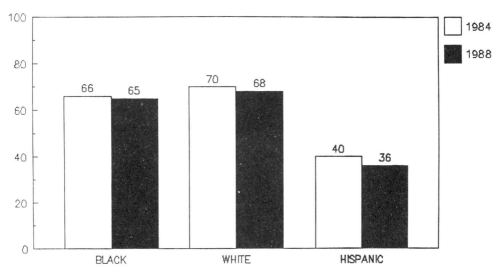

NOTE: PERSONS OF HISPANIC ORIGIN MAY BE OF ANY
      RACE
SOURCE: U.S. BUREAU OF THE CENSUS

Figure 8  Voter Registration by Race.

citizens in the electorate. Political efficacy has been defined as the sense or feeling that a person can influence political outcomes through his or her participation in the electoral process.[54] Related to political efficacy is one's belief and confidence in the integrity of the government or system. This has been described as political trust. Thus, political efficacy and trust may combine to have a tremendous impact on Black political participation.[55] If it is presumed that Blacks are cynical or suspect of the political efficacy of the government in relationship to the benefits they receive, how does their attitude differ from Whites? The study by Philip E. Secret and James B. Johnson found that Blacks have a significantly lower sense of political efficacy than Whites. However, the presumption that

Blacks have a significantly lower trust in government than do Whites was not supported.[56]

It is logical to assume that demographic and socio-economic factors do affect perceptions of political efficacy and trust. Psychologically, Blacks who may experience increased income and higher occupational status may develop a greater sense of civic responsibility. In contemporary Black politics, age may be a factor which may affect older Black voters differently than younger ones. For one thing, older voters may have a personal frame of reference to the Black Power, Black Pride and Civil Rights Movements of the 1960s, and the sacrifices in suffering and lives that made full political participation for African Americans possible. Therefore, the extent to which Black heritage and cultural consciousness have been transmitted to

# TEN STATES WITH THE GREATEST PROPORTION OF BLACKS: 1985
### (In percent)

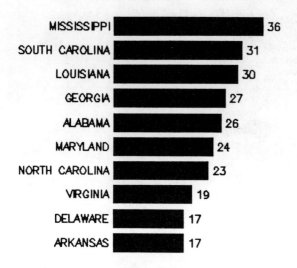

NOTE: The District of Columbia is excluded because it is treated here as a county rather than a state.

SOURCE: U.S BUREAU OF THE CENSUS

Figure 9  States with Greatest Black Population.

younger generations must be considered as a factor in Black political participation. Inevitably, research paradigms will be developed to correlate Black consciousness with socioeconomic, and political efficacy and trust factors relative to Black electoral participation.

There has been some indication in recent years of a convergence between Blacks and Whites on major social and economic issues. However, the order of priority and significance each race places on these issues are different. In a JCPS/Gallup survey in 1984, African Americans cited unemployment first, government poverty programs second, and civil rights third as principal issues of concern. Whites shared the belief that unemployment was the primary issue, but named the federal deficit and inflation as the most important secondary issues. By 1986, both Blacks and Whites listed unemployment, high cost of living and drug abuse as the most important issues. However, they differed in the ranking of these issues. In the order of priority, Blacks cited unemployment, the high cost of living and drug abuse. Almost conversely, Whites' order of ranking was drug abuse, unemployment, and the high cost of living. While African Americans advocated governmental intervention and affirmative action programs as ways of solving these problems, Whites continue to oppose governmental social programs.[57] In spite of some similarities with other population groups, African

# TEN METROPOLITAN AREAS WITH THE LARGEST NUMBER OF BLACKS: 1985
### (Numbers in thousands)

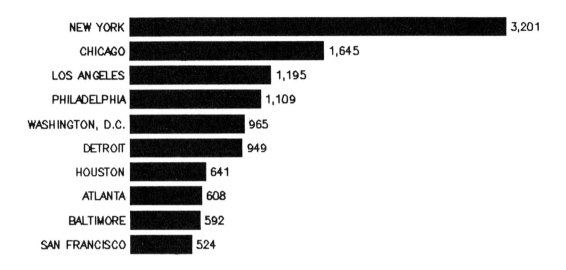

SOURCE: U.S. BUREAU OF THE CENSUS

Figure 10  Cities with Greatest Black Population.

American political participation, political concerns and problems remain quite distinct.

***Black versus White Elected Officials.*** Prior to 1965, it has been estimated that there were fewer than 300 Black elected officials in the United States. However, 1967 was a turning point for Blacks in the electoral process. It marked the election of Black mayors in two of America's largest cities—Carl Stokes of Cleveland, Ohio; and Richard Hatcher of Gary, Indiana. However, during the same election year, Elmo Bush was defeated on an all Black ticket for the mayor of East Saint Louis, Missouri by the White incumbent. Stokes and Hatcher were not the first Blacks to hold high elective office in modern times. Five Black U.S. Congressmen who were

elected from mostly Black districts in large metropolitan areas from the east, midwest and west preceded them. Edward W. Brooke assumed office as U.S. Senator from Massachusetts also in 1967. He was the first Black Senator since 1881.

The Cleveland and Gary mayoral elections were significant because as William E. Nelson and Philip J. Meranto explain that these victories

. . . were achieved on the strength of the mass mobilization of the black vote for independent political action. In these elections, black voters appeared to turn their backs on white-controlled political organizations in order to vote for politically independent black candidates dedicated to expanding black control over broad sectors of local government.[58]

# PERCENT REPORTED VOTING, BY RACE AND HISPANIC ORIGIN: NOVEMBER 1984 AND 1988

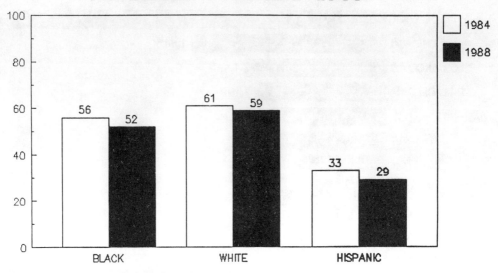

NOTE: PERSONS OF HISPANIC ORIGIN MAY BE OF ANY
       RACE
SOURCE: U.S. BUREAU OF THE CENSUS

Figure 11  Percent Voting by Race.

The elections of 1967 were important because it ushered in an era when Black candidates would routinely begin to vie against White candidates for federal, state, county and municipal elective offices. Blacks would begin to experience and assess the benefits of own-race candidate electioneering in opposition to the well established white political machines. African Americans learned the political strategy of racially polarized or bloc voting. This tactic had always been practiced by white Americans to repress the political initiatives of Blacks. The potential of Black bloc voting compelled White candidates to campaign more vigorously among Blacks and to co-opt Black leaders, often to the detriment of the entire Black community. Of course, other factors than race may influence Black as well as White voters.

Nevertheless, more than 7,000 Blacks have been elected to public office since 1967. In spite of the fact that African Americans comprise less than two percent of total elective office in the United States, they have held and continue to hold some rather impressive public offices. These offices or positions range from board/council members to, state and municipal judiciary posts, mayor, state treasurer and attorney general, lieutenant governor and governor. The most historic event was the 1990 election of L. Douglas Wilder as Governor of the State of Virginia. He was the first Black citizen to be elected governor in the continental United States.

Photo 18  L. Douglas Wilder, Governor of Virginia. Courtesy of
The Office of the Governor, Commonwealth of Virginia.

African Americans have presided as mayor of hundreds of small predominantly Black city-communities to the large majority White metropolises such as Los Angeles, Oakland, Spokane, Detroit, Chicago and Hartford. In 1990, the most diverse populated cities to elect a Black mayor were New York City (David Dinkins), and Seattle, Washington (Norman Rice). The proliferation of Black mayors, especially in cities of minority Black populations, has political analysts developing various theories of White/Black cross-over voting in situations where either race may be a majority or minority electorate.

While Black mayors may have received most of their support from Blacks, they cannot ignore White concerns. In the majority of cities, Whites own and control most of the businesses or economic enterprises. Thus, the Black mayor must look beyond his own community to the white corporate power structure, the state, and the federal government for funding and assistance. In other words, regardless of how impressive the titles of the few Black elected officials, white people still maintain overall economic and political power. Yet, in cities or districts where Blacks represent a near or complete majority, White political candidates must also be attentive to the Black electorate. There is, however, one difference. White candidates do not have to engage in the avid deracialization rhetoric to appeal to Black voters as apparently Black candidates have to or prefer to do in order to obtain white cross-over votes.

Two political scientists Monte Piliawsky and Paul Stekler have perceptively described four different types of elections that are now commonplace in the United States. They are: 1) White versus White Races—Minor Black Participation; 2) White versus White Races—Significant Black Participation; 3) Black versus White Races; and 4) Black versus Black Races.[59] For each type of election, Piliawsky and Stekler has analyzed the kinds of race politicking that has taken place, referring to

actual mayoral elections such as New York, New Haven, New Orleans, Atlanta or Detroit as examples. In the same work, the scenarios which might occur in Black Mobilization/White Crossover and White Mobilization/Black Crossover coalitions are described. This study is seminal in nature and, thus, requires more theoretical development and empirical support. It will serve as an excellent investigative topic or thesis for students of Black politics. The phenomenon of Black mayors in America is, indeed, an interesting study.

The increase in Black elected officials nationwide is the result of a growing and more politically conscious African American electorate. The number of BEOs is more pronounced at municipal than at state and federal levels. The most striking incidence of African Americans holding elective offices is reflected in the mayoralties of large urban cities. The large disproportionate number of Blacks living in cities, caused partly by White flight to incorporated surrounding suburb-townships and race bloc voting by Blacks, have contributed to the rise in the number of urban Black mayors. Following the election of Black mayors of Cleveland and Gary, political and social theorists have studied Black administrations to determine if the quality of life for Black residents have improved as the result of Black rather than White mayors or officials having been elected.

The findings of many of the studies leave much to be desired. Much of the research has been done by non-Blacks who may lack the ability to measure the intrinsic historical and psychological benefits many Blacks derive from being governed or managed sometimes by their own race. Secondly, most of the studies have focused on large cities or urban metropolises ignoring the fact that African American mayors preside over hundreds of small city-communities in the south and southwest. Moreover, whatever minimal benefits or advantages Black elected officials may be able to direct toward the uplift of the

African American community, they represent an improvement over 300 years of exploitation, denial and discrimination by the majority of White elected officials.

First, it is obvious and indisputable that Whites possess the power and control over the major political and economic institutions of American life. Secondly, regardless of which elective offices that Blacks may hold—barring those of President of the United States, Supreme Court Justice, Senator or Governor— they can do little to effect enough social change to enhance the collective plight of the masses of African Americans. The office of mayor, although titular and pompous, is mostly ceremonial and least of all powerful. No mayors have full control of the cities they preside over. A Black mayor usually is served with predominantly White city council members who may be insensitive to his or her initiatives to improve the condition of the Black community. Whites control the economic and corporate structures of the city, county, and state. Therefore, Black mayors and other Black elected officials may often have to compromise African American interests and appease the more powerful Whites in order to direct even minimal benefits to the Black community. To overcome this factor, Black mayors have been most effective in securing federal revenues for development of social and economic projects that benefit the Black underclass.[60]

Considering monumental odds against success, the achievements and benefits Black elected officials have been able to direct to Black communities are outstanding. As Nelson and Meranto observed in the early Cleveland and Gary experiences, Black mayors made a positive difference in the lives of Black citizens in these cities. Public housing units were constructed, day-care centers and health clinics were established, and problems of employment and drug abuse were attacked. Black entrepreneurship was assisted, and high-level minority hiring in municipal administrative and managerial positions permanently lifted thousands of African Americans into the middle income-class.[61]

A summary of the redistributive benefits that traditionally accrue to the African American community as a result of Black governing or supervising officials include:

1. More federal and private (philanthropic) funding.
2. Increase in numbers of Blacks employed in various municipal and governmental work forces.
3. Appointment of more Blacks to commissions and review boards.
4. More expenditures for municipal education and social welfare.
5. Black political power in city hall creates an environment in which Black business thrives.
6. Less police brutality (fewer Whites killing Blacks) although the crime rate remains constant.[62]

The intent here is not to suggest that race should be the only criteria the Black electorate should consider in its voter decision-making. A Black face alone does not constitute what is in the best interest of the Black community or for African American people in general. Political parties and ideologies are certainly relevant in Black voter decisions. In many cases, a White candidate may best serve the interest of the Black community.

For example, no political analyst can truthfully deny the fact that President Lyndon Baines Johnson, a white Southerner from Texas, was perhaps the greatest civil rights president in the history of the United States. Not only was more civil rights legislation passed during his administration, he appointed the first Black to serve in a presidential cabinet. More importantly, he nominated the first Black to serve on the U.S. Supreme Court, Thurgood Marshall.[63]

Photo 19  President Lyndon Baines Johnson. Courtesy of The Library of Congress.

# POLITICS OF RACE AND THE JUDICIAL SYSTEM

*Racism and the Courts.* The courts and the judicial system have seldom been apolitical relative to the rights and justice of Black Americans. Racism and prejudice that have been historically demonstrated through decisions and sentencings in cases involving Blacks have eroded any pretension of the courts being the ultimate protector of human rights and impartial dispensator of justice. With relative few exceptions, the courts have served as a form of political judiciary to preserve the unrighteous doctrine of white supremacy and to deny the humanity and freedom of African Americans.

The political and repressive nature of the American judiciary towards Blacks was early dramatized in the famous U.S. Supreme Court *Dred Scott v. Sanford* decision of 1857. In essence, the majority joined Chief Justice Roger B. Taney in the opinion that Blacks were not entitled to the rights of federal citizenship. Taney argued that Blacks had been regarded as "beings of an inferior order" with "no rights which any white man was bound to respect" for more than a century before the Constitution was adopted.[64] Even before the *Dred Scott* case, the courts had rendered mostly pro-slavery decisions.

A pattern of setback court decisions pertaining to the legal status of Black people occurred even after the passage of the Civil Rights Bill of 1866. The judicial system either nullified or restricted the intent of most of the pro-Black legislation that was passed during the Reconstruction era. In one of its most unjust and deplorable decisions, the 1896 case of *Plessy v. Ferguson*, the U.S. Supreme Court established the political secondary citizenship status of African Americans. The *Plessy v. Ferguson*, *"separate but equal"* decision provided the foundation and rationale for 58 years of racial segregation and discrimination that deprived Blacks of true equal rights and protection under the law. Two years after the "separate but equal" ruling, the Supreme Court supported the Southern states' scheme to deny Blacks the right of the ballot.

Blacks experienced a brief respite from judicial tyranny when under the "Warren Court" many of the former politically oppressive and repressive laws and codes were reversed. For a 14 year period after the Warren Court's 1954 historic *Brown v. Board of Education* desegregation decision, African Americans began to rely on the courts in their struggle for freedom and equality. However, much of the confidence Blacks had begun to have in the courts subsided with the retirement of Chief Justice Earl Warren in 1969. The Warren Court had presided during the genesis and at the height of the Civil Rights Movement. The successes that Blacks achieved during the Civil Rights Movement caused Whites to revert more to a neoconservative and racist political posture. Consequently, when Lyndon B. Johnson decided not to seek re-election in 1969, archconservative and Republican Richard M. Nixon was elected as President. Nixon began to alter the liberal constituency of the federal judicial system and, especially, the U.S. Supreme Court.

Richard M. Nixon, along with all of the conservative Republican presidents that eventually followed him in office, sought to fill federal court vacancies with judges who possessed anti-civil rights political ideologies. His first step began in 1969 with the successful appointment of the conservative jurist Warren Burger to succeed retiring Earl Warren as Chief Justice of the U.S. Supreme Court. Nixon succeeded in placing three conservative associate justices on the Supreme Court in addition to conservative Chief Justice Warren Burger before the 1972 presidential election. The three associate justices were Harry Blackmun, Lewis F. Powell, and

William Rhenquist. The senate had previously rejected Nixon's nomination of two extremely conservative Southern jurists for the judicial posts. Democrat, President Jimmy Carter (1976–1980) did not have the opportunity to fill a Supreme Court vacancy, however, he did appoint several Blacks to other federal judgeships.

The overt political nature and intent of the judicial system became even more pronounced with the election of conservative Republican Ronald Reagan in 1980. Reagan vowed during his campaign that he intended to halt the liberal trend of the Supreme Court. He would seek to fill court vacancies only with those jurists who would adhere to the "original intent" of the framers of the Constitution, and those who possessed a "strict constructionist" interpretation of the law. Indeed, during Reagan's two terms of office he was able to change the court to a solid conservative majority. In addition to elevating anti-civil rights conservative William Rhenquist to chief justice after the retirement of Chief Justice Warren Burger, Reagan was able to successfully appoint three more arch conservatives to the Supreme Court: Sandra O'Conner, Anthony Kennedy, and Antonin Scalia. O'Conner and Kennedy replaced moderate justices Potter Stewart and Lewis Powell. The Reagan constructed courts commenced to severely weaken the civil rights laws passed by Congress, and to restrict the intent of the Warren Court decisions of 1954 to 1968.[65]

The conservative politicizing of the Supreme Court was made complete under the administration of Republican President George Bush who succeeded Ronald Reagan. Bush appointed David Souter, a reticent conservative Republican from New Hampshire to succeed retiring Justice William Brennan, who was an ardent egalitarian. The Supreme Court lost it most forceful humanitarian and champion of human equality ever when Justice Thurgood Marshall retired in 1991. Besides being the first African American to serve on the Supreme Court, Marshall argued and won the decision in the 1954 *Brown v. Board of Education* desegregation case.

President Bush surprised many when he nominated appeals court judge Clarence Thomas, another Black, to fill the vacancy of Justice Thurgood Marshall. However, Judge Thomas was reputed to be a conservative Black who conformed to the Reagan-Bush strict constructionist and anti-liberal ideology. Judge Thomas' nomination caused much controversy and divided support among African Americans and, also, he was opposed by several white feminist groups. Nevertheless, after almost unprecedented debate and testimony, Clarence Thomas was confirmed as an associate justice of the U.S. Supreme Court. He is the second Black to have served on the highest court in the nation. It remains to be seen if he will ever achieve the respect and distinction as a champion of civil rights as Justice Thurgood Marshall.

The politics of race and racism is pervasive in all areas of the law enforcement and judicial systems in America. The systems are dominated and controlled by the White ruling class. Thus, racism is evident in the courts whenever and wherever a Black litigant is involved.[66] Officials of law enforcement and the courts are responsive and accountable to the controlling majority race of which they serve and are an integral part. Until racial attitudes change and until law and justice are administered equally and fairly to all citizens regardless of race or color, politics will be the basis of the American judicial system.

# • QUESTIONS AND EXERCISES •

1. Historically, how has the meaning and practice of Black politics differed from the politics of white society?

2. The ideology of racial integration has been a dominant theme of Black politics for centuries. Yet, there have been periods when Black separatists and nationalists have challenged the proponents of racial integration. Name the leaders of Black separatist and nationalists movements and discuss the periods of their greatest influence.

3. What is the essential difference between segregation and the Black concept of separatism?

4. Define and compare what might be described as Black liberalism and Black conservatism.

5. How does Black liberal and conservative philosophy differ or fit into the ideological frameworks of White liberalism and conservatism?

6. Prior to 1936, Blacks mostly supported and voted the Republican Party. What political factors occurred that led to their gradual defection from the Republican to the Democratic Party?

7. Write a brief position paper on the history of Black independent party efforts. Debate the option of an independent Black political party for the late 1990s or early 2000s.

8. How successful have Black political coalitions been with White liberals, Asians, Hispanics, Native Americans, or Jews?

9. Does the Black community benefit more from Black than from White elected officials? Discuss.

# • NOTES AND REFERENCES •

1. C.C. Rodee, T.J. Anderson and C.Q. Christol, *Introduction to Political Science* (New York: McGraw-Hill 1967) p. 6.

2. Reginald E. Gilliam, Jr. *Black Political Development* (Port Washington, NY: Dunellen Publishing Co. 1975) p. 3.

3. See Hanes Walton, Jr., *Black Politics* (Philadelphia: J.B. Lippincott Co. 1972) 2, 10.

4. For a historical essay of Black ideological non-development see, Rhett S. Jones, "In the Absence of Ideology: Blacks in Colonial America and the Modern Black Experience,"

*The Western Journal of Black Studies* (Spring 1988) v. 12(1). 30–39.

5. Read, Melvin J. Thorne, *American Conservative Thought Since World War II* (New York: Greenwood Press 1990).

6. See Philip S. Foner, *The Life and Writings of Frederick Douglas* Vol. 4. (New York: International Publishers 1955)

7. Raymond L. Hall, *Black Separation in the United States* (Hanover, NH: University Press of New England 1978) p. 1.

8. See James E. Turner, "Historical Dialectics of Black Nationalist Movements in America," *The Western Journal of Black Studies* (September 1977) v. 1(3) 164–183.

9. Harold Cruse, *Plural but Equal* (New York: William Morrow & Co. 1987) 378–379.

10. See Randall Rothenberg, *The Neoliberals* (New York: Simon Schuster 1984) 45–46.

11. Rothenberg, *The Neoliberal*, 107–108.

12. Williams S. Maddox and Stuart A. Lilie, *Beyond Liberal and Conservative* (Washington, D.C.: Cato Institute 1984) 13–14.

13. Thorne, *American Conservative Thought Since World War II*, pp. 4, 44, 81–82, 89.

14. Maddox and Lilie, *Beyond Liberal and Conservative*, p. 16.

15. W. Avon Drake, "Black Liberalism, Conservatism and Social Democracy: The Social Policy Debate," *The Western Journal of Black Studies* (Summer 1990) v. 14(2) 118–119.

16. Herb Boyd, "Black Conservatives" *Lies of Our Times* (January 1991) 2(1), p. 10.

17. Benjamin Quarles, *The Negro in the Making of America* (New York: The MacMillan Co. 1964) 88, 92.

18. Philip S. Foner, *History of Black Americans* (Westport Ct: Greenwood Press 1983) 280–281, 425.

19. Walton, *Black Politics*, 86–91.

20. Ibid., p. 100.

21. See Lenneal J. Henderson, Jr. "Black Politics and American Presidential Elections," in *The New Black Politics* edited by M.B. Preston, L.J. Henderson and Paul Puryear (New York: Longman, Inc. 1982) 7–8.

22. Ibid., p. 10.

23. Ronald W. Walters, *Black Presidential Politics in America* (New York: State University of New York Press 1988) p. 32.

24. See Lerone Bennett, Jr. *Before the Mayflower* (Chicago: Johnson Publishing Co. 1962) Penguin Books 1984. 594–597.

25. *Focus*, Joint Center for Political Studies, Washington, D.C. (January 1984) 12(1) p. 8.

26. See Adolph L. Reed, Jr., *The Jesse Jackson Phenomenon* (New Haven: Yale University Press 1986).

27. E.J. Dionne, Jr., "Jackson Share of Votes by Whites Triples in '88," *The New York Times* (Monday, June 13, 1988) p. A–13.

28. Linda F. Williams, "The 1988 Election in Review," *Focus*, JCPS (November-December 1988) 16(11&12) p. 3.

29. See Charles E. Fager, *White Reflections on Black Power* (W.B. Eerdmans Publishing Co. 1967) 41–43.

30. Stokely Carmichael, *Stokely Speaks* (New York: Vintage Books 1971) 18–19.

31. Manning Marable, "The Rhetoric Racial Harmony," *Sojourners* (August/September 1990) 19(7) p. 17.

32. Carmichael, *Stokely Speaks*, 19–21.

33. Walters, *Black Presidential Politics in America*, p. 139.

34. See Bill Strickland, "The Gary Convention and the Crisis of American Politics," *Black World* (October 1972) 18–23.

35. See John Henrik Clarke, "Black/White Alliances: A Historical Perspective," *Black Pages Series* (Chicago: Institute of Positive Education 1970) 1–22.

36. For a study of the near Black/White alliance in the South, See C. Vann Woodard, *The Strange Career of Jim Crow* (New York: Oxford University Press 1966) 60–82.

37. Maulana Karenga, *Introduction to Black Studies* (Inglewood CA: Kawaida Publications 1982) p. 254.

38. Stokely Carmichael and Charles V. Hamilton, *Black Power* (New York: Vintage Books 1967) p. 60.

39. For a discussion of race de-emphasis in coalition building see, Milton D. Morris, *The*

*Politics of Black America* (New York: Harper & Row Publishers 1975) p. 196–302.

40. See James Q. Wilson, *Negro Politics* (New York: The Free Press 1960) 155–161.

41. C. Eric Lincoln, *Race, Religion and the Continuing American Dilemma* (New York: Hill and Wang 1984) 180.

42. Part of a statement read by Julian Bond and adopted unanimously by Black American Leadership Meeting, Wednesday, August 22, 1979, NAACP National Office, New York, NY.

43. These descriptions are based on Kimberly A. Crews and Patricia Chancellier, *U.S. Population: Charting the Change.* Population Reference Bureau. Washington D.C. 1988.

44. See Robert Staples, "The Emerging Majority: Non-White Families in the United States," *Family Relations,* (1988) 37.

45. See Lucius J. Barker and Jesse J. McCorry, Jr., *Black Americans and the Political System* 2nd ed. (Cambridge: Winthrop Publishers, Inc. 1980) 183–188.

46. Daniel C. Thompson, *The Negro Leadership Class* (Englewood Cliffs: Prentice Hall 1963) 58–79.

47. Ibid.

48. Chuck Stone, *Black Political Power in America* (New York: Dell Publishing Co. 1970) 168–169.

49. Ibid.

50. See Marguerite Ross Barnett, "The Congressional Black Caucus and the Institutionalization of Black Politics," *Journal of Afro-American Issues* (Summer 1977) 5(3). 201–227.

51. See Gayraud S. Wilmore and James H. Cone, *Black Theology* (Maryknoll, NY: Orbis Books 1979) 534.

52. Woodrow Jones, Jr., H.L. Wingfield, and A.J. Nelson, "Black Ministers: Roles, Behavior, and Congregation Expectations," *The*

*Western Journal of Black Studies* (Summer 1979) v. 3(2). 99–103.

53. See Douglas St. Angelo and Paul Puryear, "Fear, Apathy, and Other Dimensions of Black Voting," in *The New Black Politics* edited by M.B. Preston, L.J. Henderson, Jr., and Paul Puryear (New York: Longman 1982) 128.

54. John C. Pierce and Addison Carey, Jr., "Efficacy and Participation: A Study of Black Political Behavior," Journal of Black Studies (December 1971) 202.

55. See Philip E. Secret and James B. Johnson, "Political Efficacy, Political Trust, Race and Electoral Participation," *The Western Journal of Black Studies* (Summer 1985) 74–83.

56. Ibid., 78.

57. See Linda F. Williams, "Significant Trends in Black Voter Attitudes," *The Black Scholar* (Nov/Dec 1986) 17(6). 24–25.

58. William E. Nelson, Jr., and Philip J. Meranto, *Electing Black Mayors* (Columbus OH: Ohio State University Press 1977) 68.

59. Monte Piliawsky and Paul Stekler, "From Black Politics to Blacks in the Mainstream," *The Western Journal of Black Studies* (Summer 1991) v. 15(2). 115–116.

60. See Hermon George, "Black Power in Office: The Limits of Electoral Reform," *The Western Journal of Black Studies* (Summer 1985) v. 9(2). 84–95.

61. Nelson and Meranto, *Electing Black Mayors,* 374–375.

62. For a comparison of studies on the results of Black elelcted officials see, Hugh A. Wilson, "Black Electoral Outcomes and Policy Impacts," *The Western Journal of Black Studies* (Spring 1987) 11(1). 24–28; and Gaither Lowenstein, "Black Mayors and the Urban Black Underclass," *The Western Journal of Black Studies* (Winter 1981) 5(4). 278–284.

63. See Carl T. Rowan, "Was LBJ the Greatest Civil Rights President Ever?" *Ebony* (December 1990) 78–82.

64. See, Dred Scott v. Sandford (60 U.S. 393, 19 How. 393, 1857.)

65. Read Christopher E. Smith, "The New Supreme Court and the Politics of Racial Equality," *The Western Journal of Black Studies* (Spring 1991) v. 15(1). 8–15.

66. George W. Crockett, Jr., "Racism in the Courts," in *From the Black Bar,* edited by Gilbert Ware (New York: G.P. Putnam's Sons 1976) 105.

# Chapter 7

# Black Economic and Entrepreneurial Concepts

## AFRICAN AMERICAN ECONOMIC THEORY AND EXPERIENCE

*Towards a Black Economic Ideology.* Various social and political ideologies of Black Americans have been discussed in previous chapters. However, economics is one of the most important areas of Black ideological leanings that still remains grossly undeveloped or unwittingly neglected. Economic ideology in this discussion means *one* that will serve as a practical and not merely a theoretical guide towards the total liberation of African Americans. The social and political theories of nationalism, religious activism, integrationism, individualism, collectivism, separatism, social democratism, and various other ideologies may be irrelevant unless either one has a specific and practical agenda to deliver Blacks

from the ranks of the "have nots" to the "haves."

It is difficult for Blacks to conform neatly to the European ideological frameworks of Karl Marx's socialism and to Adam Smith's capitalism because of their "caste" and oppressed status. Marx perceived economic inequality as a class struggle between the owners of capital and labor for a fair share of profits from production. Although a growing number of conservative Blacks posit class antagonism as the major factor of Black economic inequality, the majority of Black scholars propose that race and racism obstruct Blacks from achieving economic parity.[1]

The essential tenet of Adam Smith's capitalism is freedom, *laissez-faire* or governmental non-interference in business, and individualism.[2] Ironically, freedom is the fundamental right that Blacks have historically been denied. Moreover, Blacks have relied partly upon government economic intervention for the minimal entrepreneurial success they have achieved. The Civil Rights Movement of the 1960s resulted in a significant expansion of freedom for African Americans. The question is whether or not Blacks have now gained sufficient liberty under American capitalism, in spite of racism and discrimination, to achieve a functional extent of economic self-sufficiency as a race.

Consistent with the colonial analogy of Franz Fanon, Robert Staples, and Robert Blauner discussed briefly in chapter four, Blacks exist as an oppressed internal colony within the American polity. Capitalism thrives best under conditions where an oppressed or economically disadvantaged group or race can be exploited through discriminatory practices and minimal wages policies. White Americans have been able to maintain economic superiority by enforcing racism and restricting Black access to economic opportunity. Therefore, if Blacks are to ever achieve social and political equality they must first develop and pursue an economic ideology that will enable them to attain a substantial level of self-sufficiency in spite of racism and discrimination. Conflicting opinions among Blacks relating to the degree of integration *with* or separation *from* Whites have impeded the development of a functional economic ideology of Black liberation.

The debate and controversy that began with Booker T. Washington (the Atlanta Compromise) and W.E.B. Dubois at the end of the nineteenth century will, undoubtedly, continue unabated through successive generations of Black leaders on into the twenty-first century. The salient ideological issues resulting from Washington's historic address in Atlanta in 1895 were, first, whether or not Blacks should strive for integration or function separately within the society. Secondly, it was debated as to how much effort Blacks should expend fighting for social benefits and political participation than for creating their

own sub-economy and achieving a substantial measure of economic self-sufficiency.

History might reveal that Washington was right if he foresaw the futility and myth of equitable integration in America. On the other hand, DuBois was correct in asserting that economic achievements without political power to protect economic and business rights will not endure. Although W.E.B. Dubois became more ideologically socialist shortly before his demise in 1963, he earlier felt that Blacks could develop economic parity by incorporating their talents into White industry. However, Dubois' economic philosophy differed sharply from the pro-capitalist, Black nationalist ideology of Marcus Garvey. Garvey championed the idea that Blacks could compete economically and equally with whites on a racial basis. Garvey's economic ideology was in defiance to all the racism, bigotry and discrimination that Whites could impose on Black people. Garvey's economic ideology won the hearts and minds of millions of Blacks, but he was subdued by the political power of whites who felt threatened by his audacious rhetoric and the influence he wielded among millions of African Americans.

In the late 1990s, a school of Black conservative economists and some other Black social theorists proposed theories of the race problem in America contradictory to the ideology of the Black liberal establishment. Prominent among these conservatives are Thomas Sowell and Walter E. Williams who suggest that racism and racial discrimination are not the sole causes of the subordinate social and economic status of African Americans. They point out that certain Jewish, Hispanic, and Asian immigrant groups succeed economically in spite of racial and ethnic discrimination. Sowell and Williams criticize Black liberals' continuing emphasis and crusades of civil rights, social programs, and affirmative action. Black conservatives attempt to minimize race differentials and generally support the class antagonist theories of the European classical economists.[3]

Besides advocating Black self-help and focusing on technical and restrictive economic barriers to Black progress, Black conservatives propose no new, clear, and incisive economic ideology that the masses of African Americans adhere to that may resolve socioeconomic racial disparities. They submit instead a replication of the Protestant Ethic and capitalist ideology of hard work, education, sobriety, and conscientiousness as solutions to Black economic inadequacy. Inherent in Black conservative ideology is the presumption that virulent, persistent and entrenched racism is no longer pervasive in American society. Furthermore, in spite of many African Americans' educational preparation, skills, and virtues of character, they are still relegated to the ranks of the underemployed and unemployed. Conservative ideology implicitly absolves white dominated government and institutions of much of the blame for the economic condition of African Americans. This has endeared them to White politicians and academics.[4] Black conservative ideology is only partly consistent with Booker T. Washington's separatist and Marcus Garvey's nationalist philosophies. Contemporary Black conservatives mostly support social and economic racial integration.

A separatist Black economic ideology was espoused during the 1960s by Elijah Muhammad, the late leader and founder of the Black Muslims, and the Nation of Islam in America. Muhammad's philosophy of Black economic independence has been revived and is fostered today by one of his "disciples," Minister Louis Farrakhan. Muhammad noted that Blacks earned and contributed billions of dollars annually to the national economy (GNP). They spend billions for fine automobiles, clothes, alcohol, tobacco and drugs. The Muslim's economic plan is for their salary and wage earners to contribute from one to ten dollars a month to develop a national

equity or capital fund to buy land and to invest in Black-owned businesses. Muhammad had cited Pakistan and a few other Third World nations that had embarked upon a three to five year national savings plan and have since achieved autonomy and economic independence. The reasoning is that certainly almost thirty-million African Americans can do the same thing.[5]

Continuing in the separatist school of thought, Muhammad cited the ideological unity of other American groups in stating that

> The white man spends his money with his own kind, which is natural. You, too, must do this. Help to make jobs for your own kind. Take a lesson from the Chinese and Japanese and go give employment and assistance to your own kind when they are in need. This is the first law of nature. Defend and support your own kind. True Muslims do this.[6]

The Black Muslim's economic doctrine is limited in breadth and scope relative to its practical application to all Blacks in the United States. However, it may serve well the economic objectives of the Nation of Islam.

In reality, *absolute* separatism is improbable and certainly impractical in the United States. It is also improbable that fair, just, and equitable integration of Blacks and Whites will ever prevail. Considering these two hypotheses, what might be aspired for is a mutually tolerable and peaceful system of economic co-existence with both races establishing and maintaining areas of entrepreneurial interdependence. An ideology of economic co-existence would mean that both races may function cooperatively or separately in some areas of economic endeavor, and competitively in others. To a greater extent, Blacks would become more self-determining and at the same time remain mutually and equitably interdependent with Whites.[7]

Implications of the practicality of the ideology of Black/White economic co-existence was evident in the writing of Robert Kinzer and Edward Sagarin more than 40 years ago. Perceptively, they stated

> This joint development of the separate and the integrated philosophies of business is not only desirable, but is inevitable. It is, in fact, forced upon Blacks by outer circumstances, by the current political and economic status in the United States. . . .[8]

What is happening in the quest for Black ideological essence in economics is a movement towards a synthesis of social and philosophical thought. Equitable and peaceful co-existence, void of *absolute* integration or separatism, in many ways combine the ideologies of Washington, DuBois, and Garvey. Most remarkable, was the statement made by the Executive Director of the NAACP, Benjamin L. Hooks, in a 1992 issue of that organization's magazine, *The Crisis*. Hooks stated that "with the broadened perspective of time, it may be seen that [Booker T.] Washington was not always wrong. Much of what he advocated was useful and appropriate."[9] The point is that the NAACP is, historically, the foremost liberal and integration oriented of all Black civil rights organizations.

Collectively, African Americans represent a powerful economic force in American society. Comprising a population of over 30 million, the total money income of all Black Americans exceed the Gross National Product of all but ten or fifteen countries of the world. With such a vast economic potential, the only element that is lacking is an effective and functional ideology of economic liberation. A Black ideology of economic liberation must be derived from the consciousness of Black history and the contemporary Black condition in the United States. The effectiveness of such an ideology will be determined by its ability to produce change, to in-

cite group consciousness, to gain collective economic allegiance, and to command mass obedience to its concepts.

It is not that ideological schools of Black economic thought have not been espoused over the years, but that they have conflicted in function, objectives, and in elemental orders of priority. Black leaders such as Booker T. Washington, Marcus Garvey, Carter G. Woodson, Elijah Muhammad, Malcolm X, and Stokely Carmichael, with small degrees of difference, have stood for greater political and economic independence. On the other hand Frederick Douglass, W.E.B. DuBois, Roy Wilkins, Martin Luther King, Jr., and Jesse Jackson have placed greater priority on political coalition, social integration, and cultural assimilation. Black liberal ideology has held the main stage for almost a century. Its success as a totally liberating economic ideology is debatable.

Those African Americans who perceive own-race entrepreneurship or race-specific collective capital accumulation for Black empowerment as being anti-integration are not likely to subscribe to separatist economic ideology. Inexplicably, the conception of separatism or nationalism is not applied to other racial-ethnic populations including for example, Hispanic Cubans and certain Pacific Asian groups. These and many other racial-ethnic groups maintain their own economic, financial, and intra-group employment networks. Some liberal Black economists argue that Blacks should not be encouraged to seek careers as self-employed, small businessmen especially if the business is to be conducted in a separate, all-Black environment.[10] The implication is that such ventures are unprofitable. This raises a very important question. Why is it that every other racial-ethnic business person finds profitability in an all-Black community or environment except the Black entrepreneur?

The ideological debate over which social or racial approach that will achieve Black economic empowerment will undoubtedly continue. However, the only ideology that will count is the one that will change the traditional role of Blacks serving as consumers, buyers, renters, and employees to that of being sellers, producers, owners, and employers.

***Chronology of Black Business and Economic Initiatives.*** Trade and commerce are universal practices that have always existed among all races of mankind, and certainly in Africa. African historians write of the ancient maritime trade connections between Ethiopia, Egypt, East Africa, and the west coast of India and China. Trade in salt, gold, craft and agricultural products, and a multiplicity of other items along the West African coast via North Africa to Europe, and across the Sahara during the pre-colonial era is well established. In the West African region, the origin of most African Americans, women were noted for their economic acumen as sellers in the marketplace. The involuntary voyage of Africans to the New World and their conscription into slavery did not destroy their proclivity for business and trade. With opportunity, they continued to practice trade and commerce in America.

Blacks who had obtained their freedom from indentured servitude before slavery was officially inaugurated in the colonies, engaged in numerous entrepreneurial activities along with Whites as early as 1634. When the colonies began to pass various slave codes and discriminatory acts in the mid 17th century, the business and economic opportunities of Africans were severely diminished and repressed. Nevertheless, a few "free" Blacks of the North during the pre-Revolutionary period managed to successfully operate small service oriented business enterprises. After the Revolutionary War, a few Blacks in the North began to operate a variety of business enterprises. Specifically, Blacks in Philadelphia and New York were fairly represented in the catering and restaurant businesses. Notable in the annals of African American history are the phenomenal economic exploits of James Forten and Paul Cuffee. Forten was a prominent sailmaker in Philadelphia who had by 1832 amassed a fortune of more than $100,000. Cuffee was a successful merchant, shipbuilder, and sea captain. Both Forten and Cuffee were active abolitionists and civic leaders.[11]

The social and economic system in the South restricted or made impossible Black business and economic initiatives before the Civil War. There were strict laws prohibiting the literacy of Blacks and forbade giving them instructions in the conduct and activities of business. However, these laws did not always apply to free Blacks who often had blood ties to influential white businessmen and slave owners. The free Black businessman in the South was allowed to function in the lines of business that required hard labor and menial service, and in areas where he rendered service to his own people. These entrepreneurial opportunities existed generally in large southern cities such as New Orleans, Norfolk, Savannah, Mobile, Baltimore, Richmond, Charleston, Macon, and Atlanta. Free Blacks served as barbers, butchers, mechanics, artisans, minor retailers, restaurateurs, and hotel and tavern keepers in almost all the Southern cities during the ante bellum period. Blacks in the North and in the Northwest Territory had equal or even better business opportunities.[12]

The economic development of Blacks increased significantly in the South after 1865, the end of the Civil War, and during the Reconstruction period. In spite of limited capital, White hostility, and competition, Blacks went into business in a variety of unprecedented areas whenever they could obtain funds and had the opportunity. African Americans learned the art and technique of conducting many types of businesses by observing and assisting White businessmen. In the North, Black businesses continued at their nominal rate of growth. Several Blacks invented or modified various products. This enabled some of them to develop small manufacturing and production enterprises.

However, the failure of Reconstruction in 1877 and the renewed oppression of African people drastically decreased Black economic development in the South. With the loss of political power that they had enjoyed briefly during Reconstruction, racism and segregation became more intense. Whites restricted the leasing and ownership of business property to Blacks. Black patronage was limited to their own people. To make matters worse, White businessmen encroached rapidly into the Black community. This situation continues into the late twentieth century.

The re-intensification of racism forced Blacks to do for self and to turn to each other for resources and mutual benefit. The only major organization not owned, operated and controlled by Whites or dependent on White funds for existence was the Black church. The Black church was the spiritual, social, political, and economic center of the Black community and of Black life. Throughout the network of Black churches and religious denominations North and South, benevolent and mutual aid societies were formed to aid the sick, bury the dead, care for the disadvantaged, and to assist in the development of the Black community. The Black church learned, taught and practiced the art of pooling the resources of many in order to care for the needs or misfortunes of a few. From this statistical reality and capability, the idea of Black self-insurance was conceived and several insurance companies were established.[13]

From 1865 to 1915, concurrent with the development of church mutual aid societies, Black fraternal orders were being formed. The church, benevolent societies, and the fraternal orders amassed huge capital funds from assessments, dues and fees. Often church mutual aid societies and the fraternal orders joined in ventures to form banks as well as insurance companies. The first Black-owned and administered banks were organized in 1888. The Capital Savings Bank of Washington, D.C. opened October 1888, and the Grand Fountain United Order of True Reformers Bank opened in Richmond, Virginia. In successive years, banks in Chattanooga, Tennessee and in Birmingham Alabama opened. More than 50 banks were organized by 1914.

The two largest Black insurance companies existing today were founded by two former slaves and barbers. John Merrick, a former agent of the Order of True Reformers, was the principal organizer of North Carolina Mutual of Durham in 1898. In 1905 Alonzo F. Herndon bought the assets of several church mutual aid associations and formed what is now called the Atlanta Life Insurance Company. African American insurance companies remain the largest single Black industry in the United States. Black insurance companies were organized because White companies believed that Blacks were not good insurable risks. The success of Black insurance companies is a prime example of what African Americans are capable of achieving independent of Whites. Of course when Black insurance companies proved the profitability of insuring members of their race, White companies began to compete in the Black community for policyholders.

Significant development of Black businesses continued between the years 1900 and 1929. Major African American publishers and newspapers were established during this period. The most extraordinary Black business woman of this time was Madame C.J. Walker. She organized a large company that manufactured hair and skin preparations, and other cosmetic products. The 1920s was an era when African Americans experimented and practiced various types and categories of American business and capitalism. However, it must be remembered that segregation was the law of the land and its tenets were rigidly adhered to in the South. In studying the plight of Black businessmen and professionals, Gunnar Myrdal described precisely the situation when he wrote that

> On the one hand, they [black people] find that the caste wall blocks their economic and social opportunities. On the other hand, they have, at the same time, a vested interest in racial segregation since it gives them what opportunity they have.[14]

Although segregation was explicit and mandated in the Southern states, it was implicit and selective in many businesses and business situations in the North. Segregation in business, public accommodations, and schools did not begin to dissipate until after the Court's desegregation ruling in 1954.

One cannot say for sure which factors contributed most to the marked increase in Black business and economic development during the first quarter of the twentieth century. To a great extent, it was the National Business League founded by Booker T. Washington in 1900 that provided the social and psychological stimulus for Black business and economic achievements. The purpose of the National Business League was to give encouragement and inspiration to potential and practicing Black business persons. More than 600 state and local branches of the organization existed by the end of 1915. Without a doubt, Marcus Garvey's ideology of Black economic self-determination, Black pride rhetoric, and his mass following sustained the momentum of African American business progress through the 1920s. African American business growth and development continued in spite of the racial violence and racism that followed the end of World War I. Some historians note that the race riots tended to drive Blacks closer together. Consequently, Blacks "thus aroused, then, became not only racially con-

scious, but economically conscious. From this realization [Blacks] began to enter business in a larger measure."[15]

The Depression (1929–1933) took its toll in the number of Black businesses that failed. However, many Black businesses survived this critical period. According to historian Lerone Bennett Jr., by 1939, 57,195 Black-owned retail and service establishments existed with annual income far exceeding 100 million dollars. Their total income represented less than one percent of the National Income.[16]

A marked improvement in Black economic progress occurred after World War II. There was a rise in Black per capita income from a pre-war $384 to $1,070 in 1956. Black participation in the defense and peace-time industries from 1940 to 1950 accounted for much of the increase. In addition, significant occupational advances were made by African Americans from 1940 to 1956. A shift from farm jobs to non-farm and urban occupations accompanied with a resumption of migration from rural areas to the cities and from the South to the North contributed to much of the economic improvement of the Black population. Even before the Civil Rights Movement began in 1956, one in every three urban Black families owned their own home.[17] Black economic progress was minimal in comparison with White advancement during this period. Nevertheless, following World War II Blacks experienced a new era of political and economic consciousness. One might conclude that a broader Black "middle-class" began to develop during the two decades following 1945.

Politico-psychological influences resulting from the 1954 school desegregation ruling, the Montgomery Bus Boycott, and the Black Power/Black Pride Movement contributed to the upsurge in African American business and economic development through the 1970s. During the dramatic unfolding of these three phenomena, Blacks revived their interest in building and patronizing their own

# PER CAPITA MONEY INCOME BY RACE AND HISPANIC ORIGIN: 1986 AND 1987
## (in 1987 dollars)

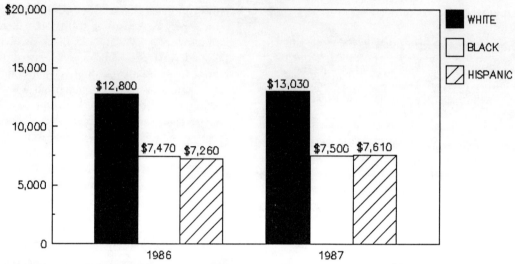

NOTE: PERSONS OF HISPANIC ORIGIN MAY BE OF ANY
      RACE
SOURCE: U.S. BUREAU OF THE CENSUS

Figure 12  Per Capita Money Income by Race.

businesses. White establishments that practiced segregated services, seating, or eating policies were boycotted by Blacks. Consequently, Black entrepreneurs began to build new businesses or improve existing facilities to accommodate members of their own race. A new capitalist spirit was generated among African Americans and many started business enterprises with less than one-thousand dollars as initial capital.

For example, it is reputed that Berry Gordy started Motown Records the largest Black recording company ever with a credit union loan of $700 in 1949. John H. Johnson began Johnson Publishing Company with $500 in 1942. Johnson Publishing Company is now America's largest and most successful Black publishing firm. Its publications include

*Ebony* and *Jet*. In the personal care and appearance business, George E. Johnson started the Johnson Products Company with $250. His company was the first Black owned firm to be listed on the American Stock Exchange. Today these companies and more than a hundred others in various commercial and industrial areas gross millions in annual sales.[18]

Black entrepreneurship grew steadfastly from 1970 to 1980. Earl G. Graves, publisher of the country's leading Black business indicator periodical, *Black Enterprise*, publishes an annual list of the top 100 Black businesses. To be eligible to appear on the list, a company must have been fully operational in the previous calendar year and be at least 51 percent Black-owned. It must manufacture or own the product it sells or provide industrial or consumer services. During the eight year period from 1972 to 1980, the total gross receipts of the top 100 Black firms increased from $459 million to $1.2 billion. When the list of the 100 top Black enterprises was established in 1973 a firm had to report at least one-million dollars in gross sales. In 1979, the minimum was raised to $5 million. More than 40 firms exceeded this figure.[19] Two factors may explain Black business growth during the 1970s.

Black business expansion from 1970 to 1980 might be attributed in part to the Civil Rights Movement and the momentum of the Black Power ideology of the 1960s. Correlated to this factor was the creation in 1969 of the Office of Minority Business Enterprise (OMBE) in the Commerce Department by President Richard M. Nixon. This office had the responsibility of coordinating and working with other federal agencies to provide advisory services and financial aid to minority enterprise, in addition to the Small Business Administration (SBA). The OMBE was Nixon's response to the demands of African Americans for Black power. Consequently, Nixon reaped political benefits by giving the government a role in reviving and fostering the concept of Black capitalism.

The Office of Minority Business Enterprise established field offices nationwide for the purpose of channeling technical assistance and aiding the loan-applications of minority businesses, in conjunction with numerous local Business Development Organizations. Within a few years after the establishment of OMBE, federal loans and guarantees and SBA assistance quadrupled. Federal procurement set-aside programs were initiated, and privately capitalized Minority Enterprise Small Business Investment Companies (MESBIC) were initiated during this period. More than a dozen federal agencies and twice as many private organizations have functioned since the 1970s to promote, advise, and to in-

crease Black entrepreneurship. It is remarkable that in spite of the difficulty of debt financing and the widespread credit discrimination that Black entrepreneurs experience, they have continued to grow in spite of adverse economic cycles. The number of Black owned banks, savings and loan institutions, and insurance companies have managed to remain relatively stable even into the 1990s taking into consideration that a few failed, and others were merged or amalgamated.

While it is undeniable that these organizations and efforts have been responsible for much of the success of Black economic development, they have been and continue to be politically motivated. Thus, their funding and effectiveness have vacillated with the political trends and attitudes of Whites toward Blacks and other ethnic-racial minorities. For example in the 1980s and during the conservative Reagan Administration, MESBIC which provides start-up capital to Black business, experienced a freeze in funding and a relative budget reduction. Private community development organizations have never had a sterling record of supporting Black business growth and development. America has funded and demonstrated greater support for the economic development of its former war enemies, Japan, Germany, and Russia than it has for the economic uplift of its 30 million, taxpaying African American citizens.

In less than two decades, the top 100 Black companies increased gross revenues from $474 million in 1972 to more than $7.169 billion in 1990. The total income of African Americans was only $15.25 billion in 1956, but in 1990 it totalled more than $200 billion. However, Black business advancement is merely fractional compared to that of White corporate America. But then, it is pointless to always compare or to use white Americans as a frame of reference for Black progress without qualifications. America's current superior economic status can be attributed partly to the fact that it benefitted from more than 250 years of free slave labor during its early development. Black business and economic development has been fraught with the impediments of racism, oppression, and discrimination. Black business growth and development began on a large scale since 1954. For every ethnic group, including Whites, it has taken time to build a financial base or capital foundation in order to eventually achieve economic formidability or self-sufficiency.

# MEANING AND CONCEPTS OF BLACK ECONOMIC DEVELOPMENT

*Dialectics of Black Capitalism and Economic Empowerment.* The problem of defining *Black* economic development lies in the attempt to differentiate it from a global concept of economic development. Conventional economic theory cites human resources, natural resources, capital formation, and technology as key processes and fundamental factors that define and measure economic development.[20] The inherent objective of economic development in this sense is to produce goods and services to satisfy human needs and wants. Thus, economic development means the process of improving the production capability of a country or society in order that it may meet the consumption requirements of its people.

Black economic development differs from general economic development only in the sense that it is race-specific. It is race-specific because Blacks are a politically oppressed people and comprise a disparate segment in the American society. Therefore, as an oppressed race, political liberation is equally fundamental to all of the other factors of economic development. Beyond these distinctions, the production and consumption analysis of economic development is applicable to

African Americans. In conformance with and adaptation to the conventional concept of economic development, Professor Louis C. Green defines Black economic development "as a purposeful, conscious, comprehensive undertaking designed to progressively alter the discrepancy between Black America's consumption pattern and its productive potential."[21] The inference of Green's definition is that Blacks consume enormously more than they can independently produce without depending almost totally on the White economic power structure.

Of the four key factors and processes of economic development, human resources (professional and occupational skills) and capital formation have been proposed as the most important and effective toward developing the Black economy.[22] Black economic development and self-determination can occur only if African Americans acquire the professional, technical and scientific training and skills to produce goods and services necessary for the sustenance of the Black community. Moreover, they must be able to produce sufficiently enough to promote economic exchanges and develop interdependent relationships with other groups. There has always been a correlation between the economic advancement of African Americans and the number of Black academic professionals, scientists, engineers, technicians, etc. graduated from American colleges and universities.

Black economic productive ability will increase to the extent that African Americans acquire education and training in the fields of business, science, and technology and use their talents and skills toward own-race uplift and development. In the 21st century, those races or ethnic groups who are significantly represented in the fields of business, science and technology will determine who is to be oppressed, who is to be liberated, who is to be independent, and who is to be empowered. The relative small number of Blacks in the areas of agriculture, business, economics, military science, computer science, engineering, and various applied sciences perpetuates a colonial dependency on Whites in spite of the progress that resulted from the Civil Rights Movement of the sixties.[23] However, individual educational achievements and skills by Blacks alone are insufficient. Attendant to Black human resource development, there must exist a collective ideology and commitment to Black economic liberation. Consequently, studies in African American history, culture, sociology, and politics are also imperative for the development of an ideology of liberation.

The second most important factor of Black economic development is capital formation or capital acquisition. Having a legacy of slavery and oppression, Blacks have not had the opportunity of having wealth and capital transferred from generation to generation. In recognition of this fact, Black leaders such as Marcus Garvey and Elijah Muhammad proposed that Blacks should pool their financial resources. On a limited scale, both Garvey and Muhammad proved that through collective and cooperative savings a race or group can amass large amounts of capital for the purpose of production and development. The previous discussion of how some of the early Black economic institutions developed from the collective contributions of the church, fraternal, and mutual aid societies is a case in point.

Capital stock or equity financing is also an undeveloped strategy of economic development among African Americans. In cases where enterprising Blacks have studied, mastered and practiced the science of finance and investments, they have succeeded in contributing significantly to the building of a viable segment of the Black economy. Booker T. Washington had suggested during the early part of the century that Blacks should assume the initiative and aggressively enter those areas of business in which Whites offer little resistance.[24] In other words, find a niche in the market and then develop it to its fullest potential. Washington's advice has proven to be sound and profitable. When whites were reluctant to insure or to loan money to African Americans, Black-owned and operated insurance companies and banks were developed. Black publishing companies were organized under the same premise. This was also the case in the Black personal and hair care area of business. Although Black-owned hair care products manufacturers and distributors face fierce competition from White companies, they still manage to hold their own and to dominate the African American segment of the market.

The example in the Black hair care business was set first by Madame C.J. Walker. By 1917, she had established a million-dollar hair products company in Indianapolis, Indiana. Since Madame C.J. Walker, numerous Black cosmetic, hair and personal care companies have been formed and continue to prosper. The Soft Sheen Products Company, organized in 1964, has through recent acquisitions developed into a $85.4 million hair-care manufacturer linking Black America to African and Caribbean markets. Increasingly since the 1980s, Black industrial/service companies are seeking global markets for their products.

The Pro-line Corporation is another outstanding example of Black entrepreneurship in the hair-care and cosmetics industry. Pro-line, a Dallas based company, in 1991 became the second largest Black-owned manufacturer and distributor of hair-care products with sales exceeding $35 million. Comer J. Cottrell started Pro-line Corporation in Los Angeles, California, on January 5, 1970 with a capitalization of $600, a borrowed typewriter, a 700 square foot office and warehouse. After initially producing and marketing a single oil based hair spray, the company now produces and distributes a multiple line of Black cosmetics. Pro-line products are presently being manufactured and sold in

Photo 20  Comer J. Cottrell, Pres. Pro-line. Courtesy of Pro-line Corporation.

Nigeria, Kenya, and the Ivory Coast. Pro-line products are also sold throughout the Islands of the Caribbean and Taiwan. Pro-line, as well as other Black-owned industrial/service companies, will continue to succeed and increase in numbers as they develop innovative products and creative marketing and advertising strategies.

Reginald F. Lewis, a former Black Wall Street attorney, represents a new breed of Black businessmen and financiers emulative of the most successful white capitalists. Buying one established American company and then availing himself of the leverage buyout

practice, he acquired several other companies. Through junk bond financing, Lewis manipulated and executed a $985 million leveraged buyout of Beatrice International, a food manufacturing and distribution conglomerate that operates in 31 countries. Lewis' company, TLC, became the first Black-owned concern to surpass the $1 billion mark.[25]

African American embracement and practice of American capitalism have not been without criticism from a few Black scholars and social theorists. The eminent sociologist, E. Franklin Frazier, described Black business as a social myth and argued that the accumulation of wealth by a few Blacks would not solve the race problem in America. He further stated that the myth "served to exaggerate the economic well-being of [Blacks] in the United States and to whet the appetites of the black bourgeoisie. . . . "[26] Frazier's criticism of African American business initiatives or Black capitalism was followed during the early 1970s by two books: *The Myth of Black Capitalism,* by Earl Ofari; and *Black Awakening in Capitalist America,* by Robert L. Allen. In 1983, Manning Marable wrote the book, *How Capitalism Underdeveloped Black America,* also highly critical of Black capitalism.[27]

Ofari, Allen, and Marable, basically, are critical of capitalism as a political system in America. They argue that capitalism is the basis and cause of racial oppression, injustice, and class antagonism in the United States—beginning with slavery. Ofari's statement that: "There is no value in trading in white corporate exploitation for black exploitation," sum up the critics' opposition to Black capitalism.

Those who criticize Black capitalism offer no viable or realistic alternatives that will improve the economic condition of Black Americans. Conceding that capitalism is an exploitative system, the critics do not propose immediate and practical ways of changing the system or the White racist order. What opponents of Black capitalism fail to realize is that it is not capitalism per se that is racist and that oppresses, but the problem begins with humans whose corrupt values and morals direct and control the system. Any politico-economic system is subject to be perverted into immorality and corruption, including socialism.

In the absence of a viable alternative, African American entrepreneurs continue to make small but meaningful progress towards building a foundation for eventual Black economic liberation. There are tens of thousands of relatively small Black businesses em-

ploying, for the most part, millions of African American workers and professional staff members. Historically, Black-owned and operated banks, savings and loan associations, and insurance companies have assisted African Americans in their business capitalizations, home mortgages, and health coverages. What is needed more than an ever increasing level of Black business development, is a collective or mass ideology of Black economic liberation.

Black business ownership is essential for the development of African American communities. This is especially so since the black and white races still occupy, basically, segregated neighborhoods. When Whites own businesses located in the Black community, the profits from those enterprises are returned to white Americans for the development of their communities and social institutions. Seldom if ever do white businesses invest in or develop the Black community from which they derive their profits. Race of ownership and control of business determines which community reaps the majority reward from entrepreneurship. Therefore in discussing Black economic development, a sharp distinction must be made between Black *proprietary* versus *participatory* entrepreneurship.

Proprietary Black entrepreneurship means Black majority ownership of the capital assets of an enterprise with Blacks having decision-making power over the personnel, materials, resources, and all matters pertaining to its economic as well as social functions. Participatory Black entrepreneurship exists where Blacks share only marginally or not at all in the ownership of the business, even though they may participate at high management levels. Participatory entrepreneurial Blacks have no ultimate decision-making responsibility or power relative to the execution of the firms' activities or the allocation of its economic resources.[28] Following the 1960s Civil Rights Movement, many African Americans were placed symbolically on corporation boards and in vice corporate management positions. Ordinarily, these Blacks possess neither the power nor influence to alter corporate policy to favorably affect African American entrepreneurs or the Black community. Social integration and participatory entrepreneurship are of little benefit without a commensurate measure of Black proprietary economic power and influence. Although profit is the life-blood and primary motive of business activity, Black-owned businesses often make policy on behalf of the economic, political, and social interests of the Black community.

Proprietary and participatory Black entrepreneurship constitute a form of Black/White economic coexistence that will exist in the United States indefinitely. Consistent with this projection, William M. Harris, a prominent urban planner, has proposed a three phase model for the development and empowerment of the Black community. The first phase involves building a sense of community through Black consciousness raising programs. The second phase is devoted to the identification of problems, goals formation, and strategies for eliminating barriers to economic development. During this phase, participation or contribution by non-Blacks or outside groups is limited to technical assistance towards the achievement of goals and objectives. The third phase tests the operation of plans designed to promote self-development and greater self-sufficiency of the Black community.[29]

A discussion of Black economic development and empowerment is not complete without mentioning the reparation demands that were made to the White religious community by James Forman, May 4, 1969. Forman's famous Black Manifesto, in essence, demanded that Whites pay reparations to Black people for two centuries of forced slavery and another hundred years of Black servitude to the white power structure.[30] Proponents and opponents of the Manifesto and

reparation demands were debated during the 1970s. The issue was raised again in 1990 when Japanese citizens demanded and received reparations for the humiliation and economic losses that they suffered because of their internment during World War II.

David H. Swinton, an economist, attempted to calculate in dollar amounts the approximate social costs of slavery, segregation, and discrimination.[31] The noneconomic costs of human indignities, pain and suffering would also be added. The economic costs would consist of lost value from denied opportunities, wages and salaries, including restricted opportunity to acquire capital and labor on the same terms as Whites. Swinton roughly calculated that it would require restitutions of more than $650 billion to repair the damage of slavery and racial discrimination. The point is that there has not been a concerted national economic program or "Marshall Plan" to enable African Americans to recover fully from the loss and destruction of slavery and Jim Crow. The question of the Black Manifesto and reparations have not been fully debated, investigated or resolved and may be expected to reemerge as a Black political issue from time to time.

However, Flournoy A. Coles observes that Black economic development is inevitably

. . . dependent upon, and limited by, its external environment—the national economy. Thus, black economic development programs and efforts must be directed toward effecting necessary changes within both the black economy and the national economy of which it is a part.[32]

***Economic Theory and Black Economic Development.*** Capitalism is the political and economic system on which economic theory relating to Black people is based. This is so because beginning in the fifteenth century, Blacks or Africans were the unwilling participants and capital factors who enabled Europe and America to rise to economic prominence through slavery, colonization, and exploitation. The economic advantages derived from African slave labor made the European and American industrial revolutions possible and created the basis for modern capitalism. Questions relevant to Blacks in the construct of economic theory regarding capitalism are: 1) Is capitalism of necessity inherently and humanly exploitative? 2) Can capitalism as a politico-economic system thrive without racism?

Capitalism has been subject to various ideological definitions and interpretations. In the simplest sense, capitalism subscribes to the political policy of private ownership of capital, and other material or abstract means of production and distribution under conditions of free enterprise and competition. Capital itself means anything used in the furtherance of production. Capitalism becomes corrupt in practice when it extends its ownership prerogative to include human labor. Since management and labor are the two human factors of production, both are innately independent, and are of equal status, and exchangeable at mutual or fair cost. The other factors of production are capital and land. Production requires voluntary cooperation between the capital owner and profit-seeker, and the labor furnisher and wage earner. When capitalists force or exploit laborers to work for free, then capitalism becomes a tyrannical economic system.

This is precisely what happened when the Europeans subjugated Africans and forced them to serve as free labor in the building of the Americas and Europe. Without a fair exchange of value between capital and labor, Africans were converted into capital and expropriated as property. Thus, in the fifteenth century, the Atlantic Slave Trade began, and it dramatically enhanced the economic fortunes of the Caucasian race throughout the world. Slavery and, subsequently, European

colonization created a new aspect of economic theory—the economics of racial discrimination. Considering the sordid history of capitalism, even in the absence of slavery, the question as to whether White capitalism can thrive without racism in America has not been resolved.

Economic discrimination does not occur in a vacuum but is made possible and compounded by social and political racism. Institutionalized social and political racial discrimination restrict the opportunity for Blacks to become sufficiently educated and trained in proportionate numbers to compete with Whites for professional and occupational jobs. Inadequate education and the lack of job skills cause many Blacks to be denied equal employment opportunity and income. Consequently, the rationale for Black economic discrimination is established. Institutional racial discrimination in the workplace and in the financial sector, impedes the ability of African Americans to accumulate capital and income necessary for business and community development.

Some economists describe the lack of adequate education, technological training, and job skills that characterize an overwhelming number of Blacks as human capital deficiency. In essence, this means that Blacks do not generally possess the right qualifications that will enable them to increase their economic productivity or to compete on an equal basis with Whites. Consequently, racism and economic discrimination leads to their unemployment. The social effects of unemployment are often reflected in increased rates of crime, delinquency, violence, drug and alcohol abuse, and family breakups. There still exists a gap in the years of schooling and academic performance between Blacks and Whites. As a result, Blacks continue to function at a competitive disadvantage relative to Whites in the American labor markets.[33]

Economists seem to agree that, at least in theory, economic discrimination prevails at a tremendous cost to the total economy and society. When all members or segments of the society are not producing up to their maximum potential, Gross National Product is reduced. In almost any reputable economics textbook, one may find graphical illustrations or models showing the negative economic cost of racial discrimination. If this is the case, a pertinent question is, why are Blacks denied equal education, and access to employment opportunity?[34]

Besides the economic costs of racial discrimination, significant social costs are also incurred. Billions of dollars in unemployment compensation, welfare payments, and social programs have to be borne by society. Increased rates of crime, violence, and other forms of social deviance require that billions more dollars be spent for law enforcement and penal costs partly as a result of racial discrimination.

In spite of societal losses, there are some who enjoy short-term gain from economic discrimination and the exclusion of Blacks and women from the labor force. Many whites perceive that they have a vested interest in obstructing Black participation in various professional and occupational fields. Economic discrimination can be profitable to those who enjoy increased wages and salaries, and higher social status as a result of a limited professional and technical work force.

Karl Marx's theory of *surplus value* may not be entirely irrelevant to the growing numbers of unemployed Blacks. Technological innovations and advances, especially since the 1970s, have made employment unlikely for low-skilled and poorly educated African Americans. Consequently, there has been an ever increasing unemployed "reserve army" of the Black underclass. Federal job-training programs and other government/private projects designed to assist and to reduce the untrained-unemployed poor have been inconsis-

tent, and only minimally effective. Even among the so-called middle class Blacks, underemployment and inequality of income have been rising for the past two decades. Furthermore, many educated, skilled, and semi-skilled Blacks are technically unemployed.[35] This factor has created a new "super-reserve" labor force that in effect will depress salaries and wages and, thus, reduce even lower the income level of the Black community.

Since 1977, college attendance by Blacks has decreased. In the long-run, this means that the reserve army of the Black unemployed will increase. As America loses or moves more of its heavy industry abroad or to Third World countries, domestic capital requirements and technology will change. Corporate demand for technological skills in the computer, electronic, and information industries will increase at an increasing rate. New capital accumulation and technical changes will cause technological unemployment, and contribute toward an even larger reserve army of unemployed African Americans. Blacks more than any other racial-ethnic minority are under represented in the highly skilled electronic-information technical fields.

According to Marxian theory, capitalists will substitute capital for labor in the productive process. The new capital accumulation will cause Blacks, who are not appropriately trained, to suffer high rates of unemployment. Even average educated and semi-skilled Blacks will have to work for minimal wages because of unemployment and underemployment caused by capital accumulation and substitution for labor, and technological change. Capitalists may experience increased profits (surplus value) because of their opportunity to exploit the reserve worker force.

The discussion of Marxian theory is relevant to the continuing controversy pertaining to the economic fairness or justice of capitalism. The problem of disparity in African American education and training may be more of a political than of an economic nature. Certainly, economic and political factors conjoin to maintain Blacks in a subordinate position in American society. The political system has not yet eliminated all the economic barriers to Black access to higher education and to highly skilled occupational training. Consequently, economic discrimination and the reserve army of the Black unemployed will continue to increase.

To a greater extent, the most important factor determining the economic progress of Blacks is the state or condition of the aggregate American economy. This idea is based on the belief that as general business conditions improve investments, factory output, wholesale and retail sales will increase. Consequently, the unemployment rate will decline and Black economic development will inevitably occur and grow in proportion with the national economy. While this may be a logical assumption, it provides for no immediate change in the economic plight of African Americans. For one thing, the nation is not politically united on which economic theory to pursue that will achieve general business revival and economic growth.[36] Until the 1970s, the economic theories of John Maynard Keynes on consumption, saving and investment prevailed. Since the mid 1970s, politicians and economists have begun to embrace or experiment with Arthur Laffer's "supply-side" economic theory.

Ostensibly, Blacks fared well under Keynesian economic theory since it advocates government intervention in monetary and fiscal policies to promote employment and relieve poverty. Simply put, Keynesian theory proposes general tax cuts that would increase public purchasing power in order to create demand for goods and services. Capital investment and factory production increases as a result of accelerated demand. The result is a reduction in the unemployment rate caused by the creation of new jobs or re-hiring. The Keynesian theory focuses on the demand-side of the economy.

Supply-side economics was politically espoused as a recessionary fighting policy during the Reagan Administration. Supply-side theorists argue that government regulations and intervention encumber the vital functioning of the marketplace and the economy. Supply-side economists propose tax cuts basically for corporations, business, and the wealthy. Such tax cuts provide business the incentive for investment and reinvestment in large capital expenditures. Concurrently, the rich would be encouraged to purchase high-cost luxury items. The new investment and spending resulting from the tax cut incentive are supposed to increase total national output and stimulate general economic growth.[37] Under the supply-side scenario, certain economic benefits such as employment opportunities and other fiscal amenities would "trickle-down" to Blacks and the poor. Thus, supply-side economics is popularly referred to as the trickling-down theory relative to its effect and benefit to African Americans.

One can hardly dispute the presumption that the economic welfare of Blacks is significantly effected by the prosperity or decline of the total economy. Everyone benefits from sound and productive economic theories and policies. However, the concept suggests that racial disparity is the norm, and that African Americans should be content at maintaining their same relative economic position with Whites. While the fate and fortunes of Blacks may rise and fall with fluctuations of the economy, the matters of fair distribution of income and economic justice are not addressed.

## BLACKS IN THE MAJOR CORPORATE STRUCTURE AND MARKETPLACE

*The African American in White Corporations.* Prior to the 1940s and World War II, Blacks were employed in major white businesses mostly in menial and unskilled jobs. This does not include the brief period following Reconstruction. Even during the period of industrial expansion and the development of the corporate idea after 1890, Black workers were displaced in major corporations primarily because of the urging and protest of White workers.[38] However, the emphasis in this topic is on the employment of African American white-collar workers in major corporations. White-collar work is referred to here as clerical, technical, managerial, and administrative salaried positions.

The number of Blacks in white-collar positions in American corporations was relatively insignificant until 1940. Prior to this time, Blacks possessed primarily agricultural and personal service skills that were not compatible to the office and technical demands of commercial and industrial enterprises. Manpower shortages of the war and in the defense industries (1939–1945) resulted in the training and hiring of Blacks in certain up-scaled jobs and occupations. This did not occur, however, until Black leaders threatened a mass March on Washington in 1941 to protest federal discrimination in the defense industries. Consequently, President Franklin D. Roosevelt signed into law Executive Order 8802 the Fair Employment Practices Commission (FEPC) which forbade discrimination by federal contractors based on race.

After the war, Black veterans benefitted from the educational provisions of the GI Bill, which allowed them to further their academic education or to obtain vocational and craft skills. These factors, plus the migration of large numbers of southern Blacks to large cities and to the North, placed political pressure on the government to act upon the deplorable racial discrimination that prevailed in the private sector. From 1950 to 1960, the genesis of the Civil Rights Movement, the increase in African American white-collar workers was, comparatively, dramatic.[39] Only after the U.S. Supreme Court's desegregation ruling of 1954, and the passage of the Civil Rights Act of 1964 did Blacks begin to be employed in significant numbers as lower and mid-level salaried managers and administrators in major white corporations.

Equal Employment Opportunity legislation and Affirmative Action programs were responsible for a substantial increase in Black male and female managerial, administrative, and clerical workers from 1965 to 1977. This growth continued until 1980. The number of African Americans employed in major corporations increased at a decreasing rate from 1980 to 1985. In spite of what appears as remarkable increases, the growth of African American white-collar workers is minute in comparison with that of Whites during the same periods. By 1985, the total number of Black officials, managers and professionals in companies was less than five percent of the U.S. total. Under the Reagan and Bush Administrations of the 1980s and early 1990s, Equal Employment Opportunity and Affirmative Action programs became virtually ineffective in encouraging white businesses and corporations to hire Blacks. In addition, the 1980s marked an era of corporate, streamlining, mergers and acquisitions sparked by adverse economic conditions. Corporate downsizing caused many of the "soft" non-income producing and token staff positions that many Blacks held to be eliminated.[40]

What is being discussed in this topic is Black participatory entrepreneurship mentioned and defined earlier in this chapter. For the most part, the managerial and administrative positions that Blacks hold in major White owned and controlled corporations are non-line positions lacking in policy-making authority. A study by Jaslin U. Salmon found that in major corporations, African Americans hold mostly dead-end administrative positions and tend to be placed in staff rather than line positions.[41] Apparently, the goal of many of the major white corporations is to achieve mere minority representation rather than allowing for meaningful integration of African Americans into their policy-making structure. The proverbial "glass ceiling" generally restricts Black entry to top executive positions in white corporations. Consequently, Black participatory status in White businesses can never completely suffice for Black proprietary entrepreneurship.

Growth in the number of Black professional participants in white businesses has been relatively significant since the 1940s. Some Blacks have managed to become successful corporate managers in spite of racial barriers. Yet, the phenomenon has not taken place without racial antagonism and political fallout. Corporations must still deal with the racist attitudes and internal problems that often result after Black professionals are hired.[42]

A recent study of Black corporate officials found that 90 percent of them believed that affirmative action and Equal Employment Opportunity programs and guidelines greatly or somewhat influenced their firms to hire them. Those who were hired after 1975 had attained education levels equal to or above those of Whites. More than half of the respondents complained that mentor support on the job had been below average or none at all. Ninety-seven percent indicated that they had personally experienced discrimination and racial prejudice, and that they had also experienced feelings of social isolation, mental stress, and cultural alienation on the job. These findings and others not reported here underscore the ominous effects of race, racism, economics and politics in corporate America.[43]

*The Black Consumer.* The African American population exceeds 30 million according to the 1990 census. This segment of the population earns over $200 billion annually. In terms of Gross National Product and numbers, the Black population ranks with some of the world's largest countries. For a few examples, the Black population in the United States is larger than that of Canada, Czechoslovakia, Australia, Peru, Kenya and North Korea. The economic and market potential of this large "internal colony" are astronomical. Yet, insofar as economic returns from being so largely represented in American society, Blacks profit the least entrepreneurially. Most of the disposable income of African Americans goes into the coffers of White businessmen and out of Black neighborhoods and communities.

The reasons that African Americans do not capitalize on their own market potential have been explicitly stated and implicitly alluded to in the preceding topics of this chapter. However, it is important to summarize and to re-enumerate them again here. Black entrepreneurs and African Americans in general: 1) lack a collective and unified economic liberation ideology; 2) are restricted economically and politically from obtaining adequate education and business training; 3) have difficulty in procuring capital and credit. Slavery and racial oppression prevented any legacy of transferred or inherited wealth and; 4) inability to organize for co-operative effort, possibly because of self-alienation. (Refer to chapter on Black psychology).

The Black consumer still represents a vastly undeveloped and only partially investigated market for two reasons. First, prior to the 1950s, White merchants, feeling that Blacks had no purchasing alternative, made no special or unique appeal to the African American market. Secondly, any effort in media advertising to appeal specifically to African Americans using Black models and symbols offended White readers and audiences. However, following the successes of the boycotts of the Civil Rights Movement, and the development of Black consciousness attitudes of the 1960s, white corporations began to understand the importance and profitability of culture in appealing to the African American market.

Cultural as well as socio-political influences are the primary reasons that major sellers have modified their marketing strategies to fit the specific behavioral characteristics and requirements of the Black consumer. While national manufacturers and retailers were once reluctant to direct their general media advertisements to African Americans, they now find it necessary to use Black models, Black music and Black situation comedies to appeal to the Black reader and audience. However, racism is not entirely absent from media programming. Advertisers are still careful to present Blacks in situations they feel are acceptable to Whites. In order to target Blacks specifically and not alienate Whites, marketers advertise very liberally in the Black print media.

Few meaningful studies have been done that reliably characterize Black consumer behavior. The problem is that the African American market is not monolithic in nature. It is composed of various subsegments based on income, education, social standing, and degrees of Afrocentric cultural and political consciousness. Non-Black market analysts and researchers find it difficult to interpret the complex nature of African American consumption behavior. Considering the logic of the DuBoisian "dual consciousness" theory, many African Americans may adopt some consumer characteristics and behaviors similar to Europeans or Whites. Still, if families of the two races are given the same income, education, and occupational background, differences in spending patterns would become evident because of historic cultural and social "separateness."

The German economist or statistician Ernst Engel developed the theory that as a family's income increases the percentage spent on: 1) food will decrease; 2) housing and household operation will remain the same; 3) the amount spent on clothing, transportation, education, health, and for savings will increase.[44] However, the consumption and expenditure patterns of low and average income Black families might be inversely related to Engel's theory. At least one study showed that for each category and for specific items, the amount spent by Black families proportionately exceeded those spent by White families. For example, except for families with extremely low-income, spending for automobiles puts Blacks ahead of Whites at low-income levels and reverses the position at high income levels.[45]

Differences in social and political statuses based on race, inevitably, causes variances in consumption and expenditure patterns of Whites and Blacks. Credit privileges and terms, housing and neighborhood discriminatory factors, and differences in social values and political perceptions all contribute toward the need to construct different paradigms for studying and assessing the Black consumer. Poor Black families who traditionally have been unable to acquire certain luxury items or have been denied access to various status symbols may spend irrationally and excessively on a single item in contradiction to Engel's family consumption and expenditure laws. Given the same income, White families will spend more on recreation than Blacks. At increased income levels Blacks will spend less on housing or homes, and Whites will spend more on homes, including vacation homes, and boarding away from home (hotel, motels, etc.).[46] Blacks spend a greater proportion of their income on hair and personal care products than Whites.

The potential market and power of the Black consumer will be a major factor in the realization of economic empowerment of

# SELECTED CHARACTERISTICS OF
# BLACK HOUSEHOLDS: 1985

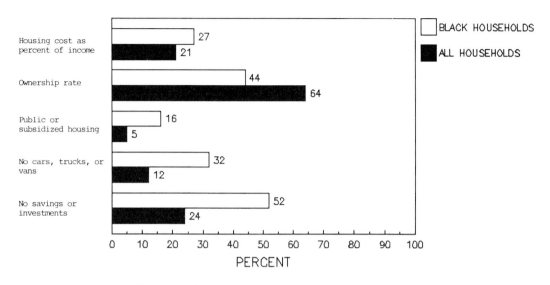

SOURCE: U.S. BUREAU OF THE CENSUS

Figure 13  Characteristics of Black Households.

African Americans. The key to Black economic prosperity may lie in a more profound analysis and exploration of Black consumer patterns and characteristics. The Black entrepreneur cannot presently compete in all consumer goods categories with White businesses. However, as African American proprietors gain in competitive equality, they will capture not only a greater share of the Black consumer segment, but they will and have already begun to attract consumers worldwide.

---

# · QUESTIONS AND EXERCISES ·

---

1. Compare the Black economic development ideologies of early twentieth century Black leaders such as Booker T. Washington, W.E.B. DuBois and Marcus Garvey with late twentieth century economists Louis C. Green, Thomas Sowell; and Islamic leaders Elijah Muhammad or Louis Farrakhan. (Research required)

2. Define Black business within the context of American entrepreneurship.

3. Discuss some of the many factors which contributed to the establishment of Black-owned banks, insurance companies and other businesses during the latter part of the nineteenth and early twentieth centuries.

4. How did the U.S. Supreme Court's desegregation ruling of 1954 effect the growth and development of Black enterprises?

5. Critique and discuss the various federal, corporate and foundation programs for Black economic development which were initiated since the 1960s.

6. Can capitalism exist as a viable politico-economic system without class exploitation and racism?

7. Differentiate between proprietary and participatory Black entrepreneurship.

8. Evaluate supply-side economics and its "trickle-down" theory relative to Black economic and community advancement.

9. Is reparations a viable Black economic development option?

10. How does the Black consumer market differ from general market demands and patterns?

## · NOTES AND REFERENCES ·

1. See William J. Wilson, *The Declining Significance of Race* (Chicago: The University of Chicago Press 1978).

2. For a synopsis of socialism and capitalism see, Paul A. Samuelson and W. D. Nordhaus, *Economics* (New York: McGraw-Hill Book Co. 1989) 823–845.

3. Read Thomas Sowell, *Race and Economics* (New York: Longman 1975); and Walter E. Williams, *The State Against Blacks* (New York: McGraw-Hill 1982).

4. Samuel L. Banks, "Don't Blame the Victims," *Baltimore Afro-American* (May 4, 1985) p. 5.

5. Elijah Muhammad, *Message to the Black Man* (Chicago: Muhammad Mosque of Islam No. 2, 1965) 192–199.

6. Ibid., p. 174.

7. Talmadge Anderson, "Black Entrepreneurship and Concepts toward Economic Coexistence," *The Western Journal of Black Studies* (Summer 1982) v. 6(2) 80–88.

8. Robert H. Kinzer and Edward Sagarin, *The Negro in American Business* (New York: Greenberg Publisher 1950) p. 169.

9. Benjamin L. Hooks, "Publishers Foreword," *The Crisis* (February 1992) 99(2) p. 4.

10. Andrew F. Brimmer, "Small Business and Economic Development in the Negro Community," in *Black Americans and White Business* edited by E. M. Epstein and D. R. Hampton (Encino and Belmont CA: 1971) 265.

11. See Lerone Bennett Jr., "Money, Merchants, Markets: The Quest for Economic Security," *Ebony* (November 1973) 72–74.

12. J. H. Harmon, A. G. Lindsay and Carter G. Woodson, *The Negro as Business Man* (College Park MD: McGrath Publishing Co. 1929, Reprint 1969) 2–6.

13. For a brief chronology of Black economic and educational development from 1865 to 1915 see, John Hope Franklin, *From Slavery to Freedom* (New York: Alfred A. Knopf 1967) 382–412.

14. Gunnar Myrdal, *An American Dilemma* (New York: Harper and Brothers 1944) p. 305.

15. Harmon, Lindsay and Woodson, *The Negro as a Business Man*, 24.

16. Lerone Bennett, Jr., "Money Merchants, Markets: The Quest for Economic Security," *Ebony*, Part 11. (1975) p. 77.

17. Emmet J. Hughes, "The Negro's New Economic Life," *Fortune* (September 1956) 127–131.

18. Compare the growth in revenue of 100 Black companies from their date of origin to 1972 in *Black Enterprise* (May 1973) 37–67.

19. *Black Enterprise* (June 1980) 119–120.

20. Samuelson and Nordhaus, *Economics*, 885–895.

21. Louis C. Green, "Political Economy of Black Economic Development," *The Western Journal of Black Studies* (Winter 1984) v. 8(4) 216.

22. See Talmadge Anderson, "Black Affirmative Action: Strategies towards Self-help and Self-determination," *Humboldt Journal of Social Relations* (F,W/S,S, 1986/87) 14(1&2) 185–194.

23. Talmadge Anderson, "Economic Self-Reliance through Appropriate Education," *The Black Collegian* (Sept/Oct 1978) p. 4.

24. See Booker T. Washington, *The Negro in Business* (New York: AMS Press 1907 rptd. 1971).

25. See, "Defining a New Generation," *Black Enterprise* (June 1988) 103–104. Also see, *Black Enterprise* (November 1987).

26. E. Franklin Frazier, *Black Bourgeoisie* (New York: Collier Books reprint 1962) 144–145.

27. See Earl Ofari, *The Myth of Black Capitalism* (New York: Modern Reader 1970) 85; Robert L. Allen, *Black Awakening in Capitalist America* (Garden City, NY: Anchor Books 1970) 274–275; and Manning Marable, *How Capitalism Underdeveloped Black America* (Boston: South End Press 1983) 133–167.

28. Anderson, "Black Entrepreneurship and Concepts toward Economic Coexistence," p. 84.

29. William M. Harris, Sr., *Black Community Development* (San Francisco: R&E Publishers 1976)

30. R. S. Lecky and H. E. Wright, (editors), "Reparations Now? An Introduction," in *Black Manifesto* (New York: Sheed and Ward, Inc. 1969) 1–4.

31. David H. Swinton, "Racial Inequality and Reparations," in *The Wealth of Races* edited by Richard F. America (New York: Greenwood Press 1990) 154–162.

32. Flournoy A. Coles, Jr. *Black Economic Development* (Chicago: Nelson Hall 1975) p. 12.

33. See, Clifton R. Wharton, Jr., "The future of the Black Community: Human Capital, Family Aspirations, and Individual Motivation," *The Review of Black Political Economy* (Spring 1986) 14(4) 9–16.

34. Talmadge Anderson, "Black Economic Liberation Under Capitalism," *The Black Scholar* (October 1970) 2(2) 11–14.

35. Study the employment statistics in G. D. Jaynes and R. M. Williams, Jr., *A Common Destiny* (Washington, DC: National Academy Press 1989) 271–328.

36. Theodore Cross, *The Black Power Imperative* (New York: Faulkner 1984) 476–482.

37. See also, Ronald Johnson, "Supply-side Economics: The Rise to Prominence," *The Review of Black Political Economy* (Winter 1983) 12(2) 189–202.

38. Herbert Hill, *Black Labor and the American Legal System* (Madison, WI: The University of Wisconsin Press 1985) 1–34.

39. For a chronology of white-collar growth figures see, John W. Work, *Race Economics and Corporate America* (Wilmington, DE: Scholarly Resources, Inc. 1984) 39–84.

40. Derek T. Dingle, "Will Black Managers Survive Corporate Downsizing?" *Black Enterprise* (March 1987) 49–55.

41. See Jaslin U. Salmon, *Black Executives in White Businesses* (Washington, DC: University Press of America 1979)

42. For an understanding of the psychological and social affects many Blacks experience in white businesses see, George Davis and Glegg Watson, *Black Life in Corporate America* (Garden City, NY: Anchor/Press 1982)

43. Talmadge Anderson and William M. Harris, "A Socio-historical and Contemporary Study of African Americans in U.S. Corporations," *The Western Journal of Black Studies* (Fall 1990) 174–181.

44. Most students of the social sciences are familiar with Engel's laws. This reference is from William F. Schoell, *Marketing* 2nd ed. (Boston: Allyn and Bacon 1985) 203.

45. See Carolyn S. Bell, *The Economics of the Ghetto* (New York: The Western Publishing Co. 1970) 131.

46. Ibid., 135.

# Chapter 8

# African American Arts and Humanities

## AFRICAN AMERICAN CULTURAL CREATIVITY

*The Black Aesthetic.* The term aesthetic is of Greek origin and it is used to describe that which is artistically beautiful. It connotes a sensitivity to beauty or an act or feat interpreted as being creative, artful, and in good taste. Aesthetics can relate to objects or materials within the physical realm such as paintings, sculpture and crafts; and to those concrete and abstract human activities, behaviors or motions, that appeal to the senses as dance, music and drama. However, an absolute universal aesthetic does not exist. Aesthetics or beauty can be an individual perception, but more often it is based on the values and ideals of a group or society. Thus, culture, race, and tradition may determine or influence the aesthetical nature and beauty of an object or phenomenon. In other words,

beauty is relative, and a sense of aesthetic relativism must prevail if the art of peoples of different cultures is to be fairly evaluated and appreciated.

Aesthetic evaluation is not immune from psychological attitudes of ethnocentrism, egoism and prejudice or the oppressive influences of political racism. These negative aspects of aesthetic appraisal are the reasons that African American and African cultural inventions have been relegated to an inferior status by European and Western critics of the arts and humanities. Even without aesthetic racism and prejudice, beauty in the classical Western or white European sense cannot be applied always to African or African American arts.

For example, the European term and concept of "art" is not easily translatable into any of the various African cultures. When the European colonizers raided African villages and societies in the 17th and 18th centuries under the guise of making scientific inquiry, they discovered an assortment of African "art objects." Many of these objects were in the form of figurines, masks, carved ivory, and castings in bronze and brass. The Europeans routinely classified these objects as primitive African art in contrast to the white man's "civilized" societies.[1] Physical paraphernalia were not the only aspects of African culture that were classified as crude or primitive by the Europeans. African dance, music and song were also described as primitive or savage in nature.

In the African tradition and frame of reference, objects, dance, music, and song were not perceived as art but as functional creations and symbols of life. The artifacts and activities were used and employed in birth, marriage, harvest, festive, and burial rituals and ceremonies. In contrast, the European conceptualization of the value of art is its inherent uselessness, antiquity or fossilization. Eurocentrically, art is a thing of beauty to be seen or from which to derive personal sensual pleasure or sensation. In African societies, "art" objects, music, dance, pantomime or drama "were a functioning, collective and integral part of society, not a cultural appendage."[2] More succinctly, Carlton W. and Barbara J. Molette describe the Black aesthetic as being "related to its usefulness, that is, art-for-peoples' use . . . in contrast to the Eurocentric elitist art-for-art's sake tradition."[3]

Black or African American art and art forms are often treated and viewed as "less-than" or unrefined by white American art and literary critics. Stemming from the slave, colonial and nadir periods of American history, Black song, music, dance and poetry were regarded as curios and primitive until the second decade of the twentieth century. However, by the 1940s, the unique, soul-stirring, and "beautiful" nature of Black arts became so appealing to Euro-Americans and Europeans that they began to imitate, emulate and to co-opt African American music,

dance and rhetoric unabashedly. Still, Black cultural creativity is categorized as *fine art* only to the extent that it conforms to European classical culture and standards. White Western culture and arts are paraded universally as the model and experience to be pursued by all other peoples and cultures. White scholars have historically attempted to define, validate or invalidate the aesthetic achievements of the non-white world.

The essence of the Black aesthetic is that the arts and writings of African Americans be judged and based upon their own social, political and economic history. Black arts and literary works are truly authentic when they reflect the condition and experience of African Americans in relation to the broader society and the world. To preserve Black aesthetic authenticity, the concept of beauty, values and standards of white European culture cannot be superimposed upon the culture and worldviews of Black people.

From an Afrocentric perspective, beauty can be seen in the perseverance and triumphs of an oppressed people. Beauty is not limited to how an object, an individual or a group appears, but what it, he/she or they contribute to the survival, function, and betterment of the race and of mankind. African Americans can least afford to perceive art and beauty only in terms of looks or its uselessness, antiquity and sensual appeal. Blacks or Africans who have been viewed and portrayed as a primitive, savage and ugly people, have enlightened the world with the beauty of their soul and spirit. Their aesthetic creativity is reflected in their struggles, song, music, dance, drama and literature.

The 1960s marked a rebirth or renaissance period of Black arts and literature that had begun during the 1920s. The Black community abounded with a myriad of creative politically and socially oriented music, song, African dance, theater, poetry and literary productions. White critics were quick to assess these works as protest, political and propagandistic having little if any aesthetic or artistic merit. What Whites did not understand was that Black artists and their works were consistent with the functional nature of Black aesthetics. The renaissance of Black arts and writings during the 1960s served as the driving force that led to the development of African American studies nationwide, and it continues to fuel the political fires of Black liberation on into the 21st century.

The Black aesthetic is derived from the unique culture of African Americans. The culture of African Americans reflect the cumulative historical, social, political and economic forces that have shaped or molded it over a given period of time. Authentic Black creativity, then, is developed out of the cultural context of the universal Black experience. Cultural creativity begins first with own-group interests. For example, an out-group who appreciates the visual or performing arts of Blacks should also appreciate the cultural context from which they are derived. Any criticism must take into consideration the culture and standards of value of African American and African peoples. While cross-cultural comparison of Black arts is perhaps inevitable, critical analysis from others that is purely ethnocentrically motivated must be accepted with reservations or rendered invalid.

The Black aesthetic has influenced the cultural and social complex of American society. The music, song, dance and rhetoric of African Americans are appreciated and imitated all over the world. The Black aesthetic is inherent in all aspects of Black life. The aesthetic qualities of Black protest chants and tactics have been widely copied. The Black aesthetic includes the silent and dignified rebellion of Rosa Parks, the aesthetical and moving oratory of Martin Luther King, Jr., and Jesse Jackson. Some of the greatest literary achievements, works of art, drama, music and song were developed during and following the Civil Rights Movement of the 1960s.

There has always been something aesthetical about right and justice.

However, these aesthetic and artistic qualities have not served to successfully alter the racism, social injustice and economic inequality suffered by African Americans. White America has assimilated much of African American music, dance, art forms and rhetoric while subordinating African people as a race. Manning Marable sums up race relationships in America when he states that

> . . . whites' affinity and tolerance for blackness are largely cultural, not racial. Many whites have learned to appreciate African-derived elements of music, dance, and religious rituals, but would not endorse the sharing of power or material privileges, which would undermine the stratification of race.[4]

***The Harlem Renaissance.*** Although Blacks had established their artistic and literary capabilities long before the Reconstruction era, the Harlem Renaissance is generally cited as the flowering period of Blacks in the arts and humanities. The Harlem Renaissance or "New Negro Movement" as it was sometimes called, began after World War I and continued throughout the 1920s until the Depression of 1929. During this period, African Americans made phenomenal advances in visual and performing arts (music, dance, theater, art) but the most significant gains were made in the literary field. Prior to the 1920s, much of Black arts and writings were compromising and imitative of Whites, excluding the earlier protest or moralizing writers. The Harlem Renaissance was the period when Blacks broke away from tradition and developed a revitalized sense of racial pride and self-expression.

The Harlem community of New York City may have been the hub of African American artistic and literary activity, but its effects and the participant-contributors ranged nationwide. The development and flourishing of

Black cultural activity during the 1920s may be attributed to several complementary factors. Without attempting to rank them according to weight or significance they were: 1) the mass migration, urbanization and industrialization of Blacks following the war; 2) the considerable increase in the number of Black graduates from Black colleges in the South and North; 3) the influence of Marcus Garvey toward the development of Black racial pride and awareness and; 4) the attraction of White tourists, patrons, scholar-writers, and publishers to the activities of Harlem.[5]

The most renown Black writers and poets of the Harlem Renaissance period were James Weldon Johnson, Claude McKay, and Countee Cullen. African American artists, theater groups, and writers came together during the 1920s and produced imaginative Black theater and musical productions. Some of the most notable theater personalities, dancers, musicians and performers included Paul Robeson, Josephine Baker, Florence Mills, Eubie Blake and Noble Sissle. This was a welcomed departure from the Blackface and Minstrelsy shows which served only the comic and stereotypical interests of Whites prior to the Twenties. The Harlem Renaissance period launched the vanguard of nationally renown Black singers, musicians; and jazz—the music created by Blacks. Blues singer, Bessie Smith; jazz bandleaders, Jelly Roll Morton, King Oliver, Duke Ellington, and Louis Armstrong are only a few famous artists who began their careers during the New Negro Movement. The African idiom in painting and sculpture began during the 1920s when foundations and galleries were established for the development of Black artists and for the exhibition of their works.[6]

The crux of Black cultural activity that occurred during the Harlem Renaissance subsided somewhat during the Depression and race-riot torn years of the 1930s and 1940s. However, during the World War II period be-

tween 1940 and 1945, Black political activity increased concomitantly with the cultural development that continued from the Harlem Renaissance. During the early forties, Black political leaders A. Philip Randolph, Walter White, Adam Clayton Powell and their respective organizations were petitioning the Roosevelt Administration for civil rights and social justice. At the same time noted Black musicians Dizzy Gillespie, Charlie Parker, and Theolonious Monk were making their debut. In art, Charles White, Elizabeth Catlett, and Romare Bearden were outstanding during this period. On stage Katherine Dunham, Pearl Primus, and Eartha Kitt received rave reviews. Richard Wright and Langston Hughes produced major works during this period. Harlem remained a major center of Black cultural and political activity.[7]

Political struggle and freedom incite cultural creativity in the arts and humanities. A review of African American history will reveal that the artistic and literary production of Blacks have increased during and following major political triumphs gained through civil rights struggles. Based on this theory, many writers compare the Civil Rights Movement and its aftermath of the 1960s and 1970s with the Harlem Renaissance period. Some humanist scholars refer to the decades of the sixties and seventies as the New Black Arts Movement.

The Harlem Renaissance of the 1920s and the New Black Arts Movement of the 1960s and 1970s differed significantly with the exception that both eras resulted in a tremendous increase in Black creative and literary productivity. The motivating force of the Harlem Renaissance was one of Black self-discovery and race vindication. In short, it could be referred to as a vindicationist movement. By vindication, it is meant that African Americans wanted to prove that they were equally talented as whites. They wanted to correct the traditional stereotypes that Whites had imposed upon them. With their new-founded race pride, Blacks discovered that they possessed artistic talents and literary skills that even Whites took heed of and admired. The prevailing social philosophy and objective of many of the Black artists and writers were the integrationist-assimilationist ideal. The Black idiom and political activism was implicitly but not blatantly stated in the works of the Renaissance artists and writers. With the exception of Marcus Garvey's adherents, the Harlem Renaissance involved what might be called the Black bourgeoisie segment. It did not engage the masses as participants, but only as patrons and observers.[8] Social injustices were not abated during the 1920s.

The New Black Arts Movement developed out of political struggle for social justice, economic equity, and educational opportunity. It was a non-violent (sometimes violent) confrontation between Blacks and Whites. The Black arts and literary works were inspired by and, for the most part, were the products of the movement. All social stratifications of the Black community, including students, were constructively engaged one way or the other in the liberation struggle. The movement was divided into two ideological factions. One faction sought integration and cultural fusion and the other introduced separatism or Black nationalism and cultural distinctiveness as solutions to the country's race problem. The New Black Arts Movement revived interest in the mother country, Africa. It was the aim of the African American intellectual to improve the plight of the masses. The New Black Arts Movement served as the foundation for Black Studies programs and departments. It was the beginning of the era when African American intellectuals would assume the authority for the interpretation of the Black cultural and historical experiences. In conjunction with the Civil Rights Movement, not only did the cultural and educational plight of Blacks improve, but the entire social and economic

structure was effected. The masses benefitted significantly from the New Black Arts Movement.

One might recall that Garveyism represented a microcosm of the separatist-nationalist and "back-to-Africa" sentiment during the Harlem Renaissance. Carter G. Woodson introduced [Black] History Week in 1926. Furthermore, the artistic legacy and, the books and writings of the Harlem Renaissance were the initial and sometimes only Black authored sources of reference toward the development of African American studies programs established in colleges and universities beginning in 1968. In assessing and comparing the Harlem Renaissance with the New Black Arts Movement four decades later, one might conclude that both movements reinforced and complemented each other. If the Harlem Renaissance had not occurred and proven culturally and artistically fruitful, the New Black Arts Movement would have been without foundation or focus. Consequently, it would have inevitably faltered and failed.

# AFRICAN AMERICAN MUSIC

*A Prologue to Black Music.* African American music is one of the cultural arts that is the most indigenous to American society. Black people have been the primary source of a folk and popular music that is native American. One that is not a derivative of European forms and types of music. Black music is so rhythmically and harmonically distinctive that it has been difficult for others to culturally comprehend, perform and imitate.[9] The types of music and song that Blacks have contributed to American musical culture are spirituals, gospel, blues, jazz and, more recently, rap.

The foundation and rhythmic forms of Black music is basically African. One of the major scholarly studies validating the fact that African musical characteristics were retained and practiced by Blacks, in spite of slavery and the ante bellum period, is Melville Herskovits' book, *The Myth of the Negro Past*.[10] Since this classic work was published in 1941, numerous scholars have substantiated that Black Americans have retained the cultural, tonal, rhythmic and technical musical traditions of Africa in their music. Not only in the United States, Africa has influenced the music, song and dance of Latin America, South America, the Caribbeans, and all other regions where Africans were transported during the Atlantic Slave Trade.

Initial studies of African retentions in Black American music were related to religious songs and music—spirituals and gospel. However, technical analyses have revealed that African patterns of melody, harmony and rhythm are also found in blues, Jazz and other forms of African American music. For example, melodically, Lazarus Ekwueme points out that the roots of the "blue notes" in Black American blues songs, spirituals, work chants and folk songs lie in African music. The blue note is the presence of the flattened third and seventh degrees in the major scale.[11] Rhythm patterns common in Africa are prevalent in the music of African Americans. Ekwueme states that it is not uncommon to find that Black American musical patterns

> use quarter notes in combination with dotted quarters, resulting in a proportional time value of two against three. The employment of two versus three, in combination and sometimes "in contradiction," is a basic character of African musical rhythm. The presence of mixed rhythmic units of duple and triple time and combinations of these in a counterpoint of rhythms contribute to that lilting, propelling force in the black man's music characterized as syncopation.[12]

Various writers have noted that the "call and response" and the "call and refrain" characteristics and forms of Black music have been derived exclusively from African musical traditions.

African American music, undoubtedly, contains some elements of European cultural, musical, and performance practices. However, Black American music has been able to maintain its own distinctiveness and identifiable African characteristics of melody, harmony and rhythm. Moreover, in a popular and quantitative sense, Black music has influenced and caused the modification of Euro-American concepts of melody, rhythm, harmony and instrumental deployment. In any of its forms, Black music can be emotional and intense, melancholy and blue, meditative and tender, or dynamic and explosive. It is an artful and abstract testimony of the slavery, suffering, oppression, resilience and freedom experiences of African Americans. For African Americans and Africans, music is more than entertainment. It is functional and therapeutic to their religious, social and political existence.

*The Spiritual and Gospel Music.* The African American spirituals may be categorized as folk music in the sense that they have been handed down and often revised from generation to generation. The original authors or composers are generally unknown or have been forgotten. Spirituals in their purest form evolved out of the slave experience of the African American. Alain Locke wrote that the spirituals are Blacks' "great folk-gift, and rank among the classic folk expressions in the whole world because of their moving simplicity, their characteristic originality, and their universal appeal."[13] W.E.B. DuBois was even more profound and poetic in his acclaim of the African American spiritual. DuBois stated in essence that the Black folk-song (spiritual) is the rhythmic cry of the slave. And that it stands not only as music indigenous of

America, but as the most beautiful expression of human experience originated on this side of the seas—and remains as the singular spiritual heritage of the nation and the greatest gift of Black people.[14] The acclaim of spirituals is well deserved. They have are appreciated by all races and have been performed in most nations of the world.

According to Eileen Southern, a renown Black musicologist, the specific time of origin of the spiritual is unknown. It is known that spirituals were sung by Blacks many years before the first collection of slave songs was formally published in 1867. Spirituals began their rise into national and international prominence in 1871 when a student concert troupe was formed at Fisk University under the leadership of George L. White. The idea for the student concert group was motivated by the dire need for funds for the operation of Fisk University, an institution that was organized primarily for Blacks after the Civil War. The concert troupe eventually became known as the Fisk Jubilee Singers. They were catapulted into national and international fame when they were invited by Henry Ward Beecher to perform in Brooklyn and, subsequently, in Boston on the occasion of the World Peace Jubilee in 1872. Praise of the group's performance was so astounding that they went on to perform before crowned heads of state in Europe, Germany, Switzerland, and Great Britain. In a few years, they had raised over $150,000 that was used to erect a new building on the Fisk University campus called, Jubilee Hall.[15]

The success of the Fisk Jubilee Singers encouraged the formation of similar spiritual choirs at Black institutions in Hampton, Virginia; Tuskegee, Alabama; and Atlanta, Georgia. But as music historians point out, the character of the genuine folk-spirituals had been transformed from the plantation and Black church to concert stages. Although spirituals have undergone an adaption and a change of original venue, they still represent a valuable contribution to American culture.

Evidence suggests that prior to 1871, the development of the spiritual took place in the independent Black churches of the North during the 1770s and 1780s. Although, indeed, spirituals of some nature were also sung in the South. When Richard Allen and fellow worshippers walked out of the white Methodist church in Philadelphia and eventually organized the African Methodist Episcopal Church, Allen compiled a hymnal for the use of his congregations. The hymnal contained songs already in circulation, folk songs, and many original and unorthodox songs. A distinction was made between hymns and spirituals which may have been the earliest record of a formal collection of spirituals. The verses of these spirituals were undoubtedly transferred and improvised by ministers and church members as they were called or visited from one congregation to the other throughout the country.[16]

The notion that Black spirituals are sorrowful songs is a one-dimensional perspective. An analysis of the verses and words will reveal the psychological and therapeutic value of these songs to an enslaved and oppressed people. Religious in nature, they generally expressed hope for divine deliverance from bondage, burdensome toil and suffering. Most of the song reflected the yearnings of Blacks to escape to a refuge called heaven. For example a song that was commonly sung was as follows:

### STEAL AWAY

Steal away, steal away,
Steal away to Jesus;
Steal away, steal away home,
I aint' got long to stay here.

This song has dual connotations. It expresses a desire for spiritual relief from suffering. On the other hand it is recorded that the song served as a coded message to signify an actual escape plan, secret meeting or slave uprising. Another song having similar implications was:

## DEEP RIVER

Deep river, my home is over Jordan
Deep river, Lord,
I want to cross over into campground,
Lord, I want to cross over into
   campground
Lord, I want to cross over into
   campground[17]

Various interpretations have been given to these early Negro spirituals. One cannot say whether spirituals were sung for their opiate affect or whether they were to be taken literally. From a contemporary Black perspective, spirituals have essentially the same meaning and significance as they did during the ante bellum period whether they are presented in concert arrangements or in folk performances.

African American gospel song and music, in contradistinction to any other gospel forms, evolved out of the Black church. Its development did not begin in the traditional or conventional denominations of the church such as the Baptist, Methodist, Presbyterian and Catholic, but in the more fundamentalist Pentecostal or "sanctified" churches. In fact, the footstamping, handclapping, and rhythmic body movements associated with the performance of gospel music was deemed as being somewhat sacrilegious in traditional worship services. However, in essence, Black gospel music is a derivation of and transition from spiritual songs. The primary difference between spiritual and gospel performances is the obligatory accompaniment of the piano and electric organ. Tambourines, drums, guitar, and brass musical instruments are also commonly used in the accompaniment of gospel songs. The performance of spirituals is mostly *a cappella* solemn and intense, but also

moving and emotional. Gospel music has a beat similar to that of Black secular music with its riffs, ostinatos, call and response, obligatos, voice exclamations, and rocking in time.[18]

Black gospel music gained in general popularity from 1945 to 1955. Its growing popularity led to the formation of gospel choirs that toured and performed, mainly for Black church goers, in rented halls and auditoriums throughout the country. Gospel music was no longer limited to the small sanctified or storefront churches but began to gain national appeal. By the late 1960s and early 1970s, gospel music became widely accepted and performed in the Baptist, Methodist and other traditional congregations. Through recordings, radio and televisions programs, it was received into the homes of listeners and viewers nationally and internationally. The noted gospel singer, Mahalia Jackson, performed at one of the inaugural parties for President John F. Kennedy. Eventually, gospel was being performed at Carnegie Hall.[19]

Initially, gospel music created much controversy and division because some perceived its beat and style to be inappropriate or sacrilegious relative to religious worship service. Earlier gospel stars, and some present gospel artists and groups, perform at night clubs and in various other secular settings. Sister Rosetta Tharpe, one of the first national gospel singers, started in the church and then moved to the night club circuit. In 1957 another gospel artist and group, Clara Ward and the Ward Singers, performed at the Newport Jazz Festival. Other noted gospel artists such as James Cleveland, Andrae Crouch, and Shirley Caesar—at one time—refused to perform outside of the church or a religious milieu. Since Black gospel music is appreciated at the Newport Jazz Festival and at Carnegie Hall, some questions may remain relative to its characterization as sacred or secular music.[20] However, in the 1990s, the indications are that gospel music is overwhelmingly a stable and continually growing tradition of the Black church.

Gospel singing has been adopted and is appreciated among most African American church groups because it is more culturally related to the African custom of performer-audience participation. During gospel performance, the congregation respond by singing along, clapping their hands and tapping their feet in harmony and rhythm with the singer or choir. Thomas A. Dorsey, gospel writer and the Father of Gospel Music, was of the opinion that traditional hymns and church music failed to enliven or to instill the spirit of rejoicing among church members. In commenting on the pre-gospel era Dorsey stated that: "The people were singing so dead, so disinterested in the church. The church needed something to fire them up."[21] African traits of harmony, rhythm, beat and style of performance are unmistakably evident in the music of African Americans. Thus, spirituals, gospel, blues, jazz and rap music are Afrocentrically cultural and ethnic related.

***The Blues and African Americans.*** M u s i c historians are not sure of the specific origin of blues music and song in America. It is known and acknowledged that the blues evolved and developed out of the oppressed and hopeless experience and condition of Southern Blacks during or after the Civil War. The antecedents of the blues were the melancholic and sorrowful work chants and field hollers of the Black slave, prisoner, railhand, and sharecropper. The rhythm, beat and melody structures of the blues are clearly consistent with the musical cultures of West Africa with residual strains evident of Central, Southern and Eastern Africa.[22] In the South during the early 1900s, it was commonplace to find in most towns a Black blues player picking a guitar on a street corner or itinerate blues troubadours performing their sorrowful songs at honky-tonks and parties in the Black community.

The blues prior to the 1920s might be categorized as the down-home country blues.

W. C. Handy is generally regarded as the Father of the Blues because, according to some music scholars, he was the first person to *write* or orchestrate the blues. Two of his most popular blues compositions were *Memphis Blues* (1912), and *St. Louis Blues* (1914). However, big band orchestrated blues may be viewed as the musical bridge to jazz. This style of blues is to be distinguished, partly, in style and adherents from the folk blues songs and music that may have developed among Blacks earlier in the South. W.C. Handy and Gertrude "Ma" Rainey, the earliest known *professional* blues singer, are credited for having popularized the blues through the commercial record business. This style of blues, performed in European orchestral form, appealed to urban Blacks and to some Whites alike.

The tonal quality and structure of the blues are related to spiritual and gospel music. However, the blues is generally secular or worldly in content and motive. Early blues artists and enthusiasts were leery and dubious of a religion or a god that would relegate Black people to such an oppressed social and economic position. Blues music and song are based on the immediate and material reality of Black life. They reflect the hurt and pain of lost jobs, lost loves, sexual desires, infidelity, hardship, white racism, despair and anguish. Yet, some blues have a degree of spiritual flavor because of some performers exclamatory injection of phrases like, "Oh Lordy" or "God have mercy."

The blues is basically a folk music having verses and stanza that have been passed along and sometimes modified from one blues singer to another. The songs have rhyming lines and, closely, parallel the poetic form. The traditional or more frequently performed blues is a twelve-bar, three-line stanza song. The first line is repeated twice and the third is a response to the previous lines. The singer "calls-and-responds" to his/her self in a falsetto, slurring, shouting, whining, moaning style. Variations in blues form may include a reduction to eight measures or an expansion to sixteen measures. The verses may vary from two to six lines with complex repetitions of lines or phrases.[23]

The early classical "down-home" blues artists included Huddie (Leadbelly) Ledbetter and Blind Lemon Jefferson. Blind Lemon's songs were almost always autobiographical. The following are typical three-line stanza songs of Blind Lemon Jefferson:

### (hardship)

I stood on the corner and almost bust my
    head
I stood on the corner and almost bust my
    head
I couldn't earn enough to buy me a loaf
    of bread.

### (sexual imagery)

Mmmmm-mm, black snake crawling in
    my room
Mmmmm-mm, black snake crawling in
    my room
And some pretty mama better get this
    black snake soon.[24]

A popular blues stanza rendered by contemporary blues artists Bobby Blue Bland is similar to this:

### (loneliness or forlornness)

I'm driftin' and driftin' like a ship out on
    the sea
I'm driftin' and driftin' like a ship out on
    the sea
And I ain't got nobody, in this whole
    world to care for me.

The uniqueness of the blues melody is its altered harmonic scale or "blue notes" that reflects the Africanisms mentioned in the dis-

cussion of the gospel. Musicologist Eddie S. Meadows explains technically that

> In the Blues scale the concept of the neutral third is the result of the Black American's attempt to retain his African musical identity. The diatonic scale contains major and minor thirds and major and minor sevenths. Both are virtually unknown in most African cultures. Since these tones were not present in most African scales, Blacks of the antebellum period had to choose between the major and minor thirds and sevenths of the diatonic scale when making music. The compromise was to use neither the major nor minor third, but, rather, to use thirds and sevenths that wavered between the two and were therefore "neutral." Each of the tones lies at a midpoint between the major and minor intervals. Although this scale is known as the Blues scale, it permeates all Black American music: Blues, Gospels, Jazz, Spirituals, and Soul music. It can be achieved through vocal inflection, through instrumental inflections, and by striking the flatted and natural thirds and sevenths simultaneously. Blues guitarists used the bottleneck technique to achieve this same effect.[25]

In spite of the cultural dilution and commercialization of the blues, the African influence still remains.

The Southern Delta country provided the earliest and the greatest growth and development of the classical down-home blues. In the 1940s and 1950s the blues "migrated" to big cities where distinctive styles promoted by various artists developed. From the Delta basic blues form, a Memphis style emerged whose major proponents included B.B. King, Bobby Bland, Albert King, Junior Parker, and Little Milton. The blues that was played on the traditional acoustic guitar was replaced with the innovative "one-string" electric guitar techniques of B.B. King, T-Bone Walker, Albert King, and Freddie King. The blues and many of the Memphis artists moved to Chicago where a Delta based, Chicago style evolved. Famous Chicago bluesmen included Muddy Waters, Elmore James, and Howling Wolf. Many of these artists such as Sonny Boy Williamson, Willie Nix, Walter Horton, and John Lee Hooker recorded with white recording companies in Jackson, Mississippi and Memphis before moving North. Blues singer-guitarists Muddy Waters, Howling Wolf, John Lee Hooker and Lightnin' Hopkins are among those categorized as "low-down dirty" blues artists.[26] Robert Cray, Albert Collins, and Johnny Copeland are among the relatively few young Black artists carrying on the Memphis/Chicago blues traditions.

Only a fractional number of the names of renown Black blues artists are mentioned in this discussion. A complete history of the blues in America requires a full-length book. It is unfortunate that at one period of time the interest of African Americans in their blues heritage waned. However, British and other European nationalities have always loved and treasured Black blues music. When European and white American rock artists began to imitate Black blues singers and to use blues music to propel them into worldwide stardom, African American interest in the blues was revived.

*Jazz: The Musical Creation of African Americans.* More books and literature exist on jazz than perhaps on any other African American art form. However, the treatment of jazz here will be limited to a brief discussion of its origin, nature, and development, and of some its early and contemporary contributors. The most phenomenal aspect of jazz music is that it evolved from the social culture of Blacks, descendants of slaves of the American South. Because jazz grew fast in popularity, and was appreciated and imitated by white American and European musicians from its inception, some critics are reluctant to classify it as Black music. Nonetheless, most scholars and music historians acknowledge the African roots and origin of jazz.

Non-blacks have contributed toward jazz development but the basic "rhythmic language" of the music is derived from the musical culture of African Americans. Jazz is an instrumentation extension of the spiritual, gospel, and blues.

The rhythmic complexity, the execution and maintenance of two or more rhythms simultaneously, the inflections, and the syncopation of jazz are indisputably African in nature. Their is no precedent of these musical characteristics in the European art of music.[27] Much of the African characteristics of jazz are reported to have been derived from the Congo and Angola regions of Africa. New Orleans, the birthplace of jazz, had a large population of Blacks from these African regions resulting from the Atlantic Slave Trade.[28] On holidays and allowed recreational occasions, slaves would assemble in New Orleans at a place known as Congo Square. In Congo Square, they would perform their native African festive music and dances. The slaves dressed in their finest. The women, men and children danced and shouted to the rhythms of the bamboula and tom-tom drums. They used anklet bells and other crude, but ingeniously devised, castanet and marimba type instruments.[29]

By the late nineteenth and early twentieth century, a distinct Black music began to develop in Storyville, a renowned red-light district of New Orleans. The music eventually became known as jazz, although the origin of the term "jazz" is unknown. African American bands performed in the cabarets of the Storyville section of French Quarter, in street parades, and in funeral processions. Daphne Harrison describes the evolution of jazz as a music that "rose from the brothels, the party houses, the river saloons, and whisky joints, from the funeral processions, the blue hollers and the street cries of Southern Blacks, and merged imperceptibly with the European quadrilles, waltzes, folk tunes, and hymns of whites."[30] White orchestras under the influence of Black musicians developed a type of Dixieland jazz which became publicly popular outside of the New Orleans area. This "jazz" was perceptively different from the authentic timbre of African American jazz.

The closing of Storyville and the beginning of the Black migration to Northern cities around 1917, caused Black musicians to disperse from New Orleans and to introduce jazz music in the urban areas of the North and Midwest. Black combos continued to play the blues-rag-jazz type of music that they had been accustomed of playing. Joe "King" Oliver and Louis Armstrong were the initial and principal purveyors of Black New Orleans style of jazz in the big cities of Chicago, New York and Los Angeles.

It must be pointed out that preceding and contributing toward the development of jazz was a distinctively Black created tempo of music called ragtime. As the restrictive and inhibiting forces of slavery diminished, Blacks began to develop music and entertainment suited for their own tastes and pleasure. They were fascinated with the piano, and in the process of mastering this instrument the Black musicians created a kind of piano-rag music adaptive to the dance of Black folk. The unique syncopated music of ragtime was a natural and perfect accompaniment to the Black folk dance called the "cakewalk."[31]

White America became aware of the music while it was being played in Black minstrel shows and musical comedies during the late 1890s. They adopted and contributed to the style of ragtime. Ragtime reigned in popularity in America and Europe until about 1917. Ragtime, essentially, became a synthesis of African American and European musical traditions. Scott Joplin (1868-1917), a Black musician and composer, is generally acknowledged as a major figure in the development and popularization of ragtime. He was famous for having published several ragtime masterpieces, one of the most notable was *Maple Leaf Rag.*

Ragtime players also performed for meager wages in saloons and in honky-tonk cafes along the Mississippi River and the eastern seaboard. A ragtime piano player could substitute for an orchestra. He could maintain a steady bass beat with his left hand while the right hand played the syncopated melody and rhythms. However, ragtime's "limited rhythmic language, and narrow emotional range" contributed to its demise. The improvisation of popular songs allowed upcoming jazz artists and bands to break away from the rhythmic and emotional restraints of ragtime. However, few will deny that ragtime was a prime musical forerunner of jazz. Later, the jazz artists of the 1920s and 1930s such as "Jelly Roll" Morton, Louis Armstrong, and Earl Hines would blend ragtime with the blues, folk and popular tunes. They also injected jazz rhythms into ragtime. Thus, to a great extent, jazz was derived or evolved from ragtime.[32]

Jazz followed almost the same route northward as its precursor the blues—from New Orleans to Memphis, Kansas City and St. Louis to Chicago. But jazz took on a new flavor in New York and spread with alacrity to Paris and London. By 1926, the music had acquired profound critics and devotees. Despite the racial origin of jazz and the racist and oppressive era in which it developed, white orchestra leaders were attracted to African American music and its musicians. Jazz sparked unprecedented interracial collaboration. It is generally known among jazz enthusiasts that famous white musicians like Glenn Miller, Tommy Dorsey, Harry James, Bennie Goodman and Jack Teagarden would avail themselves of every opportunity to visit the night clubs in Chicago and New York's Harlem to learn from and to consort with Black jazz artists. Eventually, white musicians would capitalize on jazz and receive greater economic rewards and social accolades than the Black originators of the music. Yet, white

Photo 21   Louis 'Satchmo' Armstrong. Courtesy of National Archives.

musicians played a major role in establishing jazz as a universal musical art form. White cornetist Bix Beiderbecke influenced the melodic tempo of the jazz ballad.

In the mid and late thirties, philosopher and writer Alain Locke had perceived the formation of three different jazz schools or styles. The jumping, jamming and swing style that emanated out of Chicago was termed "hot jazz." The jazz that became popular in New York, and subsequently Paris and London, stressed melody and flowing harmony. It was classified as "sweet jazz," and the more sophisticated or refined hybrid style was viewed as "classical jazz."[33] Although most Black jazzmen could be experimentally competent in all styles, Louis Armstrong, Earl Hines and Coleman Hawkins were included at that time as the principal purveyors of "hot jazz." Fletcher Henderson, Duke Ellington, Lester Young, Art Tatum, Erroll Garner, Count Basie, Lionel Hampton, and a host of other Black and White bandleaders and jazz artists ushered in the era of "sweet," sophisticated, swing, and classical jazz.

By the mid 1940s, the enthusiasm for big band swing, classic and classical jazz had climaxed. New and younger Black jazz musicians who had been mentored by the earlier jazz greats were coming on the scene. During World War II and the early 1950s not only was there rebellion against political conservatism taking place, but there was also a movement to reject conservatism and classicism in the arts and humanities. The rebellion occurred in Europe and in America. The period was referred to as the avant garde age. In music, "Be Bop" represented the avant garde approach to jazz conservatism. Charlie Parker (alto sax), Dizzy Gillespie (trumpet), Thelonious Monk (piano), Kenny Clarke (drums), Max Roach (drums), and Bud Powell (piano) were the founders of Be Bop or modern jazz movement. The new jazz was initially repudiated by many conventional jazz enthusiasts. But in a way, Be Bop was a rebellion by Black jazz artists against the White dominated music industry and racism. Be Bop was a declaration of Black musical independence.

Following the brief span of the Be Bop era, proponents of a "cool" modern jazz emerged. Many music writers label this music as west coast jazz, hard bop, or the second stage of the traditional Be Bop. The Black artists and

groups in this category included Miles Davis' quintet, Clifford Brown-Max Roach quintet, Modern Jazz Quartet, John Coltrane, Horace Silver, Charlie Mingus, Sonny Rollins, Ornette Coleman, Sonny Stitt, Eric Dolphy, Hubert Laws, and John Lewis.[34]

Jazz is antithetical to the European classical art and musical tradition. The essence of jazz is improvisation. Technical and innovative creativity in the execution of a piece, song or ballad is expected of each individual performer. Any attempt to match or duplicate the feelings of a previous artist is deemed as being unimaginative. Jazz is a living and functional art reflective of the artist's depth of emotion and feeling at a given moment or time of performance. An authentic Black jazz artist never plays the same piece of music the same way twice. Jazz does not require the player to adhere strictly to the "fossilized" rhythm, pitch, timbre or feelings and emotions of dead composers or artists as in European classical music. This freedom inherent in the expressiveness of African spirituality is perhaps why white Americans and Europeans find African American music appealing.

Black music that is not subject to European musical conventions is still denied classification as a "fine art" including jazz. It is often assumed that early jazz musicians never studied music and that Blacks only excel technically in rhythm. The truth is that most all of the Black early musicians studied music through an apprentice system, although most did not receive music degrees. Furthermore, Black musicians have also been the most innovative harmonic and melodic players in jazz.[35]

The unfortunate aspect of jazz history is that African Americans have never reaped significant economic rewards from their musical creativity. White musicians, critics, and researchers have capitalized on jazz and other Black music both economically and artistically. The leading night clubs and music halls seldom seek African American jazz artists to perform since White musicians now successfully imitate the Black jazz culture. While jazz is taught at major colleges and universities, there are few if any Blacks employed as faculty in the music departments. The fact of the matter is that while many elements of Black music and culture is accepted by white Americans, Black artists and people are not.

The commercialization and commercial specifications that influence Black jazz artists since the 1960s have resulted in the dilution of the originality and authenticity of jazz. In order to make a living, many contemporary Black jazz artists have found it necessary to cross-over or to fuse their jazz orientation and talents into the rock music culture. Unless special efforts are made on the part of African Americans to encourage young Blacks to appreciate their jazz heritage and to choose jazz careers, jazz as a Black musical art form will no longer exist.

***Rhythm and Blues—Soul Music.*** Each category and type of African American music have reflected the social, political and economic conditions of Black people during various periods of American history. While the categorization of African American music is useful for analytical or academic purposes, the music itself is a continuum of the cultural and spiritual forces from which it was derived. The rhythmic, harmonic and melodic nature of authentic Black music is African. Its emotional dynamism and spiritual excitement is founded upon the religious beliefs and practices of Black people in America.

The Black music that became known as rhythm and blues in the 1950s germinated and developed from the sound, feelings and religious aura of the Black church. Figuratively and literally, the Black church spawned the talent that created rhythm and blues in the same way it did for spirituals, gospel, blues and jazz. Many of the rhythm and blues artists formerly sang in church choirs and choral groups. In addition, rhythm and blues

music was shaped and influenced by the same social, political and economic factors of Black discontent that gave rise to the Civil Rights Movement of the 1950s and 1960s. The Black church was the spiritual force and political garrison that sustained the Civil Rights Movement. Thus, the music, lyrics and timbre of rhythm and blues reflect, substantially, the religious influence, and the social, political and economic experiences of African Americans from the 1950s through the 1970s.

It is not surprising that rhythm and blues, like the spirituals, gospel and blues had its primary development in the South with a preponderance of its artists Southern born and bred. In spite of Northern migration, the South still maintained the largest Black population. Following World War II, there existed the prospect of racial advancement. Millions of Black youth yearned for a musical medium that would be spiritually uplifting; one that they could relate to and describe their love relationships in a hopeful and inspiring manner. The traditional country and urban blues were basically melancholy and appealed mostly to the older generations. Jazz was limited in its ability to provide lyrical expression and dance rhythm that appealed to teenagers and young adults.

A more lively, upbeat and rhythmic type of music developed among young Blacks in major cities of the South and in the Northern ghettos. White record companies found it profitable to market Black music in the Black community. Prior to 1949, the term *race* was used by record companies to identify and describe Black records made by Black artists. The popular tradepaper *Billboard* substituted *rhythm and blues* (R & B) for the word *race* to designate the new Black music that began to develop by the 1950s.[36]

The phenomenon that occurred was that White youth were overwhelmingly attracted to the R & B music that was being played on spot radio programs targeted for the Black community. The records were not made available in stores assessable to Whites or in white neighborhoods. White retailers were faced with a growing demand from white youth to stock R & B records. Radio stations in major cities North and South filled the airwaves with R & B music with the primary intent of appealing to the African American market. Soon R & B became the dominant music of pop radio stations.[37]

One must be cognizant of the fact that prior to the mid 1950s and especially in the South, Whites did not generally approve of their children listening to Black music and emulating Black dance. Many Whites referred to African American popular music as "nigger music" and it was forbidden because of its "immoral" implications. Nevertheless, because of the popularity and profitability of R & B music, white artists recorded their versions of the music to cash in on and to cover the broadening market. These recordings were called "covers." The word cover was also used to describe the practice of placing a Black artist's photograph on the album cover of a White artist's recording of an R & B hit song.

The Black "sound," sexual implications and gyrations characteristic of the performance of R & B music prompted various white artists to enter the field in imitation of Blacks. White segregated audiences of the South would not think of having Black artists to perform R & B music, however, they enthusiastically accepted White imitations. Elvis Presley, who has been dubbed the King of Rock and Roll, was totally influenced by Black R & B artists. It must be emphasized that the term *rock and roll* was coined as a name for White artists' versions and performances of Black R & B music. While some white writers tend to fuse and attribute rock and roll to African Americans, the term did not originate in the Black community nor was it ever intended to refer to Black music. The hit song that propelled Elvis Presley into

fame, *Hound Dog* had been recorded three years earlier by a Black female blues singer, Big Mama Thornton.[38]

During the crux of the Civil Rights Movement, Rhythm and Blues music began to be alternatively referred to as Soul Music. At least two styles and two tempos of the music exist. One style where the lead singer is harmonically backed up by a group and they invoke the African call-and-response pattern is clearly derived from the Black gospel choir format. Another style involved group harmony where an American popular song or an original lyric is treated as a sentimental ballad. Each artist or group was capable of rendering an upbeat rhythmic-dance piece or the sentimental ballad.

The R & B groups were distinguished by their unique naturalistic names such as the Flamingoes, the Orioles, the Ravens, the Midnighters, the Drifters, and the Clovers. Male and female artists dominated the R & B or Soul field. An account of all the R & B artists from the 1950s to the 1970s would number well over a hundred. However, it is important to mention a few of the most popular artists of the period. Some of the early upbeat R & B artists included Chuck Berry, Little Richard, James Brown, and Bo Diddley. The lyrics and rhythm of these R & B stars influenced Elvis Presley and, also, such European rock groups as the Beatles and the Rolling Stones. Since R & B is an extension or modernization of the blues, bluesmen like B.B. King, Bobby Bland, Muddy Waters, Charles Brown and Amos Milburn were influential during the rise of R & B. Also in the R & B style and tradition, were individual male singers Sam Cooke, Lloyd Price, Solomon Burke, Jackie Wilson, Johnny Ace and Chuck Willis. Ruth Brown, Dinah Washington, LaVern Baker and Little Esther Phillips were among the early dynamic female R & B artists.[39]

Groups and individual singers of the 1960s and 1970s included Ike and Tina Turner, the

Impressions, the Isley Brothers, the Fifth Dimensions, Aretha Franklin, Otis Redding, Wilson Pickett, and numerous others. One of the greatest boosts to R & B music occurred when Black-owned record company, Motown, of Detroit began to discover and produce a seemingly unlimited number of R & B stars. Under the leadership of the founder, Berry Gordy, Motown produced nationally famous R & B groups and singers including Diana Ross and the Supremes, the Temptations, Smokey Robinson and the Miracles, the Marvelettes, the Jackson Five, the Four Tops, Gladys Knight and the Pips, Marvin Gaye, Martha Reeves and the Vandellas and many others.

The astounding development, growth and popularity of R & B or Soul music through the decades of the 1950s, 1960s and 1970s was, undoubtedly, the result of rising social, economic and political expectations from the Supreme Court's desegregation decision of 1954, and the subsequent Civil Rights Movement. The impact of these two phenomena also affected the family life and social relationships between Black males and females. James B. Stewart, posits that the positive expressions of Black social consciousness in Black Rhythm and Blues music of the 1960s performed a unique social function in the Black community. However, that aspect in respect of images of Black male-female relationships was lost in the R & B music of the 1970s. Stewart argues that the R & B music of the 1960s projected a highly romantic and Platonic view of male-female relationships. In contrast, much of the music of the 1970s was materialist and earthy in character. The 1970s music and song seemed to indicate more of a flippant resignation to romantic and marital breakup, and a proclivity towards sexual exploitation. The integrationist ideology that prevailed at the time led to an implicit acceptance by Blacks of general societal values.[40]

The character, pattern and style of any music changes over a period of time as artists seek to modify or expand their musical talent, and as other cultural group influences dilute or distort originality. Commercialization, profit motive, and the artificiality of electronic music have obscured the traditional R & B sound and style. In addition, the social, economic and political milieu that prevails today has changed from that of a few decades ago. The new Black musical idiom of the mid 1980s and 1990s that is reflective of the contemporary African American experience is rap music and song.

*Rap Music and the Hip-Hop Culture.* Rap music originated or evolved out of the street culture of African American and Puerto Rican youth during the mid 1970s within the New York vicinities of the South Bronx, Brooklyn, and Queens. Three radio disc jockeys (DJs), Kool Herc, Grandmaster Flash and Afrika Bambaatta, are credited with having popularized rap music. The first rap record, "Rapper's Delight," was released in 1979. "Rappers Delight" was a stunning commercial success and was marketed internationally. It listed among the top ten on the popular charts in the United States, and more than two million copies were sold.[41] Prior to this breakthrough, rap had been labeled by the entertainment media as too Black and rhetorically explicit.

Although rap has some Hispanic and White rock influences, it is overwhelmingly an African American art form. Rap was initiated by urban youth gangs who sought positive diversion from violence and drug abuse. It provided a means of relief from economic deprivation, unemployment and social despair. Blacks have always found that music, verbal dexterity, and dance are psychologically therapeutic in their struggle for survival against racism and oppression. Rap music is an art form of rhythm, rhetoric and rhymes consistent with the African musical and oral tradition. The most vivid description of Black verbal and musical dexterity may be learned from Alfred B. Pasteur and Ivory L. Toldson's explication of the Black vernacular:

> Black vernacular is both poetic and prosaic. . . . Whether written or oral, black vernacular has long been of interest to those captivated by beauty that arises from the artistic sequencing of words. Be it in the form of sermon, rap, dozens, signifying, folk tale, song (shouts, spirituals, gospels, field hollers, rhythm & blues, reggae, jazz), it emotionally stirs and seizes upon transmission. Black vernacular is explosive with emotional power.[42]

An entire culture has been created around rap music based upon the Black vernacular. The culture is commonly known as Hip-Hop.

Hip-hop music embodies a myriad of disconnected issues and phenomena from African symbolism, anarchy, Islamic fundamentalism, social protest, sexual imagery, break dancing, mural and graffiti art, Black history, pedagogy, violence, materialism, drug abstinence, egoism, to obscenity.[43] Hip-hop emerged as a rebellious art form to traditional music of the 1980s and 1990s as BeBop was to conventional jazz in the 1950s. Rap music was initially rejected and spurned by MTV and the music media. But today, its purveyors and fans includes people of all socio-economic classes, races and ethnic groups. Some of the contemporary rap groups are, Public Enemy, L.L. Cool J., The Two Live Crew, Heavy D and the Boyz, Dr. Jeckyill and Mr. Hyde, and a host of others including a growing number of female rappers.

The most intriguing and appealing aspect of rap music is inherent in the execution of its rhythm, rhetoric and rhyme. In addition to body dexterity and imagery, Houston A. Baker, Jr. describes rap music as "hybridity"

> Black sounds (African drums, bebop melodies, James Brown shouts, jazz improvs, Ellington riffs, blues innuendoes, doo-wop croons, reggae words, calypso rhythms). . . . But the most acrobatic of the techniques is the verb and reverb of the human voice pushed straight out, or emulated by synthesizers, or emulating drums and falsettos—the rhyming, chiming sound that is a mnemonic for black urbanity.[44]

Rap music has already outlasted the time span definition of a musical fad. Styles of rap will continue to develop as it widens in musical scope and popularity. Thus, in addition to spirituals, gospel, blues, jazz, and rhythm and blues; rap music represents one more musical art form that Blacks have contributed to American popular culture.

# AFRICAN AMERICAN VISUAL AND PERFORMING ARTS

**Black Art and the Evolution of the Black Artist.** In a general sense, art is the creation of things or imagery by humans that display or manifest form, beauty or perceptions that interest or attract. Usually, art is considered as the product of, by and for a particular culture or society, although it may be assessed—appreciated or depreciated—by other cultures. A society or culture determines the merits and functions of its own art. The universal appeal of an art object or concept may not be deliberate but simply incidental. The discussion here is related to African American creations in the visual arts—painting and sculpture. Each race, culture or ethnic group is endowed with its distinctive ability to paint, draw and sculpt.

Black art, in this context, may be defined as the African American creative influences and contributions in the fields of painting and sculpture in America. Black art is demonstrably racial in context and reflects the symbolism of Africa and the social experiences of Black people in the United States and the world. Black art as an aesthetic ideology began to develop in the twentieth century when African American artists gradually declined to succumb totally to European and white American concepts of art forms, beauty and social reality. Like Black music, Black art first developed to serve the interest of the Black public or community. Subsequently, its quality and appeal broadened and won the acclaim of other peoples. At least from an Afrocentric perspective, the works of African American painters or sculptors that do not reflect to some degree the Black art concept and idiom fall into the category of general art.

Black art portrays social, political and economic realities from a Black perspective. It offers an alternative to the stereotypes of African Americans created by Europeans and white Americans. Black art treats those aspects and paradigms of the Black past and present that have enabled African Americans to survive and to prevail against slavery, oppression and racism. Black art reflects the condition, hopes, despair, aspirations, triumphs, losses, imagination, joys, and sorrows of Black people. The Black artist seeks to define and redefine universal phenomena from an African oriented worldview. The elements of protest and politics can be manifested in Black art without neutralizing or nullifying its aesthetic quality and appeal.[45] While the Black artist has been unavoidably influenced by European and other cultures, threads of Afrocentrism differentiate Black art from general art.

The Black painter and sculpture have historically been confronted with the task of withstanding the belittlement and non-recognition of the white American art critic. Even within the inclusive rationale of cultural relativism, the works of African American artists are rarely accorded the status of *fine art*. Consequently, proponents of the Black Arts Movement refuse to appease white historians and critics who systematically ignore and omit the works and accomplishments of African American artists. As a result, a proliferation of African American art organizations, museums and galleries were established, especially, during and after the 1960s.

The inherent talent and skill of African American artists are attributable to their African heritage. As the case was outlined for Black music, the African slaves brought to the New World a variety of skills that might be classified as arts and crafts. West Coast and Equatorial Africa from which most African Americans descended were noted for the arts of wood and metal sculpture, metal forging, wood carving, ivory and bone carving, weaving, and pottery. In America, testimony of the artistic skills and abilities of the African slaves can be seen in the intricate ironwork designs of colonial mansions and, especially, in the forged balconies and grill work of many of the public and domestic buildings of New Orleans. Architecture and building were the outlets that provided much of the opportunity for the slaves to ply or demonstrate their craft and art abilities.[46]

When Blacks were introduced to the European tradition of easel painting on canvas and to sculpture mediums in the nineteenth century, their works were highly imitative of the art subjects, styles and techniques of Europe. Of the few Black artists that can be documented, Edward M. Bannister (1828–1901) was the first to achieve distinction as a painter. Edmonia Lewis (1845–1890), a woman, was the first Black sculptor of note. Henry O. Tanner, painter (1859–1937) and Meta Warrick Fuller, sculptor (1877–1968), departed from the European orientation and produced some works which related to their Black heritage and existence. The works depicting Black subjects by Tanner and Fuller may have been the first to inspire the Black art concept.

It was not until around 1928 when philanthropist William E. Harmon established a foundation to aid and develop African

American artists did Black art began to receive recognition. The Harmon Foundation, through its financial awards and exhibitions, influenced the development of art education programs at many African American colleges and universities. Initially, most African Americans strived to be recognized as "mainstream" artists rather than as "Negro" artists. However, there was an attitudinal change by 1931. At the Harmon Foundation sponsored exhibition of 1931, Black subjects and backgrounds predominated and according to Alain Locke, the quality, profundity and vitality of the work improved as these artists came to closer grips with familiar and well-understood subject matter.[47] The psychology of oppression and racism caused earlier Black artists to avoid producing works relevant to their own race and experience. More than a half-century ago Locke, the formally trained philosopher wrote that for the Black artist:

> A real and vital racialism in art is a sign of artistic objectivity and independence and gives evidence of a double emancipation from apologetic timidity and academic imitativeness.[48]

The adoption of a Black aesthetic ideology should not prevent an African American artist from expanding beyond this realm.

The New Deal programs of President Franklin D. Roosevelt during the Depression years was a windfall for the growth and development of Black and White actors, writers, and artists. As a measure to decrease the massive unemployment in large cities like New York and Chicago, the federal government became the patron of thousands of artists by paying them through the Works Progress Administration (WPA) to produce murals, easel paintings, etchings, sculpture, and other art that eventually were placed in public buildings and museums. The purpose of the program was to put unemployed artists to work, to develop a trend and a body of art

that depicted the American ethos, and to democratize art—to bring it into the daily life of the average citizen. Many Black artists who had begun to develop during the Harlem Renaissance period were helped immensely by the WPA program.

The Black subject was the major theme of African American art during this period. The works of Aaron Douglas and James Lesesne Wells were within this culturally conscious realm. Other such artists from the Depression through World War II include Augusta Savage, sculptor (1900–1962); Charles Alston, painter-sculptor-muralist (1907–1972); Hale Woodruff, painter (1900–1980); Ernest Crichlow, painter (1914); William Carter, painter-muralist (1909); Eldzier Cortor, painter (1915); Charles Sebree, painter-illustrator (1914–1985); Romare Bearden, painter-Collagist (1914-1988); and Charles White, painter (1918). The works of one of the most noted contemporary artists, Jacob Lawrence, painter, have shown a consistent allegiance to the Black experience.[49]

The 1950s and 1960s spawned a large cadre of politically-conscious Black artists. The works of these artists reflected a strong sense of Black pride, Black culture, civil rights themes, militancy, and Pan-Africanism. It was during this period when a major school of Black artists rejected the Eurocentric idiom of "art-for-arts-sake" and substituted it for "art-for-peoples'-sake." Under the aura and momentum of the Black Power, Black Pride, and Civil Rights Movements, the number of Black museums, galleries, community art centers dramatically increased all over the country. The Studio Museum of Harlem was organized in 1969 as a facility where artists could display their work, hold meetings and conduct other art related activities. It is now a major African American cultural center in New York. Among the prominent art exhibited there are the works of the famous Harlem Renaissance photographer, James Van Der Zee.

During the 1960s, the African Community of Bad Relevant Artists (AfriCobra), a coalition of Black artists, was founded. The purpose of AfriCobra was to establish a Black aesthetic school of thought derived from traditional African art and African American culture. While the artists agreed to sustain their artistic individuality, AfriCobra set forth certain collective principles characteristic of the Black aesthetic as follows:

Free Symmetry," meaning rhythmic syncopation in design, music, and movement; "Shine," meaning luminosity through dynamic contrasts of color, form, and spacial relationships; "Jam-packed and Jelly-tight Compositions," meaning form-filled and full-field surface design; "Awesome Imagery"; and "Koolaid Color."[50]

All African American artists do not subscribe to the Black aesthetic concept. Some reject the notion that there should be an identifiable Black art aesthetic.

African American art, like Black music, is influenced by the social and economic conditions of Blacks, and by changes in their political ideology. The Black Arts period of the 1960s fostered many positive sociopsychological changes in the Black community. In many African American lower and middle-income homes, Black or African oriented paintings and sculptor are now a part of the decor where only previously European and Victorian art were owned. Many African American churches replaced the symbolic blond, blue-eyed portrait of Christ with a Black one in harmony with their own race and image. The popular social theory of the past two decades has been cultural pluralism. However, cultural pluralism and diversity translates into cultural specificity and identity.

As a result of the cultural and civil rights movements of the 1960s, there now exist in various areas of the arts hundreds or perhaps thousands of Black artists. However, since the late 1970s there has been a retrenchment in civil rights and in progressive race relations in the United States. Consequently, many Black artists and African Americans in general have increased their interest in Black art and African culture.

One such artist is Earl Jackson of Ann Arbor, Michigan. His visits to West and East Africa during the late 1980s inspired the painting, *"Following the Path."* The painting is about African American women walking in the footsteps of their foremothers. The older women are dressed in African styled clothing and carrying large parasols. The young women and girls are dressed in Western style clothing. The older women are taking them onto sacred ground (for women only) to teach and celebrate the beauty, power, elegance and mystery of their womenhood.

*Black Theater and Dance: A Synopsis.* Creativity in the entertainment arts has always been an acclaimed and popular tradition of African Americans. However, African Americans as a race have never reaped just and equitable reward for the amusement and artistic enrichment they have contributed to the American society as the result of their creative talents and skills in the entertainment world. During their voyage from Africa as slaves, Blacks were forced on the decks of the slaveships to act, dance and entertain their captor crews. In the New World, the ritualistic acts, symbols, music, song and dance of Africans provided amusement and entertainment for Whites on plantations, city squares and riverboats throughout the South. When free Blacks of the North formed their own playhouses and shows they were often greeted with laughter and derision from white spectators. In theater, more than in any other area of entertainment, Black actors and actresses were forced or exploited to perform in stereotypical, comic and buffoonish roles to satisfy the prejudicial humor of white Americans.

Photo 22   "Following the Path," Oil Painting, 20 1/2" × 32", copyright 1988 by Earl Jackson.
Used with permission.

Even in the twentieth century, Blacks are generally cast by Whites in stereotypical roles in theater, film and television. The racism and discrimination that are so pervasive in American and European stagecraft provoked and inspired the development of Black theater. However, before a definition of Black theater is stated, it is necessary to discuss the early history of the Black American in theater and drama.

It is generally believed that the beginning experience of Blacks in drama in America was in the minstrel shows which originated among slaves. The slaves would entertain themselves by mimicking the mannerisms, walking and talking styles of their masters. Whites found the slave performances amusing and began to adopt and to develop a Whites wearing blackface type of entertainment called minstrelsy patterned after the slave

acts. Whites in blackface started a theatrical trend of projecting Blacks as lazy, shiftless, simple, dialect speaking people with kinky hair and large lips. Blacks did not participate themselves in the minstrel shows until after the Civil War. When Blacks began to form their own minstrel shows they re-blackened their faces and painted their lips to amuse white audiences. Black minstrelsy had the advantage of incorporating original Black routines, materials and dances.[51] The minstrelsy was a popular form of entertainment for almost a century. However, its negative impact upon the image and psyche of Black and White Americans has endured.

The African American's attempt to provide an alternative to the caricature of the minstrelsy began in New York with the formation of a Black theater company that eventually led to the organization of the African

Grove Theater in 1821. Understandably, serious African American theater at that juncture in history would have a European frame of reference. The repertory of the African Grove Company included such productions as *Tom and Jerry*, Shakespeare's *Othello and Hamlet, and Richard the Third.* Two of the foremost Black actors of the time were James Hewlitt and Ira Aldridge. The first drama that was written and directed by a Black man was by the African Grove's producer-director, Henry Brown. The play was entitled, *The Drama of King Shotaway* and it was performed by the African Grove Company.[52]

Some music historians believe that other Black dramatic companies existed between the time of the decline of the African Grove Theater and the Civil War. There is reference to the Creole Dramatic Company of New Orleans that performed from 1859–1870. A few Black musical companies were active during the late nineteenth century including the Hyers Sisters Combination out of Sacramento, California, and The Original Colored Opera Company of Washington, D.C. It is important to note that after 1876 Black actors, singers and dancers were often used in the performances of the classic, "Uncle Tom's Cabin."[53]

As the minstrel shows declined in popularity around 1890, they were replaced with forms of Burlesque and Vaudeville musical comedies. These shows allowed for the use of Black females as principal performers and in chorus lines. While the musical comedies were still "minstrel" in format, they did provide the opportunity for African Americans to engage in playwriting and musical composition. The first show to be produced and stage-managed by Blacks having structure, continuity and combined music with plotline was a musical titled, *A Trip to Coontown* written by Bob Cole in 1898. In the same year, Will Marion Cook composed the music and Paul Laurence Dunbar wrote the lyrics to

*Clorindy, the Origin of the Cakewalk.* The skit played in a major Broadway theater.

On the negative side, some African American actors and showpersons such as Ernest Hogan, Bert Williams, and George Walker contributed to the development of stereotypical images of the Black race by performing as dimwits and buffoons on stage. They acquired substantial personal wealth for playing these roles but, undoubtedly, were affected psychologically. Certainly, the dignity of African people was tarnished. From a positive perspective, these showpersons paved the way for hundreds of African Americans to receive training and to practice more serious stagecraft in the decades that followed.

During the Harlem Renaissance period, Black theater flourished along with the Black musical, visual and literary arts. Several Black theaters and theater companies were active in Harlem during the 1920s. The Lincoln, Lafayette and the Cresent were the most notable theaters. By the end of the decade these theaters had produced such famous actors as Paul Robeson and Charles Gilpin. Robeson gained fame for his role in *All God's Chillun Got Wings* and Gilpin played the leading role in *The Emperor Jones.* The Federal Theater Project under the sponsorship of the WPA during the Depression of the 1930s enabled Black actors to receive serious professional training. Subsequently, in the 1940s, African Americans were cast in roles of greater depth and humanity. In 1943, Paul Robeson was the first Black to play the title of *Othello* on Broadway.[54]

The 1950s were marked by the organization of various small production companies, the most successful included the two companies of the Negro Art Players. Blacks were beginning to write and produce numerous plays. The most significant of the period was Lorraine Hansberry's award winning play, *Raisin in the Sun.* The concept of Black Theater, art-for-people's-sake came to fore at the height of the 1960s Civil Rights Movement.

Small and some large Black community theaters mushroomed in major cities and on college and university campuses throughout the country. Integrationist ideals competed against Black Pride and Black Separatist ideology, and the theater productions reflected these contentions. Many of the plays focused on American racism and dwelled on themes relevant to the political and economic plight, and social experience of the Black community. Two successful Black oriented productions *The Wiz* and *For Colored Girls Who Have Considered Suicide When the Rainbow Is Enuf* played on Broadway in the mid 1970s.

Private and public funding of the arts are effected directly by the state of the economy and political administrations. A major factor contributing to the upsurge of Black community theater in the 1960s and 1970s was the funding support received from the National Endowment of the Arts, federal and municipal programs, and corporate foundations. Adverse economic conditions and the conservative posture of the Reagan and Bush Administrations of the 1980s and 1990s caused a decrease in the availability of funds and resources in support of Black theater. Nevertheless, Black theater is active and thriving in major American cities such as Chicago, New York, Atlanta, Los Angeles, and Seattle.

Now that a historical synopsis of Black theater has been stated, a definition of the term and concept is in order. Black theater is a dramatic reflection of the culture, values and experiences of African Americans. Its performance portrays their hopes, despair, joys, sorrows, triumphs, failures, fortunes and tragedies. Black theater is functional beyond its propensity to entertain because its objective is to inform, communicate, and to relate the social, political and economic experiences of Black people with other peoples of the world. Black theater reflects the reality of racism, colonialism and oppression and yet sustains its artistic commitment. Black theater is

an aesthetic vehicle for social change. Black theater must define and evaluate its self based upon the cultural values, standards and experiences of African Americans. Black theater is to be differentiated from general and other cultures' theater.

African American music, song and dance are integral in the performance of Black theater. African derived music and dance have generally accompanied the performance of Black theater since the days of the minstrelsy to the present. African derived and oriented dances include the juba, calinda, and bamboula. African American influenced dances are the hambone, Charleston, shuffle, cakewalk (ragtime), slow drag, bebop, and Lindy Hop (jitterbug). In addition, a myriad of African American originated dances developed along with the rhythm and blues music of the fifties, sixties and seventies.[55]

Beginning in the 1960s, "native" African dance and dancers were often presented or fused with Black theater. A significant number of Black theater and dance companies were formed during the Black Arts era of the 1960s, and many still exist. Some are separately identified as Black or African Dance Theater.

# THE LITERATURE OF AFRICAN AMERICANS

*A Commentary on Black Literature.* The concept of Black literature is used in the same context as Black music, Black art and Black Theater. It is the creative written and oral expression of people of African descent and, particularly, related to the cultural and socio-political experiences of African Americans. Black literature, as used in this text, is consistent with the own-race or self-defining, self-evaluating and self-legitimating stance that a school of African Americans assumed in the 1960s. The portraiture of Black literature projects the reality and mythology of Black life and experience. The portraiture of Blacks or Africans is considerably different from reflections in white American literature—history, life or culture. Much of the literature of African Americans reflects over 250 years of struggle and protest that, generally, American history and literature omits.

The concept of Black literature may not be shared by all African American writers. There are those who seek to avoid having their work being racially classified and being identified as Black writers. Consequently, a distinction might be made between Black literature and literature by Black writers. Some Black writers may seek to under-play the significance of their race with the view that they may gain broader acceptance of their work. Writers identified as African Americans may face the risk or problem of being under-read and under-represented in the White dominated literary world. Thus, the ethnological, racial or political character of the literature may have to be accommodated in order to gain White appeal.

On the other hand, the rising phenomenon of race pride and consciousness which began during the Harlem Renaissance and were revived in the 1960s have caused African Americans to prefer and to seek literature derived from a Black perspective. After centuries of seeing themselves through the eyes of others, books by Black authors and periodicals on the African American experience have increased in academic and popular appeal. Still in most schools and in many fields, Black writers are unknown. There is no reason why Black literature or the literary works of African Americans should not be given equitable recognition and treatment. Black literature, like Black history, is an integral part of American literature.

White writers are not usually confronted with the need to conceal their racial identity or obscure their Eurocentric experience and orientation in order to gain universal recogni-

tion. White European and American societies have historically sought to achieve cultural literary hegemony. Because of their economic and military power in the world, they have virtually succeeded. Those in power can influence literary definitions and popular perceptions. Therefore, it is important to realize that to an extent power contributes to the universal appeal of white American and European literature. Consequently, White literary works are read more, emulated and pursued by many other cultures.

In the absence of literary capitulation, a race or culture must create or produce its own literature, and critique and support its own writers. Universal interest or appeal of a race's or culture's literature may occur but it is often incidental. Black literature incorporates a historic, political, folkloric, parabolic, metaphoric and sometimes mythological style characteristic of that expressed in Asante's book, *The Afrocentric Idea.*[56] Whether one reads the addresses or writings of David Walker, Frederick Douglass, Booker T. Washington, W.E.B. DuBois, Langston Hughes, Martin Luther King, Jr., Margaret Walker, Malcolm X or Jesse Jackson, the uniqueness of Black literary expression is evident. It is a style that attracts and maintains much universal appeal without compromise. Yet, there have been times in the history of African Americans writers, when life and liberty were at stake, that accommodation may have been prudent.

***Black Writers from 1746 to 1899.*** Black literary expression that can be documented in the United States began as early as the 1746 when Lucy Terry, a semi-literate slave wrote a ballard poem called, "Bars Fight" recreating an Indian massacre which occurred in Deerfield, Massachusetts. Jupiter Hammon, a slave, through his owner published a poem in 1761 titled, *An Evening Thought, Salvation by Christ, with Penitential Cries.* In 1786, Hammon wrote a prose piece, *An Address to the Negroes of the State of New York* and delivered it before the African Society of New York City which was published the following year. However, Phillis Wheatley is the most recognized Black poetess of this period. She was born in Senegal, brought to America as a slave, and educated in her master's household. With the help of her owners, she published numerous poem, letters and memoirs of her life. Wheatley's poems reflected the traditional European genre of the time.[57] There were, undoubtedly, numerous undocumented narratives, folktales or pieces of prose that could be construed as literary expressions of slaves during the eighteenth century.

The slave poets of the eighteenth century are not viewed as having made a significant contribution to African American life and history beyond vindication—or having proven that Blacks possessed the ability to master European literary style and thought. Hammon and Wheatley have been dismissed by Black cultural nationalists as being irrelevant because of the accommodationist and servile themes of their prose and poetry. For example, Hammon published a poem in 1783 entitled, "The Kind Master And The Dutiful Servant." The poem seems obviously supportive of the slave system as one verse reads:

Dear Master, that's my whole delight,
    Thy pleasure for to do;
As for grace and truth's in sight,
    Thus far I'll surely go.[58]

Phyllis Wheatley's poem, "On Being Brought From Africa To America," expressed gratitude for her having been kidnapped and taken as slave from Africa:

'Twas mercy brought me from by Pagan land,
    Taught my benighted soul to understand
That there's a God, that there's a Saviour too:
    Once I redemption neither sought nor
        knew,
Some view our sable race with scornful eye,
    "Their color is a diabolic die,"
Remember, Christians, Negroes, black as Cain,

May be refin'd and join th' angelic train.[59] A few literary scholars look beyond the groveling nature of these slave poems to find some esoteric implications of religious sarcasm and subversion. However, the slave writers of the eighteenth century reflect the same three optional attitudes and responses to oppression as African American writers of the twentieth century: 1) accommodate, 2) protest or 3) escape.[60]

The nineteenth century marked the beginning of an era of Black protest writers and poets. The seeds for the future development of Black consciousness, cultural nationalism, revolutionary nationalism and Pan-Africanism were sown by writers and orators such as David Walker, Henry Highland Garnet, Frederick Douglass, and James Forten. Antislavery and political thought began to develop in Black writings at a prolific rate. The century would also give rise to one of the most staunch accommodationists, Booker T. Washington.

David Walker's *Appeal* published in a pamphlet in 1828 was a drastic change from the servile themes of the slave writers of the 1700s. Walker's writings were precursory to the Black pride proponents of the twentieth century. An excerpt from the *Appeal* reads:

They think because they hold us in their infernal chains of slavery, that we wish to be white, or of their color—but they are dreadfully deceived—we wish to be just as it pleased our Creator to have made us. . . . Now, I ask you, had you not rather be killed than be a slave to a tyrant, who takes the life of your mother, wife, and dear little children? . . .[61]

Building upon the resistance literature of David Walker, Henry Highland Garnet espoused a more militant paper entitled, "An Address to the Slaves of the United States" urging the slaves of the South to rise up in arms. The writings and addresses of Frederick Douglass are masterpieces of literary eloquence and dynamism. While Douglass writings were void of the strident and violent themes that characterized the works of Walker and Garnet, he was equally effective in the art of moral suasion.

The literary excellence of early African American writers is reflected even in their letters and petitions to government authorities. James Forten's series of letters to the Pennsylvania legislature protesting a bill that would cease the migration of free Blacks to Philadelphia are often included in anthologies of African American literature. Expressions of protest and anguish appeared in the works of renown Black poets such as Frances Ellen Harper and Paul Laurence Dunbar during the mid 1800s. William Wells Brown is recognized as being the first African American to publish a novel in 1853. The novel entitled, *Clotel: Or the President's Daughter* was first published in England. Brown was born a slave and was self educated.

Paul Laurence Dunbar was one of the most profound African American poets who wrote of Black life with realistic and functional simplicity. Dunbar was the first to gain national recognition as a Black poet. He dignified the language of the vernacular or the dialect of common Black people by using it formally with emotion and compassion in his poetry. Dunbar's poetry and short stories reflected the psychology of the oppression of Black people. This is clearly evident in one of his most often quoted poems, "We Wear the Mask:"

> We wear the mask that grins and lies,
> It hides our cheeks and shades our eyes—
> This debt we pay to human guile;
> With torn and bleeding hearts we smile,
> And mouth with myriad subtleties.
>
> Why should the world be overwise
> In counting all our tears and sighs?
> Nay, let them only see us while
> We wear the mask.

> We smile, but, O great Christ, our cries
> To Thee from tortured souls arise.
> We sing, but oh the clay is vile
> Beneath our feet, and long the mile;
> But let the world dream otherwise
> We wear the mask.        (1895)

It is not inconceivable that the noted Black psychiatrist Franz Fanon could have been inspired by this poem by Paul Laurence Dunbar when he wrote of European colonialism in his book, *Black Skin, White Masks*, in 1967.

The literature, writings or oratory of African Americans have generally served an ideological and a functional purpose. Certainly, the writings and addresses of Booker T. Washington projected his accommodationist philosophy towards the oppressed social, political and economic condition of Black people in the South. His book, *Up from Slavery*, revealed how his accommodationist ideology originated and the nature of his personal experiences under slavery which shaped and molded it. His most famous contribution to ideological literature was made at the Atlanta Exposition of 1895 in an address that has since been called the "Atlanta Compromise."

**Black Writers and Literature of the Twentieth Century.** The literary achievements of Black writers and poets of the eighteenth and nineteenth centuries laid the foundation for the proliferation of African American literature in the twentieth century. Race riots and oppression at the beginning of the century raised the racial consciousness of Blacks and caused a cohesion among Black writers and intellectuals. While the aura of the 1920s revived and stimulated African American creativity in music, art and theater, the Harlem Renaissance was basically a literary movement. The Renaissance or the "New Negro Movement" brought to fore writers and poets of future fame such as Claude McKay, Langston Hughes, Countee Cullen and Jean

Toomer. Scholar-writer and civil rights activists W.E.B. DuBois and James Weldon Johnson became dominant figures in the fight for freedom and justice during this period. During and following the Renaissance period, many Black novelists and fiction writers emerged. Such writers include Nella Larsen, Jessie Redmon Fauset, Wallace Thurman and Rudolph Fisher.[62]

The essence of the Black rebellious spirit and sentiment of the period was militantly set forth by Claude McKay in his poem "If We Must Die." The plight, despair and aspirations of African Americans were poetically expressed in Langston Hughes' "The Negro Speaks of Rivers." Perhaps Hughes was the most accomplished and acclaimed poet of the period. Although W.E.B. DuBois' sociological classic, *Souls of Black Folk* and his novel, *The Quest of the Silver Fleece* were written earlier, these works influenced the spirit of the Renaissance movement. The Black intellectual James Weldon Johnson established his literary reputation in 1927 with a collection of folk sermons in verse entitled, *God's Trombones*. Today, he is mostly remembered as the author of the poem "Lift Every Voice and Sing" which has been put to music and now serves as the Black National Anthem.

The number of Black writers, novelists and poets from the 1930s through the 1970s are too numerous to comment on individually. However, it may serve study and research purposes to list *some* of the major contributors to African American literature who followed in the spirit of the Harlem Renaissance:

Richard Wright, novelist (1908–1960)
Sterling Brown, poet, critic
James Baldwin, novelist, essayist
    (1924–1990)
Frank Yerby novelist
Ralph Ellison, novelist, essayist
Chester Himes, novelist
Robert Hayden, poet (1913–1980)
Zora Neale Hurston, novelist (1903–1960)

John O. Killens, novelist
Margaret Walker, poet, novelist
Arna Bontemps, poet, novelist
    (1902–1973)
Ann Petry, novelist, critic
Melvin B. Tolson, poet (1900–1966)
J. Saunders Reddings, author, critic
Gwendolyn Brooks, poet
Leroi Jones (Amiri Baraka) poet,
    playwright, essayist
Don L. Lee (Haki A. Madhubuti) poet,
    writer
Julius Lester, writer, essayist, critic
Paule Marshall, novelist, writer
Addison Gayle, essayist, critic
Maya Angelou, writer, poet
Sonia Sanchez, poet, playwright
Nikki Giovanni, poet
Toni Cade Bambara, poet
Mari Evans, poet
Alice Childress, playwright, novelist
Ishmael Reed, novelist, poet
Ernest J. Gaines, novelist
Clarence Major, poet, novelist
Ed Bullins, dramatist, essayist
Toni Morrison, novelist
Alice Walker, poet, novelist

A new orientation or a redefinition of African American literature and poetry developed with the advent of the 1960s and the Civil Rights Movement. Amiri Baraka (Leroi Jones) was the leading change agent and promoter of the new "relevant" Black literature. Baraka deplored a Black literature that capitulated totally to the Eurocentric tradition, and that was void of a Black identity, ethos or cultural frame of reference. Several other young Black writers and poets believed that Black literature should reflect the reality of the Black experience and conform to the needs of Black people.[63] The New Black Arts movement of the sixties differed from the Renaissance of the 1920s in that it fostered a conscious form of Black cultural nationalism.

The sixties was a period of racial violence, social unrest and reformation. Consequently, there emerged a school of "revolutionary" Black writers and poets. These writers wrote in the angry vein of David Walker, Henry Highland Garnet and simulated the tone of Claude McKay's poem, "If We Must Die." Often the style and format violated traditional prosaic and poetic standards. Self-satire, Black love, revolutionary rhetoric, social criticism, ghetto strife and African-ness characterized some of the writings of the revolutionary poets. The poetry was delivered in a manner to elicit intermittent response from the audience.

The most creative, prolific and critically acclaimed novelists of the 1970s and 1980s have been Black women. While there are numerous such women writers, Toni Morrison and Alice Walker are foremost in the eyes of many critics. According to one positive critic, Morrison is a powerful fiction writer whose works abounds in mystical occurrences—conjurations, superstitious manifestations and spiritual visitations. She artistically interweaves the physical and spiritual worlds in an African continuum so characteristic of true African-Americaness.[64] Morrison's novels include *Song of Solomon* 1977; *Tar Baby* 1981; and *Beloved* 1987. Alice Walker is a novelist, essayist and poet. She is the author of a number of collections of short stories and poems. Her novels include *Meridian*, and *The Color Purple*. Walker focuses on sensitive and controversial subjects relating to Black male/female relationships and the pains and burdens of Black life. Her works borders on the feminist idiom to the extent that it may be perceived to portray negative images of Black men. The film made from her novel, *The Color Purple*, received mixed reviews among African Americans.

The theme and focus of the literary works of Black writers are not static, but change as they are effected by social, political and economic factors that impact upon African American life and experience. The Black consciousness movements of the 1920s and 1960s have generated such a voluminous quantity and quality of books, novels, essays and other writings on and by African Americans that Black literature can no longer be ignored or relegated to an insignificant status in the field of American humanities.

# · QUESTIONS AND EXERCISES ·

1. Why is it essential that each race or culture establish and maintain foremost its own aesthetical standards?

2. What is meant by the term cultural relativism?

3. Give a philosophical or functional rationale why a painting by one of the European classical artists might sell for $30 million. Can such art valuation occur in African cultures? Why? Why not?

4. Study the *Negritude* movement of the West African and Caribbean nations that followed the Harlem Renaissance in the United States. Make cultural, intellectual and ideological comparisons of the two movements. (Research required)

5. What is the difference between African American spirituals and gospel music?

6. While the term "blues" music may be generically ascribed or found to exist in most

cultures, what are the unique and distinguishing characteristics of Black blues music and song?

7. Most music scholars and historians credit jazz music as having been created by African Americans. However, a few argue that it has European origins. Discuss.

8. Write a paper on the beginning, development and popularizing of rap music in America.

9. What is *Black* theater?

10. The names of several African American writers, novelists and poets are listed in the chapter. Critique or review the major work of any three of the writers, essayists, novelists, playwrights or poets listed.

## • NOTES AND REFERENCES •

1. See Culverson Blair, "Perspective on African Art Criticism," *Black World* (July 1975) XXIV(9) 23–24, 71–78.

2. Phyllis R. Klotman, edited, *Humanities through the Black Experience* (Dubuque: Kendall/Hunt Publishing Co. 1977) 1.

3. Carlton W. Molette and Barbara J. Molette, *Black Theater* (Bristol, IN: Wyndham Hall Press 1986) 38.

4. Manning Marable, "The Rhetoric of Racial Harmony," *Sojourners* (August/September 1990) 17.

5. See Nathan Irvin Huggins, *Harlem Renaissance* (New York: Oxford University Press 1971); also, James A. Emanuel, "Renaissance Sonneteers," *Black World* (September 1975) p. 34.

6. For a chronology and biographies of Black artists and literary figures of this period refer to H.A. Ploski and James Williams, edited, *The Negro Almanac* 4th ed. (New York: John Wiley & Sons 1983).

7. The political-cultural nexus of the 1940s is treated more fully in Acklyn R. Lynch, "Reflections on Black Culture in the Early Forties," *Black Books Bulletin* (Spring 1978) 6(1).

8. See also Robert Hayden's Preface to *The New Negro* edited, Alain Locke (New York: Atheneum 1969) p. ix.

9. Alain Locke, *The Negro and His Music* (Washington, DC: The Associates in Negro Folk Education 1936) 1–7.

10. Melville J. Herskovits, *The Myth of the Negro Past* (Boston: Beacon Press 1958; Harper & Brothers 1941).

11. Lazarus E. N. Ekwueme, "African-Music Retentions in the New World," *The Black Perspective in Music* (Fall 1974) 2(2). 134–135.

12. Ibid., p. 135.

13. Locke, *The Negro and His Music*, p. 18.

14. DuBois also described spirituals as "the sorrow songs." See chapter 14 in, W.E.B. DuBois, *The Souls of Black Folk* (New York: The New American Library 1969. reprint) p. 265.

15. Eileen Southern, *The Music of Black Americans* (New York: W.W. Norton & Co. 1971) 249–251.

16. See Eileen Southern, "An Origin for the Negro Spiritual," *The Black Scholar* (Summer 1972) 8–13.

17. Several Black spirituals and speculated interpretations are presented in Christa K.

Dixon, *Negro Spirituals* (Philadelphia: Fortress Press 1976).

18. See Portia K. Maultsby, "The Use and Performance of Hymnody, Spirituals and Gospels in the Black Church," *The Western Journal of Black Studies* (Fall 1983) v. 7(3). 161–171; also, Mark H. Davis, "The Black Sacred Song," *The Western Journal of Black Studies* (Summer 1978) v. 2(2) 140–141.

19. Horace Clarence Boyer, "Contemporary Gospel Music: Sacred or Secular?" *The Black Perspective in Music* (Spring 1979) 7(1). 5–6.

20. Ibid., 7–11.

21. An interview with Thomas A. Dorsey by *Black Books Bulletin* (Spring 1977) 5(1). p. 22.

22. See J.H.K. Nketia, "The Study of African and Afro-American Music," *The Black Perspective in Music* (Spring 1973) 1(1) 7–15; also, Samuel Charters, *The Bluesman* (New York: Oak Publications 1967) 15–22.

23. Southern, *The Music of Black Americans*, 333–335.

24. The stanzas stated here and below are from personal record collection. For an excellent pictorial, biographical and autobiographical history of the Blues see, Paul Oliver, *The Story of the Blues* (Philadelphia: Chilton Book Co. 1969).

25. Eddie S. Meadows, "African Retentions in Blues and Jazz," *The Western Journal of Black Studies* (Fall 1979) v. 3(3) p. 183.

26. See Michael Haralambos, *Right On: From Blues to Soul in Black America* (New York: Da Capo Press 1979) 20–27.

27. Grover Sales, *Jazz: America's Classical Music* (Englewood Cliffs, NJ: Prentice-Hall 1984) 26–28.

28. Robert F. Thompson, "Kongo Influences on African American Artistic Culture," in Joseph E. Holloway, ed. *Africanisms in American Culture* (Bloomington, IN: Indiana University Press 1990) 148–150.

29. F. Ramsey; Jr., and C.E. Smith, eds., *Jazzmen* (New York: Limelight edition 1985) 7–9.

30. Daphne Duval Harrison, "Jazz: The Serious Music of Black Americans," *The Western Journal of Black Studies* (Fall 1978) v. 2(3). 198.

31. Southern, *The Music of Black Americans*, 311–314.

32. Sales, *Jazz: America's Classical Music*, 50–56.

33. Locke, *The Negro and His Music*, 84–87.

34. The Categorization of jazz schools and artists are as varied as there are music writers and historians. Most of the writer-analysts of jazz have been White. Their concepts may be in variance with Black jazz enthusiasts and historians. For an interesting work by a White writer see, Ira Gitler, *Swing to Bop* (New York: Oxford University Press 1985).

35. Lewis Porter, "Some Problems in Jazz Research," *Black Music Research Journal* (Fall 1988) 8(2). 200.

36. Arnold Shaw, "Researching Rhythm & Blues," *Black Music Research*, Institute for Research in Black American Music (Fisk University 1980) p. 71.

37. For a chronology of R & B music development see, Rochelle Larkin, *Soul Music* (New York: Lancer Books 1970).

38. Shaw, "Researching Rhythm and Blues," p. 72.

39. For a more comprehensive study of R & B or Soul music the book by Peter Guralnick, *Sweet Soul Music* (New York: Harper & Row 1986) is recommended.

40. James B. Stewart, "Relationships between Black Males and Females in Rhythm and Blues Music of the 1960s and 1970s," *The Western Journal of Black Studies* (Fall 1979) v. 3(3). 186–195.

41. Nelson George, "Rapping Their Way to Gold," *Black Enterprise* (June 1982) 223.

42. Alfred B. Pasteur and Ivory L. Toldson, *Roots of Soul* (Garden City, NY: Anchor Press 1982) p. 28.

43. See Ronald Jemal Stephens, "What the Rap is About: Some Historical Notes on the Development of Rap Music and the Hip-Hop Movement," *Word* (Spring 1991) 1(1); and Elizabeth A. Wheeler, "Most of my Heros Don't Appear on no Stamps": The Dialogics of Rap Music," *Black Music Research Journal* (Fall 1991) 11(2).

44. Houston A. Baker, Jr., "Hybridity, the Rap Race and Pedagogy for the 1990s," *Black Music Research Journal* (Fall 1991) 11(2) 220–221.

45. See Addison Gayle, "Blueprint for Black Criticism," *First World* (Jan/Feb 1977) 41–45; also Randy Williams, "The Black Artist as Activist," *Black Creation,* (Winter 1972) 3(2) 42–45.

46. James A. Porter, *Modern Negro Art* (New York: Dryden Press 1943) p. 27; and Alain Locke, *Negro Art: Past and Present* (Washington: DC: Associates in Negro Folk Education 1936) p. 15.

47. Locke, *Negro Art: Past and Present*, p. 61.

48. Ibid.

49. G.C. McElroy, R.J. Powell and S.F. Patton, eds., *African-American Artists 1880–1987* (Washington, DC: Smithsonian Institution 1989).

50. Ibid., 103–104.

51. See Larry Thompson, "The Black Image in Early American Drama," *Black World* (April 1975) 54–69; and Sterling Brown, "Negro in American Theater," in *The Oxford Companion to the Theater*, edited by Phyllis Hartnoll (London: Oxford University Press 1967) 672.

52. Eileen Southern, "The Origin and Development of the Black Musical Theater," *Black Music Research Journal* (1981–1982) 2–5.

53. Ibid., 7–9.

54. See Allan Morrison, "One Hundred Years of Negro Entertainment," in *International Library of Afro-American Life and History* ed. Lindsay Patterson (Washington, DC: ASALH 1976) 3–7.

55. For a study of Black dance and music see, Samuel A. Floyd, "Afro-American Music and Dance," *The Western Journal of Black Studies* (Fall 1989) v. 13(3).

56. Read Molefi Kete Asante, *The Afrocentric Idea* (Philadelphia: Temple University Press 1987).

57. Ploski and Williams, *The Negro Almanac,* 984, 998, 1001.

58. Jupiter Hammon, *America's First Negro Poet* ed. S.A. Ransome, Jr. (Port Washington NY: Kennikat Press, 1970) 59.

59. Phillis Wheatley, *Poems On Various Subjects, Religious and Moral* (Philadelphia: 1786; facism. New York: AMS Press, 1976) 13.

60. See Arthur P. Davis and Saunders Redding, eds. *Cavalcade* (Boston: Houghton Mifflin Co. 1971) p. 3.

61. Brad Chambers, ed., *Chronicles of Black Protest* (New York: Mentor Books 1968) 58.

62. Houston A. Baker, Jr., *Black Literature in America* (New York: McGraw-Hill Book Co 1971) 140–143.

63. See also, Chestyn Everett, " 'Tradition' in Afro-American Literature," *Black World* (December 1975) 20–35; and Bernard W. Bell, "Contemporary Afro-American Poetry as Folk Art," *Black World* (March 1973) 16–26.

64. Clenora Hudson- (Withers) Weems, "Toni Morrison's World of Topsy-Turvydom: A Methodological Explication of New Black Literary Criticism," *The Western Journal of Black Studies* (Fall 1986) v. 10(3) 134.

# Index